THE WILEY BICENTENNIAL—KNOWLEDGE FOR GENERATIONS

*E*ach generation has its unique needs and aspirations. When Charles Wiley first opened his small printing shop in lower Manhattan in 1807, it was a generation of boundless potential searching for an identity. And we were there, helping to define a new American literary tradition. Over half a century later, in the midst of the Second Industrial Revolution, it was a generation focused on building the future. Once again, we were there, supplying the critical scientific, technical, and engineering knowledge that helped frame the world. Throughout the 20th Century, and into the new millennium, nations began to reach out beyond their own borders and a new international community was born. Wiley was there, expanding its operations around the world to enable a global exchange of ideas, opinions, and know-how.

For 200 years, Wiley has been an integral part of each generation's journey, enabling the flow of information and understanding necessary to meet their needs and fulfill their aspirations. Today, bold new technologies are changing the way we live and learn. Wiley will be there, providing you the must-have knowledge you need to imagine new worlds, new possibilities, and new opportunities.

Generations come and go, but you can always count on Wiley to provide you the knowledge you need, when and where you need it!

WILLIAM J. PESCE
PRESIDENT AND CHIEF EXECUTIVE OFFICER

PETER BOOTH WILEY
CHAIRMAN OF THE BOARD

Introduction to Database Management

Mark L. Gillenson, Paulraj Ponniah, Alex Kriegel,
Boris M. Trukhnov, Allen G. Taylor, and Gavin Powell

with Frank Miller

BICENTENNIAL
1807
WILEY
2007
BICENTENNIAL

Credits

PUBLISHER
Anne Smith

ACQUISITIONS EDITOR
Lois Ann Freier

MARKETING MANAGER
Jennifer Slomack

SENIOR EDITORIAL ASSISTANT
Tiara Kelly

PRODUCTION MANAGER
Kelly Tavares

PRODUCTION ASSISTANT
Courtney Leshko

CREATIVE DIRECTOR
Harry Nolan

COVER DESIGNER
Hope Miller

COVER PHOTO
©AP/Wide World Photos

Wiley 200th Anniversary Logo designed by: Richard J. Pacifico

This book was set in Times New Roman by Techbooks, printed and bound by R.R. Donnelley. The cover was printed by R.R. Donnelley.

Microsoft product screen shot(s) reprinted with permission from Microsoft Corporation.

This book is printed on acid free paper.∞

To order books or for customer service please, call 1-800-CALL WILEY (225-5945).

ISBN-13 978-0-470-10186-5

Printed in the United States of America

10 9 8 7 6 5 4 3 2 1

PREFACE

College classrooms bring together learners from many backgrounds, with a variety of aspirations. Although the students are in the same course, they are not necessarily on the same path. This diversity, coupled with the reality that these learners often have jobs, families, and other commitments, requires a flexibility that our nation's higher education system is addressing. Distance learning, shorter course terms, new disciplines, evening courses, and certification programs are some of the approaches that colleges employ to reach as many students as possible and help them clarify and achieve their goals.

Wiley Pathways books, a new line of texts from John Wiley & Sons, Inc., are designed to help you address this diversity and the need for flexibility. These books focus on the fundamentals, identify core competencies and skills, and promote independent learning. Their focus on the fundamentals helps students grasp the subject, bringing them all to the same basic understanding. These books use clear, everyday language and are presented in an uncluttered format, making the reading experience more pleasurable. The core competencies and skills help students succeed in the classroom and beyond, whether in another course or in a professional setting. A variety of built-in learning resources promote independent learning and help instructors and students gauge students' understanding of the content. These resources enable students to think critically about their new knowledge and apply their skills in any situation.

Our goal with *Wiley Pathways* books—with their brief, inviting format, clear language, and core competencies and skills focus—is to celebrate the many students in your courses, respect their needs, and help you guide them on their way.

CASE Learning System

To meet the needs of working college students, *Introduction to Database Management* uses a four-part process called the CASE Learning System:

▲ **C:** Content
▲ **A:** Analysis
▲ **S:** Synthesis
▲ **E:** Evaluation

Based on Bloom's taxonomy of learning, CASE presents key topics in databases in easy-to-follow chapters. The text then prompts analysis, synthesis, and evaluation with a variety of learning aids and assessment tools. Students move efficiently from reviewing what they have learned, to acquiring new information and skills, to applying their new knowledge and skills to real-life scenarios.

Using the CASE Learning System, students not only achieve academic mastery of database *topics*, but they master real-world *skills* related to that content. The CASE Learning System also helps students become independent learners, giving them a distinct advantage in the field, whether they are just starting out or seeking to advance in their careers.

Organization, Depth, and Breadth of the Text

▲ **Modular Format.** Research on college students shows that they access information from textbooks in a non-linear way. Instructors also often wish to reorder textbook content to suit the needs of a particular class. Therefore, although *Introduction to Database Management* proceeds logically from the basics to increasingly more challenging material, chapters are further organized into sections that are self-contained for maximum teaching and learning flexibility.

▲ **Numeric System of Headings.** *Introduction to Database Management* uses a numeric system for headings (e.g., 2.3.4 identifies the fourth subsection of Section 3 of Chapter 2). With this system, students and teachers can quickly and easily pinpoint topics in the table of contents and the text, keeping class time and study sessions focused.

▲ **Core Content.** The topics in *Introduction to Database Management* are organized into 12 chapters.

Chapter 1, Introducing Data and Data Management, introduces students to fundamental concepts relating to data and data management. Among the topics covered are the role data plays as a business resource, how business practices can be used to understand data collection requirements, and potential data management concerns such as data accuracy, data security and data accessibility.

Chapter 2, Introducing Databases and Database Management, examines the nuts and bolts of what makes up a database and a database management system (DBMS). The chapter introduces students to key database concepts such as data repository, data dictionary, database software, data abstraction, data access and transaction support, and basic database types, such as production databases, decision support databases and mass deployment databases. The chapter also covers the evolution of the hierarchical, network, relational, and object-oriented database models, and describes the primary database system architectural components, as well as the people and procedures involved in creating a DBMS.

Chapter 3, Data Modeling, explores the process of creating a data model. The chapter begins by introducing the design process, the use of data diagrams, the main types of databases (transactional databases, decisions support systems and hybrids), and the goals of data modeling. It also examines the incorporation of business rules into the design process. It then looks at the key components of a relational database model: entities, attributes and relationships, including an introduction to some fundamental database objects such as tables, views and indexes, and the various types of relationships (binary, unary, and ternary) that might be included in a database model. The chapter concludes by examining modeling tools and comparing some data models based on different businesses.

Chapter 4, Designing a Database, focuses on the process of creating a relational database design. It covers the entity-relationship to relational table conversion process, and describes how to convert simple entities, and various types of binary and unary relationships to relational tables, including choosing the foreign keys needed to establish and maintain relationships. Two case studies in which E-R diagrams are converted relational tables are included. The chapter then delves into the process known as normalization, which helps identify duplicate data and optimize data storage, and provides an in-depth look at the three normal forms.

Chapter 5, Implementing a Database, examines the final physical design issues and the basic implementation process. It introduces the types of utilities available for object creation and examines data integrity and performance optimization needs. It concludes with a section on database object implementation, and how to create basic tables, indexes, and views.

Chapter 6, Understanding the SQL Language, introduces the SQL language standard and the types of variations that have been added by different DBMSs. It covers basic language components through simple command examples, such as the use of the SELECT statement to retrieve values from a single table and to evaluate expressions. The chapter also introduces the concept of operators and SQL language functions. The chapter concludes with a discussion of DDL and DML statements, including the standard SQL syntax for selected commands such as INSERT, UPDATE, DELETE, CREATE, ALTER and DROP.

Chapter 7, Data Access and Manipulation, examines the use of the SELECT statement for data access and data manipulation. It covers using the SELECT statement to run data retrieval queries and how to build queries with SELECT statement keywords, as well as various methods for filtering the result set and organizing the data returned by a query. The chapter also describes how to use joins and subqueries to combine the results from multiple tables into a single result. The chapter concludes with a look at the basics of using batches and scripts to execute sets of statements as a group and to save these so that they can be retrieved and executed later.

Chapter 8, Improving Data Access, covers a variety of topics related to improving data access, including improving access performance, simplifying access, and protecting table data from unauthorized access. The chapter introduces the concept of bottlenecks and examines the types of symptoms they are likely to cause, and the most likely solutions to correct performance problems. The chapter also looks at how to design indexes and views to support and control data access and help improve query response. The chapter concludes with a discussion about using procedures and functions both to automate database operations (including data access queries) and to control access to database data.

Chapter 9, Database Administration, focuses on administration roles and responsibilities. The chapter begins with a look at how administration roles can be justified, and then examines the different roles of data administrators and database administrators, and the responsibilities related to each. The chapter concludes with an examination of about issues relating to administration tasks, such as choosing the proper utilities and using automation appropriately.

Chapter 10, Transactions and Locking, focuses on the basics of transactions, which are a key part of almost all database applications. It covers ACID properties and transaction commands, and the differences between implicit and explicit transactions. It next examines possible concurrency problems and methods used by various DBMSs to avoid those problems. It concludes with a look at SQL Server transaction support, including isolation level support and methods for detecting and clearing deadlocks.

Chapter 11, Data Access and Security, covers a topic that is critical to any database design. The chapter begins by introducing data server and database connectivity concepts and requirements. From there, it moves on to including server and database access requirements in the database design and implementation, focusing on a two-tier security system with separate server-level and database-level principals, including their role in the connection process. Finally, it introduces access permissions and data protection methods as a way to protect against and recover from data loss.

Chapter 12, Supporting Database Applications, looks at the three most common database configurations for application support. It starts with a look at centralized database configurations and variations on the traditional client/server model. Then, it looks at distributed database configurations that might be used to support enterprise applications, including options for implementing a distributed data environment and the role of replication in maintaining distributed data. It concludes with an examination of issues related to supporting Internet-based applications.

Pre-reading Learning Aids

Each chapter of *Introduction to Database Management* features the following learning and study aids to activate students' prior knowledge of the topics and orient them to the material.

▲ **Pre-test.** This pre-reading assessment tool in multiple-choice format not only introduces chapter material, but it also helps students anticipate the chapter's learning outcomes. By focusing students' attention on what they do not know, the self-test provides students with a benchmark against which they can measure their own progress. The pre-test is available online at www.wiley.com/college/gillenson.

▲ **What You'll Learn in This Chapter**. This bulleted list focuses on subject matter that will be taught. It tells students what they will be learning in this chapter and why it is significant for their careers. It will also help students understand why the chapter is important and how it relates to other chapters in the text.

▲ **After Studying This Chapter, You'll Be Able To.** This list emphasizes capabilities and skills students will learn as a result of reading the chapter. It sets students up to synthesize and evaluate the chapter material, and relate it to the real world.

Within-text Learning Aids

The following learning aids are designed to encourage analysis and synthesis of the material, support the learning process, and ensure success during the evaluation phase:

▲ **Introduction.** This section orients the student by introducing the chapter and explaining its practical value and relevance to the book as a whole. Short summaries of chapter sections preview the topics to follow.

▲ **"For Example" Boxes.** Found within each section, these boxes tie section content to real-world examples, scenarios, and applications.

▲ **Figures and tables.** Line art and photos have been carefully chosen to be truly instructional rather than filler. Tables distill and present information in a way that is easy to identify, access, and understand, enhancing the focus of the text on essential ideas.

▲ **Self-Check.** Related to the "What You'll Learn" bullets and found at the end of each section, this battery of short answer questions emphasizes student understanding of concepts and mastery of section content. Though the questions may either be discussed in class or studied by students outside of class, students should not go on before they can answer all questions correctly.

▲ **Key Terms and Glossary.** To help students develop a professional vocabulary, key terms are bolded in the introduction, summary, and when they first appear in the chapter. A complete list of key terms appears at the end of each chapter and again in a glossary at the end of the book with brief definitions. Knowledge of key terms is assessed by all assessment tools (see below).

▲ **Summary.** Each chapter concludes with a summary paragraph that reviews the major concepts in the chapter and links back to the "What You'll Learn" list.

Evaluation and Assessment Tools

The evaluation phase of the CASE Learning System consists of a variety of within-chapter and end-of-chapter assessment tools that test how well students have learned the material. These tools also encourage students to extend their learning into different scenarios and higher levels of understanding and thinking. The following assessment tools appear in every chapter of *Introduction to Database Management:*

▲ **Summary Questions** help students summarize the chapter's main points by asking a series of multiple choice and true/false questions that emphasize student understanding of concepts and mastery of chapter content. Students should be able to answer all of the Summary Questions correctly before moving on.

▲ **Applying This Chapter** questions drive home key ideas by asking students to synthesize and apply chapter concepts to new, real-life situations and scenarios.

▲ **You Try It** questions are designed to extend students' thinking, and so are ideal for discussion or writing assignments. Using an open-ended format and sometimes based on Web sources, they encourage students to draw conclusions using chapter material applied to real-world situations, which fosters both mastery and independent learning.

▲ **Post-test** should be taken after students have completed the chapter. It includes all of the questions in the pre-test, so that students can see how their learning has progressed and improved. The post-test is available online at www.wiley.com/college/gillenson.

Instructor Package

Introduction to Database Management is available with the following teaching and learning supplements. All supplements are available online at the text's Book Companion Web site, located at www.wiley.com/college/gillenson.

▲ **Instructor's Resource Guide.** Provides the following aids and supplements for teaching an introduction to databases course:

   ▲ *Sample syllabus.* A convenient template that instructors may use for creating their own course syllabi.

   ▲ *Teaching suggestions.* For each chapter, these include a chapter summary, learning objectives, definitions of key terms, lecture notes, answers to select text question sets, and at least 3 suggestions for classroom activities, such as ideas for speakers to invite, videos to show, and other projects.

▲ **PowerPoint Slides.** Key information is summarized in 10 to 15 PowerPoint slides per chapter. Instructors may use these in class or choose to share them with students for class presentations or to provide additional study support.

▲ **Test Bank.** One test per chapter, as well as a mid-term, and two finals: one cumulative, one non-cumulative. Each includes true/false, multiple choice, and open-ended questions. Answers and page references are provided for the true/false and multiple choice questions, and page references for the open-ended questions. Questions are available in Microsoft Word and computerized test bank formats.

Student Project Manual

The inexpensive *Introduction to Database Management Project Manual* contains activities (an average of five projects per textbook chapter) designed to help students apply textbook concepts in a practical way. Easier exercises at the beginning graduate to more challenging projects that build critical-thinking skills.

ACKNOWLEDGMENTS

Taken together, the content, pedagogy, and assessment elements of *Introduction to Database Management* offer the career-oriented student the most important aspects of databases as well as ways to develop the skills and capabilities that current and future employers seek in the individuals they hire and promote. Instructors will appreciate its practical focus, conciseness, and real-world emphasis.

We would like to thank the following reviewers for their feedback and suggestions during the text's development. Their advice on how to shape *Introduction to Database Management* into a solid learning tool that meets both their needs and those of their busy students is deeply appreciated.

Tahir Aziz, Long Beach City College
Debbie Green, Virginia College
Keith Hoell, Katharine Gibbs School

We would also like to thank Carol Traver for all her hard work in formatting and preparing the manuscript for production.

BRIEF CONTENTS

CONTENTS

1

INTRODUCING DATA AND DATA MANAGEMENT

Starting Point

Go to www.wiley.com/college/gillenson to assess your knowledge of data and data management.
Determine where you need to concentrate your effort.

What You'll Learn in This Chapter

▲ The role of data and data management as a business resource
▲ Identifying business processes and related data
▲ Potential concerns about data management

After Studying This Chapter, You'll Be Able To

▲ Understand the role of data and databases as a business resource and be able to use data to gain a competitive advantage
▲ Evaluate your organization's core business and primary processes to identify data collection requirements and sources in order to develop a data management system for your organization
▲ Identify potential human data sources and the data you can expect to retrieve based on organizational roles
▲ Identify key data management concerns in your organization and understand how to protect your organization's data from loss or corruption

INTRODUCTION

We live in a true information age where data is a critical resource. Today, perhaps more than ever before, knowledge is power. This chapter provides an introduction to data and some fundamental points about data management. We start with the role that data has played and continues to play as a business resource. We then look at how business practices help you understand data collection requirements. Finally, we take a brief look at some potential data management concerns.

1.1 Understanding the Role of Data and Databases

It may sometimes seem to you as if every aspect of your life is categorized and tracked from birth to death. In addition, you have direct access to more information than you could ever possibly use through the Internet.

We are being drowned in a veritable sea of data. Much of it is potentially valuable, but the situation has reached the point where data is being gathered so fast that much of it may never be put to use. Although the terms *data* and *information* are often used interchangeably, it is important to understand the distinction between them. **Data** (sometimes called "raw data") is a stream of facts that is not organized or arranged into a form that people can understand or use. Raw data has very little value. For instance, a retail store register captures a variety of raw data, such as the barcode associated with a purchased item, its price, the date and time, and so on. Each of these pieces of data has little meaning in isolation. However, when that raw data is organized by combining it with other similar data and is analyzed, meaningful information, such as the total number of sweaters sold at a particular store on a particular day, can be generated. **Information** is data that has been organized in such a way as to be meaningful and useful to people. One way to convert raw data into information is to use a database. A **database** is an ordered collection of related data elements intended to meet the information needs of an organization and designed to be shared by multiple users. Databases are our most powerful tool for organizing data into potentially valuable information.

Data is indispensable to every kind of modern business and government organization. Data, the applications that process the data, and the computers on which the applications run are fundamental to every aspect of every kind of endeavor. When speaking of corporate resources, people used to list such items as capital, plant and equipment, inventory, personnel, and patents. Today, any such list of corporate resources must include the corporation's data. It has even been suggested that data is the most important corporate resource because it describes all of the others.

Data can give a company a crucial competitive advantage. We routinely speak of data and the information derived from it as competitive weapons in hotly contested industries. For example, FedEx had a significant competitive advantage when it first provided access to its package-tracking data on its Web site. Then, once one company in an industry develops a new application that takes advantage of its data, the other companies in the industry are forced to match it to remain competitive.

This cycle continually moves the use of data to ever higher levels, making it an even more important corporate resource. Examples of this abound. Banks provide their customers with online access to their accounts. Package shipping companies provide up-to-the-minute information on the whereabouts of a package. Retailers send manufacturers product sales data that the manufacturers use to adjust inventories and production cycles. Manufacturers automatically send their parts suppliers inventory data and expect the suppliers to use the data to keep a steady stream of parts flowing.

1.1.1 A Practical Example

Let's take a look at a practical example. Airline companies need an overwhelming amount of data to survive. This includes internal data about their own resources and personnel, but also data about their customers' travel habits and factors that influence their business such as changes in fuel costs or actions taken by competitors.

To understand this, take a look at one small part of the airline business, the process of ticketing and seat reservation. Examine the individual tasks involved in the ticketing and seat reservation process. Let's say that a customer wants to make a trip from New York to Miami on a Monday. Are there any promotional discount plans? The ticketing agent must find and offer a suitable discount plan, if available. Although the agent has the desk, equipment, and other resources, he or she needs information about the available discount plans.

The next task involves checking possible routing options and connecting flights. To perform this task, the agent needs information about the different routing options and connecting flights on Mondays. After going through the routing options and flight times, let's say that the customer has picked a specific routing option. The next task in the process is verifying seat availability. What information does the agent need to complete this task? The agent must have information about seat availability in each leg of the journey. The agent needs different types of information for every task of the process. Figure 1-1 shows information needed for the ticketing and seat reservation process. Notice the various types of information necessary for the process.

We have considered just one process in the airline company. Even for this one process, various types of critical information are essential. Now, consider the number of additional processes involved in day-to-day business activities, each process with its own critical data set (see Figure 1-2). From this, you can start

Figure 1-1

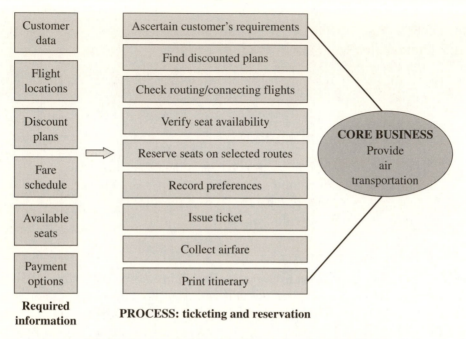

Information needed for ticketing and seat reservation.

Figure 1-2

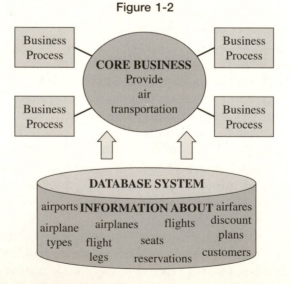

Database system needed to support airline company core business activities.

to get an idea of the volume of information needed by any business or other organization.

1.1.2 Understanding Data Management

Data is a difficult corporate resource to manage. In data, you have a resource of tremendous volume, with billions, trillions, and more individual pieces, each piece of which is different from the next. And much of it is in a state of change at any one time.

As far back as the early to mid-1960s, companies began to realize that storing each application's data separately, in simple files, was problematic for the following reasons:

▲ The increasing volume of data.
▲ The increasing demand for data access.
▲ The need for data security, privacy, backup, and recovery.
▲ The desire to share data and cut down on data redundancy (unwanted duplicate data in a database).

It soon became clear that a new kind of software was needed to help manage the data, as well as faster hardware to keep up with the increasing volume of data and data access demands. In terms of personnel, data management specialists would have to be developed, educated, and given the responsibility for managing the data as a corporate resource.

Out of this need was born a new kind of software, the database management system (DBMS), and a new category of personnel, with titles like database administrator and data management specialist. And, yes, hardware has progressively gotten faster and cheaper for the degree of performance that it provides. The integration of these advances adds up to much more than the simple sum of their parts; they add up to the database environment.

1.1.3 The Need for Data Management

It is practically impossible to buy anything, sell anything, or travel anywhere by air, rail, or sea without the fact being recorded in a database somewhere. With the recent rash of mergers of all kinds of organizations into larger entities, this data is becoming centralized. Residing in databases like the one shown in Figure 1-3, the data can be "mined" for useful information, allowing companies to find out not only who you are and where you live, but also what you like to eat, what you like to read, and who your favorite musicians and entertainers are. They know what your favorite sports teams are, and what sports you like to participate in yourself. They know where you shop and how often. They know when you are about to run out of something you buy regularly. They know when your kids are born, when they

Figure 1-3

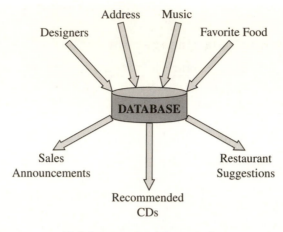

Database and mining results.

are about to enter kindergarten, when they will graduate from high school, and when they are engaged to be married. They then use the information generated from the data stored in the database, along with sophisticated mining software, to target sales efforts with a higher probability of success.

All this data is stored in databases. The databases are growing larger, not only because more data is added to them on a daily basis, but because new kinds of data are being captured and stored, based on the activities and transactions in which you participate in the course of your daily living. The amount of data being stored in databases every day, based on people's actions and transactions, is already huge, but will get even larger in the coming years.

FOR EXAMPLE

Amazon.com

Amazon.com, the largest retailer on the Web, has perfected the technique of using databases to characterize its customers. By analyzing the kinds of products you have bought or expressed interest in, Amazon.com can present you with displays of similar products that you are likely to find interesting. This sales strategy requires not only massive, well-structured databases, but also sophisticated data-mining software that finds associations and relationships in customers' past behavior in order to prediction what customers are likely to do and want in the future.

SELF-CHECK

- Explain why businesses see data management as a critical requirement.
- List companies that collect data about their customers as part of their normal business activities.

1.2 Understanding Data Sources

A single piece of data is a single fact about something that interests us. Think about the world around you, about your environment. In any environment there are things that are important to you, and there are facts about those things that are worth remembering. A thing can be an obvious object like an automobile or a piece of furniture. But the concept of an object is broad enough to include a person, an organization like a company, or an event that took place, like a particular meeting. A fact can be any characteristic of an object. In a university environment it may be the fact that student Gloria Thomas has completed ninety-six credits, or it may be the fact that Professor Howard Gold graduated from Ohio State University, or it may be the fact that English 349 is being held in Room 830 of Alumni Hall. In a commercial environment, it may be the fact that employee John Baker's employee number is 137; or it may be the fact that one of a company's suppliers, the Superior Products Company, is located in Chicago; or it may be the fact that the refrigerator with serial number 958304 was manufactured on November 5, 2004. Usually, we have many facts to describe something of interest to us in our environment.

1.2.1 Picking a Starting Point

Before you can begin organizing data into some useful form, available data must be collected. Data gathering can be tedious, but is critical. Initially, you aren't concerned about sorting the data or trying to identify what is or isn't important. Instead, you need to just get the data together in one central location. Once you have that, you can start figuring out what you can (and should) do with it.

A good place to start is with identifying the company's **core business**—its primary activity and reason for existence. Notice the numerous activities in a company. For example, look at the activities in a car rental business. Different departments are engaged in various activities, like the examples in Figure 1-4. What are the activities in the department that manages the fleet? This department studies the demand for different types of cars. It examines the usage and status at individual branches. It places orders to replace cars that need to be

Figure 1-4

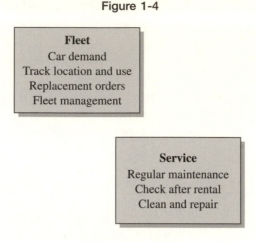

Departmental activities.

retired soon. All these and many more activities within the fleet management department are aimed at supporting the core business of the car rental company, which is renting cars to customers. The servicing department's activities are focused on keeping each car in top condition. Each car must be thoroughly checked after each rental and maintained. Again, the activities of the servicing department, although different from those of fleet management, are also aimed at supporting the core business of the car rental company, namely, renting cars to customers.

Here is a sample of the core businesses of a few types of organizations:

▲ Retail grocery store: buy groceries from vendors and sell to retail customers.
▲ Stock brokerage: buy and sell stocks and bonds for individuals and institutions.
▲ Auction company: enable customers to sell and buy goods through auctions.
▲ Computer consulting: provide consulting services.
▲ Airlines: provide air transportation to customers.
▲ Car dealership: buy and sell cars.
▲ Department store: buy and sell consumer goods.
▲ University: provide higher learning to students.

After you identify what a business is and what it does, you can start to understand the data involved.

1.2.2 Identifying Primary Processes

The core business of an organization typically is to provide goods or services to its customers. The functions of each person and every department in the organization are directed toward accomplishing the purpose of the core business. Many distinctive processes carried out by the departments support the core business. These primary processes fulfill the purpose of the core business.

At this point, data collection can still look like an overwhelming process. Even a simple business can easily have dozens, if not hundreds, of primary processes needed to accomplish its core business goals. Trying to address all of these processes at once is not only daunting, it's nearly impossible and, in the long run, a waste of time. It's better to start by focusing on one process, like airline ticketing and seat assignment.

What tasks must be completed to complete the process? To carry out the various processes, the company needs resources and assets such as buildings, equipment, materials, people, and money. But that is not all. The company also needs information to accomplish its processes. Information is a major asset, like other tangible and intangible assets of the company, used for performing the multitude of processes. Look for the information needed to complete the task, and you have a start on collecting the company's core information resources.

1.2.3 Specific Data Sources

Information comes in a wide variety of forms. In most cases, there is no shortage of available information from which to choose. However, these data sources are not always immediately obvious. You have to work with an organization to locate the information and dig it out from its many possible hiding places.

Finding Current Information

A good place to start is business documents. These include both hard copy and electronic documents. Some are common to most organizations, such as employee records, while others are more specific to the type of organization. Examples of business documents include items such as:

▲ Employee records: includes hiring and firing records, time sheets and other payroll information, vacation records, and related records.

▲ Customer records: includes customer lists, contact information, purchase history.

▲ "Hard" assets: long-term organizational assets such as land, buildings, and equipment.

▲ Inventory records: includes inventory of items for sale as well as items for internal consumption.

▲ Accounting records: information about the organization's resources with a focus on financial resources.

Some of these documents, such as accounting records, are likely already organized to some extent and in an electronic format. Though they often cannot be used as is, they are typically easier to integrate with your database. Other documents may exist only as a hard-copy paper trail, leaving much of the organization (and data entry) up to you.

Finding Historic Information

The task in finding historic information is often not so much identifying the information you need as it is physically locating the information. The older the information, the greater the chance that it exists as paper documents only. These documents may be hidden away in old filing cabinets or in boxes somewhere in the back of a warehouse.

Sometimes you will find that there are gaps in the information, with documents lost, damaged, or destroyed. Some information might no longer apply to the core business activities. The organization may need to make a decision about how far back you need to dig through the historical record, as well as what part of that record is really important.

Be careful not to dismiss data as no longer useful just because it is old. Modern data mining software can find unsuspected relationships between old and new data, identify unexpected trends, and extract a treasure trove of business intelligence.

Using Human Sources

Employees at all levels of the organization are a vital information source during data collection. However, it's important to understand that the information provided by an employee is colored by the employee's environment. Employees are most concerned about the data they need to do their jobs, as in Figure 1-5.

Supervisors and executive staff usually focus on the big picture. They can give you an overall understanding of the organization and how things fit together. They can also provide insight into organization goals, which can directly impact

Figure 1-5

Executive	Big picture data Company overview
Managers	Day-to-day activities
Employees	Job requirements Task-specific information

Human data sources.

data requirements. Front-line managers are more concerned about day-to-day activities, so this is the data with which they are most familiar. A warehouse manager, for example, can provide information about inventory and about purchasing procedures.

Often, the richest source for data requirements and practical data are rank-and-file employees. You need to spend time talking with employees as part of any data collection process. Individual employees might not be able to describe exactly what information they need to do their jobs, but they can describe the jobs they do in detail. From this, you can get an understanding of the data they need. You also get insight into how they need to have the data made available, which can be just as important when designing and developing databases and data applications. You can usually get the most complete picture of the tasks an employee performs through direct observation. Watch what they do and how they do it. If you don't understand something or why it is being done a particular way, ask.

Understanding Data Flows

Part of the data collection process includes understanding how data flows through an organization. What are the data sources? Where or how is the data generated? The answers to these questions often help you locate the data in its purest form.

Data is similar to water, flowing from source to destination. However, with water you have streams running together into rivers, then into larger rivers, and finally into the ocean as its final destination. Data, as it travels, is likely to continue branching out to more and more locations. This is important to you, though, because the better you understand the data destinations (often referred to as **data consumers**), the better you understand both data organization and access requirements. It also helps you design and manage data access security.

FOR EXAMPLE

Hands-on Collection

You are gathering data for a retail organization. How do you find out the data requirements for supporting telephone sales? You do so by watching the sales personnel in action. Watch for both standard requirements and exceptions. How do sales personnel verify product information? How do they check stocking levels? What do they record about the products sold? What do they record about the customer? What is required to complete the transaction? These questions all help to provide direction to your data collection efforts.

SELF-CHECK

- Explain how primary processes can be used to identify data collection requirements.

- Explain why a company's organization chart can be important in determining the employees to interview and what questions to ask during data collection.

- Take a business model with which you are familiar, such as retail grocer, department store, or a school. List the primary processes needed to accomplish core business goals and the types of data needed by each.

1.3 Potential Data Concerns

Every corporate resource has to be carefully managed in order for a company to keep track of it, protect it, and distribute it to those people and purposes in the company that need it. Furthermore, public companies have a responsibility to their shareholders to competently manage the company's assets. The chief financial officer, and a staff of accountants and financial professionals, is responsible for the company's financial resources, with outside accounting firms providing independent audits. Typically, vice presidents of personnel and their staffs are responsible for the administrative functions that are necessary to manage employee affairs; production managers at various levels are responsible for parts inventories; and so on. Data is no exception: it is a resource that must be carefully managed.

A database is no better than the data it contains. The data, in turn, is no better than its source. Business documents are not always accurate or up-to-date. Employees, from rank-and-file through executive staff, can be misinformed or might not understand your question. Sometimes, they might even lie. It isn't always possible to verify all of the data you collect. Still, you need to be aware of the potential for inaccuracies and be ready to correct your data as necessary. One advantage of data management systems is that some types of data inconsistencies become immediately obvious.

Data accuracy is just one of your potential concerns when working with data. You also need to consider data security. Data, as already discussed, is a critical resource. What happens if a competitor gets access to that resource, or if someone accidentally (or maliciously) deletes or modifies the data? Even if your data is accurate and secure, you also have to make it available to those that need it, while maintaining adequate security. This means having the data properly organized and accessible to those who legitimately require access.

1.3.1 Managing Data Accuracy

Data accuracy (ensuring that data is accurate and correct) begins with verifying your source and continues with careful data entry and data manipulation. Most data management systems provide tools to help ensure data accuracy through various means, such as establishing relationships between data values and setting appropriate limits on data values.

During data collection, keep in mind that even though human data sources are an important resource, they are not always accurate. The information provided by employees is filtered by the context of the job they perform and the temptation to put oneself in the best possible light. People often completely ignore some functions they perform simply because they are too familiar with their jobs. They might overlook critical steps or leave out details because they don't seem important. Occasionally, employees at different levels might feel a need to purposely hide information for various reasons, such as the belief that doing so will increase the employee's job security (if the employee is the only one that knows key information, then it's more difficult for the company to fire him or her).

You need to validate your data sources, as far as is possible. You must sometimes also apply a lifetime to the data, a description of how long the data should be considered as accurate. This can be a formal designation or more informal, based a sliding value judgment. Inaccuracies can also arise through poorly designed algorithms (formulas) used to manipulate data.

1.3.2 Managing Data Security

The term data security is somewhat flexible, depending on the context in which it is used. Say "data security" to one person, and the first things that come to mind are protecting the data against unauthorized access and modification. To someone else, it means making sure that the data is protected against corruption or loss. Both are critical concerns. In general, **data security** refers to processes and procedures implemented with the goal of keeping data safe. Basic data security categories include access security and physical security.

The tools available for ensuring data security are somewhat application- and platform-specific. This is important because data is a tempting target. Many of the most destructive viruses, Trojan horses, and other malicious software floating around the Internet right now directly target database applications.

Considering Access Security

Most database systems control **access security** (controlling user and application access to data) through support of one or more **authentication methods,** which are ways of verifying a user's identity before allowing access to the data. Different levels of access permissions are also provided. For example, you can give a user permission to view data, but not change it. Accessibility is also an issue when discussing security. You want to protect the data, but you also need to make it available to the appropriate users.

A vital part of this effort is reducing the **surface area** (a term used to refer to how exposed a database is to access and manipulation) that is vulnerable to attack. The wider your **consumer audience** (or data consumers—the people or applications who need access to data and who use data in some manner), the more difficult this task becomes. Consider a local database that contains all of your company's data. If your employees are the only people that need access to the data, protecting the data is a relatively easy task. The issue of who needs access, as well as the level of access required, is typically well defined. In many cases, you can implement many of the security requirements as an extension to existing network security.

As your potential consumer audience increases, so do your potential security concerns. What if people outside of your company need access to the data, possibly accessing your network resources remotely through the Internet, as shown in Figure 1-6?

Figure 1-6

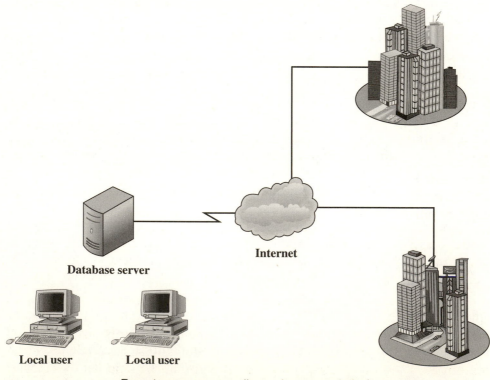

Remote consumer audience (user population).

Now you have less control over the user population. Though not shown in Figure 1-6, additional tools such as network firewalls often come into play. Rather than providing direct access to the data like you have in this example, you might instead provide indirect access, such as through a Web-based application. You will find that there are no one-size-fits-all solutions. Instead, it's likely that you will need to design a custom-access solution matched to the specific access requirements, and be ready to modify the solution and access as needs evolve.

Considering Physical Security

Protecting the data against physical corruption or loss is the role of **physical security.** This usually comes down to three basic tasks:

▲ Protecting the server
▲ Ensuring the storage media
▲ Duplicating the data

Protecting the server is usually a matter of providing physical security, locking the server away from prying eyes and busy fingers. A dedicated, secure server room is the rule in most organizations, with access to server hardware strictly limited.

Ensuring the storage media means making sure that it is reliable and provides a safe location for your data. One of the most common ways of doing this is through fault-tolerant disk systems. A **fault-tolerant disk system,** usually based on Redundant Array of Independent Disk (RAID) technologies, is designed to protect the data in the event of a hard disk failure. Usually, when a hard disk fails, all data on the disk is lost. RAID systems use different configurations based on multiple hard disks that keep the data available and protected should any one hard disk fail. When this happens, it's usually an easy matter to replace the failing disk and reestablish the data protection.

Duplicating data can be accomplished through making a literal duplicate copy, or **mirror image,** of the data. You could keep a copy of the database on one or more additional servers. However, these data image solutions can be expensive to implement and difficult to maintain. It's more likely that you implement the duplication of data through data backups, data copied to a different storage destination and available should data loss occur. You can back up the data to another computer, such as a network file server, or to removable media such as magnetic tape or DVD disk. If something does happen and the database is lost or corrupted, you restore the data from the backup, recreating the database and its data. Of course, any data changes made since the last time you ran a data backup will be lost and must be reposted to the database manually.

1.3.4 Managing Data Organization

For the huge amount of data being captured to be useful, it must be organized. Organization forces a structure on the data, helps to reduce the amount of physical space the data requires, and can help to minimize the time required to locate and retrieve the data that you want. In fact, your only hope for making sense out of the flood of data is to organize it in a way that allows fast, efficient retrieval of the information you want, regardless of how large the dataset is. The longer you wait to organize your data, the harder it will be to do. Whether you are just starting out and as yet have not collected any data, or whether you are in an established organization that has been collecting data for years, there will never be a better time than right now to decide the best way to organize your data so that you can quickly receive answers to the questions you will want to ask both now and in the years to come. After you decide what kinds of information you are likely to want to extract from the data, you can design a database that will make it easy to do so.

Data standards also play a critical role. For the data to be useful, it needs to be organized and entered in the same way for each data object. You need to collect the same data about each instance of an object, and store it the same way each time. For example, when collecting employee data, you would use the same format for storing each employee's name, employee ID, hiring data, and other information about that employee. You need to refer to the data using the same terminology to avoid confusing data consumers and application programmers.

Because of its importance, organization will be your next major task after data collection. This means identifying what is important and deciding how to represent it in a database. You must identify the key items that you want to track, typically referred to as entities, and the information that you want to keep about them, typically referred to as attributes. However, this is just the start of the process. You will need to consider how different entities influence and relate to one another, account for data that depends directly on other data, and so on. Only then can you start seriously designing a database application.

1.3.5 Managing Data Access

We've already mentioned **data access,** the process of allowing users or applications to retrieve data from a database. After all, a database isn't of any use to anyone if they can't retrieve the information that they need from it. Your data security design directly impacts user access. When you organize your data, one of the goals is to optimize performance when accessing and retrieving data.

As you prepare to build your database application, you'll spend much of your time deciding on the database objects you need to include in the database, both for data storage and to support data retrieval. Most solutions also mean programming custom executable objects to support data entry, manipulation, and retrieval.

The term commonly used to refer to data access is a **data query.** A query, though it often implies simple data retrieval, can also be used to insert new data or manipulate existing data. Most database systems use a standard set of commands known as the Structured Query Language, or SQL, to query database data. That is why you often hear modern databases referred to as SQL databases.

When you set up your database, you must determine who needs access to the data and what level of access they need. Not all users need access to the same data. Access requirements are related to users' responsibilities and the business functions (primary practices) they perform (Figure 1-7). Think back to the processes relating to airline ticketing and seat assignment. Ticket agents need access to a great deal of information such as flights, available seats, and ticket prices. There is even more information about the airline, though, to which the ticket agent should not have access, such as confidential financial records.

In addition to determining who needs access, another design decision you'll need to make fairly early is exactly how to give users access to the database. Typically, a very limited number of users have direct access to the database. This is usually restricted to database administrators and, possibly, database programmers. Nearly everyone else accesses the database indirectly through another application. The specific application type depends on the access requirements.

Users responsible for day-to-day activities typically access a database through one or more applications designed to perform specific tasks. For example, ticket

Figure 1-7

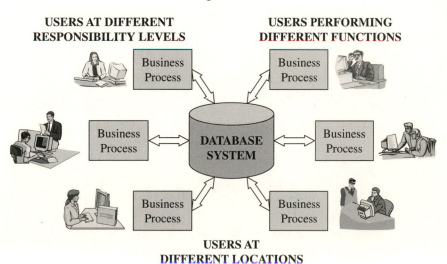

Information access requirements by responsibility and role.

FOR EXAMPLE

The Galileo Spacecraft and Its Data

The Galileo spacecraft has been studying the Jupiter system for several years. It has sent back huge amounts of data. By studying a small fraction of that data, scientists have inferred the existence of a global ocean under the ice covering the surface of Jupiter's moon Europa and the probable existence of a similar ocean under the surface of another of Jupiter's moons, Callisto. However, the large majority of Galileo's data remains unstudied, because in its unorganized state, it is very difficult to extract useful information from it, unless you already know what you are looking for. Organizing the data into a database would be of tremendous benefit, but NASA has no funding for such a massive effort.

agents for an airline would have an application designed to sell tickets and assign seats. A user in a department store working a point-of-sale terminal would have an application designed to post to sales and inventory records. People working in the accounting department would have an application designed to work with financial accounting records. Application requirements relate back to the core business and primary processes.

Other access requirements could add another layer of isolation between the data consumer and the database. Rather than communicating directly with the database, an application might send and receive data through a Web service, which, in turn, is the application that communicates with the database.

SELF-CHECK

- Lists key concerns relating to data management.
- Explain how your network environment can influence your access and security design.
- Explain the need for different levels of data-access security based on responsibilities and roles.
- Identify tools you might need to implement physical data security.
- Compare and contrast direct database access, indirect access by local clients, and indirect access by remote clients.

SUMMARY

In this chapter, you learned fundamental concepts relating to data, its role as a business resource, and requirements for data management. You compared data requirements from both historic and modern perspectives, including a look at a specific business process and related data requirements. You investigated the need for data collection and how to identify data sources based on core business activities and primary processes. You were also introduced to some of the fundamentals of data management and potential concerns related to data management.

KEY TERMS

Access security

Authentication method

Consumer audience

Core business

Data

Data access

Data accuracy

Data consumer

Data query

Data security

Database

Fault-tolerant disk system

Information

Mirror image

Physical security

Surface area

ASSESS YOUR UNDERSTANDING

Go to www.wiley.com/college/gillenson to evaluate your knowledge of data and data management.

Measure your learning by comparing pre-test and post-test results.

Summary Questions

1. The terms data and information mean the same thing. True or false?
2. What is a database management system?
   (a) an organization responsible for database maintenance and administration
   (b) specialized software designed to implement, support, and maintain databases
   (c) a manual method of record-keeping phased out with the introduction of computers
   (d) an end-user application designed to give users access to data
3. Which statement best describes the role of data in business?
   (a) Data collection and organization is a low-priority effort with few benefits for a business.
   (b) Data is important to business in the information technology sector only.
   (c) All businesses freely share data about their customers in a cooperative environment.
   (d) Data can provide a competitive advantage in hotly contested industries.
4. Which of the following statements best describe the use of business documents during initial data collection?
   (a) You should collect all business documents except those relating to personnel records.
   (b) Limit collection efforts to documents in electronic format only as hard-copy documents seldom contain useful information.
   (c) You should collect all available business documents, including both electronic and hard-copy documents.
   (d) It is safe to assume that all business documents you locate are complete, accurate, and applicable to the current business environment.
5. When interviewing employees to collect data, you should limit yourself to executive staff, supervisors, and managers only. True or False?
6. A good place for identifying the starting point for data collection is an organization's core business. True or False?

7. How do primary processes relate to data collection activities?

   (a) Primary processes give you a way of validating data accuracy.

   (b) The tasks required to complete primary processes identify critical business data sources.

   (c) Primary processes DO NOT relate to data collection activities.

8. Executive staff personnel are a good source for what kind of information?

   (a) an overall understanding of the organization and its goals

   (b) critical details of day-to-day activities at all levels

   (c) details of the tasks required to perform primary processes

   (d) identification of data paths within the organization

9. How do primary processes relate to an organization's core business?

   (a) The primary processes and core business are one in the same.

   (b) The primary processes fulfill the core business.

   (c) The primary processes are those business activities occurring outside of the core business.

   (d) The primary processes provide a clear and concise definition of the core business.

10. Which of the following is an advantage of records in an electronic format versus those in hard copy only?

    (a) The records relate to current business activities.

    (b) The records can typically be used as is, without additional modification.

    (c) The records are typically already organized for you.

11. Which of the following is typically NOT a goal in data management?

    (a) keeping data physically secure

    (b) making all data available to all employees

    (c) ensuring that the data is timely and accurate

    (d) ensuring that the data is organized for easy retrieval

12. Raw data is just as useful and valuable as organized data. True or False?

13. For what purpose are authentication methods implemented?

    (a) to verify users before allowing access to data

    (b) to set access limits through defined permissions

    (c) to provide physical security for critical data

    (d) to maintain data organization

14. For what reason would you implement RAID technologies as part of your design?

    (a) to provide user authentication

    (b) to limit user access permissions

(c) to provide fault-tolerant data storage

(d) to organize data for easy retrieval

15. Which of the following is NOT a reason for organizing data in a database?

    (a) to provide fault tolerant storage

    (b) to reduce the space required for storage

    (c) to optimize data retrieval times

    (d) to force a structure on the data

16. Database backups are an example of which of the following?

    (a) data organization

    (b) access security

    (c) physical security

    (d) user access methods

Applying This Chapter

1. You are trying to justify a computerized data management system to your supervisor. You work in a service industry that deals directly with customers. How could collecting information about your customers provide a competitive edge? What kind of software would you need to detect trends and make projections about customer activities?

2. You have been asked to design a database application for a company in the retail industry. The company sells through physical stores, through telephone sales, and through e-commerce over the Internet. How can you determine the best sources of information for each of the sales efforts? How can you determine what information you need to collect from each of the sales efforts?

3. Your company has implemented a database management system to track all business-related data from the company. Access to the data should be limited to employees only. How can you ensure this? What other access protections should you place on the data? What guidelines should you use in determining levels of user access? What methods can you use to protect the data against loss or corruption?

Data Collection and Organization

You are heading up the data collection efforts for your company's new database project. You are responsible for determining what information you need to collect and how it should be collected.

1. Discuss how you can identify the primary processes within a company.
2. What might the company have available that would let you associate employees with the jobs they perform?
3. Why is it important to collect all available information during the initial collection process?

Data Management

You are responsible for identifying data management concerns within your organization. Your company includes employees that telecommute and must access the local network via the Internet. Both local employees and telecommuters will need access to data in the database.

1. Explain why it is important to both implement access security and assign access permissions to data. What guidelines should you use for assigning permissions?
2. Discuss possible options for providing employees with access to data. Compare available options for local employees and telecommuters.

2

INTRODUCING DATABASES AND DATABASE MANAGEMENT SYSTEMS

Starting Point

Go to www.wiley.com/college/gillenson to assess your knowledge of databases and database management systems.
Determine where you need to concentrate your effort.

What You'll Learn in This Chapter

▲ Key database concepts and components and their importance
▲ The evolution of database implementation models and their significance
▲ Database system architecture and components
▲ How hardware and software work together to create a database management system

After Studying This Chapter, You'll Be Able To

▲ Understand basic database components and deployment models in order to build an appropriate data environment to support the core business processes of your organization
▲ Critically evaluate database models to determine an appropriate model to support your organization's information requirements
▲ Determine appropriate hardware and software to support the overall architecture of your organization's database environment

INTRODUCTION

No one can deny the importance of information in today's data-driven world. Vital to putting all of this information to use is the ability to organize, manipulate, and retrieve data on demand. Therein lays the importance of databases and database management systems. In order to understand databases and how to get the most out of them, you need to understand key terms and have a basic concept of the components involved and how they fit together in a coherent architectural model. That is the goal of this chapter.

In this chapter, we lift away some of the protective covers to look into the nuts and bolts of what makes up a database and a database management system (DBMS). Keep in mind throughout this chapter that databases and DBMSs have different roles and different components. The database, while a complicated entity in itself, at its core is simply where we store the data. The DBMS contains all of the other components that make the database a viable storage and retrieval tool.

2.1 Introduction to Key Database Concepts

Today, almost all organizations depend on their database systems for the crucial information they need to run their business. In every industry, from the small mom and pop business to multinational enterprises and government agencies, database systems are the norm for information storage and retrieval. Commerce, whether traditional brick and mortar or Internet-based e-commerce, thrive or die based on how they use the data they collect. Database and Web technologies have merged into something significantly more powerful than either one alone.

The Information Technology (IT) department of today's organization has the primary responsibility for designing, supporting, and maintaining database systems. However, IT personnel aren't the only ones who need at least some understanding of database technologies and what they can do for a business. Data, in today's rapidly changing environment, is everybody's business.

2.1.1 Database Approach to Data

As you learned in Chapter 1, a database can be defined as an ordered collection of related data elements intended to meet the information needs of an organization and designed to be shared by multiple users, as described in Figure 2-1.

Let's break the characteristics of a database down:

▲ A database is an ordered collection. It is a collection of data elements—not a random group, but a collection put together deliberately, with proper order. The data elements are linked together in the most logical manner.

Figure 2-1

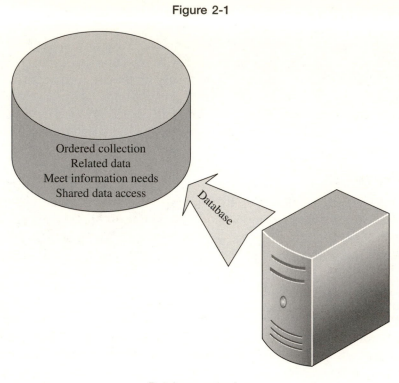

Ordered collection
Related data
Meet information needs
Shared data access

Database

Database overview.

▲ A database contains related data elements. The data elements in a database are not disjointed structures, but are instead interrelated and pertinent to the particular organization.

▲ A database is designed to meet information needs. The collection of data elements in a database is there for a specific purpose, to satisfy organizational information needs. In a bank's database, you find data elements pertinent to the bank's business, such as customers' bank balances and ATM transactions. You won't find unrelated data that doesn't apply, or at the very least, you shouldn't. Information like a customer's favorite color or whether or not the customer likes dogs doesn't fit in the mix.

▲ Database data is shared. All authorized users share information stored in an organization's database so that all user groups can collaborate to accomplish the organization's objectives.

2.1.2 Understanding Basic Concepts

In order to understand databases, you need to understand several basic concepts and must be familiar with the terminology used. These include:

▲ Data repository

▲ Data dictionary

▲ Database software

▲ Data abstraction

▲ Data access

▲ Transaction support

We take a little time to review each of these in the following sections.

Data Repository

All data in the database resides in a **data repository.** This is the data storage unit where the physical data files are kept and the central storage location for the data content. The physical structure of the data repository is database specific.

Data Dictionary

The data repository contains the actual data. Let's say that you want to keep data about your customers. There are two aspects of this data. One aspect is the structure of the data consisting of the field names, field sizes, data types, and so on. The other part is the actual data values stored in the fields.

This first part, relating to the structure, typically is stored separately from the database values as the data dictionary or data catalog. A **data dictionary (data catalog)** contains the data element structures and the relationships among data elements. The data dictionary and the data repository work together to provide information to users.

Database Software

Though sometimes referred to as databases, products like Microsoft Access, SQL Server, MySQL, Oracle, Informix, and similar products are technically the software that manages data and databases. These are **database software** or **database management systems (DBMS),** which support storing, retrieving, and updating data in a database. The database software, or database management system (DBMS), is not the database itself, but lets you store, manage, and protect the data in a database.

Data Abstraction

Consider a situation where you want to store information about customers. Data about each customer consists of several fields such as customer name, street address, city, state, zip code, credit status, and so on. Depending on users' requirements and roles in an organization, different users consider the data from different levels of data abstraction. **Data abstraction,** in this context, is a way of looking at data that breaks it down into its basic components and groups the components to give you different ways of looking at the data. It gives you the ability to hide the complexities of data design at the levels where they are not required.

Consider the requirements of a retail business. Sales personnel need general information about customers and inventory, but only limited information. The warehouse manager needs different information about inventory, such as suppliers and inventory costs. A database programmer needs a more complete understanding of the data to know what is available for use in the application design. A database administrator needs access to all information about any database entities, not just database data, but schema and design information as well.

Data Access

The database approach includes the fundamental operations that can be applied to data. Every database management system provides for the following data access basic operations:

- ▲ READ data contained in the database.
- ▲ ADD data to the database.
- ▲ UPDATE individual parts of the data in the database.
- ▲ DELETE portions of the data in the database.

Database practitioners, who are personnel such as database designers and programmers, refer to these operations by the abbreviation **CRUD:**

- ▲ C: create or add data.
- ▲ R: read data.
- ▲ U: update data.
- ▲ D: delete data.

Transaction Support

Consider the process for entering an order from a customer into the computer system. The order entry clerk types in the customer number, the product code, and the quantity ordered. The order entry program retrieves the customer data so the clerk can verify the customer data, retrieves and displays product information and inventory data, and finally completes the order and updates inventory or creates a back order. All these tasks perform a single primary task, entering a single order comprised of a single order entry transaction. A **transaction** is a series of statements or commands that execute as a group, like the statements represented in Figure 2-2. All of the statements must either run successfully or all must be rolled back, backing out the results as if the statements were never run. This compensates for errors that might occur during transaction execution.

When a transaction is initiated it should complete all the tasks and leave the data in the database in a consistent state. For example, if the initial stock is 1000 units and the order is for 25 units, the stock value stored in the database after

Figure 2-2

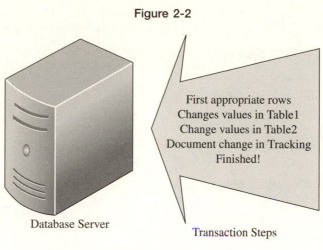

Database Server   Transaction Steps

First appropriate rows
Changes values in Table1
Change values in Table2
Document change in Tracking
Finished!

Transaction.

the transaction is completed must be 975 units and there must be an order in file documenting the sale of the 25 units.

2.1.3 Database Use

Figure 2-3 illustrates the primary types of databases and their uses. **Production databases** support the core business and operational systems of an enterprise. Most databases fall in this category. More recently, with increasing demand for information,

Figure 2-3

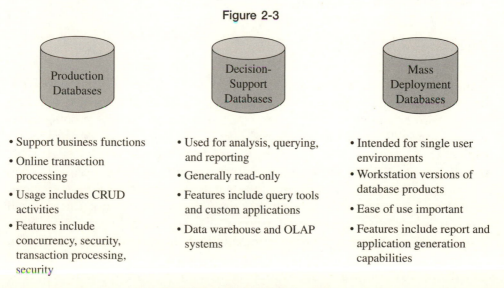

Production Databases

- Support business functions
- Online transaction processing
- Usage includes CRUD activities
- Features include concurrency, security, transaction processing, security

Decision-Support Databases

- Used for analysis, querying, and reporting
- Generally read-only
- Features include query tools and custom applications
- Data warehouse and OLAP systems

Mass Deployment Databases

- Intended for single user environments
- Workstation versions of database products
- Ease of use important
- Features include report and application generation capabilities

Database types and their uses.

FOR EXAMPLE

Choosing an Appropriate Deployment Model

You are a database designer and administrator for a business with offices throughout the United States. All of the database and other IT support personnel are located in the home office in Chicago, Illinois. You support a single database server named "Ol_Faithful" with access provided to the remote offices through remote networking.

The company recently acquired another company in the same industry, primarily to get its customer list and other business intelligence. Your job is to make the data available as quickly as possible with minimal interruption to current procedures and user access to current data. The new database server, named "OurData," is physically located in St. Louis, Missouri, and runs a different DBMS than your existing database server. Also, you determine that you can't import data from the new server into the existing server without first upgrading Ol_Faithful to a more powerful computer with larger hard disks.

How does this situation fit into the implementation models? What you need is to change your current centralized model into a distributed model, but with all of the servers physically located in the same place. Bring the OurData server to Chicago. That's where all of your support staff is located, and your infrastructure is designed to support centralized data access from Chicago. Once you have the server physically in place, you can provide access through a distributed model based on a heterogeneous data environment. This buys you time until you can upgrade Ol_Faithful and combine the data onto one server.

---

databases are serving another important function. These **decision support databases** are designed to support advanced data mining and provide support for strategic decision making in an organization. Production databases and decision support databases are typically large-scale databases designed to support several users' needs within an organization. When a company uses both, the production database has the added role of acting as the data source for the decision support database.

Individuals and single departments might also use private databases (referred to in the figure as mass deployment databases), but this is typically discouraged unless required for security or other reasons. However, having multiple databases does not necessarily mean implementing multiple database servers. Instead, you can implement multiple databases through a single server.

Businesses implement databases using either a centralized model or a distributed model. In the **centralized model,** you have a single, centrally located database server. This server and the database it hosts contain all of the business data. This model is relatively easy to implement, but can become difficult to support if you have to provide data access for remote users.

The **distributed model** uses multiple database servers with the data spread across the servers. Each server typically contains its own unique set of data. Servers are usually deployed in different physical locations. The database servers can all use the same DBMS, or use different database products, giving you a **heterogeneous data environment** made of mixed database types, operating systems, and hardware platforms. Potential drawbacks include the need for reliable communication between the database servers and the fact that different database products don't always interface well with each other.

SELF-CHECK

- Explain basic database concepts relating to data and transactions.
- Discuss how the basic building blocks of a database work together to provide a data environment.
- List business factors that would determine whether it would be better to deploy a centralized or distributed database model. Be sure to include cost as part of the determining factors.
- Compare the role of the data repository with that of the data dictionary and describe how the two interact.

2.2 Understanding Basic Database Models

The basic database models are:

▲ Hierarchical database model
▲ Network database model
▲ Relational database model
▲ Object-oriented database model

The original implementations of the hierarchical and network approaches to database are both called navigational approaches because of the way that programs have to "navigate" through hierarchies and networks of data to find the data they need. Both of these technologies were developed in the 1960s and, relative to the other approaches, are somewhat similar in structure.

Our focus is on **relational databases,** which are databases based on the relational model, and hybrid databases, which are based on an integration of different models in one database. The relational database approach became commercially viable in about 1980. It is currently the preferred database model and is implemented in applications from simple desktop storage to massive enterprise-level applications. The object-oriented approach has proven useful for a variety of niche applications. In this approach, data items are treated as objects, which are individual items that can be defined and described. The importance of the object-oriented approach is that some of the key object-oriented database concepts have found their way into some of the mainstream relational systems and provide a hybrid object/relational database system.

2.2.1 The Hierarchical Database Model

The **hierarchical database model** is based on a hierarchical data organization. In the business world, many data structures are hierarchical in nature. You can trace a hierarchy by division, subdivision, department, and employee. Figure 2-4 illustrates one such model showing the hierarchy of customer, order, and order line item. A customer can have one or more orders, and an order can have one or more line items.

Each data structure representing a business object is at one hierarchical level. The data segment at the top level of the hierarchy is known as the root data segment (as in an inverted tree). The relationship between each pair of data structures at levels next to each other is a parent-child relationship. CUSTOMER is a parent data segment whose child is ORDER. Each child can have one parent,

Figure 2-4

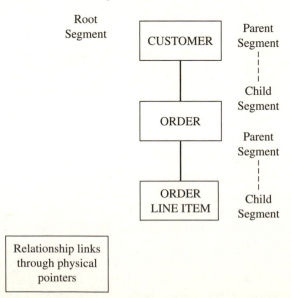

Hierarchical database model.

> **FOR EXAMPLE**
>
> ### Hierarchical Storage in the Real World
>
> Though it isn't based on the hierarchical database model, hierarchical storage has seen rapidly growing interest recently with the use of extensible markup language (XML) files. XML files are commonly used for local data storage and for data transfer over the Internet. XML is not a database type, but is instead a data storage and presentation format. XML is used as an internal format, or at least a formatting option, in several database systems. However, some new database systems, designed primarily for small, low-volume databases, are based on XML data files and storage structures. Even though they use hierarchical storage, they are not hierarchical model databases.

but a parent can have multiple children. You might want to separate orders into phone orders and mail orders. In that case, CUSTOMER may have PHONE ORDER and MAIL ORDER as two child segments. The parent/child links are maintained through **physical data pointers** that are embedded in the data records. The parent has a pointer to the child record and the child has a pointer back to its parent.

2.2.2 The Network Database Model

The network database model overcomes some of the limitations of the hierarchical database model and is more representative of real-world information requirements. The network database model can represent most business information. As you can see in Figure 2-5, the model doesn't attempt to force the data into hierarchical levels. Notice the six data elements of sales territory, salesperson, customer, order, order line item, and payment as nodes in a network arrangement.

The **network database model** expresses relationships between two record types by designating one as the owner record type and the other as the member record type. For each owner, there are one or more member types. The owner record type works somewhat like a hierarchical model parent and the member record type like a hierarchical child. Each member type and its corresponding owner record type form a set, which represents the relationship. A key difference between this and the hierarchical model is that each child (member) can have multiple parents (owners). The relationships between the owner and member are maintained by physical pointers in the data records. The owner points to its members and each member points to its owner or owners.

Figure 2-5

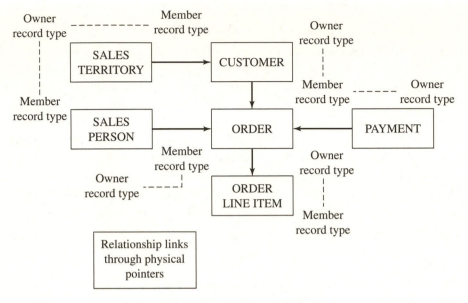

Network database model.

2.2.3 The Relational Database Model

The relational database model is superior to the earlier models. In business, many data structures and their relationships cannot be readily placed in a hierarchical arrangement. Also, in both the hierarchical and network models, you use physical pointers to connect related data. The **relational database model** establishes the connections between related data occurrences by means of logical links implemented through **foreign keys,** which define and maintain relationships through logical pointers. Figure 2-6 illustrates the relational database model.

Just like the network database model, no hierarchical levels are present in the relational model. As in the network model, the lines connect the various data structures with no restrictions. Instead, the model is based on two-dimensional tables. A **table** is the fundamental object in a relational database, and is made up of rows and columns. In general, each table represents a single **entity,** which is a single definable type of item that you want to track in your database. Each entity is described by its **attributes,** the information you can track and record about the entity. The table columns store attribute data describing the entity. Each row represents a single, unique instance of that entity. This is typically enforced through a **primary key** that enforces uniqueness on a key column or set of key columns. By doing this, it enforces uniqueness on the table.

The primary key is also used in defining relationships. When you create a foreign key in the referencing table, it must point to a column with the same value set in the referenced table. Typically, the foreign key points to the primary

Figure 2-6

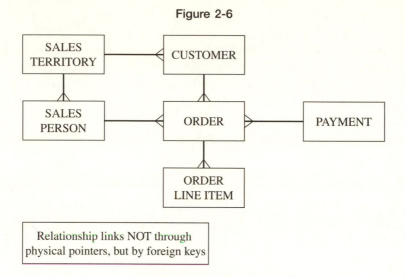

Relational database model.

key in the referenced table, or it can also point to a column that has been specifically configured as unique.

For example, the CUSTOMER table represents the data for all customers. Columns in the CUSTOMER table describe the customer with information such as the customer ID value, name, address, and so forth. The ORDER table represents the data content for all orders and the information describing each order.

In the relational model you define relationships between different data elements. A **relationship** is an association defined and established between two data entities. Consider the relationship between CUSTOMER and ORDER. Each customer might have one or more orders. Each customer occurrence must be connected to all related order occurrences. In the relational model, a foreign key field (column) is included in the ORDER data structure to define that relationship. For each customer order in ORDER, the foreign key identifies the related customer. To look for all the orders for a particular customer, you search through the foreign key field of ORDER and find those orders with that customer's ID value in the foreign key field.

The foreign key enforces and maintains the relationship between CUSTOMER and ORDER. This replaces the physical pointers used in the hierarchical and network models. Even though this model does not use physical data pointers to define relationships, it does still use them. Physical data pointers are used in many implementations of the relational model to identify where data rows are physically stored to help optimize data retrieval.

2.2.4 The Object–Oriented Database Model

Object-oriented databases integrate object orientation with database technology. Object orientation enables a more precise, truer depiction of real-world objects, so an object-oriented database can provide a better representation of real-world information requirements than earlier data systems. Object orientation allows a developer to hide the details of implementation and concentrate on true representation, combining features of object orientation such as abstract data typing and distinctive object identities with database capabilities such as transaction processing, concurrency control, recovery, and security. **Concurrency control** deals with ensuring data accuracy and reliability in a multi-user environment. For example, concurrency control can prevent two users from modifying the same data at the same time.

Object-oriented databases evolved to address some of the limiting features of relational databases. For example, even though recent versions of relational database systems support binary large objects (BLOB) data types, some can handle only limited data types. A **data type** is a way of describing the kind of data that can be stored in a column or table. **BLOB data types** are used to store large quantities of binary data, such as a digital photograph or an executable file. Object-oriented database systems include additional data types, including multimedia-specific data types optimized for storing audio and video data and user-defined data types. Object-oriented systems also support user-defined functions.

In the relational data model, each table does not necessarily represent a real-world entity accurately. You might have to combine two or three tables to fully represent the entity. The added flexibility and enhanced data types in the object-oriented data model avoids this and improves the representation of real-world entities.

A detailed discussion of the object database model is beyond the scope of this book, except in how it relates to a hybrid model, sometimes referred to as the object-relational database model. This is the model you are most likely to see implemented in the database applications of most businesses.

2.2.5 The Object-Relational Database Model

The most popular and most powerful of the modern database system applications, including Oracle and Microsoft SQL Server, are built on an **object-relational database model.** These applications are built on a historically relational database platform, but integrate many features from the object database model such as more flexible data types and the ability to create user-defined data types and user-defined functions. Based on current industry trends, it's likely that this merging will continue, blurring the lines between the relational and object database models. Object-relational database management systems (ORDBMS) present viable solutions for handling complex data types. The object-relational model combines the ability of object technology to handle advanced types of relationships with features of data integrity, reliability, and recovery found in the relational realm. A sample table, such as you might see in an object-relationship

Figure 2-7

Product Number	Product Name	Unit Price	Image
16386	Wrench	12.95	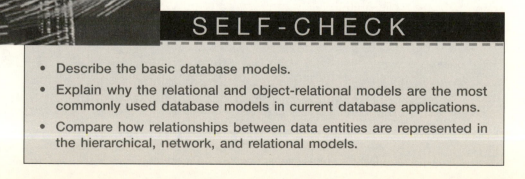
19440	Hammer	17.50	
21765	Drill	92.99	
24013	Saw	26.25	
26722	Pliers	11.50	

Object-relational database table.

database, is shown in Figure 2-7. Notice in this example that the data includes large-object image data.

It is now common to see the **Unified Modeling Language (UML)** used when creating data models for relational database management system (RDBMS) based applications. UML was developed in 1997 specifically as the modeling language to describe data models for object-oriented database systems.

SELF-CHECK

- Describe the basic database models.
- Explain why the relational and object-relational models are the most commonly used database models in current database applications.
- Compare how relationships between data entities are represented in the hierarchical, network, and relational models.

2.3 Database Components

How do you determine the architecture of a building? You look at the building blocks and the arrangement of the components in the structure. These building blocks and their arrangement make up the building's architecture. You can look at the overall architecture of a database environment in much the same way. What are the pieces that make up the architecture? How do they fit together to make a cohesive whole?

Essentially, a database environment is responsible for data storage, retrieval, manipulation, and a wide range of support activities. The data repository constitutes one piece of the overall architecture. You need specialized software to manage and make use of the data. You need hardware to store and process the data. You need people, including users (the data consumers) and practitioners (personnel such as database programmers and administrators). You need procedures that relate to users and processing, providing guidelines for the storage, management, and use of data. Figure 2-8 illustrates the possible architecture of a database environment in an organization. Pay close attention to the individual components and how they are connected.

Figure 2-8

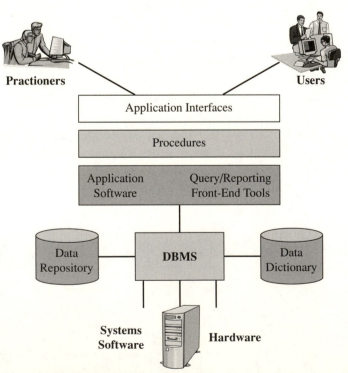

Database environment overall architecture.

You've already been introduced to some of these, specifically the data repository, data dictionary, and database software, here shown as the DBMS. Let's take a brief look at each of these functional building blocks, which include the following:

▲ **Data repository:** stores the organization's data in databases. This is essential in every database environment.

▲ **Data dictionary:** contains the definition of structures of the data stored in the data repository.

▲ **DBMS:** the Database Management System software needed to manage storage, use, and protection of the data stored in the database.

▲ **Systems software:** includes the operating system, network operating system, and utility programs that are needed to support and work with the DBMS.

▲ **Hardware:** hardware is part of the underlying infrastructure and includes processors, storage devices, and network connections.

▲ **Network:** part of the hardware, but outside of the computer providing local and remote communication paths. Can include the Internet as a remote communication backbone.

▲ **Application software:** suite of application programs to perform business processes that use the database.

▲ **Front-end tools:** these include query tools, report writers, and other front-end tools that supplement the application programs for data access and usage.

▲ **Procedures:** procedures relate to instructions and guidelines for use by database practitioners and end users to streamline the operations in the database environment.

▲ **Application interfaces:** these include hardware and software components at the client workstation to connect to the database through application programs, query tools, or report writers.

▲ **Practitioners:** these include data administrators, database administrators, analysts, and programmers responsible for database design, deployment, and maintenance.

▲ **Users:** the fundamental goal of a database environment is to satisfy the information needs of the end users. The user population extends to the entire organization in need of information for performing their day-to-day tasks.

The components in the overall architecture fall into three major groups: (1) hardware, (2) software, and (3) people and procedures.

2.3.1 Hardware Components

Hardware components form the basic infrastructure over which the functions of the database environment take place. Hardware includes the individual computers and the network infrastructure that provides a communication path. Though not discussed separately here, the network also includes a software component responsible for managing communications, resource sharing, and security.

Individual computers require hardware storage to store data along with structure definitions. Processors and the computer memory components physically retrieve, process, and update the data. You need communication links between users, application servers, and databases. Figure 2-9 shows parts of the hardware infrastructure.

Databases are traditionally deployed on a mainframe or mini-computer, or in a client/server configuration. Our focus is on the client/server configuration, which uses PCs as both database servers and clients. Key hardware components include the processor, main memory, input/output (I/O) control, communications' links, and storage devices.

Ensuring that computers meet hardware requirements is critical to successful DBMS installation and reliable server performance. Manufacturers usually provide minimum hardware requirements as well as a recommended configuration. The minimum requirements are the minimum computer components needed to install and run the product. However, these are only the requirements for the smallest databases and simplest applications. Actual requirements vary

Figure 2-9

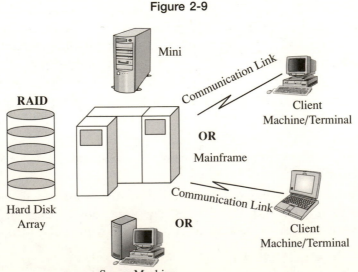

Database system hardware infrastructure.

depending on variable factors such as the size and type of database, the expected number of users, details of the database application and its processing requirements, and whether or not the server must support other applications in addition to the DBMS. Most manufacturers provide guidelines for calculating your actual server requirements.

In a database environment, servers and client workstations require powerful, fast processors. The processors in the client computers perform instructions to present data to the users in many new and sophisticated ways. There may be additional processing requirements, such as locally performed calculations, depending on the specific client application software. The processors in the application servers (database servers) must process complex requests for data from the database and perform data manipulation. As with the client, requirements vary depending on the application. A common option is to have a multiple-tier configuration for server-side processing where the database server is separate from an application server running additional application components.

Main memory provides temporary storage of data and programs. This is also where data manipulation physically occurs. On a database server, much of the memory is dedicated to **memory buffers**, memory set aside within the main memory specifically for storing database data, as shown in Figure 2-10. When data is initially requested, it is read from the hard disk and maintained in the

Figure 2-10

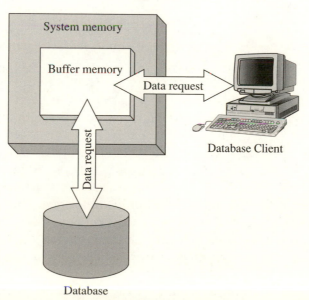

Buffer memory use.

memory buffers. Data can be read from the memory buffers for data extraction or processing as needed. In a database environment, you must move large volumes of data through the memory buffers. The data remains in memory until the space is needed and it is overwritten by new data coming into the buffers. Because of this, when a request is made for data, the memory buffers are searched first to see whether the requested data is already there. If so, then the data can be accessed from memory and used much faster than when being read from the hard disk.

Computer systems use I/O (input/output) mechanisms to move data into and out of the computer's main memory from **secondary storage,** a term used to refer to **nonvolatile storage** media that does not lose the data it contains if the computer is turned off, such as hard disks. Modern PCs improve transfer performance through **direct memory access (DMA)** channels that let devices such hard disk drives, floppy drives, video adapters, and network adapters transfer data directly to and from memory without going through the processor cache.

Another I/O concern is communication between computers. In earlier database environments, most of the processing was done locally around a centralized database. Today's database environments are different. Distributed databases have become common. Data communications components move high volumes of data between distributed databases at different locations. Communication links with sufficient capacity and speed to handle the data movement are critical. These communications links include both local communications through a local network, and remote communications through a wide-area or enterprise network. The Internet is used extensively as the communication path of choice for remote communications.

Data storage devices such as disk, tape, and CD or DVD drives are critical. Without nonvolatile data storage on secondary storage devices, there is no database. How you use secondary storage and how you are able to retrieve data from it affects the performance of the database environment. Often, storage device performance is the most limiting factor when optimizing database server performance.

Two primary concerns are capacity and speed. You were introduced earlier to the data repository as containing all of the database data. Your secondary storage must have sufficient capacity to hold all of this data along with program files, operating system files, and any other data stored locally on the computer. It must also provide for high-speed data access so that data requests are processed quickly and efficiently. Secondly, data storage should be fault tolerant. Data storage mechanisms should ensure that the database operations continue even when some malfunction affects parts of the storage. RAID technology devices are a common solution and allow you to store data so that even if one disk fails, the database operations continue. **RAID,** which stands for redundant array of inexpensive (or independent, depending on who you ask) disks, provides high-performance disk storage. Most RAID configurations also provide fault-tolerant storage.

FOR EXAMPLE

Comparing Data Storage Formats

A DBMS stores data in an operating system file. The total number of files involved and how they are structured depends on the particular DBMS. You can get an idea of common variations by comparing popular examples.

Our first example is Microsoft Access. Access uses a relatively simple storage structure, creating a single file when you create the database. The database objects are contained in this one file. This has its advantages, such as making the database extremely portable, but it is also limited, with few options for managing storage. For example, there is little you can do with the database file to improve performance.

MySQL is an open source application with versions available that you can download and use free of charge. There are also for-purchase versions that include additional tools and utilities. It is a complete RDBMS product and a popular choice for Web-based applications. When you create a MySQL database, it creates a data folder containing an.opt file, which contains option settings for the database. Separate data files are created in the database folder for each table and view that you create in the database (a **view** is a database object that supports custom data retrieval). One drawback of this storage system is that you must deal with a large number of separate files when managing a large, complicated database.

MySQL also shares log files between databases. Log files are used in most database systems to store errors, informational messages, database activity, and other database information. These shared log files include a log that tracks statements executed against the database as a way of logging transaction activity.

Microsoft SQL Server is one of the most full-featured database products on the market. It includes a wide range of features and supports something of an object-relational database model. Different versions, called editions, are available to support a wide range of database needs.

A SQL Server database is physically made up of at least two and possibly more files. One required file is the database file and contains the database objects and data. The other is the transaction log that tracks any activity that modifies the database. The data storage model is designed so you can create additional data files as needed and specify the physical file locations. You can then define the file in which a database object is created. This gives you a way of spreading a database across multiple hard disks. You have control over how the space is used and, by sharing the work between multiple drives, a way of improving database performance and I/O throughput.

The data storage component also relates to the storage of the structure definitions in the data dictionary, the database's metadata. **Metadata** is a term referring to data about data. It's the data that describes the database and database objects. The storage format is specific to the database management system software used. Structure definitions specify database and object schemas. In this context, **schema** refers to the design and structure of database objects. For example, a table's schema describes, among other items, the columns that make up the table.

Speed is of the essence for the storage devices holding the data dictionary. This is especially true because, with many database systems, the data dictionary must be accessed first before the data is accessed.

You may also have removable storage media components, such as a tape drive or writeable CD or DVD drive, to support database backups and data archiving. In a well-managed design, databases are backed up regularly. The backups are used for recovery if and when problems occur and data is lost. You can run backups to a shared storage location on the network or to local removable media. Also, periodically, you might archive old data to remove it from the active database for storage in a separate location.

2.3.2 Software Requirements

Collectively, the software component includes the specialized database management system (DBMS) (discussed further in Section 2.3.3), operating system software, and application programs. The **operating system software,** among the other tasks that it must perform, acts as the layer between the database management system and hardware. For example, when a user requests some data from the database, the database management system processes the request. It determines what data is requested and where the data is physically located. Then the DBMS has the operating system software retrieve the data from physical storage. The operating system software, in turn, interacts with physical hardware to retrieve the data.

The operating system is a required component on any computer. For desktops PCs, different versions of Microsoft Windows are the most common operating system choice. However, acceptance of the Linux operating system is growing steadily, with many hardware manufacturers offering computers with Linux already installed.

No matter which operating system you run, it serves the same function. It manages and provides access to hardware resources through software control. To do this, it includes specialized software components known as device drivers that let the operating system control the hardware devices installed in and connected to the computer. It is directly responsible for the following activities:

▲ Hardware management
▲ Process management

▲ Memory management

▲ File management

▲ I/O management

▲ Network control and communications

▲ Fault detection and recovery

Database application software can run as server applications, client applications, or, in many instances, both, running as a distributed application. Components dealing with the user interface and data presentation run at the client. Specialized data processing components run at the server, either on the database server or on a separate application server. It's common to see database application designs that include Web server-based components taking advantage of Internet technologies. Often, the Internet is used as the communication path tying the application components together.

Small applications usually consist of just a handful of forms and reports. The components available in modern DBMSs let you put together a small application easily and quickly. In addition, support components are provided to help develop even the most complex of applications within a reasonably short time. The final mix of what you can do and what you have available depends on both the DBMS and your application development environment.

2.3.3 DBMS Components

The DBMS deserves special attention. A DBMS is a collection of specialized software modules. Database administrators cannot implement, control, and manage databases without the DBMS. Every request for data must go through the DBMS. Over the years, the features and functions of DBMSs have broadened, so that today's DBMSs do not just provide data access. Instead; they contain a powerful and versatile set of tools. Figure 2-11 shows how the various software modules making up a DBMS could be grouped as major components.

Database Engine

The kernel or heart of the DBMS is the **database engine**, which coordinates the tasks performed by all other DBMS components. This helps ensure that every database operation gets completed correctly and completely. The other components depend on the database engine to perform actions for them such as storing data and other system information, retrieving data, and updating data in the database.

As an example, consider the database engine's role in processing a query. A **query** refers to an executable statement, such as a statement used to retrieve or modify data. Suppose you create a query to retrieve production data from the database. When your users run this query, the DBMS must coordinate the tasks

Figure 2-11

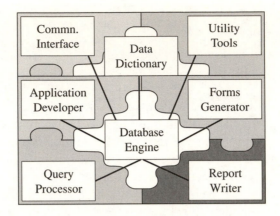

DBMS components.

needed to determine where the data is located and how it is structured. Once the structures and data location are determined, the DBMS interacts with the operating system to retrieve the requested data.

The database engine is also responsible for security, sometimes working together with the operating system. Does the user executing the query have authorization to access the data specified in the query? The database engine component coordinates the services of the security module to verify the authorization.

Some systems include an automated agent service or agent and alert system that works in close cooperation with the database engine. This service is known by various names, depending on the DBMS, but performs the same function in each case. Some descriptions of DBMS components might not identify this as a separate component, instead including it with database tools and utilities. However, its role in the DBMS and the fact that it is often implemented as a separate service or application justifies listing it as a unique component in its own right.

An agent and alert system performs background tasks that support the database service. Key among these is managing periodic activities that are scheduled for automatic execution. It ensures that these activities run when scheduled and if not, reports the error and takes appropriate corrective actions. Other tasks for which the service might take responsibility include background monitoring and managing activity logs. Background monitoring takes different forms, but is most often related to performance monitoring and detecting and reporting errors. It usually falls on the database administrator to define and configure performance thresholds and identify the error conditions the service should report. Log management includes writing error and status messages to database log files. Most systems will have one or more log files, some dedicating different logs to different components.

Nearly all systems provide some kind of support for error and activity log maintenance. If the DBMS does not include an automated agent as a separate component, you might find these functions integrated into the database engine. Performance monitoring and scheduled activities are a different story, however. If not supported by the database engine or a separate service, you will need to either find a way to use operating system utilities or buy (or build) a separate support application that handles them for you.

Data Dictionary

Another component is the data dictionary, which refers to the storage of structure definitions—the storage repository of structure definitions. In many relational databases, the data dictionary comprises a set of system tables like a directory system. The data dictionary interface software is sometimes considered a distinct component within a DBMS. However, in other manufacturers' products the data dictionary is considered an integrated part of the database engine rather than a separate component. Either way, the data dictionary is part of the database's metadata, and no matter how it is defined, its role is the same. Specifically, the data dictionary performs the following tasks:

▲ Keeps the definitions of all data structures and relationships.
▲ Describes data types of all stored data items.
▲ Specifies field sizes and formats of data items.
▲ Holds information on space allocations and storage locations for all data.
▲ Enables the database engine to keep track of the data and store it in the assigned places.
▲ Maintains indexes.
▲ Stores report and screen definitions.

Query Processor

Another key component is the **query processor**, which may be called the **query optimizer,** the DBMS component responsible for parsing, optimizing, and compiling queries for execution. Each commercial vendor adopts a standard query language or develops its own proprietary language for creating queries. **Structured Query Language** or **SQL** (pronounced see-kwil) is the standard language for relational DBMSs. Each relational database vendor enhances the standard SQL command set and adds a few features here and there, but the essential features of SQL are present in every commercial DBMS.

Now, for example, you can write a query in SQL to retrieve data from the CUSTOMER table: This might require a query such as the following:

```
SELECT *
FROM CUSTOMER
WHERE CUSTOMER_ZONE = 'North' and
CUST_BALANCE > 10000
```

What happens in the DBMS when your query is presented for execution? The database engine coordinates the services of the query processor to complete the query and return the results. The query processor parses the query and checks for obvious syntax errors. It determines the resources available to run the query and makes selections to help ensure that the query is optimized for processing. It then compiles the query for execution. It also watches for potential errors specific to query processing and, in some cases, is even able to abort queries that run too long. As shown in Figure 2-12, some DBMSs give you a sneak peak into the specific steps necessary to process the query.

Figure 2-12

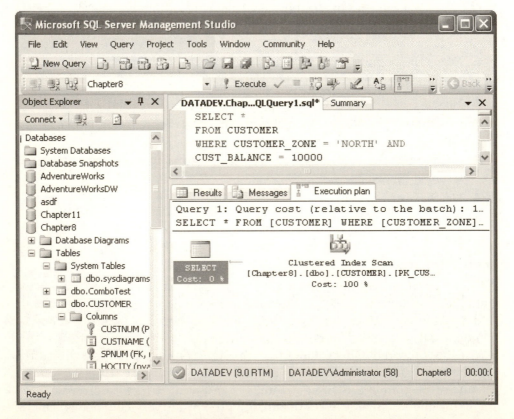

Query execution plan.

These processing steps are used as an execution plan. After the query processor parses and optimizes the query, it compiles the execution plan and writes it to memory. This execution plan is used to perform the query and return the requested data. Figure 2-12 shows one possible execution plan for our sample query. The actual execution plan can change as the database design and available optimization components change, so the execution plan you see now might not be exactly the same as the execution plan you would see on a later run of the same query.

Forms Generator

The **forms generator** component, when included with the DBMS, lets you create screen layouts or forms for data input and data display. For example, suppose you want to display the details of a customer order to your user. You need a layout to display the various data elements such as the order number, date, method of shipment, products ordered, price, and so on. You would use the forms generator to create a form to display this information in an easily readable format. You can usually include graphics and images to enhance the appearance of your forms, such as displaying the picture of the employee on a form showing employee information.

A forms generator is not included as an integrated component with all DBMS products. In fact, it is not a common component with higher-level database products. Instead it is usually found in products like Microsoft Access. Higher-level products, like Microsoft SQL Server, leave forms generation as a need to be filled by a separate application or a separate development environment.

Report Writer

The **report writer** is another component that you might or might not see included with your DMBS. Although most information access is online, a good deal of information delivery still uses printed reports. Reports may be viewed on screen before selecting and printing only the ones needed in hard copy. In some cases, reports are generated and distributed in an electronic format only, though the recipient usually has the option of printing a hard copy if desired.

Several DBMS products include a report writer component. The functionality and features are product specific or even product version specific and vary widely. Because of the additional overhead required to support this component, many manufacturers include this as an optional component.

Other DBMS Components

While application development is sometimes a function of the DBMS, through a component called an applications generator, it is usually done through a separate application development environment such as PHP, Java, or Microsoft's .NET Framework. Components provided with the development environment and the DBMS enable them to interact and communicate.

Most modern database management systems have separate modules for establishing and managing communications between databases, or more accurately, between the computers on which they are hosted. This can include DBMSs running on different computer systems and under multiple operating systems. The computers could be in different physical locations. Communications interface modules in the DBMS interact with the operating system and network software to initiate and manage the connections. They manage the data flow between databases and help to promote true global data sharing.

Another aspect of the communications interface is the link with traditional programming languages and application development environments. This is supported both through interfaces integrated in the DBMS and those included in the development environment.

Most commercial vendors have enhanced their DBMSs and equipped them with rich sets of utility tools. Others have left this up to third-party developers who create the utilities as separate applications. In some cases, the only support tools available are those defined as part of the SQL language command set.

Either way, these tools and interface modules are commonly known as the toolkit portion of database software. The toolkit is primarily intended for database administrators to perform necessary functions. Common utilities include tools to support loading data into the database and backup and restore utilities. Tools and utilities are often provided in both GUI interface and command-line interface versions. The command-line interface tools and utilities are often the preferred choice when having to manage a database remotely, especially when working over a low-speed connection.

2.3.4 Understanding People and Procedures

The term *people* refers to two broad groups: users and practitioners. Users are the data consumers, the people who need access to and who use the data to perform business-related tasks. Practitioners refer to the broad group of people involved in designing, implementing, maintaining, and administering a database solution.

Who are the users in a database environment? As shown in Figure 2-13, we can classify the users into a few groups on the basis of their data requirements, levels of their computer skills, and the frequency of data access.

▲ **Casual Users:** This group uses the database occasionally. Usually, midle- and upper-level executives fall into this group and need special considerations for providing data access. You typically have to provide these users with simple menu-driven applications.

▲ **Regular Users:** The database in a production environment serves as the information repository for the regular users to perform their day-to-day functions. This group of users retrieves data and updates the database, typically more than any other group. They work with programs that

Figure 2-13

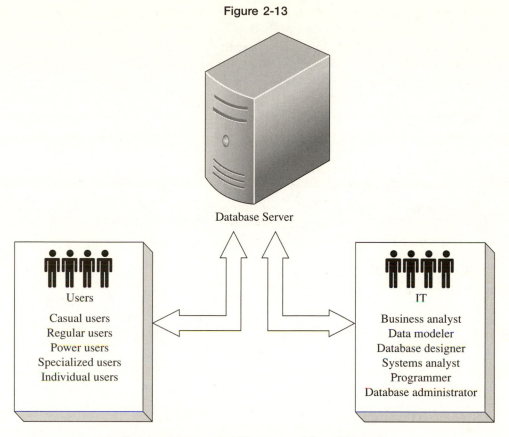

Database users and IT personnel (practitioners).

retrieve data, manipulate data in many ways, change data to current values, and also typically run periodic reports.

▲ **Power Users:** These users do not require well-structured applications to access the database. They can write their own queries and format their own reports. For the power users, you have to provide general guidance about the query and reporting tools and give them a road map of the database contents.

▲ **Specialized Users:** Business analysts, scientists, researchers, and engineers who are normally part of research and development departments need the database for specialized purposes. These users know the power and features of database systems. They may write their own applications.

▲ **Individual Users:** Some users in your organization may justify maintaining standalone, private databases for individual departments. Departments working with highly sensitive and confidential data may qualify for personal databases.

You can think of the entire group of IT personnel who create and maintain databases as database practitioners. These people keep the database environment functioning and enable the users to reap the benefits. Broadly, we can classify database practitioners into three categories: those who design, those who maintain, and those who create the applications.

▲ **Business analysts:** work with senior management, conduct special studies, and interpret management's direction for information.

▲ **Data modelers:** create semantic data models with popular modeling techniques. Often use computer-aided software engineering (CASE) tools to create data models.

▲ **Database designers:** develop and integrate user views of data and create the logical design for the database to be implemented with the selected commercial DBMS. Often use CASE tools to generate the outputs of the logical design process.

▲ **Systems analysts:** determine the process requirements of the various user groups and write application specifications. Work with the programmers in testing and implementing applications.

▲ **Programmer/analysts:** translate applications into program code. Test and implement applications. Also, write programs to convert and populate databases from previous database systems, if necessary.

▲ **Database administrators:** exercise overall control and manage the database. They perform key functions in the database environment.

Without proper methods and procedures, a database environment will eventually slip into confusion and chaos. Some procedures are essential just for keeping the database up and running. Because of this, and to ensure consistency, users and practitioners need good methods and procedures. Procedures can be manual or automated, and can include the following:

▲ **Usage:** clear and concise procedures on how to make use of the database. For example, procedures might include plain and nderstandable instructions on how to sign on and use the various functions provided by the applications. These often consist of written procedures as well as user aides, which are sometimes built into an applications help system.

▲ **Queries and Reports:** a list of available predefined queries and reports, along with instructions on how to supply the parameters and run them, provided to users. These can include written documentation or be integrated into a database application or support application such as a Web service. Sometimes, programmers document these through the application's help system.

▲ **Routine Maintenance:** consists of tasks such as monitoring usage of storage, allocation of additional space whenever necessary, keeping track of access patterns, and looking out for problem areas. The database administrators must have proper procedures to perform the routine maintenance functions. With some systems, many of the functions can be configured to occur automatically as needed or on a periodic basis.

▲ **Structure Change Management:** Business conditions keep changing continuously, and the data structures must change accordingly. Every organization must have detailed procedures on how to initiate structure changes, review and approve the changes, and implement the changes. This usually involves written policies, automated procedures, and manual follow-up requirements.

▲ **Backup and Recovery:** In the event of a disaster, database administrators must be able to recover from the malfunctions and restore the database. Clearly defined and thoroughly tested procedures are required. Backup and recovery procedures stipulate the type and frequency of backups and methods for using the backups to recover after failures. Most systems have requirements for automatic periodic backups supplemented with manual backups as needed.

▲ **Database Tuning:** As the volume of data increases and the number of users multiplies, the load increases and database performance tends to degrade. Database administrators must monitor performance and find ways to tune the database and optimize performance. Tuning procedures help them understand how to locate problem areas and to apply techniques for improving performance. With many systems, some tuning can take place automatically through periodic procedures. However, most tuning activities require manual intervention and should include follow-up testing to verify that you have actually improved database performance.

Many of these activities are considered part of ongoing periodic management and support activities. These account for many of the job requirements for the typical database administrator.

SELF-CHECK

- List and describe database architectural components.
- Explain the difference between required and recommended hardware.
- Compare common data storage methods, including benefits and shortcomings of each.
- Describe common DBMS components and how they are related.

SUMMARY

You learned about databases and database management systems in this chapter. You were introduced to basic database concepts and database types. You compared the hierarchical, network, relational, and object-oriented data models. You also learned about database system architectural components.

KEY TERMS

Attribute

Binary large object (BLOB) data type

Centralized model

Concurrency control

CRUD

Data abstraction

Database engine

Database management system (DBMS)

Database practitioner

Database software

Data catalog

Data dictionary

Data repository

Data type

Decision support database

Direct memory access (DMA)

Distributed model

Entity

Foreign key

Forms generator

Heterogeneous data environment

Hierarchical database model

Main memory

Memory buffer

Metadata

Network database model

Nonvolatile storage

Object-oriented database model

Object-relational database model

Operating system software

Physical data pointer

Primary key

Production database

Query

Query optimizer

Query processor

RAID

Relational database model

Relational database

Relationship

Report writer

Schema

Secondary storage

Structured Query Language (SQL)

Table

Transaction

Unified Modeling Language (UML)

View

ASSESS YOUR UNDERSTANDING

Go to www.wiley.com/college/gillenson to evaluate your knowledge of databases and database management systems.

Measure your learning by comparing pre-test and post-test results.

Summary Questions

1. Companies adopting the database approach to data typically use a combination of data-driven and process-driven development methods. True or False?

2. Which of the following relate to storing and managing data structure information?

   (a) data repository

   (b) data abstraction

   (c) data dictionary

   (d) data access

3. In the distributed model of database implementation, all of the database servers must use the same DBMS. True or False?

4. Which of the following statements correctly describes a transaction?

   (a) All statements in a transaction must be completed or rolled back as a group.

   (b) A transaction must consist of a single executable statement.

   (c) If an error occurs during processing, a transaction leaves data in an inconsistent state.

5. Which of the following correctly lists the words making up the abbreviation CRUD?

   (a) consistency, redundancy, utility, data store

   (b) create, read, update, delete

   (c) columns, rows, users, data

   (d) create, reply, understand, distribute

6. Which of the following is a common hybrid database model?

   (a) object-relational

   (b) hierarchical-object

   (c) network-relational

   (d) hierarchical-network

7. In the relational model, a relation refers to which of the following?

   (a) the association between two data tables

   (b) a foreign key definition

    (c) a unique occurrence of a data entity

    (d) a two-dimensional table

8. In the hierarchical model, a parent can have multiple children and a child can have multiple parents. True or False?

9. Which database model organizes data into sets containing owners and members?

    (a) hierarchical model

    (b) network model

    (c) object-oriented model

    (d) relational model

10. Which database model is most commonly used in modern database design?

    (a) hierarchical model

    (b) network model

    (c) object-oriented model

    (d) relational model

11. The hierarchical database model uses physical data pointers to associate parents and children. True or False?

12. Which data model is able to most completely describe complex data types and real-world entities?

    (a) hierarchical model

    (b) network model

    (c) object-oriented model

    (d) relational model

13. Database architecture components are described as falling into how many major groups?

    (a) one

    (b) two

    (c) three

    (d) four

14. Hardware and file management are the responsibility of which of the following?

    (a) application software

    (b) operating system

    (c) database

    (d) DBMS

15. Database and DBMS are synonymous terms for the same concept. True or False?

16. Which term specifically describes personnel responsible for modeling, designing, and implementing a database?

   (a) practitioners

   (b) power users

   (c) specialized users

   (d) administrators

17. Which of the following would typically be supported by automatic periodic procedures?

   (a) data backup

   (b) database tuning

   (c) routine maintenance

   (d) all of the above

18. What is SQL?

   (a) a specialized DBMS product

   (b) the standard language for relational DBMSs

   (c) an acronym referring to the DBMS query processor

   (d) a popular third-party forms generator

19. Which component would you find included by default in Microsoft Access, but not Microsoft SQL Server?

   (a) query processor

   (b) utilities

   (c) forms generator

   (d) report writer

20. Secondary storage refers to which of the following?

   (a) local hard disk

   (b) main computer memory

   (c) memory buffers

   (d) processor cache

Applying This Chapter

1. You are part of a team designing a database and database application that will support point-of-sale retail sales, inventory control, and financial accounting. The company has three locations, but all IT personnel will work out of the home office only. What deployment model should you use? What aspect of a database system will ensure that inventory is updated correctly when posting sales to customers? What is the role of the data repository in this design?

2. You are comparing DBMS products as the platform for supporting a retail sales application. You plan to use a standard product from an established manufacturer. Everything should run on standard PC hardware. The database must support inventory tracking, customer records, and customer orders, including a complete sales history. The company plans to eventually expand into e-commerce over the Internet. To support this, you must be able to have both a description and a picture of each product. Should you use a traditional model or hybrid model DBMS? Which model best supports your data requirements?

3. You are comparing DBMS products as the platform for a new e-commerce application. You have identified the tables that you need and the attributes that each table needs to support, such as relationships between tables, uniqueness, and so forth. Compare and contrast features supported by different commercial DBMS products.

   TIP: Use the manufacturer Web sites to research features and functionality.

4. You are deploying a database application based on Microsoft's SQL Server DBMS. You need to identify implementation requirements and product features. You need to justify where additional software packages will be needed. Why is a separate development platform needed for application development? How can you determine the initial database server hardware configuration? What hardware components are critical to optimum performance? What two general categories of users must you support?

YOU TRY IT

Database Fundamentals

All Good Things is a startup company entering the highly competitive Internet sales market. You are responsible for identifying database requirements for the company.

1. What are potential justfications for including a decision support system in the design?
2. Discuss the importance of transaction support in the proposed database environment.
3. What are issues that might justify the need for multiple database servers in a distrubuted model?

Database Models

You work for an established company. The company has used a mainframe-based database system for several years. Several departments have deployed their own individual database servers. You are responsible for consolidating the data on these servers and the mainframe database files on one or more PC-based database servers. All servers will be left online during initial deployment and testing.

1. Discuss potential concerns when supporting a heterogenous database environment with DBMSs using different database models.
2. Compare benefits and potential concerns in the relational and object-relational database models?
3. Identify the models most likely used for the mainframe database and discuss possible data design and migration concerns.

Database Components

You work for a company that operates a chain of dry cleaning and alteration shops. Customer drop-offs and alteration requests are recorded manually on multi-part carbonless forms. The current cash registers cannot retain more than one day's worth of information. The company has traditionally outsourced its data processing needs. You were hired to bring those activities internal, basing them at the company's home office.

1. Discuss the various database users that the database solution must support and their probable data requirements.
2. Why will form design be important when developing end-user applications for counter personnel? What might you use as a guide for initial entry form design?
3. What should you use as a guide for determining the reports that the application should be able to provide?
4. If all development is to be managed in-house, what IT roles must be filled to facilitate design, development, and ongoing support?
5. Discuss procedures needed to support the database solution. Identify whether manual procedures, automated processes, or both are required.

3

DATA MODELING

Starting Point

Go to www.wiley.com/college/gillenson to assess your knowledge of data modeling.
Determine where you need to concentrate your effort.

What You'll Learn in This Chapter

▲ The database design process and the initial design decisions in database design
▲ The three general categories of databases and their impact on database design
▲ Database modeling goals
▲ The role of business rules
▲ The importance of entities, attributes, and relationships
▲ Basic database objects: tables, views, and indexes
▲ Basic relationship types: binary, unary, and ternary
▲ Creating and reading an E-R diagram

After Studying This Chapter, You'll Be Able To

▲ Identify the tasks included in each database design step
▲ Accurately represent the business structure of your organization by identifying the business rules associated with it
▲ Determine the appropriate functional type of database you need in your organization by analyzing the business and user applications it will support
▲ Identify entities, attributes, and relationships
▲ Create a model including one-to-one, one-to-many, and many-to-many relationships
▲ Properly use cardinality and modality in describing relationships
▲ Recognize requirements for intersection data
▲ Develop an entity-relationship (E-R) model that uniquely identifies and describes each instance of an entity within your organization and its attributes, as well as show the associations and relationships between entities
▲ Read an E-R relational data diagram

INTRODUCTION

This chapter focuses on the process of creating a data model. A **data model** represents real world business data in the form of a database design. The chapter begins by introducing the design process, the main types of databases, and the goals of data modeling. It then looks at the key components of a relational database model: entities and relationships. The chapter concludes by comparing some data models based on different businesses.

3.1 Understanding Database Design

Before you start designing your database, you need to know something about the design process and what is involved. You need to understand how the data will be used, so you must identify the database type, which will help define both data and application requirements. You must also consider how business rules can impact your final design.

3.1.1 Understanding the Design Process

Typically, database and application design is considered a three part process, made up of

▲ Conceptual design

▲ Logical design

▲ Physical design

During the **conceptual design** (Figure 3-1), you lay the groundwork. This is when you interview all of the **stakeholders,** which includes everyone with any interest in the project, about their data requirements. This is when you identify

Figure 3-1

Conceptual Design	Logical Design	Physical Design
Data requirements	Logical framework	Physical modeling
Information requirements	Applicable data	Database objects
Collection needs	Data services	Object placement
Data locations	Data modeling	Optimization

Conceptual design.

Figure 3-2

Conceptual Design	Logical Design	Physical Design
Data requirements Information requirements Collection needs Data locations	Logical framework Applicable data Data services Data modeling	Physical modeling Database objects Object placement Optimization

Logical design.

what the application needs to do. This is also where you identify the data requirements and collect the information you need. You aren't concerned about how things will get done or which of the data you collect you actually need, you're just pulling together everything you can find.

You start organizing the data during the **logical design** process (Figure 3-2). This is where you sort through the data to identify what information applies to the project and start putting together a basic logical framework. You identify the basic type of database application that you need based on processing requirements. You start thinking about data services you'll need to support the application. You also go back to the stakeholders for verification, to ensure that your vision meets their expectations.

Data modeling occurs during logical design. During the process of data modeling, you identify entities and attributes, distinguish relationships between the entities, and make initial decisions about database tables. The framework is still somewhat tentative at this point. You may find roadblocks to implementing your design that force you to rethink and rework your logical framework.

Implementation details come in during **physical design** (Figure 3-3). The focus moves from logical modeling to physical modeling. This is where you make final decisions about how the data will be represented in the database. You've already identified your attributes and now you decide how to store them. You decide on the physical database objects that your solution will require. You make decisions that will help you settle on a hardware platform, such as physical object placement, to optimize both space use and database performance. At the end of this process you should have a complete physical design that you will in turn use to install and configure your database server and create the physical database.

Throughout the design process, it's important to realize that the conceptual, logical, and physical design are all interrelated, and that you'll move back and forth between them during the design process.

Figure 3-3

Conceptual Design	Logical Design	Physical Design
𝒢ℴ	✍	✓
Data requirements Information requirements Collection needs Data locations	Logical framework Applicable data Data services Data modeling	Physical modeling Database objects Object placement Optimization

Physical design.

3.1.2 Determining the Database Type

Early in the modeling process, you need to identify the functional type of database you need. This directly impacts your design requirements. You identify the functional type by looking at the business and the user application or applications the database will support.

Databases functionally fall into three general categories:

▲ Transactional

▲ Decision support system (DSS)

▲ Hybrid

This chapter focuses on the transactional database model as its primary example, but we must also consider the other models and their core concerns. The core data modeling concerns are much the same in each of these models.

Designing a Transactional Database

A **transactional database** is designed to support the processing of business transactions, such as the sales of a product. The primary function of the database is to support the addition of new data and the modification or deletion of existing data. This is performed at a granular level, typically working in very small chunks, such as individual records. The database design must be optimized to support these activities.

The transactional database model is the one used in the vast majority of database applications. Almost every business you can imagine uses a transactional database as its production database. For example, a retail business needs to be able to quickly process individual sales and inventory changes. Think about the checkout lines at the local discount store and it's easy to see why optimizing these operations is critical. A bank needs to quickly and accurately process each change to each account, hundreds or thousands of incremental changes every hour. A library has to track each book coming in and going out as an individual change. The database for each of these organizations needs to be optimized to process these changes.

The traditional model for a transactional database is a client-server database environment where the database services users within a single company. A more expansive version of this is the **online transaction processing (OLTP)** database. The difference is one of scale. With this model, you must consider a much larger network environment, possibly a global enterprise network, and larger user base. A typical feature of this model is Internet-based access with Web services and Web applications. Because of the larger user base, concurrency requirements for OLTP database models can be critical. **Concurrency** relates to supporting multiple users who need concurrent access, access to the same data at the same time. You are also concerned about **throughput,** how much data can you process, and how fast can you process it.

Designing a Decision Support Database

A **decision support system (DSS)** is designed to support business decisions made primarily at the management and executive level. Common types of decision support databases include data warehouses, reporting database, and data marts. With each of these, the primary goal is retrieving and evaluating, rather than modifying, data. Speed in accessing data and data throughput are critical concerns. When you do add data to the database, it's usually done by adding large amounts of data all at once, a process known as **bulk loading** (Figure 3-4).

A **data warehouse** database stores historical data. It can typically use the same data modeling approach as a transactional database model. The key difference between data warehouse databases and transactional databases is that the

Figure 3-4

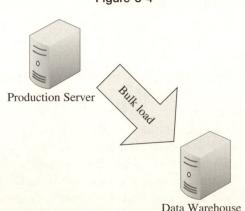

Bulk load.

data warehouse often contains many years of historical data to provide effective forecasting capabilities. An OLTP database is typically used as the source database for the data warehouse. A **data mart** is essentially a small subset of a larger data warehouse. The data mart is typically based on the modeling technique as its parent data warehouse. A **reporting database** is often a specialized data-warehouse-type database containing only active (and not historical or archived) data. They are typically small in comparison to the data warehouse, similar in size to the source OLTP database. In fact, they can be smaller than the OLTP database because they often have more limited data requirements and contain a selected subset of the data.

Consider the retail example again. In many cases, the company will also have a DSS that relies on a data warehouse. Information collected by the transactional database is periodically written to the data warehouse.

How would a retail business use the information? One way is by determining ordering and stocking levels. It's important to most businesses to keep inventory levels to a minimum. Ever wonder how a business decides the best time to discount summer items and put Halloween costumes out for sale, or when to bring out Christmas trees? A DSS lets the retailer adjust inventory stocking levels based on variations needs, such as seasonal requirements. It tells the retailer when to rotate the stock and can even provide suggestions as to the best physical product placement inside the store.

Another example is using a DSS to help identify new products that the business might want to stock. Data mining applications can make associations between products or customer purchases you might otherwise overlook. A DSS can help the business target advertising so that it better matches specific customers' purchase patterns. That's one of the ways marketing efforts specifically target different groups. In a chain store, this is important because purchase habits vary by geographic location, and can even vary by neighborhood in the same city.

Designing a Hybrid Database

A **hybrid database** is simply a mixture containing both OLTP-type concurrency requirements and data warehouse-type throughput requirements. In less-demanding environments (or in companies running smaller operations), a smaller hybrid database is often a more cost-effective option, simply because there is one rather than two databases. This costs less because there are fewer computers, fewer software licenses, fewer people, and fewer support requirements. This is not, however, your only cost-effective option. You could also deploy the solution as two databases running on the same database, with no increase in software costs and likely little, if any, change to the hardware configuration. Because the database meets the same data support requirements as the other models, the data modeling requirements are also the same.

Figure 3-5

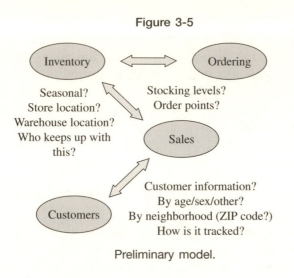

Preliminary model.

3.1.3 Understanding Modeling Goals

Database design is critical because all applications written against that database model design are completely dependent on the structure of that underlying database. If the database model must be altered at a later stage, applications based on the database model probably must be changed and perhaps even completely rewritten. That can get very expensive and time consuming. You should design the database model using tools such as flowcharts, Entity Relationship Diagrams, and anything else that might help to ensure that what you intend to build is not only what you need, but will actually work. **Entity-Relationship Diagrams (ERDs)** are graphical depictions of entities and how they relate to each other. From an operational perspective, the most important objective is fulfilling application needs.

Your modeling could, and often does, start with just a few notes and a simple design. Consider the preliminary modeling shown in Figure 3-5. Think about what's involved with a large retailer or discount store. This could easily represent the start of the modeling process. You've identified a few of the key entities such as inventory, customers, and orders. Sales might be hard to think of as some kind of physical object, but it is a critical part of your entities, and the point where inventory and customers cross paths. The additional notes are questions that could have come to mind while sketching this out, data that you want to include, or ideas that deserve additional follow-up. Obviously, Figure 3-5 is just the start of the design process, with more entities to be identified and more data to be tracked down.

The design must support the business objectives. For a retailer, that means stocking the appropriate inventory and selling it to customers at a profit. The structure should represent business structures as accurately as possible. Figure 3-5 represents a start, identifying key elements and where they intersect. As you continue to build this out, the process can mean compromising in some of the design or deviating from "correct" design processes to create a structure that looks more like your business and is optimized to meet your access needs.

Your design should aim for a well-structured database model that is simple, easy to read, and easy to comprehend. Each table in a database model should preferably represent a single subject or topic, a single entity, but don't over design by creating too many tables. OLTP databases can thrive on more detail and more tables, but not always. Data warehouses can collapse under their own weight when data is divided up into too many tables. At the same time, ensure that the design is **scalable,** that it can grow to meet your needs. As you get toward the end of the design process, issues like scalability can force you to go back to earlier design steps and rethink decisions that you made at that time in the light of real-world requirements.

For example, in a chain store with multiple locations, you might initially build a design based around keeping all of the data in one central location and using remote communications to support each of the individual stores. There could be several reasons why this solution won't scale to meet your needs. The combined inventory tables could turn out to be larger than expected, or you might have more tables than you wanted to support in your final design. Communication support could be an issue, as it might be more cost effective to farm database servers out to different locations than to upgrade the communications support to meet the access requirements.

3.1.4 Understanding Business Rules

The importance of understanding the nature of the business is paramount to understanding how best to model that business in a database. Because of this, part of your design process is incorporating business rules. **Business rules** are essentially the processes and flows of whatever is involved in the daily workings of that organization. A good place to start is asking the following questions:

- ▲ What does the organization do to operate?
- ▲ What limits are placed on how the business performs daily tasks?
- ▲ How does the business make its money?

Business rules cover a wide area of subjects, not all directly relating to your database design. However, you must identify those that do impact the design and ensure that they are included. Essentially, business rules cover:

- ▲ Any types of organizational policies of any form and at all levels of the organization.
- ▲ Any types of calculations or formulas (such as loan amortization calculations for a mortgage lending company).
- ▲ Any types of rules and regulations (such as rules applied because of legal requirements, self-imposed restrictions, or industry-standard requirements).

A relational database model cannot avoid defining some business rules. They will impact what data is kept in the database, limits placed on that data, data relationships, and how they are defined.

Supporting Business Rules—Database System

Let's go back to the "generic" retailer that we've been using as an example. What are some of the specific business rules that you might need to consider? We've already established inventory levels as an issue. Your business rules could start out as executive statements made about inventory goals such as the following:

▲ High-value items are defined as items that cost us $1000 or more each.

▲ There should be no more than three of any high-value items in stock and on order at any time.

In most cases, you could enforce this through the database system. Assume that you have an inventory table that includes quantity on hand and quantity on order. The logic used would be some variation of the following (expressed below as pseudocode):

```
IF cost >= $1000 AND
((quantity on hand) + (quantity on order)
+ (new order amount)) <= 3
THEN
   Allow the order
ELSE
   Cancel the order
```

First, check to see if the cost is greater than or equal to $1000. If not, you don't do any additional checking. If so, then add up the quantity on hand, already on order, and the new order amount. If this total is less than or equal to 3, then you can place the order. If not, the order is canceled.

To take this one step further, you could have set stocking levels or order points defined in the database. In that case, you would use similar logic in the order point calculations to ensure that the order point is never set higher than 3 for items costing $1000 or more.

Supporting Business Rules—Application

Other applications of business rules are better handled through the application or through logic implemented specifically for that purpose. Take the following requirement for all credit card purchases at our retailer:

▲ All credit card purchases must be approved by the card company.

This is something that you would probably handle through the application. When the customer tries to pay by credit card, the application must first get an approval. This is usually done passing the credit card number and amount to a credit card authorization service and then waiting for approval. The approval is often accompanied by some kind of verification code for tracking and audit history, just in case there is any kind of question in the future.

What if there's a problem, such as the phone lines being down, or the company providing authorization being unavailable for some reason. You might have an additional business rule, such as:

▲ If credit card purchases cannot be automatically approved, then manager override is required.

FOR EXAMPLE

Using Business Rules

Business rules will relate directly to the business for which you are designing the database. The types of business rules you encounter for a retail sales company will probably be quite different than the rules for a credit card company. In either case, the rules will be a design factor.

Consider a situation where you're designing a database for a company that sells home improvement products. You might have a small number of customers, such as contractors, who are allowed to charge their purchases and pay later. When someone tries to charge an order, the person making the sale must determine the following:

- Does the customer have an established account?
- Does the customer have credit available?
- Can the customer charge these types of items?
- Does the customer get the same discount on the order when charging?

Each of these would result in business rules. You would have a rule that you can make charge sales only if the customer has an account and is not over the credit balance. Any other attempts to charge an order would be blocked. Also, you must have a way to keep track of the customer's current balance and credit limit. If the customer can charge only certain items, there would have to be some way of identifying these items in the database and associating them with customers as appropriate. If the customer normally gets a discount, but the amount changes when the order is charged, the change would need to apply automatically. Discount amounts would have to be stored somewhere in the database and associated with the customer.

Once again, you would build this into the application. It would need to recognize that automatic approval didn't occur because of a problem. Maybe you would want to write the application so that the salesperson must manually report the problem. The application would then need a way of accepting and verifying the manager override and allowing the transaction.

SELF-CHECK

- List the steps in the design process and decisions that must be made in each.
- Explain the importance of business rules and how they can be identified.
- Compare the roles of transactional and decision support databases.
- Explain why a small business might use a hybrid database to support its database applications.

3.2 Understanding Relational Database Models

Our focus is on relational database design, or more specifically, object-relational database design. For our purposes, this means creating a relational database design that also supports data integrated from the object database model. This includes **large object (LOB) data,** which is usually binary data such as pictures or sound clips.

When do you need to support LOB data? One of the first examples that come to mind is online retailers. Customers want to see what they're buying, and one way of supporting this is by storing pictures along with other inventory information in the database. When the user requests an item, the application can return both a written description and a digitized photo of the item. Some sites even provide multiple views or three-dimensional views that let you rotate the item and see it from all angles. Music or video downloads are another example. You could store a song, as well as a short preview, in the database as a way to optimize retrieval. Of course, this is just one part of the data needed to describe your database entities.

Accurately describing the entities making up your data model is critical. In order to model data for a relational database you must be able to recognize entities. You must be able to uniquely identify each instance of an entity. You identify the information that you need to track about each of the entities. Together, these give you your basic working set of data.

In the real world, entities never really stand alone; they are typically associated with each other, or intersect in some fashion. Parents are associated with their children, automobile parts are associated with the finished automobile, firefighters are associated with the fire engines to which they are assigned, and so forth. Customers and the items they buy intersect at the point of sale. Recognizing and recording the associations and intersections among entities provides a far richer description of an environment than recording the entities alone. In order to intelligently and usefully deal with the associations or relationships between entities, you must be able to identify and describe both the entities and the relationships.

3.2.1 Entity-Relationship (E-R) Modeling Concepts

Let's start by making sure that we all have the same idea in mind when discussing database concepts. We're focusing on **entity-relationship (E-R) modeling**. This is a model commonly used for designing relational databases and is based on business entities and the relationships between them.

As you've already learned, each "thing" that you want to track in the database is an entity. Many entities are physical objects such as people or product inventory. Some are less tangible, such as loan balances or interest rates. Your data modeling process begins with digging through the data you've accumulated and identifying the entities.

While you are doing this, you will also identify attributes, the information that describes the entity. Each entity type will have its own attributes. The data collected for employees, for example, will be somewhat different than the data collected for customers, and very different than the data collected for inventory items.

Entities

Your best starting points are physical entities, the things you can see and touch, and related business processes. That's because these are the entities that are usually the easiest to recognize and understand. For some of your most obvious physical entities, all you have to do is look around.

Let's take another look at the retailer example we've been using during this chapter. Assume you need to develop a data model for a department store. What are some of the entities that immediately come to mind? Physical entities for a department store database might include product inventory, vendors, customers, and employees. Now, let's focus more closely on one of these entities—employees. Each hourly employee must have a time card or other way of tracking time worked. That's another entity. Pay rates, as a group, might also be considered as an entity and kept in a separate table. You might want to track vacation time accrued and used as another separate entity.

Now, let's stop for a moment, to look at pay rates closer. What's the advantage to tracking pay rate as a separate entity? Each employee will probably just have one base pay rate? Consider the situation though, where you have set pay rates and the employee's pay rate must match up with one of these. You would track pay rate as a separate entity then so that you could use those values to validate the pay rate assigned to an employee.

Sometimes, something might initially look like a single entity, but as you look closer, you need to break it down into two or more entities. Take purchase orders placed with your vendors, for example. You issue a purchase order to a specific vendor to order inventory items. There are two basic parts to the purchase order. First, is the general information—things like who the order is for, the date it is being placed, the purchase order number, and so forth. The second part is the list of individual items that you are ordering. Each of these should be treated as a separate entity. That's because each is a separate, physical "thing," that you can see, touch, and describe. Each item is further described by its place in the item list, the quantity you are ordering, the item cost, and so forth. These are all pieces of data that can vary by item, the item attributes.

Attributes

As you define your entities, you also need to define attributes, which as you already learned, is the information you track about an entity. Attributes, for the most part, will be entity-specific, because you don't keep the same information about every entity. For employees, you might track information such as:

▲ Hire date
▲ Pay code or rate
▲ Social security number (for United States employees)
▲ Employee number
▲ Home address and phone number

This isn't meant as a complete list. The attributes that you need to track about an entity vary not only by entity, but also by business. Some businesses might, for security reasons, want to keep a recent employee picture or biometric data (uniquely identifying information about a person, such as a fingerprint, voice print, or retinal pattern) for employee verification. However, if you don't use biometric verification, there's no reason to track it. Attributes should include all information that is needed for business purposes, and *only* information that is needed for business purposes. Any other information is, at best, a waste of space and, when dealing with people, a possible invasion of their privacy.

One attribute will be used as the entity's identifying value, referred to as the entity's **identifier** or **primary key.** It must be something that distinguishes each instance of that entity from every other instance of that entity. Examples you might encounter include:

▲ Each employee is identified by his or her employee ID number.
▲ Each customer is assigned a unique customer number.
▲ Each inventory item has a unique inventory number, used to identify and track that item.

In the United States, a common choice for the employee primary key is the employee's social security number (SSN). Every employee is required to have one by law, so you know that it will be present as an attribute. Also, each employee's SSN is unique, so it uniquely identifies each instance of the entity employee.

Why doesn't everyone use the SSN as the primary key? You might want to treat that information as sensitive, to help prevent identity theft, for example. In that case, you need to "make up" a primary key. It's common to have the database system or application generate these values for you automatically. Many database systems let you add an attribute that is commonly known as an identifier, based on integer values and often using a one-up numbering system to identify each entity instance.

This is another case where it's important that you understand the context in which a term is used. The term *identifier* can refer to any value you choose as the entity's primary key. It can also refer, as we have just seen, to an automatically generated value that is used as an identifier or primary key.

Note that in the case of employees, you must uniquely identify each individual employee. For inventory items, you would probably just want to identify each unique type of item. For example, you would want to uniquely identify 12-foot fiberglass ladders as a unique type of item, but if you have 100 ladders, you wouldn't want to keep track of each one of them separately. Instead, you would manage them as a group, identifying the group and the number of items in that group that you have on hand.

Be careful to select a value that doesn't change as the primary key attribute (identifier). Each item probably has a unique shelf location, for example, but there's also a possibility that the location could change in the future. Typically, once an identifying attribute is assigned to an item, it rarely (if ever) changes.

Relationships

That brings us to relationships. We discuss relationships in detail later in this chapter, but let's look at a couple of simple examples now to introduce the concept. Looking at employees and Figure 3-6, each employee must turn in a weekly time card in order to get paid. This gives us a relationship between employees and time cards, employees and pay checks, and possibly, depending on how you want to track things in the database, between time cards and paychecks. You also have

Figure 3-6

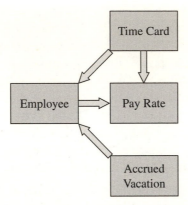

Employee and associated entities.

a relationship between employees and managers. Each employee has a manager, and each manager is responsible for one or more employees.

Breaking down one of these relationships, each time card is associated with a unique employee, as shown in Figure 3-7. The time card is the **referencing entity** and the employee is the **referenced entity.** The employee identifier is included with each time card as a foreign key and ensures **referential integrity,** establishing and maintaining that relationship and making sure that the referencing entity is associated with a unique instance of the referenced entity. A foreign key is always based on a unique value in the referenced entity, usually the entity's primary key.

Now, think about purchase orders. As you should remember, we created two entities for each purchase order, one to contain the general header information and the other to contain the individual line items. The obvious identifier for the header information is the purchase order number. That same number could be embedded in each line item row to associate the line item with the purchase order. It might

Figure 3-7

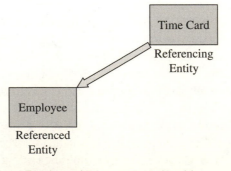

Employee/time card relationship.

also have a second use. Let's say that you plan to keep all line items for all purchase orders in a single table. You need a way to uniquely identify each item. An obvious choice is to use two columns together as the primary key, the purchase order number and the item's line item number, with each combination creating a unique value.

As the name implies, relationships are essential to a relational database. Identifying and defining relationships is a major part of the data modeling process. You will find, as you go through the process, that more and more relationships become apparent. A key part of the design is identifying which relationships are important and including only those relationships in your design. Otherwise, you risk the design becoming too complicated and confusing to be of any use. Keep in mind that your database doesn't sit alone in the universe as an isolated entity.

3.2.2 Introducing Basic Database Objects

Our eventual goal is creating a physical database which is made up of **database objects.** To help keep our focus on that goal, we need to take time to introduce a few basic database objects. These are objects that are created as part of the database and are stored with the database. Database objects can be somewhat DBMS-specific. Some database systems do not support a full range of potential database objects. The objects discussed here are three of the most commonly used objects in the relational database model: tables, views, and indexes.

Tables

For each entity that you identify in your business, you will have at least one table for storing the unique occurrences of that entity. Sometimes, in order to improve performance and minimize wasted space in data storage, it might take two or more tables to describe a single entity.

In a database table, the columns represent the attributes, the information that you want to track about an entity, as shown in Figure 3-8. The rows are the individual occurrences of that entity. Each row will be uniquely identifiable. This uniqueness can be enforced in various ways, but is most often enforced through a primary key. You base the primary key on one or more table columns. If the table doesn't have a column that uniquely identifies each row, you'll need to add one. One way is to add a column known as an identifier column, as mentioned earlier, that generates a unique value for each row you add to the table.

Two additional terms you need to know are record and field. Some database management systems use the term **field** to refer to table columns and individual attributes. They use the term **record** to refer to table rows, each instance of a particular entity.

In the retail example we've been using, you can already see some of the tables that you would likely include in the database, such as employees, time cards, pay rates, accrued vacation, inventory, purchase orders, customers, and sales (which you might refer to as customer orders).

Figure 3-8

Customer Table

Customer Number	Customer Name	Postal Code
01102	Tom's Store	63122
23441	Livermore Things and Stuff	94550
12001	Polly's Place	23450

Customer View

Customer Number	Customer Name
01102	Tom's Store
23441	Livermore Things and Stuff
12001	Polly's Place

Sample table and view example.

Views

Once you deploy your database and as you define user access requirements and create your application, you'll usually find that the tables and columns that you define don't necessary match up directly with users' data requirements. What do you do then? You can use another database object, known as a view, to further organize the data for viewing and manipulation. You will typically create a view because you want to limit user access to table data, want to provide custom data, or want to combine the contents of two or more tables.

When you create a view, you define the **base objects,** the objects used to create the view, which will be tables or (in some cases) other views. As part of the process, you identify the columns displayed through the view. Users who access the data through the view see only those columns included in the view definition, thereby limiting the user's access. You might do this as a security measure to protect sensitive data or simply to avoid confusing the user with too much unnecessary data.

A simple example of this is shown in Figure 3-8. The Customer table has three columns: Customer Number, Customer Name, and Postal Code. If you want to limit users to just the Customer Number and Customer Name, you could create the view shown. You would then give users access to the view, but not the underlying table.

Views can provide a customized look at table information. You can reorder the columns and have them appear in any order you want. You can also define columns that are computed based on the contents of other columns. For example, you could have a view based on employee records and time cards. The database stores the employee's rate of pay and hours worked, but you create a view that multiplies these values and returns instead the amount the employee should be paid.

During database design and data modeling, you often end up breaking data up into smaller, more specific entities and creating smaller tables. This is done for various reasons, but it may be that many of these tables provide little useful information when standing alone. Instead, to get any really useful information it may be necessary to combine the contents of two or more tables. You can create a view based on these tables, extracting the columns that you need and presenting them in the order that best suites the users' requirements.

Indexes

Indexes are a key part of database organization and optimization. A database **index** has a similar function to an index in a book: it organizes and sorts the data and provides a pointer to the specific physical location of the data on the storage media.

An index can be based on one or more table columns. The database engine organizes the data based on both the columns selected and the order in which they are selected. You can define multiple indexes on a table, each with a different set of key columns, thereby organizing the data in different ways. The query processor selects the optimum index or indexes to use for data retrieval.

Why different indexes? Here's an example. Your database includes a Customer table. Most reports run against the table sort data by last name and then first name. It makes sense to have an index that uses the columns containing the last name and first name values to make it easier to retrieve the data in that order. However, you also run reports by geographic region, sorted by postal code and address. To support this, you might create a separate index based on the columns containing address information.

Most database management systems automatically create an index for a table's primary key, sometimes called the **primary index.** In that case, additional indexes are called **secondary indexes.** Indexes can also be referred to as clustered and nonclustered. The primary index is usually a clustered index. With a **clustered index,** the data is physically sorted in the index order. This is used to organize the data in the order in which it is most often needed. Secondary indexes are usually all nonclustered indexes. **Nonclustered indexes** organize the data for retrieval, but through the index only, and have no effect on the table.

The most common type of index used in modern databases is the **balanced tree** or **B-Tree** (also called a **binary tree**) index, based on nodes with pointer values directing you, in the end, to the desired data. An example of a primary index created as a B-Tree index, along with index node contents, is shown in Figure 3-9, illustrating how pointers are used to search for a specific record.

Figure 3-9

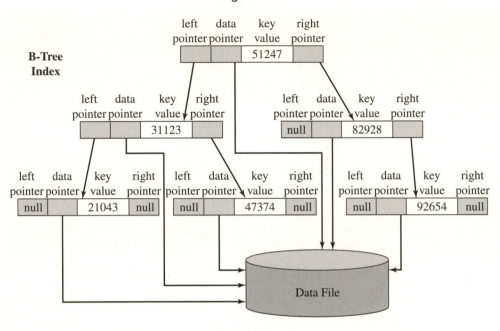

B-tree index.

FOR EXAMPLE

Entities, Attributes, and Objects

Suppose that you are creating a database for a private golf course. It includes full members who have access to all facilities and limited members who are allowed on the course and in the Pro Shop only. The Pro Shop keeps a small inventory of items available for purchase and also keeps track of tee time reservations and golf carts.

There are several entities that should come to mind immediately, such as members, employees, inventory, and golf carts. These are all tangible entities. What about intangible entities? One already mentioned is tee times, and others will probably come to mind as you think about activities around a golf course and private clubhouse.

However, some decisions might not be as obvious as they would seem at first glance. For example, how many tables will you need to track the member entity? Should full and limited members be tracked in the same table or do you need separate tables? This points out the need for gathering as much information as possible before you make modeling decisions. Right now, you probably don't know enough about the data requirements to make that decision, so you need to go back to your human data sources and ask more questions.

Each **node** contains two pointers to nodes on the left and right sides. **Leaf nodes,** which are the nodes located at the bottom of the index, also contain a pointer to where the data for the key value is physically stored. To see how this works, trace the search for a data record with the key value 92654. You search at the root node containing index value 51247. The search value 92654 is greater than 51247, so follow the right pointer from the root and go to the index record with key value 82928. From here, you follow the right pointer which takes you to the index record with key value 92654. This is the index record you are looking for. The data pointer from this index record gives the physical location needed to retrieve the data record.

SELF-CHECK

- Explain the role of entities, attributes, and relationships in data modeling.
- Describe how logical entities relate to physical tables.
- Explain the term **referential integrity** and how it is maintained in a relational database.

3.3 Understanding Relationships

You saw some simple relationship examples in the last section. However, to understand relationships you need to look at them in greater detail. There are three basic relationship types:

▲ **Binary relationship:** a relationship between two types of entities.
▲ **Unary relationship:** a relationship with another occurrence within the same entity.
▲ **Ternary relationship:** a relationship directly involving three entity types.

The majority of the relationships in most relational databases are binary relationships. An entity can have separate binary relationships with any number of other entities in the database. Each binary and unary relationship can also be described as one-to-one, one-to-many, or many-to-many. These terms are described a little later in this chapter.

This section uses examples based on a fictitious company. The company has a sales staff that sells directly to its customers. Salespersons are assigned specific

Figure 3-10

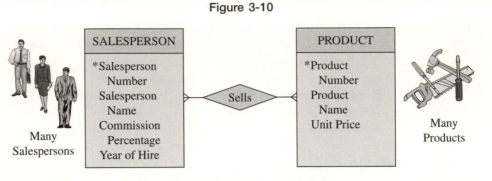

A sample binary relationship.

customer accounts and normally sell to those accounts only. Each customer also has a backup salesperson who handles the customer's needs if its primary salesperson is unavailable.

3.3.1 Binary Relationships

The simplest kind of relationship is known as the binary relationship—a relationship between two entity types. Figure 3-10 shows a small E-R diagram with a binary relationship between two entity types: salespersons and products. The diamond-shaped box represents the relationship.

The E-R diagram in Figure 3-10 tells us that a salesperson "sells" products. Conversely, products are sold by salespersons. That's good information, but we can do better than that with a very small increase in effort. Just knowing that a salesperson sells products leaves open several obvious and important questions. Is a particular salesperson allowed to sell only one kind of product, or two, or three, or all of the available products? Can a particular product be sold by only a single salesperson or by all of the salespersons? Might we want to keep track of a new salesperson who has just joined the company but has not been assigned to sell any products yet (assuming that there is indeed a restriction on which salespersons can sell which products)?

Figure 3-11 shows three binary relationships of different **cardinalities**, which is the maximum number of entities that can be involved in a particular relationship. Figure 3-11a shows a **one-to-one (1-1) binary relationship,** which means that a single occurrence of one entity type can be associated with a single occurrence of the other entity type and vice versa. A particular salesperson is assigned to one office. Conversely, a particular office (they are all private offices) has just one salesperson assigned to it. Note the "bar" or "one" symbol on either end of the relationship in the diagram indicating the maximum one cardinality. The way to read these diagrams is to start at one entity, read the relationship in the diamond, pick up the cardinality on the other side of the diamond

Figure 3-11

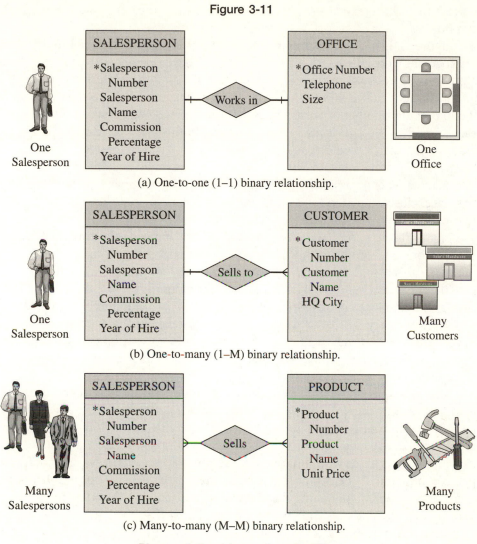

(a) One-to-one (1–1) binary relationship.

(b) One-to-many (1–M) binary relationship.

(c) Many-to-many (M–M) binary relationship.

Binary relationships and cardinalities.

near the second entity, and then finally reach the other entity. Thus, Figure 3-11a, reading from left to right, says, "A salesperson works in one (really at most one, since it is a maximum) office." The bar or one symbol involved in this statement is the one just to the left of the office entity box. Conversely, reading from right to left, "An office is worked in by (is assigned to) one salesperson."

The symbols used here represent one standard way of documenting an E-R model, but are not the only possibility. Your options will depend somewhat on the modeling tool you use. Some modeling tools show all relationships as simply a line between the entities with no additional information provided.

Others include a textual description of the relationship, without the mapping symbols.

Figure 3-11b shows a **one-to-many (1-M) binary relationship** between salespersons and customers. The "crow's foot" device attached to the customer entity box represents the multiple association. Reading from left to right, the diagram indicates that a salesperson sells to many customers. Note that "many," as the maximum number of occurrences that can be involved, means a number that can be 1, 2, 3, . . . n. It also means that the number is not restricted to being exactly one, which would require the "one" or "bar" symbol instead of the crow's foot. Reading from right to left, it says that a customer is sold to by only one salesperson. This is reasonable, indicating that in this company each salesperson has an exclusive territory and thus each customer can only be sold to by one salesperson from the company.

Figure 3-11c shows a **many-to-many (M-M) binary relationship** between salespersons and products. A salesperson is authorized to sell many products; a product can be sold by many salespersons. By the way, sometimes "many" can be either an exact number or have a known maximum, in either the 1-M or M-M case. For example, a company rule may set a limit of a maximum of ten customers in a sales territory. Then the "many" in the 1-M relationship of Figure 3-3b can never be more than ten (a salesperson can have many customers but not more than ten). Sometimes people will include this exact number or maximum next to or even instead of the crow's foot on the E-R diagram.

Many database products do not have an option for directly defining many-to-many relationships. Instead, you must include an intermediary or mapping table in the physical design to implement them. In the previous example, the table would have two columns, one identifying the salesperson and one identifying the product. It would have a unique row for each valid salesperson/product combination. Whether or not you define this as a separate entity in your data model and include it in the **data diagram** (the graphic depiction of the data model) depends on your modeling standards. If used, the entity is known as an **associative entity.** This concept is described in more detail later in this chapter.

Figure 3-12 shows the addition of the **modality** to the relationships—the minimum number of entity occurrences that can be involved in a relationship. In our particular salesperson environment, every salesperson must be assigned to an office. On the other hand, a given office might be empty or it might be in use by exactly one salesperson. This situation is recorded in Figure 3-12a, where the inner symbol, which can be a zero or a one, represents the modality—the minimum—and the outer symbol, which can be a one or a crow's foot, represents the cardinality—the maximum. Reading Figure 3-12a from left to right tells us that a salesperson works in a minimum of one and a maximum of one office, which is another way of saying exactly one office. Reading from

Figure 3-12

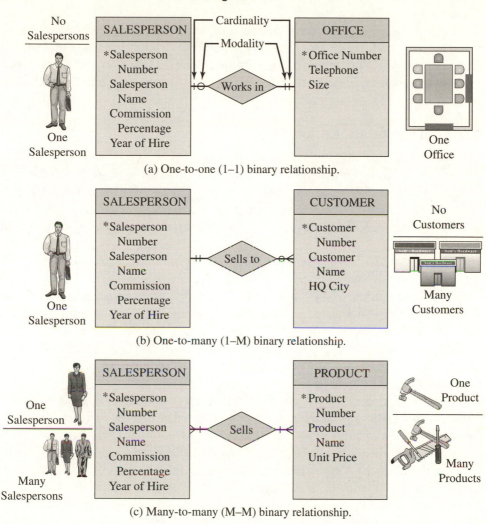

(a) One-to-one (1–1) binary relationship.

(b) One-to-many (1–M) binary relationship.

(c) Many-to-many (M–M) binary relationship.

Binary relationships and modalities.

right to left, an office may be worked in or assigned to a minimum of no salespersons (i.e., the office is empty) or a maximum of one salesperson.

Similarly, Figure 3-12b indicates that a salesperson may have no customers or many customers. This allows for the case in which we have just hired a new salesperson and have not as yet assigned a territory or any customers. On the other hand, a customer is always assigned to exactly one salesperson. If a salesperson leaves the company, the company's procedures require that another salesperson or, temporarily, a sales manager be immediately assigned the departing salesperson's customers.

Figure 3-12c says that each salesperson is authorized to sell at least one or many of our products and each product can be sold by at least one or many of our salespersons. This includes the extreme, but not surprising, case in which each salesperson is authorized to sell all of the products and each product can be sold by all of the salespersons.

3.3.2 Unary Relationships

Unary relationships associate occurrences of an entity type with other occurrences of the same entity type. Thinking about this as a physical database, it relates data in a table to itself. Take the entity "person," for example. One person may be married to another person and vice versa. One person may be the parent of other people; conversely, a person may have another person as one of his parents.

Figure 3-13a shows the one-to-one unary relationship called "Backup" involving the salesperson entity. The salespersons are organized in pairs as backup to each other when one is away from work. Following one of the links, say the one that extends from the right side of the salesperson entity box, we can say that salesperson number 137 backs up salesperson number 186. Then, going in the other direction, salesperson number 186 backs up salesperson 137. Notice that in each direction the modality of one rather than zero forbids the situation of a salesperson not having a backup.

Some of the salespersons are also sales managers, managing other salespersons. A sales manager can manage several other salespersons. Further, there can be several levels of sales managers, that is, several low-level sales managers can be managed by a higher-level sales manager. Each salesperson (or sales manager) is managed by exactly one sales manager. This situation describes a one-to-many unary relationship. Consider Figure 3-13b and follow the downward branch out of its salesperson entity box. It says that a salesperson manages zero to many other salespersons, meaning that a salesperson is not a sales manager (the zero modality case) or is a sales manager with several subordinate salespersons (the many cardinality case). Following the branch that extends from the right side of the salesperson entity box, the diagram says that a salesperson is managed by exactly one other salesperson (who, of course, must be a sales manager).

Unary relationships also come in the many-to-many variety. One classic example of a many-to-many unary relationship is known as the bill of materials problem. Consider a complex mechanical object like an automobile, an airplane, or a large factory machine tool. Any such object is made of basic parts like nuts and bolts that are used to make other components or subassemblies of the object. Small subassemblies and basic parts go together to make bigger subassemblies,

Figure 3-13

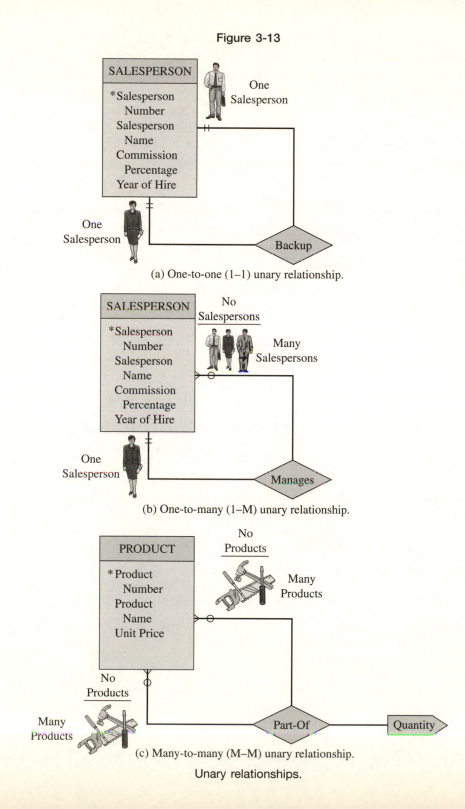

(a) One-to-one (1–1) unary relationship.

(b) One-to-many (1–M) unary relationship.

(c) Many-to-many (M–M) unary relationship.

Unary relationships.

and so on until ultimately they form the entire object. Each basic part and each subassembly can be thought of as a "part" of the object. Then, the parts are in a many-to-many unary relationship to each other. Any one particular part can be made up of several other parts, while at the same time itself being a component of several other parts.

In Figure 3-13c, think of the products sold in hardware and home improvement stores. Basic items like hammers and wrenches can be combined and sold as sets. Larger tool sets can be composed of smaller sets plus additional single tools. All of these single tools and sets of all sizes can be classified as products. Thus, as shown in Figure 3-13c, a product can be part of no other products or part of several other products. Going in the reverse direction, a product can be composed of no other products or can be composed of several other products.

3.3.3 Ternary Relationships

A ternary relationship involves three different entity types. Assume for the moment that any salesperson can sell to any customer. Figure 3-14 shows the

Figure 3-14

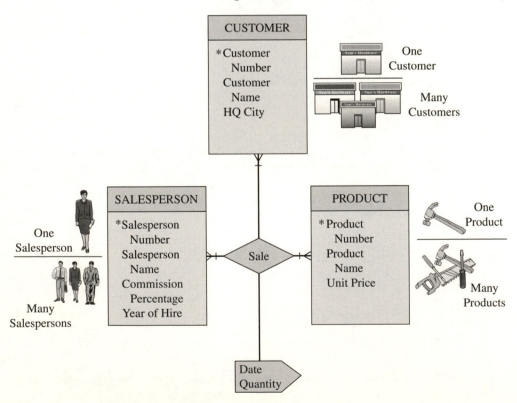

Ternary relationship.

most general many-to-many-to-many ternary relationship between salespersons, customers, and products. It means that we know which salesperson sold which product to which customer.

Each sale has **intersection data** consisting of the date of the sale and the number of units of the product sold. Often, rather than trying to consider these as ternary relationships, it's easier to look at them as sets of binary relationships.

3.3.4 Breaking Down Many-to-Many Relationships

One of the keys to having a well-designed data model and database is how well you've handled many-to-many relationships. Some designers try to find excuses not to use them. If the relationships are overlooked, you can end up stuffing a table with unnecessary, duplicated data. If you try to avoid using many-to-many relationships, you end up with a poorly designed model that wastes space and results in less than optimum performance.

Generally, we think of attributes as facts about entities. Each salesperson has a salesperson number, a name, a commission percentage, and a year of hire. At the entity occurrence level, for example, one of the salespersons has salesperson number 528, the name Jane Adams, a commission percentage of 15 percent, and the year of hire of 2003. In an E-R diagram, these attributes are written or drawn together with the entity, as in the E-R diagrams you have seen. This certainly appears to be very natural and obvious. Are there ever any circumstances in which an attribute can describe something other than an entity?

Consider the many-to-many relationship between salespersons and products back in Figure 3-12c. As usual, salespersons are described by their salesperson number, name, commission percentage, and year of hire. Products are described by their product number, name, and unit price. But what if there is a requirement to keep track of the number of units, call it "quantity," of a particular product that a particular salesperson has sold? Can we add the quantity attribute to the product entity box? No, because while a particular product has a single product number, product name, and unit price, there will be lots of quantities, one for each salesperson selling the product. Can we add the quantity attribute to the salesperson entity box? No, because while a particular salesperson has a single salesperson number, salesperson name, commission percentage, and year of hire, there will be lots of quantities, one for each product that the salesperson sells. It makes no sense to try to put the Quantity attribute in either the salesperson entity box or the product entity box. While each salesperson has a single salesperson number, name, and so forth, each salesperson has many quantities, one for each product he sells. Similarly, while each product has a single product number, product name, and so forth, each product has many quantities, one for each salesperson who sells that product. But an entity box in an E-R diagram is designed to list the attributes that simply and directly describe the entity, with no complications involving other entities. Putting quantity in either the salesperson or the product entity box just will not work.

Understanding Intersection Data

The quantity attribute doesn't describe either the salesperson alone or the product alone. It describes the combination of a particular occurrence of one entity type and a particular occurrence of the other entity type. The quantity 170 doesn't make sense as a description or characteristic of salesperson number 137 alone. She sold many different kinds of products. To which one does the quantity 170 refer? Similarly, the quantity 170 doesn't make sense as a description or characteristic of product number 24013 alone. It was sold by many different salespersons.

In fact, the quantity 170 falls at the intersection of salesperson number 170 and product number 24013. It describes the combination of or the association between that particular salesperson and that particular product, and it is known as intersection data. This is similar to the mapping table described earlier, but containing data in addition to the associations. Figure 3-15 shows the many-to-many relationship between salespersons and products with the intersection data, quantity, as represented in a special five-sided intersection data box. Notice that the intersection data box is attached to the relationship diamond between the two entity boxes. That is the natural place for it to be drawn. Pictorially, it looks like it is at the intersection between the two entities, but there is more to it than that. The intersection data describes the relationship between the two entities. We know that an occurrence of the Sells relationship specifies that salesperson 137 has sold some of product 24013. The quantity 170 is an attribute of that

Figure 3-15

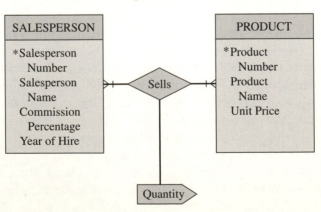

Intersection data.

Figure 3-16

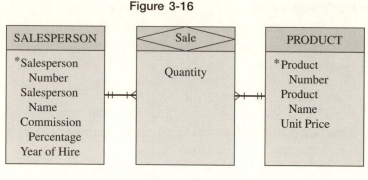

Associative entity.

relationship occurrence further describing the relationship. We know not only that salesperson 137 sold some of product 24013 but also how many units of that product that salesperson sold.

Using Associative Entities

Since we know that entities can have attributes and now we see that many-to-many relationships can have attributes, does that mean that entities and many-to-many relationships can in some sense be treated in the same way within E-R diagrams? Indeed they can, although it is a matter of choice and not a requirement! Figure 3-16 shows the many-to-many relationship Sells converted into the associative entity Sale. An occurrence of the Sale associative entity does exactly what the many-to-many relationship did: it indicates a relationship between a salesperson and a product, specifically sales, and includes any intersection data that describes that relationship. Note very, very carefully the reversal of the cardinalities and modalities when the many-to-many relationship is converted to an associative entity. Sale is now a kind of entity in its own right, and you must think of the new relationships as follows. A salesperson can be involved in many sales (where in this case *sale* means that a salesperson has been involved in selling a type of product over some period of time), but a particular sale can only involve one salesperson! Similarly, a product can be involved in many sales, but a particular sale can involve only one product.

If the many-to-many relationship E-R diagram style of Figure 3-15 is equivalent to the associative entity style of Figure 3-16, which one should you use? This is one of those instances in which this type of diagramming is an art with a lot of leeway for personal taste. The fact is that you can use either one, but you may find yourself working for a company that has set standards for these diagrams and expects you to use the one that has been chosen for its standards.

Defining Uniqueness

Since, as we have just seen, a many-to-many relationship can appear to be a kind of an entity, complete with attributes, it also follows that it should have a unique identifier, like other entities. In its most basic form, the unique identifier of the many-to-many relationship or the associative entity is the combination of the unique identifiers of the two entities in the many-to-many relationship. So, the unique identifier of the many-to-many relationship of Figure 3-15 or the associative entity of Figure 3-16 is the combination of the Salesperson Number and Product Number attributes.

Sometimes, an additional attribute or attributes must be added to this combination to produce uniqueness. This often involves a time element. For example, if we wanted to keep track of the sales on a weekly basis, we would have to have a date attribute or a week number attribute as intersection data and the unique identifier would be Salesperson Number, Product Number, and Date. If we want to know how many units of each product were sold by each salesperson each week, the combination of Salesperson Number and Product Number would not be unique because for a particular salesperson and a particular product, the combination of those two values would be the same each week! Date must be added to produce uniqueness, not to mention to make it clear which week a particular value of the Quantity attribute applies to a particular salesperson product combination.

The third and last possibility occurs when the nature of the associative entity is such that it has its own unique identifier. For example, a company might

---

FOR EXAMPLE

Describing Relationships

It is common to have multiple relationships between one entity and other entities. Consider this situation. Your company does telephone sales to established customers. Each customer has a customer ID. Each employee is identified by an employee ID. Whenever an order is placed, it must include both the employee ID of the employee creating the order and the customer ID of the customer placing the order.

Here, we have two separate one-to-many relationships. One is between customers and orders—each customer can have multiple orders. The other is between employees and orders—each employee can create multiple orders. Even though they are related, there is no need to explicitly identify a relationship between employees and customers. This is taken care of for you, because the two are associated through the order entity.

specify a unique serial number for each sales record, in which case the combination of Salesperson Number, Product Number, and Date isn't needed. Another example would be the many-to-many relationship between motorists and police officers who give traffic tickets for moving violations. The unique identifier could be the combination of police officer number and motorist driver's license number plus perhaps date and time. But, typically, each traffic ticket has a unique serial number, and this would serve as the unique identifier.

SELF-CHECK

- Compare binary and unary relationships.
- Give one example each of a one-to-one, one-to-many, and many-to-many relationship.
- Discuss the role of using a mapping table when implementing a many-to-many relationship.
- Explain the role of intersection data.

3.4 Comparing Data Models

At this point, you can put what you learned together and start creating basic data models using E-R diagrams. It's best to take a careful, organized approach to things rather than trying to do it all at once. Start by identifying entities, and for each of the entities, appropriate attributes. Then, identify the associations between the entities. If an association becomes obvious while you are still identifying entities, jot it down so that you'll remember it when you start defining relationships. Also, keep in mind that during the process of defining relationships, you might discover additional entities or find that you need to break an entity down into two or more smaller entities.

Before looking at data models in detail, we're going to talk a little about modeling tools and their uses. When selecting a tool, choose one that you feel comfortable using. Most of the options available on the market are very similar, so it becomes a matter simply of personal choice.

Often, the easiest way to understand concepts like these is to see them in use. That's what we're going to do here, comparing E-R models for two different fictional companies. This gives you an opportunity to see both similarities and differences between the two models. We use the term *entity* throughout in these descriptions because that's what they still are. They don't become tables until we create our physical model and start implementing the database.

3.4.1 Choosing a Modeling Tool

Hopefully, you've been convinced of the importance of documenting your database model. The easiest way to find errors in your logic is to draw them out and review the logical diagram. This will help you see mistakes like a table standing alone when it should be related to one or more other tables. You have three basic options for data modeling:

▲ Manual
▲ Generic draw program
▲ Custom modeling program

It could be that the only modeling tools you need are a pencil and a piece of paper. When designing a relatively simple database with only a few relationships, this is often the fastest method. You could possibly have the model finished before you could even get a modeling application up and running. And as a "just in case note", be sure and use a pencil so you can erase your mistakes.

A common option is to use a generic drawing or modeling program. Some, like Microsoft Visio, include templates and symbols specific to database modeling so that you can produce models similar to the ones you've seen here. It also includes an object modeling template you can use to create **object-relation models (ORM)** for object-relational databases. ORMs, because of their flexibility, also are sometimes used when modeling relational databases.

There are also applications available that are specifically designed for database modeling. Some are model-specific while others support a variety of standard modeling languages and templates. If you only plan to design and implement one, or very few, databases in your career, there probably isn't much justification for buying an application specific to that purpose. However, if you plan to do this on a regular basis, you may find it worth your while.

One advantage of both Visio and some drawing applications is that you have some flexibility in what is shown in your model. For example, Figure 3-17 shows two different options for how Visio could document the same relationship. The one on the left is the default—a simple line with the arrow pointing to the referenced table. The one on the right looks more like the drawings you've seen in this chapter, indicating that this is a one-to-many relationship. You have the option of showing as many or as few details of the relationship as you want.

Another advantage of drawing programs that include modeling templates and modeling applications is that they do some of the checking for you to help you avoid errors. For example, depending on the application, you might

Figure 3-17

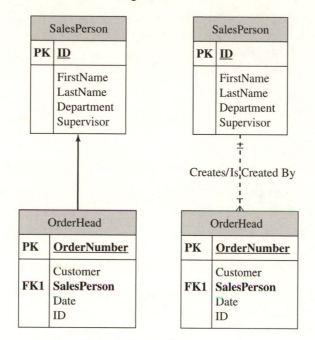

Visio database diagrams.

be forced to identify the key columns in the referenced and referencing entities when defining a relationship. You might also be forced to provide cardinality and modality information for each relationship. This added functionality can help you avoid mistakes when designing a very large or very complicated database.

3.4.2 The General Hardware Company

Figure 3-18 is the E-R diagram for the General Hardware Company, parts of which we have been using throughout this chapter. General Hardware is a wholesaler and distributor of various manufacturers' tools and other hardware products. Its customers are hardware and home improvement stores, which in turn sell the products at retail to individual consumers. Again, as a middleman it buys its goods from the manufacturers and then sells them to the retail stores. How exactly does General Hardware operate? Now that we know something about E-R diagrams, let's see if we can figure it out from Figure 3-18.

Begin with the SALESPERSON entity box in the middle on the left. SALESPERSON has four attributes, with one of them, Salesperson Number, serving as

Figure 3-18

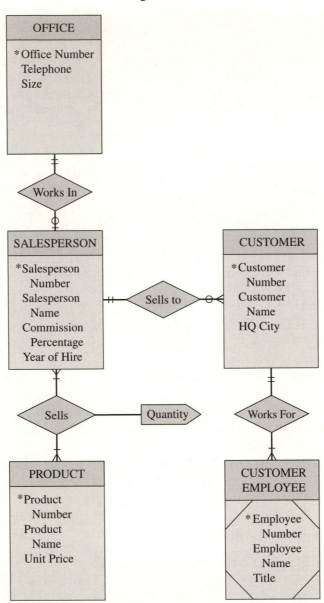

General Hardware.

the unique identifier of the salespersons. Looking upwards from SALESPERSON, a salesperson works in exactly one office (indicated by the double ones or bars encountered on the way to the OFFICE entity). OFFICE has three attributes. Office Number is the unique identifier. Looking back downwards from the OFFICE entity box, an office has either no salespersons working in it (the zero modality symbol) or one salesperson (the one or bar cardinality symbol). Starting again at the SALESPERSON entity box and moving to the right, a salesperson has no customers or many customers. Remember that the customers are hardware or home improvement stores. The CUSTOMER entity has three attributes and Customer Number is the unique identifier. In the reverse direction, a customer must have exactly one salesperson.

From the CUSTOMER entity downward is the CUSTOMER EMPLOYEE entity. According to the figure, a customer must have at least one but can have many employees. An employee works for exactly one customer. This is actually a special situation. General Hardware has an interest only in maintaining data about the people who are its customers' employees as long as their employer remains a customer of General Hardware. If a particular hardware store or home improvement chain stops buying goods from General Hardware, then General Hardware no longer cares about that store's or chain's employees. Furthermore, while General Hardware assumes that each of its customers assigns their employees unique employee numbers, those numbers can only be assumed to be unique within that customer store or chain. Thus the unique identifier for a customer employee must be the combination of the Customer Number and the Employee Number attributes. In this situation, CUSTOMER EMPLOYEE is called a dependent entity. As shown in the CUSTOMER EMPLOYEE entity box in Figure 3-18, a dependent entity is distinguished by a diagonal hash mark in each corner of its attribute area.

Returning to the SALESPERSON entity box and looking downward, there is a many-to-many relationship between salespersons and products. A salesperson is authorized to sell at least one and possibly (probably, in this case) many products. A product is sold by at least one and possibly many salespersons. The PRODUCT entity has three attributes, with Product Number being the unique identifier. The attribute Quantity is intersection data in the many-to-many relationship, meaning that the company is interested in keeping track of how many units of each product each salesperson has sold.

3.4.3 Good Reading Bookstores

Figure 3-19 shows the E-R diagram for Good Reading Bookstores, a chain of bookstores that wants to keep track of the books it sells, their publishers, their authors, and the customers who buy them. The BOOK entity has four attributes; Book Number is the unique identifier. A book has exactly one publisher. Publisher Name is the unique identifier of the PUBLISHER entity. A publisher may have (and generally has) published many books that Good Reading carries; however, Good Reading also wants to be able to keep track of some publishers that currently have no books in Good Reading's inventory. (Note the zero modality symbol from PUBLISHER towards BOOK.) A book must have at least one author but can have many (where in this case "many" means a few, generally

Figure 3-19

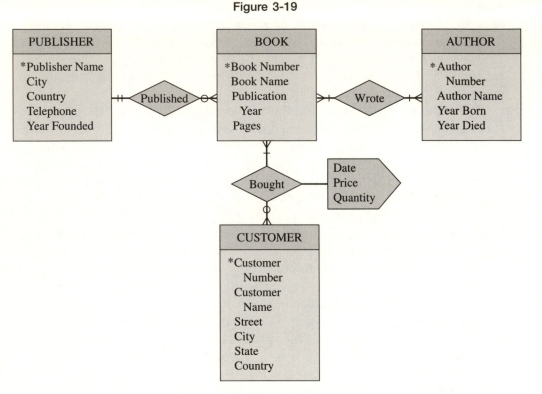

Good Reading bookstores.

two or three, at most). For a person to be of interest to Good Reading as an author, she must have written at least one and possibly many books that Good Reading carries. Note that there is a many-to-many relationship between the BOOK and AUTHOR entities but no intersection data.

Looking downward from the BOOK entity box, a book that Good Reading carries may not as yet have been bought by any of its customers (maybe it just came out) or may have been bought by many of its customers. For a customer to be of interest to Good Reading, he must have bought at least one book and possibly (hopefully!) many. Date, Price, and Quantity are intersection data in the many-to-many relationship between the BOOK and CUSTOMER entities. Does this make sense? Might a customer have bought several copies of the same book on the same date? After all, that's what the presence of the Quantity attribute implies. Might she have then bought more copies of the same book on a later date? Yes to both questions! A grandmother bought a copy of a book for each of three of her grandchildren one day, and they liked it so much that she returned and bought five more copies of the same book for her other five grandchildren several days later.

- Describe the relationship in Figure 3-17, including all of the information available in the diagram.
- Explain why it is helpful to study other data diagrams before creating your own data model.

SUMMARY

This chapter introduced data modeling and the use of data diagrams. We started with a general look at the design process and some of the decisions you must make about the type of database you need to design and your design goals. We looked at relational database modeling and the E-R model in some detail, including an introduction to some fundamental database objects. You were introduced to the various types of relationships that might be included in your database model. Finally, we talked about modeling tools and compared two example data diagrams.

KEY TERMS

Associative entity	Data model
Balanced tree index	Data warehouse
Base object	Decision support system (DSS)
Binary relationship	Entity-Relationship diagram (ERD)
Binary tree index	Entity-Relationship (E-R) modeling
B-tree index	Field
Bulk loading	Hybrid database
Business rules	Identifier
Cardinality	Index
Clustered index	Intersection data
Conceptual design	Large object (LOB) data
Concurrency	Leaf node
Database object	Logical design
Data diagram	Many-to-many (M-M) binary relationship
Data mart	

Modality

Node

Nonclustered index

Object-relation model (ORM)

One-to-many (1-M) binary relationship

One-to-one (1-1) binary relationship

Online transaction processing (OLTP)

Physical design

Primary index

Primary key

Record

Referenced entity

Referencing entity

Referential integrity

Reporting database

Scalable

Secondary index

Stakeholder

Ternary relationship

Transactional database

Throughput

Unary relationship

ASSESS YOUR UNDERSTANDING

Go to www.wiley.com/college/gillenson to evaluate your knowledge of data modeling.
Measure your learning by comparing pre-test and post-test results.

Summary Questions

1. Entities and attributes are identified during logical design. True or False?
2. A transactional database must support which of the following activities?
   (a) adding new data
   (b) changing existing data
   (c) deleting data
   (d) all of the above
3. Your design must ensure that any customer purchases at least $20.00 in merchandise. This is an example of which of the following?
   (a) entity definition
   (b) business rule
   (c) attribute
   (d) relational integrity
4. Each table in your database typically represents which of the following?
   (a) an entity
   (b) an attribute
   (c) a relationship
   (d) a data diagram
5. You are defining an employee entity. Which of the following would you likely use as the identifier?
   (a) first name
   (b) last name
   (c) employee ID
   (d) hire date
   (e) none of the above
6. A foreign key is based on a unique value in the referenced entity. True or False?
7. Which statement best describes attributes?
   (a) You should have a table for each attribute defined in your model.
   (b) Any attribute can be used as an entity's identifier.
   (c) Attributes describe entities.
   (d) Attributes are used in object modeling only.

8. Which statement best describes an identifier?

   (a) The identifier must be defined by a single attribute.

   (b) It is seldom necessary to specify an identifier for an entity.

   (c) An identifier must uniquely identify an entity.

9. Which statement best describes a clustered index?

   (a) A table is physically sorted in clustered index order.

   (b) A clustered index is used to enforce referential integrity.

   (c) A table can have up to 249 clustered indexes.

10. A table's primary index is based on the table's primary key. True or False?

11. Which statement best describes how views are defined?

    (a) A view can be based on one table only.

    (b) A view can be based on one or more tables.

    (c) A view can have tables, but not views, as base objects.

    (d) A view can be based on one or more tables or views.

12. Which statement describes the role of a foreign key in a relationship?

    (a) A foreign key enforces uniqueness on the referenced table.

    (b) A foreign key enforces referential integrity in a relationship.

    (c) A foreign key enforces uniqueness on the referencing table.

    (d) A foreign key has no role in a relationship.

13. A unary relationship refers to any one-to-one relationship. True or False?

14. A relationship between two entities is referred to as which of the following?

    (a) a binary relationship

    (b) a unary relationship

    (c) a ternary relationship

15. A supervisor is responsible for several employees. This describes what type of relationship?

    (a) one-to-one

    (b) one-to-many

    (c) many-to-many

16. The line connecting two entities in an E-R diagram has a crow's foot at either end. This describes what kind of relationship?

    (a) one-to-one

    (b) one-to-many

    (c) many-to-many

17. Which term refers to the maximum number of entities that can be involved in a relationship?

    (a) cardinality

    (b) modality

    (c) intersection

    (d) association

18. What kind of relationship can be used when relating an entity to instances within itself?

    (a) one-to-one

    (b) one-to-many

    (c) many-to-many

    (d) all of the above

19. Which of the following can you use to create E-R diagrams?

    (a) pencil and paper

    (b) a generic drawing program

    (c) a custom modeling program

    (d) all of the above

20. When reading an E-R diagram, how is a "one" relationship identified?

    (a) by an arrow

    (b) by a bar

    (c) by a crow's foot

    (d) no special symbol is used to identify a "one" relationship

Applying This Chapter

1. Each customer may have a charge account, known as the AccountBalance entity. Each AccountBalance entity is related to only one customer. Complete the E-R diagram in Figure 3-20 to show this relationship.

2. You are creating a data model for a transactional database. What are the primary kinds of activities that the database must support? The Purchase Order entity must be modeled as two entities, one with header information and the other with detailed line items. How can you keep an association between these two entities? How is the association enforced?

3. The city of Chicago, Illinois, wants to maintain information about its extensive system of high schools, including its teachers and their university degrees, its students, administrators, and the subjects that are taught. Each school has a unique name, plus an address, telephone number, year built, and size in square feet. Students have a student number, name,

Figure 3-20

CUSTOMER	
PK	**ID**
	Name
	City
	PostalCode
	Phone

AccountBalance	
PK	**AccountNum**
	CustomerID
	Current
	Due
	PastDue

Partial E-R diagram.

home address, home telephone number, current grade, and age. With regard to a student's school assignment, the school system is only interested in keeping track of which school a student currently attends. Each school has several administrators, such as the principal and assistant principals. Administrators are identified by an employee number and also have a name, telephone number, and office number. What attributes are described for the entity STUDENT? Which attribute should you use as the entity's identifier? What is the relationship between student and school? What is the relationship between schools and administrators?

Creating a Data Model

The following is a description of the company Lucky Rent-a-Car:

Lucky Rent-A-Car's business environment is, obviously, centered around its cars. A car was manufactured by exactly one manufacturer. A manufacturer manufactured at least one and generally many of Lucky's cars. A car has had many maintenance events (but a brand new car may not have had any yet). A car may not have been rented to any customers (again, the case of a brand new car) or to many customers. A customer may have rented many cars from Lucky and to be in Lucky's business environment must have rented at least one. Rental Date, Return Date, and Total Cost all relate to the many-to-many relationship between CAR and CUSTOMER.

1. What is intersection data and how is it represented?

2. What are the one-to-many relationships described here?
3. Sketch the E-R diagram.

Reading an E-R Diagram

The E-R diagram for the World Music Association (WMA) is shown in Figure 3-21. Musicians are tracked, even if not currenlty employed by an orchestra. For the purposes of this diagram, assume there are no instances where two different musicians have earned the same degree from the same university.

1. What are the one-to-many relationships shown in the diagram? Many-to-many?
2. What intersection data is shown in this diagram?
3. What tables would you create, based on the diagram?
4. Fully describe the information provided in this E-R diagram.

Figure 3-21

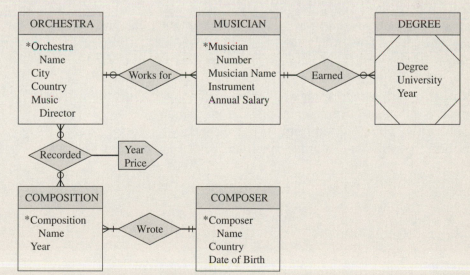

WMA E-R diagram.

4

DESIGNING A DATABASE

Starting Point

Go to www.wiley.com/college/gillenson to assess your knowledge of database design.
Determine where you need to concentrate your effort.

What You'll Learn in This Chapter

▲ Entity-relationship to relational table conversion processes
▲ Associative table requirements
▲ Standard normalization forms

After Studying This Chapter, You'll Be Able To

▲ Convert stand-alone entities to tables
▲ Identify entity relationships by type and conversion requirements
▲ Convert unary entity relationships to database objects
▲ Convert binary entity relationships to database objects
▲ Compare E-R diagrams and the resulting relational table designs
▲ Select appropriate foreign keys and their placement in relational tables
▲ Create associative tables, including intersection data where needed
▲ Recognize unnormalized data
▲ Normalize a database by applying the first, second, and third normal forms
▲ Normalize a database through non-loss decomposition
▲ Normalize the tables created from an E-R diagram
▲ Recognize the need for denormalization and selectively denormalize data

INTRODUCTION

As you've learned, several steps are involved in designing a database to support a business and business applications. You must collect business data in the form of business documents, employee interviews, and other data sources. You use this data to generate an entity-relationship (E-R) diagram that describes the business and its requirements. From this diagram you will create the logical and then physical design of your database.

In this chapter, we'll focus on the next step in the process: identifying the relational tables you will create based on the entities in the E-R diagram and then going through a process known as normalization, which will help you identify duplicate data and optimize data storage. Your final result is a finished relational design from which you can identify the database objects you need to implement your physical database.

4.1 Designing Relational Tables

The conversion of E-R diagrams to relational tables is a straightforward process. Typically, each entity converts to a table. For many-to-many relationships, each associative entity also converts to a table. Attributes become table columns, at least those attributes that apply to business and application requirements. During the process, rules must be followed to ensure that foreign keys appear in their proper places in the tables.

4.1.1 Converting a Single Entity

We'll start with the easiest example, converting a single entity to a table. Figure 4-1 shows a single entity from a representative E-R diagram.

The entity in this situation is named SALESPERSON. The process of creating a table based on this entity is relatively simple. You create a table, typically with

Figure 4-1

SALESPERSON

*Salesperson
Number
Salesperson
Name
Commission
Percentage
Year of Hire

SALESPERSON entity.

Figure 4-2

SALESPERSON			
Salesperson Number	Salesperson Name	Commission Percentage	Year of Hire

SALESPERSON table.

the same name, with a column for each of its attributes. This is shown in Figure 4-2. Notice that Salesperson Number is underlined to indicate that it is the entity's unique identifier and will be used as the table's primary key.

4.1.2 Converting Binary Relationships

The process becomes more interesting and more complicated when working with related tables. The process starts out much the same, identifying tables from business entities. Selecting the identifier and the primary key takes on greater importance because they are used in defining the foreign key to establish relationships between the tables.

Adding to the complication is that there is often more than one way to represent entity relationships as relational tables. It becomes a matter of identifying your options and picking the option that best meets your business and application requirements. You may also find it necessary to go back and fine tune the tables you identify as you go along.

Converting a One-to-One Binary Relationship

We'll start with the one-to-one binary relationship shown in Figure 4-3. As you can see, this is a simple relationship based on the SALESPERSON and

Figure 4-3

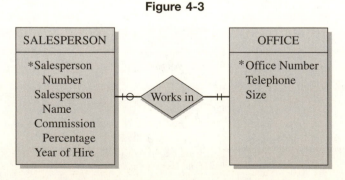

SALESPERSON to OFFICE relationship.

Figure 4-4

SALESPERSON/OFFICE						
Salesperson Number	Salesperson Name	Commission Percentage	Year of Hire	Office Number	Telephone	Size

SALESPERSON/OFFICE table.

OFFICE entities. Each Salesperson works in one Office. Office, in this case, identifies a single office cubicle.

There are at least three options for designing tables to represent this data. The first option is shown in Figure 4-4, with the two entities combined into one relational table. This design is possible because the one-to-one relationship means that for one salesperson, there can only be one office associated with the salesperson and conversely, for one office there can be only one salesperson. Because of this relationship, a particular salesperson and office combination could be stored as one record, as shown.

There are three reasons why Figure 4-4 is not a good data design. The first two can be determined from the diagram in Figure 4-3. First, the very fact that salesperson and office were drawn in two different entity boxes in the E-R diagram indicates that they are thought of separately in this business environment. This means that they should be kept separate in the database. Second is the modality of zero at the SALESPERSON entity. Reading Figure 4-3 from right to left, it says that an office might have no one assigned to it. In the table shown in Figure 4-4, a few or possibly many record occurrences could have values for the office number, telephone, and size attributes but have the four attributes pertaining to salespersons empty or null. A **null value** is an undefined value, usually used to identify that no value is provided for that attribute. Even though considered as an undefined value, it is still considered a valid value and provides useful information by the fact that the attribute is not defined. This would result in wasted storage space. It also means that the Salesperson Number cannot be declared to be the primary key of the table, because there would be records with no primary key values, which is not allowed. Before going on, there are a couple of points about storage costs and the relationship between database design and data storage that you should be aware of. Even though the cost per byte has dropped significantly over the years, wasted space continues to be an issue deserving consideration in your database design and implementation. Inefficient design and space use can lead to inefficient indexes and could mean less than optimal performance. That's not the only performance issue. As database tables (and the database as a whole) grow, access performance tends to suffer because of the increased volume of data involved. Also, just because the price of storage has dropped, installing additional storage when you run out of space can be time consuming and usually means down time for the database, which typically is very expensive.

The third reason is not visible from the partial E-R diagram in Figure 4-3. However, when you look at the full E-R diagram in Figure 4-5, the reason

Figure 4-5

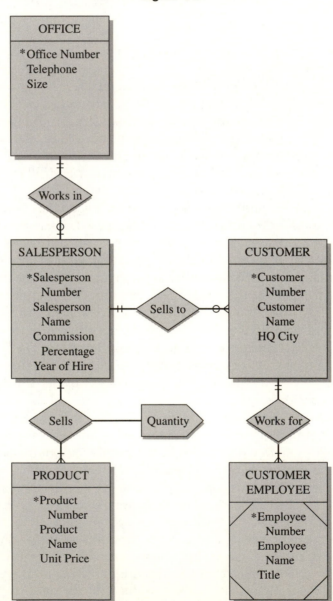

Full E-R diagram.

Figure 4-6

SALESPERSON				
Salesperson Number	Salesperson Name	Commission Percentage	Year of Hire	Office Number

OFFICE		
Office Number	Telephone	Size

Separate SALESPERSON and OFFICE tables, first version.

becomes immediately evident. The salesperson entity is involved in relationships with other entities in addition to the office entity. It is related to the CUSTOMER entity through a one-to-many relationship and the PRODUCT entity through a many-to-many relationship.

Figure 4-6 is a better choice. There are separate tables for the SALESPERSON and OFFICE entities. In order to record the relationship (which salesperson is assigned to which office), the Office Number attribute is placed as a foreign key in the SALESPERSON table. This connects each salesperson with the office to which he or she is assigned. Again, look at the modalities in the E-R diagram of Figure 4-3. Each salesperson is assigned to exactly one office, as is indicated by the two "ones" adjacent to the office entity. That translates directly into each record in the SALESPERSON table of Figure 4-6 having a value (and a single value at that) for its Office Number foreign key attribute. Each unassigned office will have a record in the OFFICE table, with Office Number as the primary key. In this case, unassigned offices aren't seen as a problem. Their office numbers will simply not appear as foreign key values in the SALESPERSON table.

The third option is shown in Figure 4-7. Instead of placing Office Number as a foreign key in the SALESPERSON table, you place Salesperson Number as a foreign key in the OFFICE table. Recall from the E-R diagram that the modality of zero adjacent to the salesperson entity says that an office might be empty. As a result, some or perhaps many records of the OFFICE table in Figure 4-7 would have no value or a null in their Salesperson Number foreign key attribute positions.

It follows that if the modalities were reversed, meaning that the zero modality was adjacent to the OFFICE entity box and the one modality was adjacent to the SALESPERSON entity box, then the design in Figure 4-7 might be preferable. Reversed modality would mean that every office must have a salesperson assigned to it, but a salesperson may or may not be assigned to an office. There are different circumstances that could result in this situation. For

Figure 4-7

SALESPERSON			
Salesperson Number	Salesperson Name	Commission Percentage	Year of Hire

OFFICE			
Office Number	Telephone	Salesperson Number	Size

Separate SALESPERSON and OFFICE tables, second version.

example, perhaps lots of the salespersons travel most of the time and don't need offices.

While we're in a "what if" mode, what if the modality was zero on both sides and we didn't have the other relationships to consider? Then we would have to make a judgment call between the designs of Figure 4-6 and Figure 4-7. If the goal is to minimize the number of null values in the foreign key, then we have to decide whether it is more likely that a salesperson is not assigned to an office or that an office is empty.

Converting a One-to Many Binary Relationship

The relationship shown in Figure 4-8 is a one-to-many binary relationship. In this relationship, each occurrence of the SALESPERSON entity is related to zero or more occurrences of the CUSTOMER entity.

Figure 4-9 shows the conversion of this E-R diagram into two relational tables. This time, the conversion is relatively simple. The rule is that the unique identifier

Figure 4-8

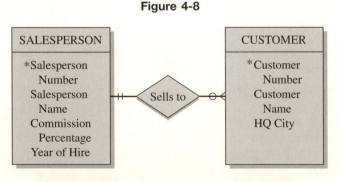

SALESPERSON to CUSTOMER relationship.

Figure 4-9

SALESPERSON			
<u>Salesperson Number</u>	Salesperson Name	Commission Percentage	Year of Hire

CUSTOMER			
<u>Customer Number</u>	Customer Name	HQ City	Salesperson Number

SALESPERSON and CUSTOMER tables.

of the entity on the "one side" of the one-to-many relationship is placed as a foreign key in the table representing the entity on the "many side." In this case, the Salesperson Number attribute is placed in the CUSTOMER table as a foreign key. Each salesperson has one record in the SALESPERSON table, as does each customer in the CUSTOMER table. The Salesperson Number attribute in the CUSTOMER table links the two, and since the E-R diagram tells us that every customer must have a salesperson, there are no empty attributes in the CUSTOMER table records.

This solution also fits the full E-R diagram in Figure 4-5. The same Salesperson Number attribute used to establish a relationship with the CUSTOMER table can also be used in the relationship between SALESPERSON and OFFICE.

Converting a Many-to-Many Binary Relationship

Figure 4-10 once again uses the SALESPERSON entity, this time in a many-to-many binary relationship with the PRODUCT entity.

Figure 4-10

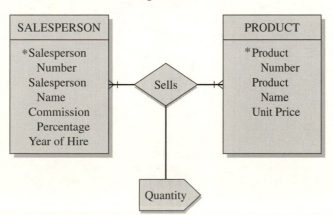

SALESPERSON to PRODUCT relationship.

Figure 4-11

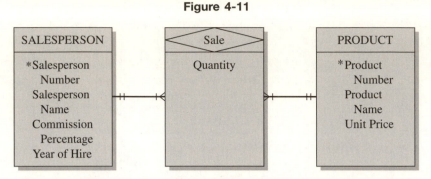

SALESPERSON, SALE, and PRODUCT entities.

Most relational DBMS systems do not directly support many-to-many relationships. Instead, you must also include an associative entity, in this case SALE, to establish the relationship. The E-R diagram in Figure 4-11 includes the associative entity.

Each of the two entities converts to a table with its own attributes but with no foreign keys (regarding this relationship). The SALESPERSON table and the PRODUCT table in Figure 4-12 each contain only the attributes shown in the SALESPERSON and PRODUCT entity boxes in Figure 4-10 and Figure 4-11. The primary key of this associated SALE table is the combination of the unique identifiers of the two entities in the many-to-many relationship. The primary

Figure 4-12

SALESPERSON			
Salesperson Number	Salesperson Name	Commission Percentage	Year of Hire

PRODUCT		
Product Number	Product Name	Unit Price

SALE		
Salesperson Number	Product Number	Quantity

Many-to-many relational tables.

key might also include another attribute, such as a date and time stamp, to ensure unique values. A key that is defined by multiple columns is called a **composite key.**

The table based on the associative entity can include additional attributes representing intersection data. This is shown as the Quantity attribute in this example. However, this is not a requirement. The associative table often includes only the data values needed to establish and maintain the many-to-many relationship.

4.1.3 Converting Unary Relationships

A unary relationship is one that is based on a single table. The problem in this case is not deciding what tables you need to create, but on how key values can be used to identify and maintain the relationship.

Converting a One-to-One Unary Relationship

In Figure 4-13 you see a one-to-one unary relationship based on the SALES-PERSON entity. Each Salesperson has one backup salesperson, someone who covers when the original salesperson isn't available.

In this case, with only one entity type involved and with a one-to-one relationship, the conversion requires only one table, as shown in Figure 4-14. For a particular salesperson, the Backup Number attribute represents the salesperson number of the backup person. The Backup Number is related to the SALES-PERSON table's primary key, Salesperson Number. Any value used as Backup Number must be a valid Salesperson Number.

Figure 4-13

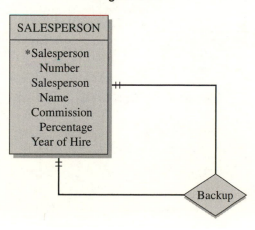

One-to-one unary relationship.

Figure 4-14

SALESPERSON				
Salesperson Number	Salesperson Name	Commission Percentage	Year of Hire	Backup Number

SALESPERSON table with Backup Number foreign key.

Converting a One-to-Many Unary Relationship

Figure 4-15 shows a one-to-many relationship based on the same Salesperson entity. You can read this as "each salesperson manages zero or more salespersons," but for the purpose of creating a related table, it's better to read this as "each salesperson is managed by a manager." The manager is also an occurrence of the SALESPERSON entity.

Figure 4-16 shows the conversion of this diagram into a relational database table. Some employees manage other employees. An employee's manager is recorded in the Manager Number. The manager numbers are actually salesperson numbers because some salespersons are sales managers who manage other salespersons. This arrangement works because each employee has only one manager. For any particular SALESPERSON record, there can only be one value for the Manager Number attribute. However, if you scan down the Manager Number column, a particular value may appear several times because a person can manage several other salespersons.

Figure 4-15

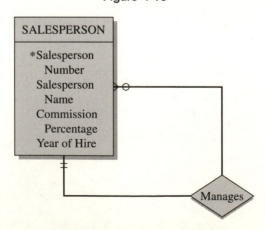

One-to-many unary relationship.

Figure 4-16

SALESPERSON				
Salesperson Number	Salesperson Name	Commission Percentage	Year of Hire	Manager

SALESPERSON table with Manager foreign key.

Converting a Many-to-Many Unary Relationship

Though not a common situation, you can have many-to-many unary relationships. One is shown in Figure 4-17. You have a situation where one product can be constructed out of a set of other products. For example, you might have the products Cup, Saucer, and Plate as separate occurrences of the PRODUCT entity. You could also have an occurrence called Place Setting, made up of a Cup, a Saucer, and a Plate.

As Figure 4-18 indicates, this relationship requires two tables in the conversion. The PRODUCT table has no foreign keys. The COMPONENT table indicates which items go into making up which other items. This is commonly referred to as a bill of materials. COMPONENT also contains any intersection data that might exist in the many-to-many relationship. In this example, the Quantity attribute indicates how many of a particular item go into making up another item.

The fact that we wind up with two tables in this conversion is not surprising. The general rule is that in the conversion of a many-to-many relationship

Figure 4-17

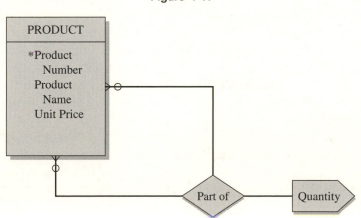

Many-to-many unary relationship.

Figure 4-18

PRODUCT		
Product Number	Product Name	Unit Price

COMPONENT		
Product Number	Subassembly Number	Quantity

Relational tables for many-to-many unary relationship.

of any degree—unary, binary, or ternary—the number of tables will be equal to the number of entity types (one, two, or three, respectively) plus one more table for the many-to-many relationship. Thus the conversion of a many-to-many unary relationship requires two tables, a many-to-many binary relationship requires three tables, and a many-to-many ternary relationship requires four tables. Ternary relationships are seldom diagramed in that form, so this chapter does not include an example of a ternary conversion.

FOR EXAMPLE

Requirements for Converting Diagram Entities

The basic requirements for creating an E-R diagram and relational tables are essentially the same. However, the reason behind these requirements becomes more evident as you get closer to your final physical model.

Consider this situation. You are responsible for the initial interviews and data gathering. You are expected to sketch out a simple E-R diagram of the company, which is then handed off to an analyst who will create the relational table design. You sketch the model and hand it off, but you haven't determined any identifiers for the entities. Can you see the problem this is going to cause?

The analyst can describe the tables, but not the relationships between the tables. In the relational model, you need two things to establish the relationship. You need a primary key in the referenced table that is used as the foreign key in the referencing table. Because you did the initial research, you are the best person to recommend identifiers for the initial entities, which are then converted to primary keys in the relational table design.

SELF-CHECK

- Describe the information you need to convert related entities into related tables and how you determine primary and foreign key columns.

- Explain why an additional table is needed when converting a many-to-many entity relationship into related tables.

- In a binary one-to-zero-or-one relationship with no other related entities, explain how can you determine which should be the referenced and which should be the referencing table.

4.2 Comparing Relational Designs

So far, we have (for the most part) taken entity relationships out of context to focus on the conversion process. You might find it easier to understand the conversion process between entities and relational tables if you could see examples based on more complete E-R diagrams. It also puts the process into more of a real-world context, letting you see how it relates to business models you might need to develop. We're going to convert the E-R models of two fictitious companies, General Hardware Company and Good Reading Bookstores. This chapter assumes that you can read and understand the E-R diagrams used in each case.

Keep in mind that you are still working in a pencil-and-paper mode, either literally or using a design or draw program. This is where you should work through your "what if . . ." scenarios and try out different data and relationship combinations. Your only real expense when making changes now is time. However, if you need to make changes to the model after you start implementing the physical database, the situation can become very expensive. Depending on where you are in the process, it might mean having to recreate the database or reload data. It might also mean having to redesign and even recode your application.

4.2.1 Designing General Hardware

Figure 4-19 is the General Hardware E-R diagram. It is convenient to begin the database design process with an important, central E-R diagram entity, such as salesperson, that has relationships with several other entities.

Thus the relational database in Figure 4-20 includes a SALESPERSON table with the four Salesperson attributes from the SALESPERSON entity box (plus the Office Number attribute, which we will return to shortly). Looking to the

Figure 4-19

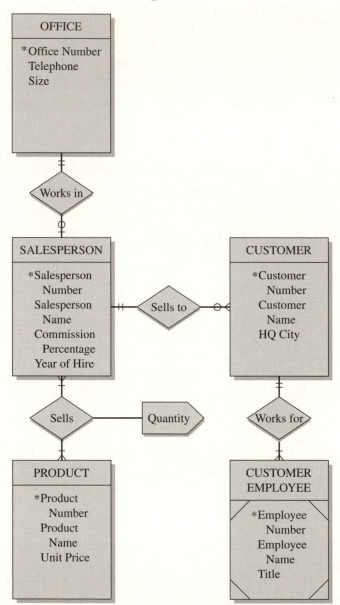

General Hardware E-R diagram.

right of the SALESPERSON entity box in the E-R diagram, we see a one-to-many relationship ("sells to") between salespersons and customers. The database then includes a CUSTOMER table with the Salesperson Number attribute as a foreign key because Salesperson is on the "one side" of the one-to-many relationship and Customer is on the "many side" of the one-to-many relationship.

Figure 4-20

SALESPERSON				
Salesperson Number	Salesperson Name	Commission Percentage	Year of Hire	Office Number

CUSTOMER			
Customer Number	Customer Name	Salesperson Number	HQ City

CUSTOMER EMPLOYEE			
Customer Number	Employee Number	Employee Name	Title

PRODUCT		
Product Number	Product Name	Unit Price

SALES		
Salesperson Number	Product Number	Quantity

OFFICE		
Office Number	Telephone	Size

General Hardware relational tables.

Customer Employee is a dependent entity of customer, and there is a one-to-many relationship between them. Customer Employee occurrences are employees who work for a particular customer and can make purchases for that customer. Because of the one-to-many relationship, the CUSTOMER EMPLOYEE table in the database includes the Customer Number attribute as a foreign key. Furthermore, the Customer Number attribute is part of the primary key of the CUSTOMER EMPLOYEE table because Customer Employee is a dependent entity and employee numbers are unique only within a customer. For example, two different customers could each have an employee number 100, representing different unique persons.

The PRODUCT table contains the three Product entity attributes. The many-to-many relationship between the SALESPERSON and PRODUCT entities is represented by the SALES table in the database. Notice that the combination of the unique identifiers (Salesperson Number and Product Number) of the two entities in the many-to-many relationship defines the primary key of the SALES table. Finally, the OFFICE entity has its table in the database with its three attributes, which brings us to the presence of the Office Number attribute as a foreign key in the SALESPERSON table. This is needed to maintain the one-to-one binary relationship between Salesperson and Office. We put the foreign key in the SALESPERSON table rather than in the OFFICE table because the modality adjacent to SALESPERSON is zero while the modality adjacent to OFFICE is one. An office may or may not have a salesperson assigned to it, but a salesperson must be assigned to an office. The result is that every salesperson must have an associated office number; the Office Number attribute in the SALESPERSON table can't be null. This requirement can be easily enforced, automatically helping prevent data errors (missing Office Number). If we reversed it and put the Salesperson Number attribute in the OFFICE table, many of the Salesperson Number attribute values could be null since the zero modality going from office to salesperson tells us that an office can be empty. Because the value might or might not be null, **data integrity,** ensuring that the data is entered and stored correctly, is harder to enforce.

One last thought: Why did the PRODUCT table end up without having any foreign keys? Simply, it is because there is no situation that requires insertion of a foreign key. It is not the "target" (it is not on the "many side") of any one-to-many binary relationship. It is not involved in a one-to-one binary relationship that requires a foreign key to ensure **relational integrity,** that is, to maintain the relationship. (Maintaining the relationship between referencing and referenced tables is also called **referential integrity.**) Finally, the PRODUCT table is not involved in a unary relationship that requires that the primary key to be repeated in the table.

4.2.2 Designing Good Reading Bookstores

The Good Reading Bookstores E-R diagram is shown in Figure 4-21. Beginning with the central BOOK entity and looking to its left, we see that there is a one-to-many relationship between books and publishers. A Publisher publishes many books, but a BOOK is published by just one publisher.

The Good Reading Bookstore's relational database tables of Figure 4-22 show the BOOK and PUBLISHER tables. Publisher Name is a foreign key in the BOOK table because publisher is on the "one side" of the one-to-many relationship and book is on the "many side." Next is the AUTHOR table, which is straightforward.

Figure 4-21

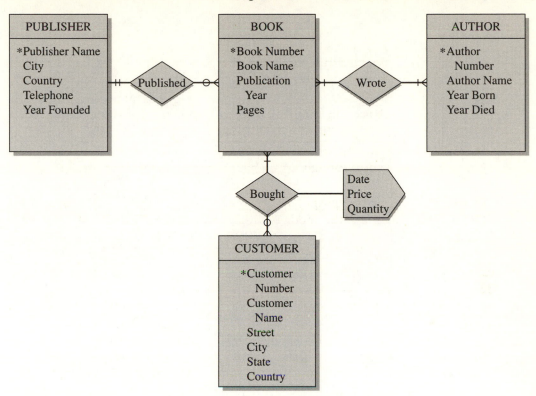

Good Reading Bookstores E-R diagram.

FOR EXAMPLE

Following Up on Your Design

You might discover during the conversion process that your E-R design isn't as complete as it should be. When this happens, you may find it necessary to go back to your original data to look for missing attributes.

Consider the following situation. You are designing a database for a customer support call center. When customers call they are automatically routed to the next available customer support agent. The agent with whom the customer speaks is, in this case, completely random. Your first choice as an associative entity might be the combination of the customer and employee identities. You would use this as the primary key.

When a customer calls back, he or she might get a different customer service agent or, by luck of the draw, the same customer service agent. This would mean the same combination of customer and employee identities, and would mean a duplicate value in the primary key. This is an illegal condition. You need an additional value, such as the date and time of the call, to produce a unique primary key value.

Figure 4-22

PUBLISHER				
Publisher Name	City	Country	Telephone	Year Founded

AUTHOR			
Author Number	Author Name	Year Born	Year Died

BOOK				
Book Number	Book Name	Publication Year	Pages	Publisher Name

CUSTOMER					
Customer Number	Customer Name	Street	City	State	Country

WRITING	
Book Number	Author Number

SALE				
Book Number	Customer Number	Date	Price	Quantity

Good Reading Bookstores relational tables.

The many-to-many binary relationship between books and authors is reflected in the WRITING table, which has no intersection data.

Finally, there is the CUSTOMER entity and the many-to-many relationship between books and customers. Correspondingly, the relational database includes a CUSTOMER table and a SALE table to handle the many-to-many relationship. Notice that the Date, Price, and Quantity attributes appear in the SALE table as intersection data. Also notice that since a customer can buy the same book on more than one day, the Date attribute must be part of the primary key to achieve uniqueness.

SELF-CHECK

- Explain the role of associative tables when defining many-to-many relational tables.

- Compare and contrast associative data and intersection data and the role of each.

- Explain how relational integrity is assured in a one-to-one or one-to-many binary table.

4.3 Normalizing Data

Data normalization is a methodology for organizing attributes into tables so that redundancy among the nonkey attributes is eliminated. Each of the resultant tables deals with a single data focus, which is just another way of saying that each resultant table will describe a single entity type or a single many-to-many relationship. Furthermore, foreign keys will appear exactly where they are needed. In other words, the output of the data normalization process is a properly structured relational database.

You should be aware that the normalization rules provided here are based on a common version of the accepted normal forms. The definitions, as they apply to relational tables, can vary somewhat depending on your reference source. If you see small differences in how they are defined in other sources, you should consider it as a difference of opinion rather than that one or the other is wrong.

4.3.1 Using Normalization Techniques

The input required by the data normalization process comes in two parts. One is a list of all the attributes that must be incorporated into the database—that is, all of the attributes in all the entities involved in the business environment under discussion, plus all of the intersection data attributes in all of the many-to-many relationships between these entities. The other input, informally, is a list of all the **defining associations** between the attributes, which are a means of expressing that the value of one particular attribute is associated with a single, specific value of another attribute. Formally, these defining associations are known as **functional dependencies.** If we know that one of these attributes has a particular value, then the other attribute must have some other value. For example, for a particular Salesperson Number, 137, there is exactly one Salesperson Name, Baker, associated with it. We know this because a Salesperson Number uniquely identifies a salesperson, and, after all, a person can have only one last name. Informally, we might say that Salesperson Number defines Salesperson Name. If I give you a Salesperson Number, you can give me back the one and only name that goes with it. These defining associations are commonly written with a right-pointing arrow like this:

$$\text{Salesperson Number} \rightarrow \text{Salesperson Name}$$

In the more formal terms of functional dependencies, the attribute on the left side is referred to as the **determinant attribute.** This is because its value determines the value of the attribute on the right side. Conversely, we also say that the attribute on the right is functionally dependent on the attribute on the left.

Data normalization is best explained with an example. In order to demonstrate the main points of the data normalization process, we will modify part of the General Hardware Company business environment and focus on the SALESPERSON and PRODUCT entities. Let's assume that salespersons are organized into departments and that each department has a manager who is not herself a salesperson. Then the list of attributes that we will consider is shown in Figure 4-23.

The list of defining associations or functional dependencies is shown in Figure 4-24. Notice a couple of fine points about the list of defining associations in Figure 4-24. The last association:

$$\text{Salesperson Number, Product Number} \rightarrow \text{Quantity}$$

shows that the combination of two or more attributes may define another attribute. That is, the combination of a particular Salesperson Number and a par-

Figure 4-23

| Salesperson Number |
| Salesperson Name |
| Commission |
| Percentage |
| Year of Hire |
| Department |
| Number |
| Manager Name |
| Product Number |
| Product Name |
| Unit Price |
| Quantity |

Salesperson entity attributes.

Figure 4-24

Salesperson Number ⟶ Salesperson Name
Salesperson Number ⟶ Commission Percentage
Salesperson Number ⟶ Year of Hire
Salesperson Number ⟶ Department Number
Salesperson Number ⟶ Manager Name
Product Number ⟶ Product Name
Product Number ⟶ Unit Price
Department Number ⟶ Manager Name
Salesperson Number, Product Number ⟶ Quantity

Salesperson entity defining associations (functional dependencies).

ticular Product Number defines or specifies a particular Quantity. Put another way, in this business context, we know how many units of a particular product a particular salesperson has sold.

Another point, which will be important in demonstrating one step of the data normalization process, is that Manager Name is defined, independently, by two different attributes, Salesperson Number and Department Number:

$$\text{Salesperson Number} \rightarrow \text{Manager Name}$$

$$\text{Department Number} \rightarrow \text{Manager Name}$$

Both of these defining associations are true. If you identify a salesperson by Salesperson Number, you can determine the salesperson's manager. Also, given a department number, you can determine the department manager. What this means is that during the systems analysis process, both of these equally true defining associations were discovered and noted. By the way, the fact that we know the department that a salesperson works in:

$$\text{Salesperson Number} \rightarrow \text{Department Number}$$

(and that each of these two attributes independently defines Manager Name) is also an issue in the data normalization process.

4.3.2 Normalizing Data by the Numbers

The data normalization process is known as a **decomposition process,** sometimes called **non-loss decomposition.** We will line up all of the attributes to be included in the relational database and start subdividing them into groups that will eventually form the database's tables. Thus we are going to "decompose" the original list of all the attributes into subgroups. To do so, we are going to step through a number of **normal forms,** which are rules for data normalization. First, we will examine what unnormalized data looks like. Then, we will work through the three main normal forms in order:

▲ First Normal Form
▲ Second Normal Form
▲ Third Normal Form

There are certain exception conditions that have also been described as normal forms. **Exception conditions** are nonstandard normal forms in addition to the three accepted standard normal forms. These include Boyce-Codd Normal Form, Fourth Normal Form, and Fifth Normal Form. They are relatively less common in practice and will not be covered here. Here are three additional points to remember:

1. Once the attributes are arranged in third normal form (and if none of the exception conditions is present), the group of tables that they comprise is, in fact, a well-structured relational database with no data redundancy.
2. A group of tables is said to be in a particular normal form if every table in the group is in that normal form.
3. The data normalization process is progressive. If a group of tables is in second normal form, it is also in first normal form. If the tables are in third normal form, they are also in second normal form.

Understanding Unnormalized Data

Figure 4-25 shows the salesperson and product-related attributes listed in Figure 4-24 arranged in a table with sample data. The salesperson and product data is taken from the General Hardware Company relational database. Note that salespersons 137, 204, and 361 are all in department number 73 and that their manager is Scott. Salesperson 186 is in department number 59 and his manager is Lopez.

The table in Figure 4-25 is unnormalized. The table has four records, one for each salesperson. But since each salesperson has sold several products and there is only one record for each salesperson, several attributes of each record must have multiple values. For example, the record for salesperson 137 has three product numbers, 19440, 24013, and 26722, in its Product Number attribute because salesperson 137 has sold all three of those products. Having such multivalued attributes is not permitted and so this table is unnormalized.

Normalizing to First Normal Form

In the **first normal form,** each attribute value is atomic, that is, no attribute is multivalued. The table in Figure 4-26 is the first normal form representation of

Figure 4-25

SALESPERSON/PRODUCT table									
Salesperson Number	Product Number	Salesperson Name	Commission Percentage	Year of Hire	Department Number	Manager Name	Product Name	Unit Price	Quantity
137	19440	Baker	10	1995	73	Scott	Hammer	17.50	473
	24013						Saw	26.25	170
	26722						Pliers	11.50	688
186	16386	Adams	15	2001	59	Lopez	Wrench	12.95	1745
	19440						Hammer	17.50	2529
	21765						Drill	32.99	1962
	24013						Saw	26.25	3071
204	21765	Dickens	10	1998	73	Scott	Drill	32.99	809
	26722						Pliers	11.50	734
361	16386	Carlyle	20	2001	73	Scott	Wrench	12.95	3729
	21765						Drill	32.99	3110
	26722						Pliers	11.50	2738

General Hardware sample unnormalized data.

the data. The attributes under consideration have been listed in one table, and a primary key has been established. In this definition of normal forms, the requirement for a primary key is not listed as part of any normal form, but is considered an assumed requirement of the initial E-R diagramming process.

As the sample data in Figure 4-27 shows, the number of records has increased compared to the unnormalized representation. Every attribute of every record has just one value. The multivalued attributes from Figure 4-25 are eliminated.

The combination of the Salesperson Number and Product Number attributes constitutes the table's primary key. The business context tells us that the combination of the two provides unique identifiers for the records of the table and that there is no single attribute that will do the job. In terms of data normalization,

Figure 4-26

SALESPERSON/PRODUCT table									
Salesperson Number	Product Number	Salesperson Name	Commission Percentage	Year of Hire	Department Number	Manager Name	Product Name	Unit Price	Quantity

Attributes defined in the first normal form.

Figure 4-27

SALESPERSON/PRODUCT table									
Salesperson Number	Product Number	Salesperson Name	Commission Percentage	Year of Hire	Department Number	Manager Name	Product Name	Unit Price	Quantity
137	19440	Baker	10	1995	73	Scott	Hammer	17.50	473
137	24013	Baker	10	1995	73	Scott	Saw	26.25	170
137	26722	Baker	10	1995	73	Scott	Pliers	11.50	688
186	16386	Adams	15	2001	59	Lopez	Wrench	12.95	1475
186	19440	Adams	15	2001	59	Lopez	Hammer	17.50	2529
186	21765	Adams	15	2001	59	Lopez	Drill	32.99	1962
186	24013	Adams	15	2001	59	Lopez	Saw	26.25	3071
204	21765	Dickens	10	1998	73	Scott	Drill	32.99	809
204	26722	Dickens	10	1998	73	Scott	Pliers	11.50	734
361	16386	Carlyle	20	2001	73	Scott	Wrench	12.95	3729
361	21765	Carlyle	20	2001	73	Scott	Drill	32.99	3110
361	26722	Carlyle	20	2001	73	Scott	Pliers	11.50	2738

Data normalized to the first normal form.

according to the list of defining associations or functional dependencies of Figure 4-24, every attribute in the table is either part of the primary key or is defined by one or both attributes of the primary key. This is actually a requirement of the second normal form, as we will see later. Salesperson Name, Commission Percentage, Year of Hire, Department Number, and Manager Name are each defined by Salesperson Number. Product Name and Unit Price are each defined by Product Number. Quantity is defined by the combination of Salesperson Number and Product Number.

These two different ways of approaching the primary key selection are equivalent. If the combination of a particular Salesperson Number and a particular Product Number is unique, then it identifies exactly one record of the table. And if it identifies exactly one record of the table, then that record shows the single value of each of the nonkey attributes that is associated with the unique combination of the key attributes. But that is the same thing as saying that each of the nonkey attributes is defined by or is functionally dependent on the primary key. For example, consider the first record of the table in Figure 4-27.

The combination of Salesperson Number 137 and Product Number 19440 is unique. Only one record in the table can have that combination of Salesperson Number and Product Number values. Therefore, if someone specifies those values, the only Salesperson Name that can be associated with them is Baker, the only Commission Percentage is 10, and so forth. But that has the same effect as the concept of functional dependency. Since Salesperson Name is functionally dependent on Salesperson Number, given a particular Salesperson Number, say 137, only one Salesperson Name can be associated with it, Baker. Since Commission Percentage is functionally dependent on Salesperson Number, given a particular Salesperson Number, say 137, there can be only one Commission Percentage associated with it, 10.

First normal form is merely a starting point in the normalization process. At this point, we have a great deal of data redundancy. Three records involve salesperson 137 (the first three records), and so there are three places in which his name is listed as Baker, his commission percentage is listed as 10, and so on. Similarly, two records involve product 19440 (the first and fifth records), and this product's name is listed twice as Hammer and its unit price is listed twice as 17.50. Intuitively, the reason for this is that attributes of two different kinds of entities, salespersons and products, have been mixed together in one table.

In some references, you will see the first normal form described differently, stated that each table within a row must be uniquely identified. Data designers who prefer that definition roll the requirement for atomic data to the second normal form. In that case, the requirements of the second and third normal forms, as described in this chapter, are combined as the third normal form. In either case, the final goal and final result remains the same.

Normalizing to Second Normal Form

Since data normalization is a decomposition process, the next step will be to decompose the table defined in Figure 4-26 into smaller tables to eliminate data redundancy. And since we have established that at least some of the redundancy is due to mixing attributes about salespersons and products, it seems reasonable to want to separate them out. Informally, we will look at each of the nonkey attributes and decide which attributes of the key are really needed to define it. For example, Salesperson Name really only needs Salesperson Number to define it. Product Name needs only Product Number to define it. Quantity needs both attributes.

More formally, second normal form does not allow **partial functional dependencies** where data is dependent on part of the primary key. That is, in a table in **second normal form,** every nonkey attribute must be fully functionally dependent on the entire key of that table. In plain language, a nonkey attribute cannot depend on only part of the key, the way that Salesperson Name, Product Name, and most of the other nonkey attributes of Figure 4-26 violate this restriction.

Figure 4-28 shows the salesperson and product attributes arranged in the second normal form. There is a SALESPERSON table in which Salesperson Number is the sole primary key attribute. Every nonkey attribute of the table

Figure 4-28

SALESPERSON table					
Salesperson Number	Salesperson Name	Commission Percentage	Year of Hire	Department Number	Manager Name

PRODUCT table		
Product Number	Product Name	Unit Price

QUANTITY table		
Salesperson Number	Product Number	Quantity

Relational tables in the second normal form.

is fully defined by Salesperson Number. Similarly, the PRODUCT table has Product Number as its sole primary key attribute, and the nonkey attributes of the table are dependent just on it. The QUANTITY table has the combination of Salesperson Number and Product Number as its primary key because its nonkey attribute, Quantity, requires both of them taken together to define it.

Figure 4-29 shows the sample salesperson and product data arranged in the second normal form structure. Much of the initial data redundancy has been eliminated. Now, salesperson 137's name is listed as Baker, his commission percentage listed as 10, and so forth only once in the SALESPERSON table. Product 19440's name is listed as Hammer, and its unit price is listed as 17.50 only once in the PRODUCT table.

Second normal form is thus a great improvement over first normal form, but has all of the redundancy been eliminated? In general, that depends on the particular list of attributes and defining associations. It is possible that second normal form can be completely free of data redundancy. In such a case, the second normal form representation is identical to the third normal form representation. This is not the case in our example.

A close look at the sample data in Figure 4-29 reveals that the second normal form structure has not eliminated all of the data redundancy. At the right-hand end of the SALESPERSON table, the fact that Scott is the manager of department 73 is repeated three times. This constitutes redundant data. All of the nonkey attributes are fully functionally dependent on Salesperson Number, but that is not the source of the problem. It's true that Salesperson Number defines

Figure 4-29

SALESPERSON table

Salesperson Number	Salesperson Name	Commission Percentage	Year of Hire	Department Number	Manager Name
137	Baker	10	1995	73	Scott
186	Adams	15	2001	59	Lopez
204	Dickens	10	1998	73	Scott
361	Carlyle	20	2001	73	Scott

PRODUCT table

Product Number	Product Name	Unit Price
16386	Wrench	12.95
19440	Hammer	17.50
21765	Drill	32.99
24013	Saw	26.25
26722	Pliers	11.50

QUANTITY table

Salesperson Number	Product Number	Quantity
137	19440	473
137	24013	170
137	26722	688
186	16386	1745
186	19440	2529
186	21765	1962
186	24013	3071
204	21765	809
204	26722	734
361	16386	3729
361	21765	3110
361	26722	2738

Second normal form sample data.

both Department Number and Manager Name. Focusing in on a particular salesperson, you should know the salesperson's department and manager's name. But, as indicated in the next-to-the-last defining association of Figure 4-24, one of those two attributes defines the other: given a department number, you can tell who the manager of that department is. In the SALESPERSON table, one of the nonkey attributes, Department Number, defines another one of the nonkey attributes, Manager Name. This is what is causing the problem.

Normalizing to Third Normal Form

In **third normal form,** nonkey attributes are not allowed to define other nonkey attributes. Stated more formally, third normal form does not allow **transitive dependencies** in which one nonkey attribute is functionally dependent on another.

In Figure 4-29, you see that in the SALESPERSON table, Department Number, and Manager Name are both nonkey attributes. Department Number defines Manager Name. Figure 4-30 shows the third normal form representation of the attributes. Note that the SALESPERSON table in Figure 4-28 has been further decomposed into the SALESPERSON and DEPARTMENT tables in Figure 4-30. The Department Number and Department Manager attributes, which were the cause of redundant data in the second normal form, were split off to form the DEPARTMENT table, but a copy of the Department Number attribute (the primary key attribute of the new DEPARTMENT table) was left behind in the SALESPERSON table. If this had not been done, there no longer would have been a way to indicate each salesperson's department, and you would have lost that relationship. Keep in mind, the goal is *non-loss* decomposition. In other words, no data is lost in the process.

The sample data for the third normal form structure in Figure 4-30 is shown in Figure 4-31. Now, the fact that Scott is the manager of department 73 is shown

Figure 4-30

SALESPERSON table				
Salesperson Number	Salesperson Name	Commission Percentage	Year of Hire	Department Number

DEPARTMENT table	
Department Number	Manager Name

PRODUCT table		
Product Number	Product Name	Unit Price

QUANTITY table		
Salesperson Number	Product Number	Quantity

Relational tables in the third normal form.

Figure 4-31

SALESPERSON table

Salesperson Number	Salesperson Name	Commission Percentage	Year of Hire	Department Number
137	Baker	10	1995	73
186	Adams	15	2001	59
204	Dickens	10	1998	73
361	Carlyle	20	2001	73

DEPARTMENT table

Department Number	Manager Name
59	Lopez
73	Scott

PRODUCT table

Product Number	Product Name	Unit Price
16386	Wrench	12.95
19440	Hammer	17.50
21765	Drill	32.99
24013	Saw	26.25
26722	Pliers	11.50

QUANTITY table

Salesperson Number	Product Number	Quantity
137	19440	473
137	24013	170
137	26722	688
186	16386	1745
186	19440	2529
186	21765	1962
186	24013	3071
204	21765	809
204	26722	734
361	16386	3729
361	21765	3110
361	26722	2738

Sample data in the third normal form.

only once, in the second record of the DEPARTMENT table. Notice that the Department Number attribute in the SALESPERSON table continues to indicate the salesperson's department.

4.3.3 Shortening the Process

As you can see, the normalization process tends to result in more and smaller tables created through decomposition. When you look back over the design process, you'll see that most of the tables identified through the normalization process had already been identified through data modeling. In fact, you should typically start as we did in the beginning of this chapter, by defining tables based on the E-R diagram.

Consider the tables defined by the E-R diagram your first draft of the database design. Once you have your relational tables identified, apply the three normal forms to each of the tables. The usual goal is normalizing to the third normal form, sometimes indicated as 3NF. Check each table and verify that each adheres to the requirements for normalization to 3NF. This will save you the time and effort of building a "supertable" (not a formal term, just a convenient description) containing every possible attribute in a relationship. Remember that when looking at normalization through full deconstruction, we focused on one primary entity. We would have to go through this process with each entity that brought with it additional relationships. It's easy to see how this could become a daunting task.

If you start with your E-R diagram, you will still find normalization requirements. Start with the first normal form and work your way through. For example, the customer table might have an attribute of Address. This violates the first normal form because this attribute is multivalued. For addresses in the United States, it includes a street address or PO Box (and possibly both), City, State, and ZIP Code. You would need to break each of these down into individual attributes to meet the first normal form. Continue the process through the second and third normal forms, creating additional related tables as necessary to meet normalization requirements.

You will often find that this is the least complicated and most efficient way to handle the normalization process. Even though some tables require additional normalization, others will already be at 3NF and not require any additional effort.

4.3.4 Denormalizing Data

The smaller tables created by the normalization process are typically the most efficient design for data entry and data modification. One reason for this is that you have eliminated duplicate data, reducing the amount of data that must be written to the database. However, there are two potential problems.

One problem is that this process can be taken to the extreme. Consider customer addresses for example. It's likely that you will have several customers in the same state. You could create a separate STATE table to contain this information and create a relationship between the CUSTOMER and STATE tables, but it's probably less work and requires less storage space to just store the 2-character state abbreviation with each customer.

The other problem is that a design that makes for efficient data entry does not always make for efficient data retrieval. During normalization, you tend to break a table down into smaller, related tables. There is a good possibility that at least some of your queries will require you to recombine that data into a single result. This is done through a query process known as **joining**, where you combine the data from two tables based on a linking column or columns. Typically, you will combine two related tables based on the foreign key, but that's not the only possibility. This can be a resource-intensive process, becoming more intensive as more tables are added.

This can be an issue in any database, but tends especially to be a problem in decision support databases where the majority of the database activity relates

FOR EXAMPLE

Finding New Tables

It's fairly common to "discover" new tables during the normalization process. Your E-R diagram includes an ORDER entity. For each order, you have the customer placing the order, the employee writing up the order, the order date, order number, and other information that applies to the order as a whole. You also have information about individual line items, such as the item ID, quantity, and selling price. There's no reason, usually, to store the extended total (quantity times selling price) because that can be calculated whenever you need it.

If you create an ORDER table, for it to be properly normalized, you will need a row for each line item in the order. That means that the customer, employee, order date, and any other general information about the order are also repeated for each line item. This could result in a significant amount of data and wasted space. A better solution is to have two tables. One, call it ORDERHEAD, contains the information that applies to the order as a whole. The other, call it ORDERITEM, contains the information for each line item. You would use the Order Number as the identifier in ORDERHEAD, and also use it as the foreign key in ORDERITEM to maintain the relationship between the two tables.

to data retrieval. If you regularly need the joined data, you could find it more efficient in the long run to denormalize the data, combine two or more normalized data tables into one less normalized table. For example, you might need to draw on data from three or four different tables to generate employee paychecks, including columns from an EMPLOYEE table, a TIMESHEET table, a PAYRATE table, and other tables in a single report. You might find it better to create a separate table named EMPLOYEEPAY that contains all of this information. Keep in mind, however, that if you also keep all of the other tables, you are introducing duplicate data into the database. Whether or not the performance increase is worth the additional overhead will have to be evaluated on a case-by-case basis.

Why the concern about performance? The more operations the database has to perform, the greater the load on resources, which can result in performance loss. If you create a new EMPLOYEEPAY table while also keeping the same data in the EMPLOYEE, TIMESHEET, and PAYRATE tables, you are forcing the database server to make additional updates anytime you add or modify data. If you change a rate in the PAYRATE table or hours in the TIMESHEET table, for example, you will also have to update records in the EMPLOYEEPAY table to reflect these changes. Introduce too many situations where duplicate updates are needed and performance eventually suffers.

SELF-CHECK

- List and describe the three normal forms.
- Explain how normalizing to the third normal form can result in additional relational tables.
- Explain the meaning of the term non-loss decomposition.

SUMMARY

This chapter discussed the process of creating a relational database design. You saw how to convert simple entities, unary relationships, and binary relationships to relational tables. This included choosing the foreign keys needed to establish and maintain the relationships. You compared examples in which E-R diagrams were converted to relational tables. You also learned about the normalization process and how apply the three normal forms.

KEY TERMS

Composite key

Data integrity

Data normalization

Decomposition process

Defining association

Determinant attribute

Exception conditions

First normal form

Functional dependency

Joining

Non-loss decomposition

Normal forms

Null value

Partial functional dependency

Referential integrity

Relational integrity

Second normal form

Third normal form (3NF)

Transitive dependency

ASSESS YOUR UNDERSTANDING

Go to www.wiley.com/college/gillenson to evaluate your knowledge of database design.

Measure your learning by comparing pre-test and post-test results.

Summary Questions

1. There is always a one-to-one relationship between entities in an E-R diagram and the tables in a database design. True or False?
2. Which statement best describes the process of converting a one-to-one binary relationship to related tables?
   (a) You should convert the entities into a single related table.
   (b) There will typically be only one way to define the tables.
   (c) There will typically be more than one way to define the tables.
3. You are converting a many-to-many unary relationship. How many relational tables will result from this conversion?
   (a) one
   (b) two
   (c) three
   (d) four
4. There is a many-to-many relationship between the Customer and Issue entities. Each combination of Customer and Issue occurrences is unique. Which should you use as the associative table primary key?
   (a) the Customer identifier
   (b) the Issue identifier
   (c) the combination of the Customer and Issue identifiers
   (d) you don't have enough information to determine the best primary key
5. Customer relates to Order as a one-to-many relationship. How should you define the relationship between the CUSTOMER and ORDER tables?
   (a) Add the CUSTOMER primary key to the ORDER table as a foreign key.
   (b) Add the ORDER primary key to the CUSTOMER table as a foreign key.
   (c) Create a new value to use as a foreign key in both the CUSTOMER and ORDER tables.
   (d) Create an associative table.
6. An associative table is needed when converting a one-to-many or many-to-many relationship. True or False?
7. When converting related entities, it is necessary to consider all relationships in which an entity is included. True or False?

8. Manager-to-Employee is a one-to-many unary relationship. You create an EMPLOYEE table. How any additional tables do you need?

   (a) none

   (b) one

   (c) two

9. Data integrity ensures that data is entered and stored correctly. True of False?

10. The usual goal in normalization is normalizing to the third normal form. True or False?

11. What statement best describes the second normal form?

   (a) Each attribute value is atomic, that is, no attribute is multivalued.

   (b) Transitive dependencies are not allowed.

   (c) Every nonkey attribute must be fully functionally dependent on the entire key.

12. If tables are in the second normal form, they may or may not also be in the first normal form. True or false?

13. Which normal form works to eliminate partial functional dependencies?

   (a) first

   (b) second

   (c) third

   (d) fourth

14. Which term is used to refer to the value on the left in the following association?

   Salesperson number → Salesperson name

   (a) independent attribute

   (b) associative attribute

   (c) dependent attribute

   (d) determinant attribute

15. In normalization, what is an exception condition?

   (a) normalization forms beyond the three standard normal forms

   (b) data that cannot be normalized

   (c) the requirement to add a table to support relationships

   (d) a table that is self-normalizing

16. Saying that a table is normalized to the Boyce-Codd normal form is the same as saying that a table is normalized to 3NF. True or False?

17. Combining data from different normalized tables into a query result is referred to as joining. True or False?

18. Which column list violates the third normal form?

(a) vendor name (primary key), alternate vendor, PO Box, city, state, postal code

(b) employee number (primary key), last name, first name, department number, department name, e-mail address, cubicle location, manager ID

(c) product SKU (primary key), description, warehouse location, quantity on hand, quantity on order, vendor

(d) order number (primary key), line item number (primary key), product SKU, quantity, selling price

Applying This Chapter

1. You can order multiple products from any vendor. A product can be ordered from multiple vendors. The identifier for the PRODUCT entity is SKU. The identifier for the VENDOR entity is Vendor Number. What kind of relationship does this describe? List the tables that would result from conversion to relational tables. Include the primary key for each of the tables.

2. You are designing relational tables for the E-R diagram shown in Figure 4-32. What foreign keys would be added during conversion (list by table)? What tables not currently identified by an entity would be added (if any)? What are the primary key attributes in the first normal form for this model?

Figure 4-32

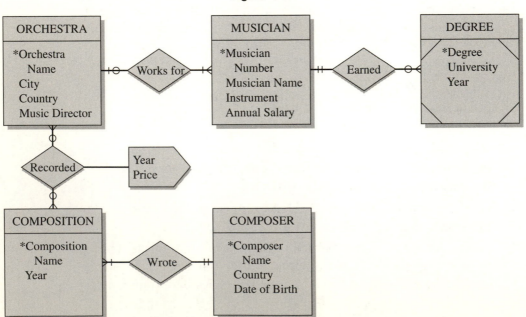

Sample E-R diagram.

3. You are designing relational tables based on the functional dependencies in Figure 4-33. List the tables and primary keys represented by this.

Figure 4-33

Salesperson Number ⟶ Salesperson Name
Salesperson Number ⟶ Commission Percentage
Salesperson Number ⟶ Year of Hire
Salesperson Number ⟶ Department Number
Salesperson Number ⟶ Manager Name
Customer Number ⟶ Customer Name
Customer Number ⟶ Salesperson Number
Customer Number ⟶ HQ City
Customer Number, Employee Number ⟶ Employee Name
Customer Number, Employee Number ⟶ Title
Product Number ⟶ Product Name
Product Number ⟶ Unit Price
Department Number ⟶ Manager Name
Salesperson Number, Product Number ⟶ Quantity
Office Number ⟶ Telephone
Office Number ⟶ Salesperson Number
Office Number ⟶ Size

Sample functional dependencies for General Hardware Company.

Creating and Normalizing a Relational Table Design

Figure 4-34 is the E-R diagram for Lucky Rent-A Car.

1. Complete Table 4-1 with the information requested.

2. For each of the relational tables in Table 4-1, list the attributes based on the E-R diagram. Indicate any attributes that violate the first normal form.

Table 4-1: Lucky Rent-a-Car

Table	Primary Key Column(s)	Foreign Key Column(s)

Figure 4-34

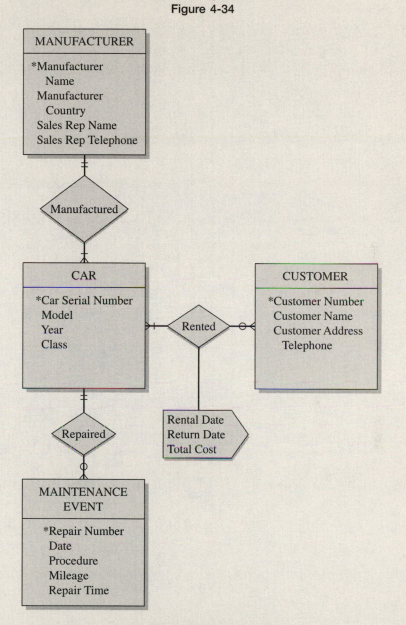

Lucky Rent-a-Car E-R diagram.

Non-loss Decomposition

Figure 4-35 is the E-R diagram for General Hardware Company.

Figure 4-35

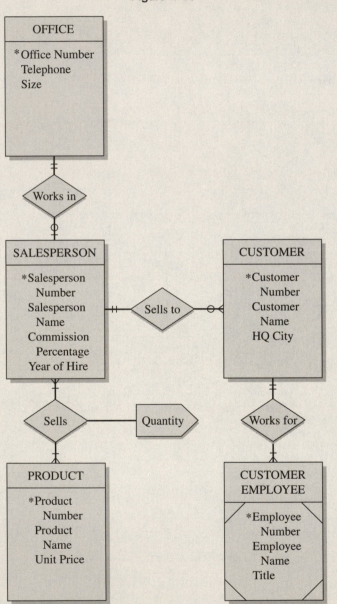

General Hardware Company E-R diagram.

Figure 4-36

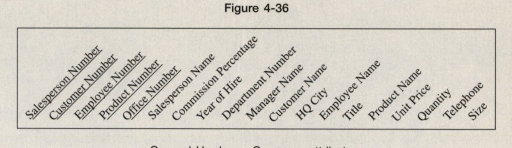

General Hardware Company attributes.

Figure 4-36 represents the attributes of the General Hardware Company taken to the first normal form.

Continue the process and apply the second and third normal forms. Show the result below.

5

IMPLEMENTING
A DATABASE

Starting Point

Go to www.wiley.com/college/gillenson to assess your knowledge of database implementation.
Determine where you need to concentrate your effort.

What You'll Learn in This Chapter

▲ Physical data design requirements
▲ Tools for creating database objects
▲ Data integrity and database performance design requirements
▲ Database object implementation

After Studying This Chapter, You'll Be Able To

▲ Recognize data integrity issues
▲ Recognize potential performance issues
▲ Modify a database design to address business requirements
▲ Use SQL language commands to create objects
▲ Use graphical utilities to create objects
▲ Enforce domain integrity
▲ Enforce entity integrity
▲ Enforce relational integrity
▲ Create tables, indexes, and views based on physical design requirements

INTRODUCTION

The better your database design, the better it will meet your business and application requirements. This means collecting business data, identifying entities and relationships, and then converting them to database tables. All this is done with your final goal in mind, implementing your physical database.

Before you can begin creating database tables you need to finish the remaining details of your database design. Review the physical design requirements and how they impact your final design. These include not only data requirements, but application requirements and requirements relating to the environment in which the database will be deployed. It may be necessary to make additional adjustments to your design to more accurately reflect the real world. Now you must not only consider entities and attributes, but also the volume of data that you must support and how it impacts your physical design requirements.

With the design process out of the way, you're ready to implement the design and deploy your database. Even here, there are additional decisions to be made. These relate to how to create database objects that match your design. The process starts with database tables and continues on through other database objects as needed, such as indexes and views.

5.1 Physical Design and Implementation

The process of completing E-R diagrams, data normalization, and conversion to relational tables does not represent the end of the design process. At best, these steps can be considered the end of the beginning. There is still work to be done before you can implement the tables you've designed and prepare to deploy your database solution. The process brings you to the starting point for physical database design.

In order to determine how best to modify the tables to improve application performance, a wide range of factors must be considered. The factors will help determine which modification techniques to apply and how to apply them.

5.1.1 Understanding Design Requirements

Keep in mind that design is an ongoing process and the dividing lines between design phases can become vague over time. Even as you move into the final design phases you may find it necessary to perform more data gathering as new questions arise. The new information is applied to your design to try to create the model that matches your needs as closely as possible in a relational database model. The remaining process is often considered to be as much art as science. The choices are so numerous and the possible combinations of modifications are so complex that even an experienced designer hopes for a satisfactory, but not a perfect, solution.

Figure 5-1

```
┌─────────────────────────────────────────────────────┐
│  Inputs Into the Physical Database Design Process     │
│  • The Tables Produced by the Logical Database Design  │
│    Process                                             │
│  • Business Environment Requirements                   │
│    ▪ Response Time Requirements                        │
│    ▪ Throughput Requirements                           │
│  • Data Characteristics                                │
│    ▪ Data Volume Assessment                            │
│    ▪ Data Volatility                                   │
│  • Application Characteristics                         │
│    ▪ Application Data Requirements                     │
│    ▪ Application Priorities                            │
│  • Operational Requirements                            │
│    ▪ Data Security Concerns                            │
│    ▪ Backup and Recovery Concerns                      │
│  • Hardware and Software Characteristics               │
│    ▪ DBMS Characteristics                              │
│    ▪ Hardware Characteristics                          │
└─────────────────────────────────────────────────────┘
```

Inputs to the physical design.

Figure 5-1 lists the inputs to physical database design, which are also factors important to the design process. These inputs fall into several subgroups. We'll take a look at each of these physical design inputs and factors, one-by-one.

The tables produced by the logical database design process (which for simplicity we will now refer to as the logical design) form the starting point of the physical database design process. These tables reflect all of the data in the business environment. In theory, they have no data redundancy (or at least minimal redundancy), and they have all of the foreign keys in place that are needed to establish the relationships in the business environment.

This does not necessarily reflect an optimum performance environment. Keep in mind that at this point, we have limited our design to database tables only. We still need to design the objects, like indexes, that will help to optimize data access. Even then, there may be additional performance issues. For example, it is possible that a particular query may require the joining of several tables, which may cause an unacceptably slow response from the database. Clearly then, these tables, in their current form, might be unacceptable from a performance point of view. This is why we need to make additional modifications and physical design changes.

One important point is that none of these factors operates in a vacuum. Each influences the others. Actions taken to help you meet the needs of one requirement better could actually make it harder to meet another set of requirements.

5.1.2 Business Environment Requirements

Two typical considerations are response time requirements and throughput requirements. **Response time** is the delay from the time that the request is made to execute a query (such as when the Enter key is pressed) until the result appears on the screen. **Throughput** is the measure of how many queries from simultaneous users must be satisfied in a given period of time by the application set and the database that supports it. In other words, throughput refers to the volume of work that must be performed and volume of data that must be moved.

One of the main factors in deciding how extensively to modify the logical design is establishing the response time requirements. This relates directly to how the application is used and the response expected by the users. In general, operational and production environments require very fast responses. Decision support environments tend to have more relaxed response time requirements. Customers placing orders through an online e-commerce site don't like to be left waiting. A service agent online with a customer needs answers quickly. Requirements can also vary by application component. You may be less concerned, for example, about how long it takes periodic management reports to run or the time required to process trend analysis data.

Throughput and response time are closely related. The more people who want access to the same data at the same time, the harder it is to keep the response time from dropping to an unacceptable level. The more potential pressure on response time, the more important the physical design task becomes. Some needs can be met through changes to the table design. This could mean changing the table structure, such as recombining tables through denormalization. It may be necessary to subdivide the data in some manner, along with distributing the physical placement of the data. The solution might also require additional database objects or an improved hardware platform.

5.1.3 Data Characteristics

How much data will be stored in the database and how frequently different parts of it will be updated are important considerations in physical design as well. You need to perform **data volume assessment,** which deals with both the number and size of the database records. You must also consider **data volatility**, which refers to how often stored data is updated.

Data volume assessment requires you to answer a number of questions so you can calculate how much data will be in the database. You need a rough idea of how many records will be stored in each table. Multiply the row size by the number of rows to get the approximate table size. Add together the table sizes to get an approximate total database size. Design decisions will hinge on whether a table is expected to have 300 or 30,000 or 3 million records. This is also affected by how efficiently the database is able to store the data. To understand this, you need to know how your database system stores data.

Figure 5-2

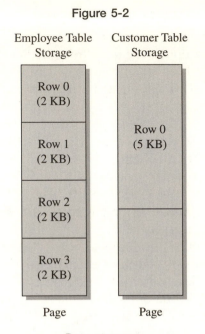

Data storage.

Take Microsoft SQL Server for example. The fundamental storage unit is a page, which is 8 KB of contiguous space. A table row cannot span pages, but a page can hold multiple rows, assuming that they are small enough.

Now, look in Figure 5-2. The maximum row size for the Employee table in this example is 2 KB. That means that four rows fit on each page with no wasted space. If you have 1000 rows in the table, you need 1000 times 2 KB, which is 2000 KB, or 2 MB to store the data.

You have a very different situation in the Customer table. The maximum row size is 5 KB. That means you can fit only one row per page. What happens to the remaining 3 KB? It's lost, wasted, and can't be used for any other purpose. That means that each row effectively requires 8 KB. If you have 1000 rows, you need 8 MB of storage.

When processing data in the Employee table, you need to work with 2 MB of data (in this example) for each 1000 rows. However, performing an operation on the Customer table means having to move around 8 MB of data. As you add rows to the Customer table, the space needed increases, as does the wasted space. If you just based your calculations on row size and didn't factor in page use, your space requirement calculations would be off by nearly 40 percent for the Customer table.

Data volatility can directly impact response time and throughput. Some data, such as active inventory records that reflect the changes in goods constantly being put into and taken out of inventory, is updated frequently. Other data, such as historic sales records, is seldom or never updated, except possibly for data from the latest time period being added to the end of the table. Data volatility is often a justification for how far you take the normalization process, but it doesn't stop there. Data volatility is an important factor in physical design decisions. It will directly impact database object design, placement, and hardware platform requirements.

5.1.4 Application Characteristics

The nature of the applications that will use the data, which applications are most important to the company, and which data will be accessed by each application form yet another set of inputs into and factors in physical design. You need to consider the **application data requirements,** what information the application needs and how it will be used. If the database is shared by multiple applications, relative application priority is another important concern.

When determining the application data requirements, you need to take a close look at how the application, or applications (if the database supports more than one), use data. You need to determine to which database tables each application requires access. You also need to know if any applications require that tables be joined. Concurrent access is another issue. This means finding out which tables are shared by more than one application and how frequently the tables are used. This information serves as one indication of how much demand there will be for access to each table and its data. More heavily used tables and tables frequently involved in joins require particular attention during the design process. Once again, issues are raised relating to response times and throughput, though now specifically at the application level.

To put this in perspective, think about a point-of-sale application for a store. Each time you make a sale, you would need to access tables used for inventory tracking and for recording sales. Because you need to get customers checked out and on their way quickly, access to these tables and the speed at which updates are performed are both critical. Demand for these tables during normal hours of operation is frequent, probably nearly constant.

You also need to understand the relative priority between all of the applications that share the database. Because tables in a database will be shared by different applications, a modification to a table proposed during physical design that's intended to help the performance of one application can hinder the performance of another application. When this happens, or could happen because of a change you want to make, it's important to know which application is more critical to business activities. Ask yourself:

▲ Which application is required to support the core business and primary processes?

▲ Which application most directly impacts company profits?

▲ Which application provides for cost savings?

The tables used to track sales in our retail example are used by the point-of-sale application, but that's probably not the only application needing access to those tables. Suppose you also have an accounting application that collects sales information and writes in the tables used to track financial accounting information. The two applications have to compete for the same resources. In this case, the higher-priority application should be the point-of-sale application, because of the need to quickly complete customer transactions.

Sometimes priority decisions are based, at least partially, on which application's sponsor has greater political power in the company. No matter how the determination is made, the changes you make and how you make them rely on these relative priorities. The higher the application's relative priority, the more important that the modifications do not adversely affect it.

5.1.5 Operational Requirements

Operational requirements include any number of ongoing activities that deal with issues relating to protecting the data and to data availability. Most operational requirements fall under the general category of data management. These can include any of a wide-ranging number of administrative tasks. Activities supporting these task requirements are sometimes integrated into one or more database applications or can be performed outside of the scope of any of the applications using tools provided with the DBMS.

Some design decisions can depend on such data management issues as data security and backup and recovery. Data security can include such concerns as protecting data from theft or malicious destruction and making sure that sensitive data is accessible only to those employees of the company who have a "need to know." Backup and recovery ranges from being able to recover a table or a database that has been corrupted or lost due to hardware or software failure, to the recovery of an entire information system after a natural disaster. Design issues include both how the data is organized and where and how the data is physically stored on the host computer. They can also include the physical location of and access to the physical computer hosting the database.

5.1.6 The Hardware and Software Environment

The hardware and software environments in which the databases will reside have an important bearing on design. Software, in this context, refers to the DBMS and its characteristics rather than the database application. Hardware characteristics relate to physical computer resources (the computer platform on which the database is deployed).

All relational database management systems are similar in that they support the basic, sometimes thought of as the classic, relational model. However, relational DBMSs differ in certain details, such as the exact nature of their indexes, attribute data type options, and SQL query features, which must be known and

Figure 5-3

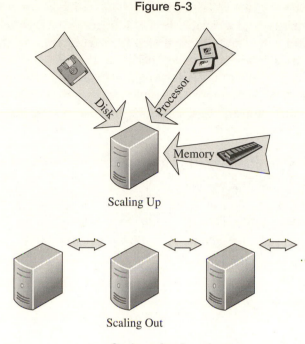

Scaling Up

Scaling Out

Scale up/scale out.

taken into account during database design. For example, different DBMS systems support different options for how data is stored and organized within the database tables. Microsoft SQL Server, for example, supports a data type that directly supports storage and manipulation of XML data. **Data types** are data storage formats used when defining database tables. Most other DBMSs, at least at this point in their development, do not include a data type designed for this purpose. XML data storage requires you to develop your own work-arounds based on more traditional data types.

Certain hardware characteristics, such as processor speeds and disk data transfer rates, are associated with the physical database design process though not directly part of it. Simply put, the faster the hardware, the more tolerant the system can be of a less than optimal physical design. In fact, some database designers might try to scale up or scale out the hardware platform rather than correcting problems found in the physical design after the database has been deployed. Options are shown in Figure 5-3. **Scaling up** refers to improving the server hardware, such as by installing additional processors, more memory, or faster disk subsystems. **Scaling out** refers to spreading the data across multiple database servers in a distributed data environment. Both are valid responses to changing conditions such as increased user support requirements or an increase in the volume of data stored on the database. However, these responses can also be used in attempt to cover up an inefficient design.

In regards to hardware characteristics and their impact on database design, you have two basic, but interrelated, options. One is to design the database for optimal performance on the available hardware platform. The other is to design a hardware platform that meets the performance requirements needed to support the database design and application needs. In the real world, the final solution is usually a compromise between the two. As a database designer and implementer you request the best (most powerful) server that you can get, but design the database understanding that it might be deployed on a less than optimal hardware platform.

5.1.7 Evaluating Implementation Options

While you think about the "what" of your physical implementation requirements, you also need to consider the "how" of the process. In most modern DBMS environments, you have two options for creating database objects. One is to use graphical user interface (GUI) utilities, when supported. The other is to use traditional SQL language CREATE statements. Each has its advantages and disadvantages.

GUI Management Utilities

Let's start with GUI-based utilities. Microsoft SQL Server 2005, for example, installs SQL Server Management Studio by default with nearly all database server editions. It can also be installed on client systems as part of a client utilities suite. MySQL, on the other hand, doesn't include a GUI-based management utility. There is, however, one that was developed by a third party and available as a free download from several Web sites, including the MySQL website. Microsoft Access, which is part of the Microsoft Office Suite, takes the opposite approach from MySQL. It has a primarily GUI environment for design, management, and even data access. Unlike SQL Server or MySQL, Access is most often used as a local data store—for example, for personal databases.

The advantage of a GUI management utility is its graphical environment. The user interface for creating a database table in Management Studio is shown in Figure 5-4 as an example. The biggest advantage of a graphical utility is that it prompts you through the process, asking for the column name, letting you choose a data type from a dropdown list, and providing you with a list of column properties that you can review and set.

We have four table columns named SerialNumber, Model, Year, and Class. The Allow Nulls checkbox sets nullability. Nullability determines whether or not you must provide a value for a column. A key icon, which you can see to the left of the column name SerialNumber, is used to identify primary key columns. Nulls are never allowed in the primary key. Null values and their use are described in more detail later in this chapter.

Figure 5-4

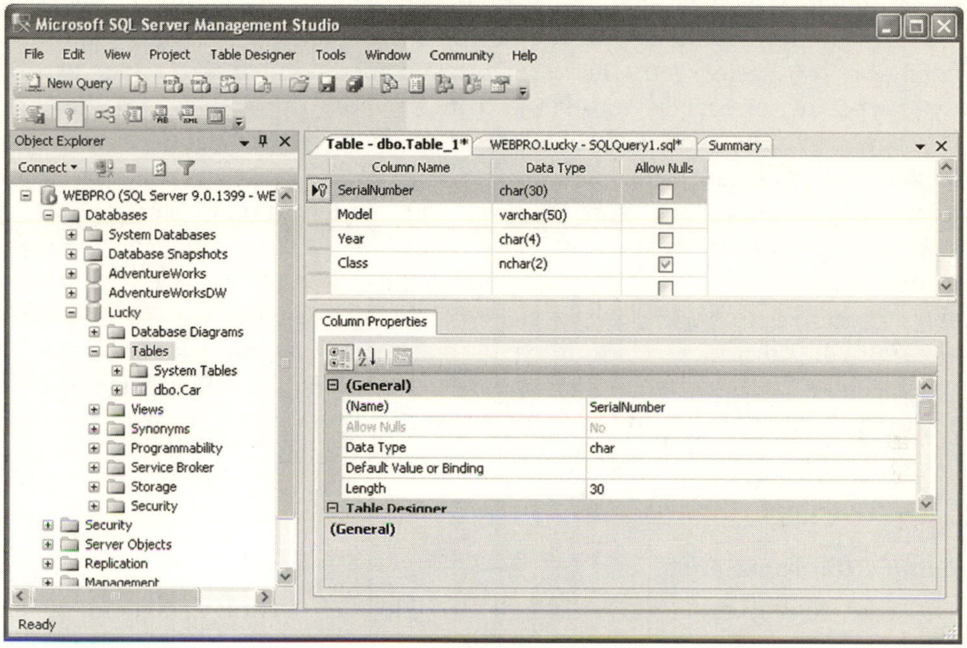

Management Studio new table dialog box.

At this point, the table is named Table_1, as you can see in the window tab. You'll be prompted to specify the table name when you save it. Additional graphical utilities let you modify table columns for existing tables and manage properties for the table as a whole.

The disadvantages might not be immediately obvious. There are usually some actions that you can take or properties that are accessible through the SQL command that are not available through the GUI-based command. The biggest disadvantage is the command environment itself. You must have access to SQL Server Management Studio, either locally or through a remote **virtual desktop**, which is a utility that lets you run the command on one computer, but see the screens and control the command remotely from another computer. This is possible with programs like Windows Remote Desktop Connection. Because Management Studio is graphic- and resource-intensive, it cannot be used in this way over a low-bandwidth connection such as a dial-up connection.

SQL Command Utilities

SQL is a standard (or more accurately, the standard) database command language. SQL command utilities are text-based utilities and are run from a command prompt. Database management systems provide a SQL command processing environment for running SQL commands. When you use GUI utilities, in some environments they work by building SQL command strings and then executing them in the background where you don't see them used. Depending on whose definition you prefer, you will see SQL commands divided into either two or three types of commands. You will learn more about these types of commands in Chapter 6. The most common categories you'll see are data manipulation language (DML) and data definition language (DDL) statements. DML statements are, like the name implies, statements used to modify data, including statements used to insert new data or delete data rows. DDL statements are used to define server and database objects, like logins, users, tables, views, indexes, and so forth.

You will sometimes see a third type of statement, data query language (DQL) statements. A DQL statement refers specifically to SELECT command queries that are used to retrieve data. Because the term *query* can be used to refer to statements used to retrieve or modify data, the SELECT statement is often rolled in as part of the DML command set.

Using SQL Commands

The standard SQL command set includes the **CREATE TABLE command,** which can be used to create a table, specify columns and data tables, and set table properties and constraints, such as identifying the primary key. **Constraints,** in basic terms, are limits or controls placed on tables and table columns. For example, a table's primary key and foreign keys (if any) are technically referred to as its primary key constraint and foreign key constraints. Another command, ALTER TABLE, lets you modify existing tables. Here's an example CREATE TABLE command:

```
CREATE TABLE dbo.Car(
SerialNumber char(30) NOT NULL,
Model varchar(50) NOT NULL,
Year char(4) NOT NULL,
Class nchar(2) NULL,
CONSTRAINT PK_Car PRIMARY KEY(SerialNumber) CLUSTERED )
ON PRIMARY
```

The full command syntax is beyond the scope of this chapter, but if you take a close look at this command example, it's relatively easy to see what the command is doing. The command name tells you that you are creating a table. The table name in this example is Car. The dbo is the relational schema and is part of the **fully qualified object name,** which is the complete object name that defines the object as globally unique. The period (.) is used as a delimiter to identify the different parts of the fully qualified name. The object name syntax is a SQL concept, but its specific implementation can vary somewhat by DBMS. The column names, along with basic column parameters, are enclosed in parentheses, along with any constraint definitions. You can see that the command creates four columns named SerialNumber, Model, Year, and Class, setting the data type and nullability for each. "NOT NULL" says a value must be provided during data entry or modification. "NULL" means that you can leave the column blank during data entry and a null value will be entered as the default. The primary key is identified as SerialNumber. The command is creating a clustered index for the primary key, so the table data will be physically sorted in primary key order. The ON [PRIMARY] clause at the end specifies the physical storage location, in this case, specifying the default storage location.

As you learned in Chapter 4, a null value is a special type of value. In some cases, you want to set the column value as unknown or undefined rather than as what you might consider "nothing" values of zero or an empty string. A null value represents "no value," either unknown, undefined, or no value applied. Even though it stands for "nothing," a null can be significant.

Consider an inventory table. One of the columns you might have is the QuantityOnHand column, the number of items that you currently have in stock. Typically, you would expect to see an integer value. A value of 0 indicates that you do not currently have any of that item in stock. But what about a null value? You could have a null entered automatically if a record is added to the table without specifying an amount for QuantityOnHand. You could then retrieve a list of items that you have never had in stock by retrieving all rows with a null value in QuantityOnHand.

One place null values can be problematic is in text fields. You use character data types to store text data. If you don't see a value, it could be a null, or it could be a zero-length string, a valid character string that happens to contain zero characters. The two might look the same to you, but a database server sees, and sorts, the two differently. A query used to retrieve zero-length strings would ignore null-valued fields. By the same token, a query retrieving records with a null value would ignore zero-length strings.

There are several advantages to using SQL commands. They are typically more powerful and more flexible than their GUI equivalents. They require minimal resources to run, so they can be used over a remote connection. You can also use them inside of a **batch** file, which is a file that contains a set of executable statements that can run as a group. In fact, you could create all of the tables for a database, and the database itself, using a batch. You could even send the batch to a user in another location as an email attachment and let that user run the batch locally.

The biggest disadvantage is that some SQL commands can be complicated and difficult to use. In order to use them effectively, you need to understand the statement syntax and available options. The order in which options are specified in SQL commands can even be an issue. Command documentation can sometimes run on for several pages for a single command. In the case of creating tables, for example, you need to know the available data types and how they are specified.

FOR EXAMPLE

Remote Updates

Consider this situation. You are a consultant and one of your clients has a database that you created as part of a business solution. The client requested some additional security features that will require you to create some new tables in the database. The application developer has already created an installation file that patches the application, but you need a way to modify the database.

You don't have remote access to the database server, can't go on site at the client's location in time to create the tables, and don't want to chance talking a local user through the process of creating the tables. The client has already loaded data, so you can't easily replace the complete database. This is a situation made for using CREATE TABLE.

You can create a SQL batch file that contains the appropriate CREATE TABLE statements. You can then attach this batch file to an email message and send it to a local user. Include instructions for running the batch file in the body of the email. The user runs the batch and updates the database, the user can now run the application setup file to patch the application, you're a hero in your client's eyes, and everyone is happy (until the next crisis).

SELF-CHECK

- List business environment requirements that can directly impact your database design.
- Create a table that compares and contrasts advantages and disadvantages of using GUI-based utilities and SQL commands to create database objects.
- Discuss why it is necessary to consider design influences as a group, rather than individually.

5.2 Adjusting Your Design to the Real World

The design considerations discussed help you adjust your physical design to meet real world requirements. Throughout this design process, you need to match your data to the business requirements while ensuring data integrity and meeting performance expectations.

You need to ensure that data is accurate when it is entered and remains accurate during updates and modifications. Two of the primary tools for ensuring this have already been mentioned, primary keys and foreign keys. Another factor already mentioned is controlling nullability.

As fast as computers have become, their speeds are certainly not infinite and the time it takes to find data stored on disks and bring it into primary memory for processing is a crucial performance issue. Data storage, retrieval, and processing speeds all matter. Regardless of how elegant an application and the database structures it uses are, it must meet performance expectations to be a success. Because of this, you may need to make changes to your table design that go beyond converting entities and applying normalization rules.

5.2.1 Ensuring Data Integrity

Modern DBMSs are designed to help you ensure data integrity. Some of these are considered to be part of the basic SQL features set while others are database specific. To understand what you have available, however, you need a better understanding of just what data integrity encompasses.

Data integrity requirements are typically broken down into key areas. These are:

▲ **Domain integrity:** ensures that the values entered into specified columns are legal.

▲ **Entity integrity:** ensures that each row is uniquely identified.

▲ **Referential integrity:** ensures that references with other tables remain valid.

▲ **Policy integrity:** ensures that values adhere to established business rules.

Domain, entity, and referential integrity issues are actually relatively straightforward. It's a little more difficult to make universal statements about policy integrity. Policy integrity requirements are business and business rule specific, as are actions taken to ensure them.

Addressing Domain Integrity

The first step in ensuring domain integrity is specifying an appropriate data type for each table column. This limits the type of data that you can store in the column and to some extent sets the data storage format. Data type also relates to data volume assessment because it determines how much space is required for storing column data.

You also control domain integrity through:

▲ **Nullability:** determines whether or not a column can contain null values. You could use this, for example, to differentiate between a zero value and a field that has never held a value.

▲ **Check constraint:** limits column values to a set list, to within a specified range, or to match a specified format. This is used for simple limits. For example, you might want to set maximum stocking levels for inventory items. One way to do this is through check constraints.

▲ **Unique constraint:** requires that values in a column or set of columns are unique. For example, you have an inventory table with each item's part number used as its primary key. You might also have a separate manufacturer part number, which is also supposed to be a unique value. You can use a unique constraint to enforce this requirement.

▲ **Default constraint:** A value entered into the column when no value is provided. Suppose you are adding new items to the inventory file, but you want don't necessarily want the ordering system to order items automatically. You can include an OrderPoint column and use the default constraint to give it a default value of zero. That way, if you don't enter a value, 0 is entered for you.

You must specify a data type for each table column, though some DBMSs allow for a default data type. You can apply nullability, check constraints, unique constraints, and default constraints to any or all table columns as appropriate.

Addressing Entity Integrity

In most cases, entity integrity is the easiest part of ensuring database integrity. Entity integrity is enforced through the primary key. Identifiers are specified during initial entity and attribute design. When you convert entities to database tables, the identifiers become the tables' primary keys.

We've already discussed different entity integrity examples. One mentioned was the inventory table, using the part number as the primary key to enforce entity integrity. Each item has a unique part number and is identified by that part number.

If an entity doesn't naturally have a primary key, you need to create one artificially. This is usually done through an identity column. An identity column is usually a numeric column, most often an integer value, generated automatically during data entry. When you specify an identity column you specify the starting value and an increment, usually a one-up count value. Some DBMSs also support automatically generated **globally unique identifiers (GUIDs)**. These are values that are generated in such a way that even if created for different tables or on different servers, each value is unique.

Addressing Referential Integrity

Referential integrity, also called relational integrity, maintains relationships between tables. Most relationships are defined and maintained through a foreign key. The foreign key is specified as one or more columns in the referencing table. It relates to one or more matching columns (with the same or compatible data types) in the referenced table. The referenced column values must be unique, so the foreign key must be related to the referenced table's primary key or a unique constraint.

Think about customer orders. Each order contains one or more inventory items. You would use referential integrity between the orders table(s) and the inventory table to ensure valid part numbers, and through these, valid inventory items.

In some cases, the requirements for ensuring referential integrity go beyond what can be accomplished through a foreign key constraint. In that situation, it might be necessary to use a trigger to enforce integrity. A **trigger** is a specialized type of executable procedure, in short, a program.

Adding Policy Integrity

It's difficult to make any blanket statements about policy integrity because the requirements will be business specific. Policy integrity requirements are defined through business rules which will naturally vary, based on businesses' specific requirements. The way in which policy integrity is enforced depends on the business rule.

In many cases, policy integrity is defined as an extension of other types of data integrity. Others require more complicated programming logic. For example:

▲ You require that each customer order must identify the employee who wrote up the order. You could enforce this through relational integrity, relating orders to employees.

▲ You require a phone number for each customer. This can be enforced through nullability requirements and by applying a check constraint.

▲ More than 8 hours worked in a day or 40 hours worked in a week must be identified as overtime. You could use a simple check constraint to limit the hours, but to calculate the overtime hours and store them separately would require more. In this case, you would likely create a trigger to perform the calculation and save the overtime hours appropriately.

Policy integrity is usually enforced through the DBMS whenever possible, as long as it does not adversely impact performance to the point that it becomes unacceptable. Policy integrity requirements, especially more complicated requirements, can also be implemented through the database application. In some cases, where the requirements are extensive, they are implemented through a separate application server.

Introducing Triggers

Triggers run, or fire, in response to events. Events can be related to data or data objects. For example, you can have triggers that fire when data is entered, updated, or modified in a table, either through the actions of a GUI-based utility or a DML

FOR EXAMPLE

Security through Triggers

Your database includes several tables that contain sensitive information. A small number of employees are allowed to view the information, but no employees are authorized to directly modify the information. You've set access limits, but you need to audit attempts to change the data in the tables.

This is a situation where you could use triggers as a security tool. You would create DML triggers on each of the tables that execute when a user attempts to modify or delete table data. You configure the trigger to run instead of the triggering statement. You could then have the trigger write information about the attempt to a separate audit table. You could include not only that the action occurred, but also what the employee attempted to do, when, and even which employee made the attempt.

statement. With a few DBMSs, including SQL Server 2005, you can also have triggers that fire when database or database server objects are created or modified, such as a trigger that fires any time you create a table; these are DDL triggers. As you learned earlier, DDL statements are statements used to create and manage server and database objects, such as tables, views, and even databases themselves. However, most current DBMS products do not support DDL triggers.

Triggers are extremely flexible in what they can do. They can include nearly any SQL language executable statement. They can be set up to run after the triggering event, the statement that causes the trigger to fire. In the case of SQL Server and some other DBMS products, you can have the trigger run in place of the statement or statements in the triggering event. Triggers can be used to enforce data integrity that cannot be enforced through normal constraints and to set limits on what can be done to server and database objects. You can also use triggers for security auditing, to block and track attempts to perform unauthorized actions.

You will typically limit trigger use to situations where you cannot enforce your requirements with a constraint, such as a check or foreign key constraint. That is because executing a trigger is more resource-intensive than enforcing a constraint and has a bigger potential adverse affect on database performance.

5.2.2 Adjusting Factors Relating to Performance

Database performance can be adversely affected by a wide variety of factors. Some factors are a result of application requirements. Normalization can sometimes be the source of your performance issues. Often, the most obvious culprit is the need for joining. Joining is an elegant solution to the need for data integration, but it can be unacceptably slow in many cases. Another common issue is the need to calculate and retrieve the same totals of numeric data over and over again. In a normalized database, you would normally calculate rather than store these values to save space. Technically, you would consider these to be redundant data. However, when performance becomes an issue, it might be better to calculate the values once and then store them with the rest of the table data. Also, the "correct" primary key and foreign keys values, from a logical design standpoint, aren't always the best choices for physical implementation.

Data volume is another issue. Data is the lifeblood of an information system, but when there is a lot of it, care must be taken to store and retrieve it efficiently to maintain acceptable performance. Certain factors involving the structure of the data, such as the amount of direct access provided and the presence of clumsy, multi-attribute primary keys, can affect performance. If related data in different tables that has to be retrieved together is physically dispersed on the disk, retrieval performance will be slower than if the data is stored physically close together on the disk.

Finally, the business environment often presents significant performance challenges. We want data to be shared and to be widely used for the benefit of the business. But a very large number of access operations to the same data can cause a bottleneck that can ruin the performance of an application environment. Also, giving people access to more data than they need to see can be a security risk.

We need to spend a little time looking at additional design changes that you might make that relate directly to managing performance issues. At this point we are not limiting ourselves to table design only. We're also looking at how we might organize the data stored in the table to make our database more efficient.

Combining Tables

Most of what you do during normalization relates to non-loss decomposition, breaking entities down into smaller and smaller related tables. While good in theory, this doesn't always result in the most efficient design. Sometimes, it's best to combine some of your design's individual tables into larger tables. In some cases, you will keep both the normalized and combined tables in your database, trading increased storage requirements for improved performance. Let's start with a look at the tables created for a fictional company, General Hardware. This is shown in Figure 5-5.

Consider a one-to-one relationship between salespersons and offices. Typically, you would use this entity definition to create two tables, but it could be created as a single table as shown in Figure 5-6. After all, if a salesperson can have only one office and an office can have only one salesperson assigned to it, there can be nothing wrong with combining the two tables. Since a salesperson can have only one office, a salesperson can be associated with only one office number, one (office) telephone, and one (office) size. A like argument can be made from the

Figure 5-5

SALESPERSON				
Salesperson Number	Salesperson Name	Commission Percentage	Year of Hire	Office Number

CUSTOMER			
Customer Number	Customer Name	Salesperson Number	HQ City

CUSTOMER EMPLOYEE			
Customer Number	Employee Number	Employee Name	Title

PRODUCT		
Product Number	Product Name	Unit Price

SALES		
Salesperson Number	Product Number	Quantity

OFFICE		
Office Number	Telephone	Size

General Hardware tables.

Figure 5-6

SALESPERSON/OFFICE						
Salesperson Number	Salesperson Name	Commission Percentage	Year of Hire	Office Number	Telephone	Size

Combined SALESPERSON OFFICE table.

perspective of an office. Office data can still be accessed on a direct basis by simply creating an index on the Office Number attribute in the combined table.

The advantage is that if we ever have to retrieve detailed data about a salesperson and his office in one query, it can now be done without joining. However, this is not a perfect solution and, in fact, has three definite negatives. First is that the tables are no longer logically or physically independent. If we want information just about offices, there is no longer an OFFICE table. The data is still there, but we have to be aware that it is buried in the SALESPERSON/OFFICE table. Second, retrievals of salesperson data alone or of office data alone could be slower than before because the larger combined SALESPERSON/OFFICE records would tend to spread the combined data over a larger area of the disk. Third, the storage of data about unoccupied offices is problematic and may require a reevaluation of which field should be the primary key. If you can justify combining the tables, it's likely that you will also keep the original, separate tables as well, in this situation.

Another way of adjusting data is to find alternatives for repeating groups. Suppose we change the business environment so that every salesperson has exactly two customers, identified respectively as their "large" customer and their "small" customer, based on annual purchases. This would result in repeating groups of customer attributes, with one "group" of attributes (Customer Number, Customer Name, etc.) for each customer. The attributes are so well controlled they can be folded into the SALESPERSON table. What makes them so well controlled is that there are exactly two for each salesperson and they can even be distinguished from each other as "large" and "small." This arrangement is shown in Figure 5-7. With this structure, the foreign key attribute of Salesperson Number from the CUSTOMER table is no longer needed.

This arrangement avoids joins when salesperson and customer data must be retrieved together. However, retrievals of salesperson data alone or of customer data alone could be slower than before because the longer combined SALESPERSON/CUSTOMER records spread the combined data over a larger area of the disk. Retrieving customer data alone is also now more difficult. As with the last example, even if you can justify this combined table, it's likely you would also keep the two separate tables as is.

Figure 5-7

SALESPERSON/CUSTOMERS									
					Large Customer	Large Customer	Large Customer	Small Customer	Small Customer	Small Customer
Salesperson Number	Salesperson Name	Commission Percentage	Year of Hire	Office Number	Customer Number	Customer Name	Customer HQ City	Customer Number	Customer Name	Customer HQ City

Combined SALESPERSON/CUSTOMER table.

Figure 5-8

CUSTOMER							
Customer Number	Customer Name	Salesperson Number	HQ City	Salesperson Number	Salesperson Name	Commission Percentage	Year of Hire

Denormalized CUSTOMER table.

Both of these are examples of **denormalization.** To optimize data retrieval performance, it may be necessary to take pairs of related, third normal form tables and to combine them, introducing possibly massive data redundancy. If all else has been done to improve performance and response times and throughput are still unsatisfactory for the business environment, eliminating run-time joining by recombining tables may mean the difference between success and failure. If designers go this route, they must put procedures in place to manage the redundant data as updates are made to the data over time.

Figure 5-8 shows the denormalized CUSTOMER table containing data from the SALESPERSON table. When combining tables in this manner, the surviving table in the one-to-many relationship will always be the table on the "many side" of the relationship. That's because you can attach one set of salesperson data to a customer record, but you cannot attach many sets of customer data to a single salesperson record without creating an even worse mess.

Figure 5-9 shows the denormalized data as stored in the combined table. Since a salesperson can have several customers, each salesperson's data will be repeated for each customer for which he is responsible. In this sample data, the

Figure 5-9

CUSTOMER							
Customer Number	Customer Name	Salesperson Number	HQ City	Salesperson Number	Salesperson Name	Commission Percentage	Year of Hire
0121	Main St. Hardware	137	New York	137	Baker	10	1995
0839	Jane's Stores	186	Chicago	186	Adams	15	2001
0933	ABC Home Stores	137	Los Angeles	137	Baker	10	1995
1047	Acme Hardware Store	137	Los Angeles	137	Baker	10	1995
1525	Fred's Tool Stores	361	Atlanta	361	Carlyle	20	2001
1826	City Hardware	137	New York	137	Baker	10	1995

Denormalized salesperson and customer data.

table shows that salesperson number 137's name is Baker four times, his commission percentage is 10 four times, and his year of hire was 1995 four times. The added storage requirement would normally be avoided unless it can be justified by the performance improvement.

Adjusting Table Attributes

You may find it necessary to make changes to your initial set of entity attributes and table columns. For instance, as mentioned before, sometimes a table simply does not have a single, unique attribute that can serve as its primary key. A two-attribute primary key might be okay, but there are circumstances in which the primary key of a table might consist of two, three, or more attributes, with the combination leading to unacceptable performance. For one thing, having to use the multi-attribute key as a foreign key in the other tables could be unacceptably complex.

The solution is similar to what you would do if there were no columns that could be used at the primary key. You can invent a new primary key for the table that consists of a single, new attribute. The new attribute will be a unique, serial number attribute, with an arbitrary unique value assigned to each record of the table. An identity column, like that discussed in the earlier example, is once again an appropriate solution. This new attribute will then also be used as the foreign key in the other tables in which such a foreign key is required.

In most cases, this new attribute will be in addition to the multiple values rather than a replacement for them. The values likely contain valid, perhaps critical, business information and therefore cannot be removed from the table. Instead, you simply choose not to use them as your primary key columns.

The CUSTOMER EMPLOYEE table in Figure 5-5 has a two-column primary key, a composite key, based on Customer Number and Employee Number (the customer employee number). You could create a new attribute, Customer Employee Number, which will be its own set of employee numbers for these people that will be unique across all of the customer companies. This is shown in Figure 5-10. If the Customer Number, Employee Number combination had been placed in other tables in the database as a foreign key, the two-attribute combination would need to be replaced by this new, single attribute.

Figure 5-10

CUSTOMER EMPLOYEE				
Customer Employee Number	Customer Name	Employee Number	Employee Name	Title

Restructured CUSTOMER EMPLOYEE table.

Customer Number is still necessary as a foreign key because it links back to the CUSTOMER table and detailed customer information. The original Employee Number attribute may still be required because that is still that company's internal identifier for the employee.

Some queries require that calculations be performed on the data in the database, returning the calculated result. If these same values have to be calculated over and over again, then it might make sense to calculate them once and store them in the database. If the raw data is updated, calculated values must be updated as well or the accuracy and integrity of the database will be compromised. This is another situation where you would use a trigger to perform the updates automatically.

To illustrate this point, let's add an attribute to General Hardware's CUSTOMER table. This attribute, called Annual Purchases in Figure 5-11, is the amount of merchandise, in dollars, that a customer purchases from General Hardware in a year. There is a one-to-many relationship from salespersons to customers, with each salesperson being responsible for several customers. Each salesperson's sales total for the year is the total of all of the sales for all of that salesperson's customers.

Suppose you need to retrieve this information quickly. This sum could be recalculated each time it is requested for a particular salesperson, but the time required to perform the calculations might make this solution inappropriate. The other choice is to calculate the sum for each salesperson and store it in the database, updating the value as the data on which it is based is updated.

Now you have to decide where to store the sum of annual purchase amounts for each salesperson. Since the annual purchases figures are in the CUSTOMER table, your first instinct might be to store the sums there, but you have to decide where. You can't store them in individual customer records because each sum involves several customers. You could insert special "sum records" in the CUSTOMER table, but they wouldn't have the same attributes as the customer records themselves and that would be very troublesome. The answer is to store them in the SALESPERSON table because there is one sum for each salesperson. The way to do it is to add an additional attribute, the Total Annual Customer Purchases attribute, to the SALESPERSON table, also shown in Figure 5-11.

Splitting Tables

It shouldn't surprise you that the larger the table, the greater the resources required to sort and retrieve the data. The bigger the table, the bigger the potential performance hit when applications must reference that table. One way to reduce the resources requirement is to split the table. There are two basic options for this, horizontal partitioning and vertical partitioning. **Horizontal partitioning** is partitioning by rows, storing different rows in different tables. **Vertical**

Figure 5-11

SALESPERSON					
Salesperson Number	Salesperson Name	Commission Percentage	Year of Hire	Office Number	Total Annual Customer Purchases

CUSTOMER				
Customer Number	Customer Name	Salesperson Number	HQ City	Annual Purchases

Modified CUSTOMER and SALESPERSON tables.

partitioning is partitioning by column, storing different columns in different tables. The tables can be stored in different tables on the same database with the best performance improvement coming when the tables are stored on different physical hard disks. You can also store the data in different tables on different servers in a distributed processing environment.

In horizontal partitioning, the rows of a table are divided into groups, written to different tables, and stored on different areas of a disk or (usually) on different disks. This may be done for several reasons. The obvious one is to improve data retrieval performance when, for example, one group of records

FOR EXAMPLE

Splitting Tables

Consider a situation where a company has offices in different geographic locations. Each location keeps an inventory specific to its warehouse's needs. You keep a master inventory list on a database server in the home office in San Diego, California. You also have a database server at each of the warehouse locations. At the warehouses, you want to minimize data storage requirements and optimize performance when performing inventory lookups.

This is a situation where you would split a table across multiple locations. The database server would store only those records appropriate to that warehouse, keeping the size of the INVENTORY table to a minimum. Reducing the table size also helps improve performance when retrieving data. You can have the database servers in each of the warehouses send updates to the server in San Diego to keep the master inventory file up-to-date.

is accessed much more frequently than the rest of the records in the table. Another is to manage the different groups of records separately for security or backup and recovery purposes. For example, you might need to access the records for sales managers in the CUSTOMER EMPLOYEE table more frequently than the records of other customer employees. Separating out the more frequently accessed group of records means that they can be stored near each other on the disk, which will speed up their retrieval. The records can also be stored on an otherwise infrequently used disk, so that the applications that use them don't have to compete with other applications that need data on the same disk. The downside of horizontal partitioning is that a search of the entire table or the retrieval of records from more than one partition can be more complex and slower.

In vertical partitioning a table is subdivided by columns, producing the same advantages as horizontal partitioning. In this case, the separate groups, each made up of different columns of a table, are created because different users or applications require different columns. For example, it might be beneficial to split up the columns of the SALESPERSON table so that the Salesperson Name and Year of Hire columns are stored separately from the others. But note that in creating these vertical partitions, each partition must have a copy of the primary key, Salesperson Number in this example. In all but one of the tables it is also used as the foreign key, relating all of the vertically partitioned tables as a set. The major disadvantage is one you've already seen. A query that involves the retrieval of complete records, that is, data that is in more than one vertical partition, requires that the vertical partitions be joined to reunite the different parts of the original records.

In some situations, vertical partitioning may be physically required by the DBMS. For example, when using SQL Server a table's row size is limited to approximately 8 KB. This is a physical limit that cannot be exceeded. If you have too many attributes, or the attributes are too large to fit in a single physical row, you must vertically partition the table into multiple tables.

S E L F - C H E C K

- List and describe key data integrity requirements.
- Explain how entity integrity can be enforced if an entity does not have a uniquely-valued attribute.
- Describe changes you might make to table design to optimize performance.

5.3 Implementing Database Objects

Physically implementing the database objects is one of the major milestones in solution deployment that you've been working toward. First you create the database, and then you create the database objects you need to support the solution. The three most basic database objects in any database design are tables, indexes, and views, so that is where we'll focus our attention.

As part of this discussion, we will introduce three SQL language DDL commands: CREATE TABLE, CREATE INDEX, and CREATE VIEW. Each of these commands supports a large number of options and command parameters, but we're going to limit ourselves to using the commands in their most basic forms as a way of starting the implementation process.

5.3.1 Implementing Your Final Table Design

We've picked apart the concept of table design as much as we can for now. Sooner or later you get to the point where you have to put up or shut up. In other words, you have to prove your design by putting it into use.

You create your database tables based on your conversions from the E-R models and any additional physical design changes you've made. Each table must have a unique name, usually something easily recognizable and easy to remember. Attributes become table columns. Each column must also have a name. Columns names must be unique in the context of the table: each table column must have a unique name, but you can reuse the same column name in different tables.

You must also specify the data type for each column. Once again, you have to make physical design decisions. The data type must be appropriate to the data the column will contain. You will usually want to choose a data type that minimizes storage requirements. For example, you will usually have multiple choices for storing integer data. The differences between the choices are the maximum value that you can store and the storage space required. The larger the maximum value, the more space you need.

Some data types can be fixed or variable length. Fixed length data types always require the same amount of storage space. For character data, they use one byte per character for ASCII data types and two bytes per character for Unicode data types, whether or not all of the characters are used or even if there is any data at all in the column. **ASCII**, the **American Standard Code for Information Interchange**, is an encoding standard for encoding English language characters and control characters. **Unicode** is a universal writing system encoding system capable of encoding any written language. With variable-length data types you set the maximum column size, but the space used is based on the actual data stored in the columns.

Data type selections can also impact performance and flexibility. DMBSs can store, retrieve, and manipulate some data types more quickly than others. What you can do with data, including the types of calculations in which the data can be used, also varies by data type.

Data types fall into general categories, with most DBMSs supporting the same basic categories. Typically, these will include:

▲ **Numeric:** For storage of integer, floating point, and scientific format numeric data.

▲ **Binary:** Fixed or variable-length flexible storage that can store a raw binary image, even files such as photos or executable program.

▲ **String:** Fixed or variable-length character storage.

▲ **Date/Time:** Stores date and time values, usually with various levels of accuracy supported.

▲ **Large object (LOB):** Used to store large blocks of text or binary data, with "large" as a relative term defined by the DBMS.

▲ **Other:** Specialized storage for data such as globally unique identifiers (GUIDs), XML data, or generic storage that can accept nearly any kind of data without having to predefine the data.

In addition to defining the data columns, you can also define table constraints. Depending on the DBMS, these can include primary key, foreign key, check, unique, and default constraints. You can specify them when you create the table or, in most cases, add them later.

The basic CREATE TABLE syntax requires you to specify the table name and column list, along with the data type for each column. For example, to create the General Hardware Company CUSTOMER table, you could use the following command:

```
CREATE TABLE CUSTOMER
(CustomerNumber as int,
CustomerName as nvarchar(40),
SalespersonNumber as int,
HQCity as nvarchar(40))
```

This is similar to the statement example you saw earlier in this chapter. This statement creates the table CUSTOMER with the following four columns:

▲ CustomerNumber that stores integer data.

▲ CustomerName that stores up to 40 Unicode characters.

▲ SalespersonNumber that stores integer data.

▲ HQCity that stores up to 40 Unicode characters.

You need to specify additional command parameters if you want to also define the primary key and any foreign keys when you create the table.

5.3.2 Implementing Indexes

If the name of the game is performance and since today's business environment is addicted to finding data on a direct access basis, then the use of indexes in relational databases is a natural. There are two questions to consider.

The first question is which attributes or combinations of attributes should you consider indexing in order to have the greatest positive impact on the application environment? There are two categories of qualifying columns. One category is columns that are likely to be prominent in direct searches. These include primary keys and search attributes. **Search attributes** are values you will use to retrieve particular records. This is true especially when the attribute and resulting table column can take on many different values, referred to as having high **selectivity.** It really isn't beneficial to build an index on an attribute that has only a small number of possible values, one with low selectivity, because of the limited benefit derived from the index. The other category is table columns likely to be used in operations such as joining that will require direct searches internally. Such operations also include queries in which data is grouped or sorted by particular values.

The second question is, what potential problems can be caused by building too many indexes? The primary issue here is the volatility of the data. Indexes are wonderful for direct searches, but when the data in a table is updated, the system must take the time to update the table's indexes, too. It will do this automatically, but it takes time. If several indexes must be updated, this multiplies the time it takes to update the table several times over, which slows down the operations that are just trying to read the data for query applications, degrading query response time down to an unacceptable level.

One final point about building indexes is that if the data volume, the number of records in a table, is very small, there is usually no point in building any indexes. If the table is small enough, it is more efficient to just read the whole table into main memory and search by scanning it. However, some DBMSs will always create an index automatically on the primary key, no matter what the table size. SQL Server falls in this category.

Figure 5-12 shows the General Hardware Company relational database with some added indexes. We start by building indexes, marked indexes A–F, on the primary key attribute(s) of each table. Consider the SALESPERSON and CUSTOMER tables. If queries that join the SALESPERSON and CUSTOMER tables are needed, the Salesperson Number attribute of the CUSTOMER table would be a good choice for an index (index G). Because Salesperson Number is the

Figure 5-12

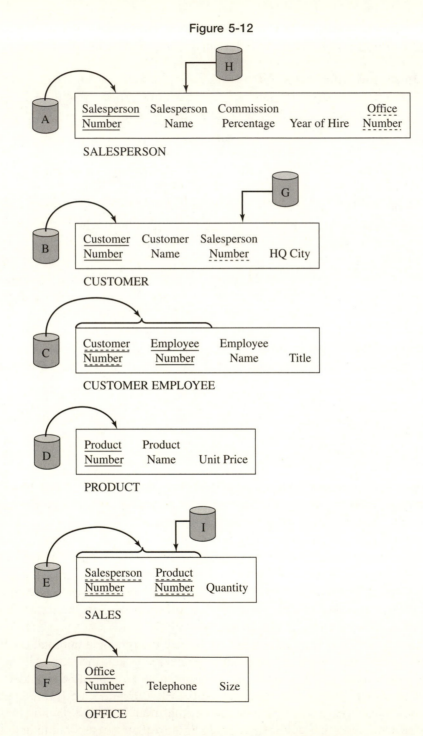

General Hardware Company tables and indexes.

foreign key, it connects those two tables in the join. If we need to frequently find salesperson records on a direct basis by Salesperson Name, then we would want an index with that as a key column (index H).

Consider the SALES table. If we have an important, frequently run application that has to find the total sales for all or a range of the products, then the query would run more efficiently if the Product Number attribute was indexed (as index I, in this example).

The SQL language statement for creating an index is the **CREATE INDEX command.** In its most basic format you specify the table on which the index is based and the index key columns, the columns used to organize the data. Columns are applied in the order in which they are listed. An index is created as nonclustered by default, which means that it does not affect the table's physical storage order. You can include the keyword CLUSTERED when you to create the index if you want the table physically sorted in index order. Because of the impact on the table sort order, a table can obviously have only one clustered index.

Suppose you want to create an index on the CUSTOMER table. You might use the following statement:

```
CREATE INDEX ix_CUSTOMER_NAME
ON CUSTOMER (Customer Name)
```

This creates an index on the CUSTOMER table using Customer Name as the only key column. This might be used, for example, to optimize an application that prints customer lists.

5.3.3 Implementing Views

A view is a way of enforcing logical controls over physical data. When based on a single table, you can limit the view to allowing access to a subset of the table's columns, a subset of the table's rows, or a combination of the two. You can also create a view based on two or more tables or, with most DMBSs and in most situations, a combination of views and tables. No data is physically duplicated when a standard view is created.

Suppose you want to limit most users' access to the SALESPERSON table. You could create a view that includes the Salesperson Number, Salesperson Name, and Office columns only. Users with access to this view, but not the table, would be limited to seeing these three columns. In fact, the users would have no way of knowing that other columns even existed.

A view is often created as a means for protecting the security and privacy of data. Using views to limit the access of individuals to only the parts of a table that they really need to do their work is an important means of protecting the company's data. Views become even more powerful when used together with access permission sets.

FOR EXAMPLE

Choosing the Correct Index Keys

You have a table with a two-column identifier, PartNumber and Salesper-sonNumber. You want to create a clustered index to optimize data retrieval, but you need to know which column you should list first when you create the index. What should you do?

The first column listed has the most effect on how the data is physically sorted. Before you can make your decision, you need to know one thing: When data is retrieved from the table, in what order is the data usually needed? If you usually need the data in PartNumber order, that's your first column. If you need it in SalespersonNumber order, then that's your choice. If the data retrieval requirements are too evenly split to tell for sure, then choose based on selectivity. If it's still too close to call, the choice comes down to your personal preference. If the order doesn't matter, then you should probably create a nonclustered index instead of a clustered index.

The SQL command to create a view is the **CREATE VIEW command.** In its simplest form you specify the view name, base object or objects, and columns to include in the view. The view content is defined through a query based on a SELECT statement. For example, to create the view we just described, you could use the following statement:

```
CREATE VIEW v_LIMIT_SALESPERSON AS
SELECT [Salesperson Number],
[Salesperson Name], Office
FROM SALESPERSON
```

As you can see in the SELECT statement column list, the column names immediately following the SELECT statement, the query returns the three columns specified as making up the view. Salesperson Number and Salesperson Name are enclosed in square brackets so that the command will recognize and process the names correctly. This is needed because the names include embedded spaces. Whenever a user accesses data through this view, the SELECT statement executes and the specified columns are returned.

To improve performance when accessing data through a view, SQL Server supports a type of view called an indexed view that *persists* the view data. In other words, it stores the result of the SELECT query on disk for faster retrieval. There is no reason to run the query unless the underlying table data changes. SQL Server places several restrictions on the creation and use of indexed views, so they cannot be used in all situations. Also, as we have already seen, there are usually trade-offs when addressing a design issue like access performance. In this case, the improved performance comes at the cost of the additional disk storage needed to keep the query result.

SELF-CHECK

- Describe the basic information needed to create a table.
- Describe the basic information needed to create an index.
- Describe the basic information needed to create a view.

SUMMARY

This chapter takes a close look at some final physical design issues and the basic implementation process. It introduced additional design requirements. You were also introduced to the types of utilities available for object creation. You learned about data integrity and performance optimization needs. You also saw how to create basic tables, indexes, and views.

KEY TERMS

Application data requirements	Globally unique identifier (GUID)
ASCII	Horizontal partitioning
Batch	Nullability
Check constraint	Policy integrity
Constraint	Referential integrity
CREATE INDEX command	Response time
CREATE TABLE command	Scaling out
CREATE VIEW command	Scaling up
Data type	Search attribute
Data volatility	Selectivity
Data volume assessment	Throughput
Default constraint	Trigger
Denormalization	Unique constraint
Domain integrity	Unicode
Entity integrity	Vertical partitioning
Fully qualified object name	Virtual desktop

ASSESS YOUR UNDERSTANDING

Go to www.wiley.com/college/gillenson to evaluate your knowledge of database implementation.

Measure your learning by comparing pre-test and post-test results.

Summary Questions

1. Data volatility refers to which of the following?
   (a) how often data changes
   (b) the size of data rows
   (c) the number of rows in a table
   (d) the number of constraints placed on a table

2. Which of the following can be used to determine relative application priority?
   (a) requirements to support primary processes
   (b) impact on company profits
   (c) cost savings provided
   (d) all of the above

3. Which of the following is an advantage of using SQL language commands to create database objects?
   (a) The commands are easier to use than graphic utilities.
   (b) The commands must run locally at the server.
   (c) Commands can run as part of a SQL batch file.
   (d) Commands prompt you for options and replaceable parameters.

4. Your database server hardware platform in not a factor in database physical design. True or False?

5. When storing numeric data, a null value is the same as a zero. True or false?

6. Domain integrity ensures which of the following?
   (a) that business rules are implemented
   (b) that each row is uniquely defined
   (c) that values entered into columns are legal
   (d) that users are members of a Windows domain

7. Which of the following is used to enforce entity integrity?
   (a) foreign key constraint
   (b) check constraint
   (c) default constraint
   (d) primary key constraint

8. Which of the following statements best describes a trigger?
   (a) A trigger is the same as a check constraint.
   (b) A trigger is a program that runs in response to an event.
   (c) A trigger can be used to override DML statements only.
   (d) A trigger is the most efficient way to enforce nullability.

9. Foreign keys are used to enforce referential integrity. True or False?

10. You would combine tables to minimize the adverse impact of which of the following?
    (a) storing very large tables
    (b) queries that join tables
    (c) domain constraint requirements
    (d) table row size

11. You can use an identity column as a table's primary key when none of the table columns contain unique values. True or False?

12. In which situation would you use vertical partitioning to split a table?
    (a) table row length is excessively long
    (b) the table contains an excessively large number of rows
    (c) none of the table columns contain unique values
    (d) all of the table columns contain unique values
    (e) both a. and b

13. In which situation would you use horizontal partitioning to split a table?
    (a) table row length is excessively long
    (b) the table contains an excessively large number of rows
    (c) a subset of tables rows are needed more often than the remaining rows
    (d) all of the table columns contain unique values
    (e) both b. and c

14. Which of the following should you use to limit column values to a set list?
    (a) unique constraint
    (b) default constraint
    (c) check constraint
    (d) trigger

15. Executing a trigger requires more resources than enforcing a constraint. True or False?

16. Which data type category is best suited to storing an employee's name?
    (a) large object
    (b) binary

(c) string

(d) numeric

17. Unicode data is stored as one byte per character. True or False?

18. SQL Server automatically creates an index based on which of the following?

(a) primary key constraint

(b) foreign key constraint

(c) check constraint

(d) default constraint

19. Selectivity refers to the number of unique values present in a column. True or False?

20. In which situation should you create a view?

(a) You want to vertically partition a table.

(b) You want to limit user access to table columns.

(c) You want to audit attempts made to modify table data.

(d) You want to physically combine tables.

Applying This Chapter

1. You are designing a database solution for an established retail sales company. The core goal is to complete point of sale transactions accurately and as quickly as possible. The solution will include four applications:

▲ An application responsible for posting and managing customer orders.

▲ An inventory control application.

▲ An accounting application.

▲ A reporting application.

You have completed your logical design and converted the entities to tables. You are trying to determine additional design changes that you must make. How can you determine which data is the most volatile? Which application has the highest relative priority and why? What types of operational requirements would relate to minimizing down time?

2. You are deploying a distributed database application with database servers in several regions. Connectivity methods and available bandwidth vary by region. How can you determine whether or not GUI-based utilities can be used for remote management? How can you have employees that do not have a DMBS background or experience make changes to database objects with minimal risk of errors? What guidelines should you use for splitting data tables by region? How should you limit local users' access to data to a subset of available table rows and columns?

Figure 5-13

MANUFACTURER			
Manufacturer Name	Manufacturer Country	Sales Rep Name	Sales Rep Telephone

CAR				
Car Serial Number	Model	Year	Class	Manufacturer Name

MAINTENANCE					
Repair Number	Car Serial Number	Date	Procedure	Mileage	Repair Time

CUSTOMER			
Customer Number	Customer Name	Customer Address	Customer Telephone

RENTAL				
Car Serial Number	Customer Number	Rental Date	Return Date	Total Cost

Lucky Rent-a-Car database tables.

3. You are preparing to deploy the database tables shown in Figure 5-13. This is the logical design for the Lucky Rent-a-Car company's database. How can you ensure that a legal value is used for the Manufacturer Name in the CAR table? How can you have Customer Number generated automatically as a one-up count of customers in the CUSTOMER table with minimal resource requirements? In the MANUFACTURER table, how can you ensure that Sales Rep Telephone is formatted properly?

YOU TRY IT

Good Reading Bookstores

You are preparing to implement a database to support Good Reading Bookstores. The current logical table design in shown in Figure 5-14.

1. For which tables and columns should you store data as date/time type data?
2. Customer numbers are a 5-digit alphanumeric string, two letters and three numbers. How can you enforce this?
3. You want to minimize disk space requirements. Which columns in the CUSTOMER table should be fixed length string types and which should be variable length string types? Explain your answers.
4. How can you determine whether character data should be stored as ASCII or Unicode?
5. How can you determine whether or not a trigger should be used to enforce data integrity?

Figure 5-14

PUBLISHER

Publisher Name	City	Country	Telephone	Year Founded

AUTHOR

Author Number	Author Name	Year Born	Year Died

BOOK

Book Number	Book Name	Publication Year	Pages	Publisher Name

CUSTOMER

Customer Number	Customer Name	Street	City	State	Country

WRITING

Book Number	Author Number

SALE

Book Number	Customer Number	Date	Price	Quantity

Good Reading Bookstores tables.

Implementation Requirements

You are designing a database to support a Customer Service company. You have already designed part of the table requirements and have some idea of data storage needs. The EMPLOYEE table will have approximately 200 rows. Managers are identified through a one-to-many unary relationship. The CUSTOMER table will have approximately 2000 rows initially but could grow to over a million rows. There is no set relationship between customers and employees. Any employee can take an initial call from any customer.

The CALL COMMENT table will need to track the customer, employee, date and time of the call, and a written summary. You include Customer Number and Employee Number as foreign key constraints referencing CUSTOMER and EMPLOYEE. You must be able to call up these summaries by employee and customer as quickly as possible. You want to provide as much space as possible for the summary.

The CALL CONTACT table will be used with a screen form that has the employee collect initial information about the customer and purpose of the call. The ONLINE CONTACT table will store a complete transcript of customers who contact the service center through an Internet chat program. Both CALL CONTACT and ONLINE CONTACT must give you a way of identifying the customer, time and date of the contact, the employee, the general call category, and whether or not the problem was resolved.

1. How can you avoid the need to store detailed information about a customer in the CALL CONTACT and ONLINE CONTACT tables?

2. Chat sessions can sometimes run on for an hour or more. What category of data type should you use to store the transcript and why?

3. What can you do to optimize performance when looking up entries in the CALL COMMENT table?

4. You may need to split the CALL CONTACT and ONLINE CONTACT tables if they become too large (contain too many rows). What should you use to filter the rows? Justify your answer.

5. At minimum, what information in the ONLINE CONTACT table would be needed to enforce entity integrity? How can you minimize the space needed to relate other tables to the ONLINE CONTACT table?

6. You want to restrict each manager to seeing information relating to employees he or she manages in the ONLINE CONTACT, CALL CONTACT, and CALL COMMENT tables. How can you enforce this, considering the volatility of the information? What could you add to these tables to optimize the data retrieval?

6

UNDERSTANDING THE SQL LANGUAGE

Starting Point

Go to www.wiley.com/college/gillenson to assess your knowledge of the SQL language.
Determine where you need to concentrate your effort.

What You'll Learn in This Chapter

▲ Basic SQL features and functionality
▲ SELECT statement fundamentals
▲ Operators and functions
▲ DDL and DML statements

After Studying This Chapter, You'll Be Able To

▲ Execute SQL statements in query mode
▲ Use embedded SQL statements
▲ Recognize required and optional keywords and parameters in SQL command syntax
▲ Use SELECT to retrieve data from database tables
▲ Use SELECT to evaluate expressions and execute functions
▲ Identify the proper use of arithmetic, comparison, and logical operators
▲ Use operators in command search conditions
▲ Identify selected functions in the standard SQL-99 function set
▲ Identify the need for function variations and accepted function categories
▲ Use aggregate functions to calculate requested values
▲ Recognize and use DDL and DML statements

INTRODUCTION

Most modern database management systems are based on the SQL language standard. You'll find, however, that most are based somewhat loosely on that standard, choosing instead to employ their own variations and additions to the SQL language. There is also some confusion as to what is considered part of the SQL language and what has been added as part of manufacturers' DBMS products.

In this chapter, you'll get a formal introduction to the SQL language standard and to the types of variations that have been added by different DBMSs. You will learn about basic language components through simple command examples. The chapter introduces representative DDL and DML command statements through the standard command syntax and gives some insight into how some DBMS providers have modified these statements to meet their particular needs and design visions.

6.1 Introducing the SQL Language

There are two aspects of data management: data definition and data manipulation. Data definition requires a **data definition language (DDL)** that instructs the DBMS software as to what tables will be in the database, what attributes will be in the tables, which attributes will be indexed, and so forth. Data manipulation refers to the four basic operations performed on data stored in any DBMS: data retrieval, data update, insertion of new records, and deletion of existing records. Data manipulation requires a special language with which users can communicate data manipulation commands to the DBMS. As a class, these commands are known as **data manipulation language (DML).** Data retrieval statements are sometimes placed in a different category, separate from DML, as **data query language (DQL)** statements. For the purposes of this chapter, retrieval statements are treated as part of the DML set.

The current relational database management system language, Structured Query Language (SQL), was developed in the early 1980s and incorporates both DDL and DML features. SQL has been declared a standard by the American National Standards Institute (ANSI) and by the International Organization for Standardization (ISO), with several standard versions issued since its initial development. Many manufacturers have produced versions of SQL, most quite similar, including mainstream DBMSs such as DB2, Oracle, MySQL, Informix, and Microsoft SQL Server.

6.1.1 Understanding SQL Features

The SQL standard defines the features supported by "standard" SQL implementations. Most vendor implementations, however, go beyond the SQL standard.

They offer the standard features and support most, if not all, of the standard command set, but provide their own extension to the language, giving them added functionality. These extensions usually take the form of additional commands or additional command options. There are also differences in how features that are not fully defined in the SQL standard are implemented.

For example, the SQL standard defines basic database objects such as tables, views, and indexes. It does not define how these features are physically implemented. Microsoft SQL Server stores database objects in one or more database files, with each file containing one or more database objects. MySQL, on the other hand, creates separate files for database objects. Each table in MySQL can be effectively thought of stored as its own operating system file.

Basic features of SQL can be described as falling within the following categories:

▲ **Data definition language (DDL):** statements used to create and maintain database objects.

▲ **Data manipulation language (DML):** statements used to retrieve and manipulate data.

▲ **Command operators:** operator symbols and keywords used to run arithmetic, comparison, and logical operations.

▲ **Functions:** special executables that return values.

▲ **Transaction control:** include statements used to initiate and complete or abort transaction processing.

What this means is that some things that you might have considered part of SQL because they are common to relational database systems are not. Instead they are features and command extensions implemented first by one DBMS provider and sometimes copied by others. For example, the SQL language specifies nothing about scheduled command execution, but this is a feature supported by Microsoft SQL Server and many others. The SQL language defines **procedures,** which are compiled sets of executable statements, in the context of the statements used to create and modify them. It does not include any specific management procedures to be included with a DBMS, but most do support a wide array of predefined management procedures that install with the database server and are treated as part of the vendor's language set.

6.1.2 Using SQL

There are two basic options for executing SQL commands: interactive SQL and embedded SQL. **Interactive SQL,** also known as **dynamic SQL,** refers to statements that you run directly, interacting with the database server. **Embedded SQL** refers to functionality that is embedded in a procedure or part of an application written in a different programming language.

Query mode execution, which is used to refer to interactive execution, and embedded SQL, are both supported by all current DBMS products. Where DBMSs differ is in how they support them and what tools they provide. There is also, many times, a difference in what is called the language set included with the DBMS. For example, when you run statements in SQL Server, you're running Transact-SQL (or TSQL) statements. Many of these support command options not supported by standard SQL. Also, a small number of commands defined in standard SQL are not included as part of the Transact-SQL language.

Interactive SQL

All DBMSs provide some sort of command interface or command prompt for running SQL commands interactively. Microsoft SQL Server, for example, supports two basic options. It provides a character-based command prompt where statements can be typed in one at a time. Statements can be executed individually or as a set of executable statements known as a **batch.** You can also load and run **scripts,** groups of SQL Server commands stored as a file. Microsoft has released various versions of its command interface over the years, retaining older versions to provide backward compatibility as new ones are released. The preferred command interface for SQL Server 2005, **sqlcmd,** is shown in Figure 6-1.

One of the biggest problems with a character-based interface is that it can be confusing and difficult to use. Sqlcmd, for example, supports a large number of startup options to let you configure the command environment. The options let you log in to a specific server, choose a working database, specify a script file to load and run automatically, and set options such as communication

Figure 6-1

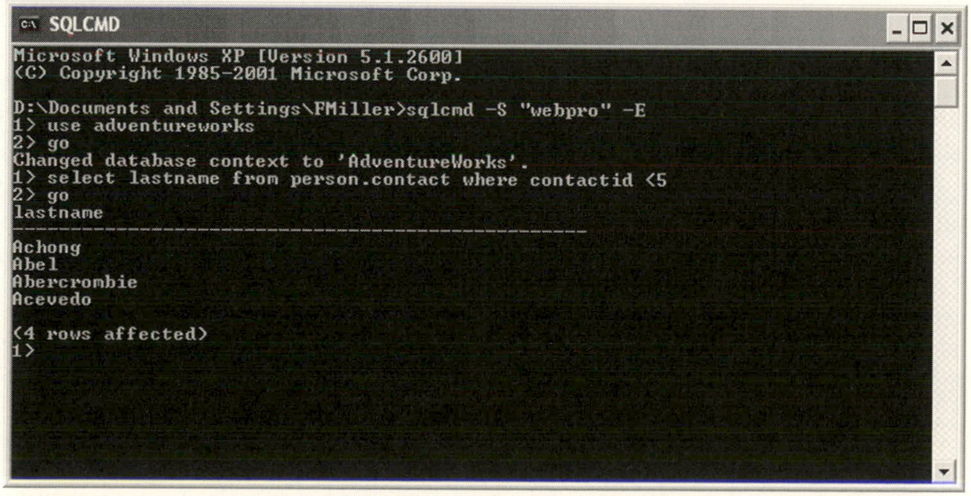

Sqlcmd command interface.

time-out values and network packet sizes for network communication. You can set default options for how data returned by queries is displayed. Set wrong, they can impair your performance and even keep you from doing what you need to do.

Using a character-based interface also requires either a thorough understanding of SQL language commands or a readily available reference. The interface is unforgiving and the error messages returned by most DBMSs are usually brief and not always helpful. Editing command strings in the interface can be difficult and even small typographic errors could lead to major problems.

The biggest advantage of using a character-based interface is that it provides a way of executing SQL language commands through operating system batch files. This can be significant with a DBMS that does not internally supported scheduled command executions. In that case, you can still run periodic activities, such as data backups, through command scheduling supported by the operating system.

SQL Server, as well as many other popular DBMS options, also provides a windowed command environment using a graphic user interface (GUI). In the case of SQL Server, it is included as part of SQL Server Management Studio, shown in Figure 6-2. The interface has menu-driven option support, making it somewhat easy to manage the command environment. You also have windowed

Figure 6-2

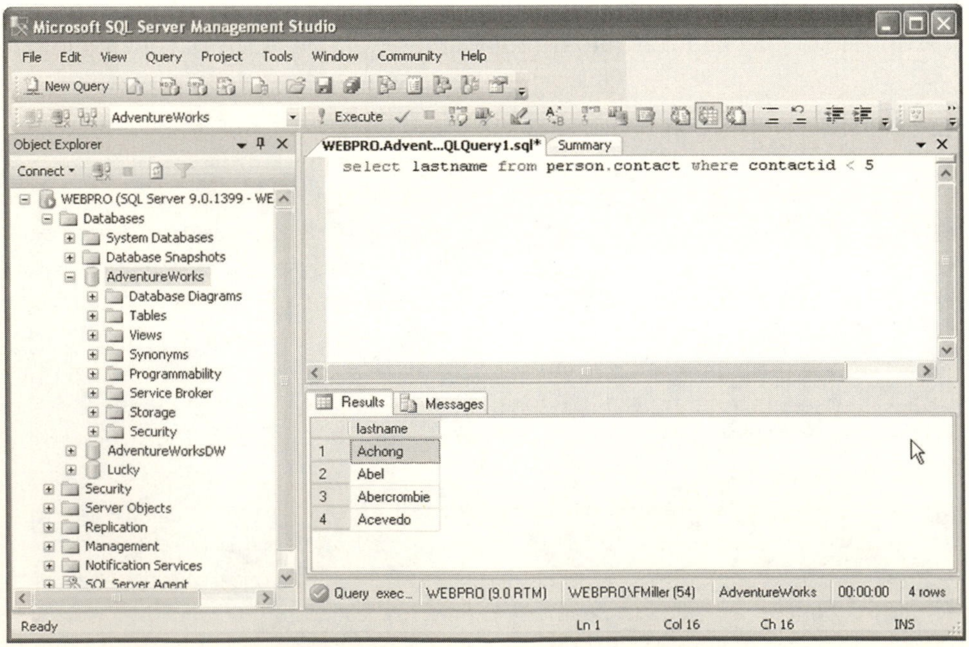

SQL Server Management Studio.

help available with access to database and database object structures, and easy access to documentation. You can check commands for syntax errors before running them and easily edit your commands using a tool called Query Analyzer.

The biggest problem with using Query Analyzer is that it is resource intensive and is not always available. If you want to run it from a client computer, which is what you would normally want to do for security reasons, then you must install the SQL Server client tools on that computer. The client tools include SQL Server Management Studio.

Embedded SQL

Embedded SQL is best suited to activities that must be performed periodically and that you want performed in the same way each time. Embedded SQL is also a critical part of any database application. Embedded SQL uses the same SQL language commands as when you are running interactive SQL statements. The difference is that they are included as part of an executable program.

SQL Server, for example, has two basic programmable objects that provide embedded SQL support. These are stored procedures and user-defined functions. Both are similar in that they are sets of executable statements, they can accept parameters to help control execution, and they can perform actions and return results. The primary difference is how they are used. Stored procedures are most often used to automate periodic procedures or to hide the details of those procedures from the users. User-defined functions are used when you want to return either a scalar value to a user or a result formatted as a table.

For example, you might create a stored procedure to process customer payments. The user would need to provide the stored procedure name, the customer ID, and the payment amount. Statements inside the stored procedure would handle the details of exactly what changes need to be made to the table or tables involved and could detect and respond to errors that might occur during the process. Not only do you ensure that the payments are posted properly, this also helps to ensure data security. Users do not need to know how the tables involved in the process are structured. Because they don't know how the data is structured, it's harder for someone to retrieve information from the database without proper authorization.

Embedded SQL is also used in application programs. The programming environment provides the connectivity tools to communicate with the database server and execute SQL commands. This can be done by passing literal command strings to the database server for execution or through application programming interfaces (APIs) that provide the necessary functionality. For example, SQL Server 2005 provides a set of.NET Framework management objects that make it easy to build management applications. Also, the data objects provided with ADO.NET support direct manipulation of database tables and other database objects. In fact, ADO.NET is able to mirror the database and table structure, down to column names and table constraints, in memory.

6.1.3 Understanding Command Basics

Whether running DDL or DML commands (as well as DQL commands, if you want to consider them separately), whether using interactive or embedded SQL, there are a few basic things that you need to understand. The first thing is that each SQL command has a specific command syntax that describes how you run the command. The **command syntax** includes the command name and any command keywords and parameters. Command **keywords,** also known as command **clauses,** are used to describe specific actions that a command will take. Command **parameters** are values that you supply so the command can run. Take a look at the following example, a simplified version of the SELECT statement:

SELECT *select_list* FROM *table* [WHERE
qualifying_conditions]

Let's break this down. SELECT is the command name. The SELECT command has various uses, but is most commonly used in queries to retrieve values from tables and views. The *select_list,* when SELECT is used in this manner, is the list of columns that you want the command to return. The *select_list* is one of the SELECT command parameters. Command syntax descriptions typically use italicized type, as in this example, to identify replaceable parameters.

FROM is a command keyword defining the FROM clause. When using SELECT to retrieve data, FROM is a required keyword. It identifies the object or objects (typically tables and views) from which you are retrieving data.

WHERE is an optional keyword and is used to filter the retrieval result. When retrieving data, if you don't include a WHERE clause, all rows are returned. The WHERE clause lets you set **qualifying conditions,** also called the **search argument,** that limit the rows returned. For example, you might want to filter a numeric column by the value it contains, or a date/time column by a range of dates. Square brackets are typically used in command syntax descriptions when describing command syntax to identify optional clauses. In actual command strings, square brackets can be used to enclose object names.

When you run any command, SQL Server parses the command before it does anything else. In this context, **parsing** is the process of reviewing the command string to verify that you've used the correct command syntax. For example, attempting to run the following would result in a syntax error:

SELECT name, street, city FORM employees

This would return an error that "FORM" is not recognized. The exact wording of the error depends on your DBMS. In most cases, you will receive an error number and a textual description of the error. With some DBMSs, you can use its help system to look up the error number and get more information. However, some DBMSs just repeat the textual error statement that you've already seen.

You need to understand that most commands, with the exception of some DDL commands, run in the context of a database. When you connect to a SQL Server database server, for example, through a command-line or graphical interface, your connection is associated with a **default database,** also known as the **working database.** When you execute a command that depends on a database, the default database is assumed. For example, when you specify a table by name or by schema and name only, SQL Server assumes the table is in the default database. Some commands, mostly maintenance commands, can run against the default database only. Other database products have similar defaults for connections, but the terminology used can vary between different DBMS products.

Each connection will also have an associated user—the user specified when you connected to the database server. The actions you can take depends on the permissions assigned that user. In some cases, you can temporarily override this by specifying to run a command using the security context of a different user, but this feature is not supported by all DBMSs.

The result returned by the command after successful completion is somewhat command specific. When you run a SELECT command to retrieve data, it returns the requested columns and qualifying rows, known as the **result set.** You might also see this referred to as a **relational result.** It will also return a message stating

FOR EXAMPLE

About SQL Compatibility

If all modern DBMSs are based on the SQL language standard, then why is there such a concern about selecting a DBMS? The difference relates primarily to the version of the SQL standard on which the DBMS is based and how close it is to that standard. You will find that the closer a DBMS is to the SQL standard, the fewer features and less functionality it supports. Moving away from the standard brings more power and flexibility, but also means that you have to deal with more proprietary command syntaxes and language components. The learning curve before you can successfully deploy a database solution increases.

Microsoft SQL Server is one of the most popular modern DBMS products. It is also one of the fastest, if not the fastest, depending on whose benchmark tests you prefer. It is also one of the most difficult to learn. An understanding of the SQL language standards will be enough to get you started so you can employ basic features, but to make use of its unique benefits, you need to learn new commands and learn about features that aren't part of the SQL standard. It also means that scripts containing executable command statements that are written for SQL Server may or may not run on another DBMS, depending on what statements you've used, and how.

how many rows were returned. DML statements usually just return a count of rows affected. You receive even less with most DDL statements. In most cases, they only return a statement that the command completed successfully.

If the command didn't complete successfully, the DBMS returns an error. Often, the errors returned give little information other than the fact than an error has occurred. One reason for this is security. One possible source of errors is that someone is trying to break into a database without authorization. The less information you provide them about why a command didn't work, the more difficult it is for them to figure out a solution without knowing the database and database object structures.

SELF-CHECK

- Briefly describe the importance of the SQL language standard.
- Compare interactive and embedded SQL.
- Explain why DBMS providers vary from the SQL standard.

6.2 Understanding SELECT Fundamentals

One of the most commonly used SQL commands is the SELECT command. As you have already learned, you use SELECT to retrieve data. You can also use SELECT to perform calculations and to retrieve the results from functions, which are special commands designed to operate on data and return a result.

6.2.1 Working with SELECT

You have already been introduced to the SELECT statement and its basic syntax. We're going to talk a bit more about SELECT because you will likely use it more than any other command. The complete SELECT command syntax is beyond the scope of this chapter, but we'll take a closer look at a few additional syntax options. SELECT statement command examples used in this chapter are all based on Microsoft SQL Server's Transact-SQL variation of the SQL standard language. Command syntax for the SELECT command, as well as for other commands discussed later in the chapter, varies for other DBMS products.

SELECT commands are considered **declarative statements** rather than being procedural in nature. This means that you specify what data you are looking for rather than provide a logical sequence of steps that guide the system in how to find the data. The relational DBMS analyzes the declarative SQL SELECT statement and creates an **access path**—a plan for what steps to take to respond to the query. The SELECT command also allows the user, in some circumstances, to exert a certain amount of logical control over the data retrieval process.

Another point is that SQL SELECT commands can be run in either an interactive query or an embedded mode. In the query mode, the user types the command at a workstation and presses the Enter key. In the embedded mode, the SELECT command is embedded within the lines of a higher-level language program and functions as an input or "read" statement for the program. When the program is run and the program logic reaches the SELECT command, the program executes the SELECT. The SELECT command is sent to the DBMS where, as in the query mode case, the DBMS processes it against the database and returns the results, this time to the program that issued it. The program can then use and further process the returned data. The only tricky part to this is that some programming environments are designed to retrieve one record at a time. In the embedded mode, the program that issued the SQL SELECT command and receives the result set must process the rows returned one at a time. However, many newer languages and programming environments are designed to recognize and process result sets. Microsoft.NET Framework, for example, includes data objects that let you access rows one at a time, in the order received, or store the entire result set in memory and randomly access its contents.

6.2.2 Using Simple Data Retrieval

Let's look at a couple of examples of simple retrieval statements. We're retrieving data from the SALESPERSON table shown in Figure 6-3.

Let's start with a simple request: "Find the commission percentage and year of hire of salesperson number 186." The SQL statement to accomplish this would be:

```
SELECT COMMPERCT, YEARHIRE FROM SALESPERSON
WHERE SPNUM=186;
```

The desired attributes are listed in the SELECT clause, the required table is listed in the FROM clause, and the restriction or predicate indicating which row(s) is involved is shown in the WHERE clause in the form of an equation. Notice that the SELECT ends with a single semicolon (;) at the very end of the entire statement. This is used to identify the end of the statement. The use of a

Figure 6-3

(a) SALESPERSON table				
SPNUM	SPNAME	COMMPERCT	YEARHIRE	OFFNUM
137	Baker	10	1995	1284
186	Adams	15	2001	1253
204	Dickens	10	1998	1209
361	Carlyle	20	2001	1227

SALESPERSON table.

semicolon is specified in the SQL standard with command statements as the end-of-statement delimiter, but its use is optional with Microsoft SQL Server. Different vendors vary in how they use end-of-statement delimiters. The result of this statement is:

COMMPERCT	YEARHIRE
15	2001

As is evident from this query, a qualifying condition (or search argument) like SPNUM, being used to filter the result set by searching for the required rows, does not have to appear in the query result. Its inclusion in the select list is optional as long as its absence does not make the result ambiguous, confusing, or meaningless.

To retrieve the entire record for salesperson 186 the statement would change to:

```
SELECT * FROM SALESPERSON WHERE SPNUM=186
```

This gives the result:

SPNUM	SPNAME	COMMPERCT	YEARHIRE	OFFNUM
186	Adams	15	2001	1253

The "*" in the SELECT clause indicates that all columns (fields) are to be retrieved.

Now, let's look at an example where you want a specific set of columns, but don't limit the rows, such as: "List the salesperson number and salesperson name of all of the salespersons." Here, you would run:

```
SELECT SPNUM, SPNAME FROM SALESPERSON
```

This gives the result:

SPNUM	SPNAME
137	Baker
186	Adams
204	Dickens
361	Carlyle

Finally, if you want to return all rows and all columns, all of the data in the SALESPERSON table, you would run:

```
SELECT * FROM SALESPERSON
```

The result would be identical to the table shown in Figure 6-3.

6.2.3 Retrieving Other Values

When using Microsoft SQL Server, you can use SELECT to evaluate expressions. These can be, for example, mathematical expressions or expressions containing SQL functions. The syntax for using SELECT to perform a calculation is:

SELECT *expression*

You can't get much simpler than that. The *expression* is any mathematical or logical expression that returns a result. Here's an easy example:

SELECT 5 + 7

When you execute the command, the database server returns a result of 12. The expression must resolve to a legal value or an error is returned. For example, the following will return a divide by 0 error:

SELECT 5/0

The syntax is similar for resolving a function. In this case, the syntax is:

SELECT *function* [(*parameter_list*)]

The *parameter_list* is in square brackets because some functions do not include any parameters. Others can accept multiple parameters, depending on what the

FOR EXAMPLE

The SELECT Statement

The SELECT statement is the basic workhorse of most database applications. To understand this, think about how a database might meet the needs of a business, such as an online sales business. A customer logs onto your Web site. When this happens, it's likely that your application will attempt to retrieve information from the customer's computer and compare it with information it has on file, using the information to recognize returning customers. How will it do this? By running a SELECT statement filtered by this identifying information. The customer wants to view information about products you have for sale. This information is often spread across multiple tables, requiring the use of one or more SELECT statements used to retrieve the information and organize the result.

The checkout process relies on a series of SELECT statements, retrieving shipping options and formulas for calculating shipping costs, the customer's preferred shipping address and possibly one or more alternate addresses. Some online vendors will also use queries against secure database tables to retrieve credit card information you've left on file. Even when using embedded SQL features that don't necessarily execute an explicit SELECT statement, they are still based on SELECT statement functionality.

function is designed to do. This syntax for evaluating expressions and functions is not supported by all DBMS products.

SELF-CHECK

- Explain the basic SELECT statement syntax.
- Explain the importance of the WHERE clause when retrieving SELECT results.

6.3 Understanding Operators and Functions

A key part of writing and understanding expressions is understanding operators. SQL operators include both arithmetic and logical operators. Logical operators are used in the WHERE clause to build search conditions that depend on more than one qualifying condition. You can also categorize operators as the following:

▲ **Unary Operator:** an operator applied to only one operand at the time; typically in the format operator operand. For example, NOT A.

▲ **Binary Operator:** an operator applied to two operands at the time, typically in the format operand operator operand. For example, A OR B.

Because of variations between different DBMS products, specific examples in this chapter are based primarily on Microsoft SQL Server.

6.3.1 Arithmetic Operators

Arithmetic operators are used for arithmetic computations. The use of the arithmetic operators is very intuitive, and they can be used in virtually every clause of a SQL statement. Because of its effect when used with numeric data, we've also included a concatenation operator in our discussion. The full list of arithmetic operators is given in Table 6-1.

While doing arithmetic in SQL is relatively easy, you must pay attention to the data type used in the operations. For numeric values, this includes the precision and scale of the result; for datetime, the range of the resulting values; and so on. Most DBMSs can convert similar data types automatically for evaluation through a process known as **implicit conversion,** but dissimilar types require **explicit conversion** (manual conversion) to a compatible type.

To add two values, as you've already seen, you could:

```
SELECT 5 + 5 total_value
```

Table 6-1: Arithmetic and Concatenation Operators

Operator	Description
+	Addition: adds two numbers. When used with SQL Server, also concatenates (joins together) strings. The use for concatenation in nearly unique to SQL Server.
−	Subtraction: subtracts one numeric value from another.
*	Multiplication: multiplies one number by another.
/	Division: divides one number by another.
%	Modulo: calculates the integer remainder of a division. For example, 15%5=0, 17%5=2, 18%5=3, and 20%5=0

This gives you the following result, with "total_value" used as the column name.

total_value
10

To concatenate (join together) numbers in SQL Server, you would need to use a different expression. Instead of numeric data, you would use numbers represented as strings. Use the + operator with values that are explicitly identified as strings, as in the following:

```
SELECT '5' + '5' total_value
```

This gives you the result:

total_value
55

6.3.2 Comparison and Logical Operators

You can use comparison operators in a SELECT statement's WHERE clause or with decision statements that take an action depending on the logical result of a comparison operation, such as: "If A > B, then perform an action." The most commonly supported comparison operators are listed in Table 6-2.

Some DBMS vendors recommend that whenever possible, you should avoid negated operators because they require more resources to process. For example, a query using >= will run faster than a query using !<.

Comparison operators can be used by themselves or together with logical operators. Logical operators are used to evaluate a set of conditions, with the returned result a value of TRUE, FALSE, or "unknown." Like comparison operators, you can use logical operators in a SELECT statement's WHERE clause or with

Table 6-2: Comparison Operators

Operator	Description
=	Equal to. The operand values are equal.
>	Greater than. The value of the left operand is greater than the value of the right operand.
>=	Greater than or equal to. The value of the left operand is greater than or equal to the value of the right operand.
<	Less than. The value of the left operand is less than the value of the right operand.
<=	Less than or equal to. The value of the left operand is less than or equal to the value of the right operand.
<>	Not equal to. The value of the left operand is not equal to the value of the right operand.
!	Not. Used to reverse the operand logic. For example, you can use != for not equal to or !< for not less than.

decision statements that take an action depending on the result of a logical operation, such as: "If A AND B are true, then perform an action." The most common logical operators are shown in Table 6-3.

In addition to these operators, there are special operators that are used with subqueries. A **subquery** is a special way of retrieving information where one query is dependent on another query. A discussion of subqueries is beyond the scope of this chapter.

We should, however, look at a couple of examples of using common logical operators. We're going to use them in the SELECT statement WHERE clause. This time, we'll be querying the CUSTOMER table shown in Figure 6-4.

Table 6-3: Logical Operators

Operator	Description
AND	Evaluates to TRUE if both Boolean expressions are TRUE.
BETWEEN	Evaluates to TRUE if the operand is within a range.
LIKE	Evaluates to TRUE if the operand matches a pattern.
NOT	Reverses the value of any other Boolean operator.
OR	Evaluates to TRUE if either Boolean expression is TRUE.

Figure 6-4

(b) CUSTOMER table			
CUSTNUM	CUSTNAME	SPNUM	HQCITY
0121	Main St. Hardware	137	New York
0839	Jane's Stores	186	Chicago
0933	ABC Home Stores	137	Los Angeles
1047	Acme Hardware Store	137	Los Angeles
1525	Fred's Tool Stores	361	Atlanta
1700	XYZ Stores	361	Washington
1826	City Hardware	137	New York
2198	Western Hardware	204	New York
2267	Central Stores	186	New York

CUSTOMER table.

First, let's look at an example where we have two conditions and both must be met for a row to qualify.

List the customer numbers, customer names, and headquarter cities of the customers that are headquartered in New York and that have a customer number higher than 1500.

In this case, you would run:

```
SELECT CUSTNUM, CUSTNAME, HQCITY FROM CUSTOMER
WHERE HQCITY='New York' AND CUSTNUM>1500
```

This gives us the result:

CUSTNUM	CUSTNAME	HQCIT
1826	City Hardware	New York
2198	Western Hardware	New York
2267	Central Stores	New York

Notice that customer number 0121, which is headquartered in New York, was not included in the results because it failed to satisfy the condition of having a customer number greater than 1500. With the AND operator, it had to satisfy both conditions to be included in the result.

To look at the OR operator, let's change the last query to:

List the customer numbers, customer names, and headquarter cities of the customers that are headquartered in New York or that have a customer number higher than 1500.

In this case, you would run:

```
SELECT CUSTNUM, CUSTNAME, HQCITY FROM CUSTOMER
WHERE HQCITY='New York' OR CUSTNUM>1500
```

This time, our result is:

CUSTNUM	CUSTNAME	HQCIT
0121	Main St. Hardware	New York
1525	Fred's Tool Stores	Atlanta
1700	XYZ Stores	Washington
1826	City Hardware	New York
2198	Western Hardware	New York
2267	Central Stores	New York

Notice that the OR operator really means one or the other or both. Customer 0121 is included because it is headquartered in New York. Customers 1525 and 1700 are included because they have customer numbers higher than 1500. Customers 1826, 2198, and 2267 satisfy both conditions.

If both AND and OR are required, AND has a higher precedence than OR. **Operator precedence** determines the order in which operators are processed, so all ANDs are considered before any ORs are considered. The following query, which has to be worded very carefully, illustrates this point:

List the customer numbers, customer names, and headquarter cities of the customers that are headquartered in New York or that satisfy the two conditions of having a customer number higher than 1500 and being headquartered in Atlanta.

The query for this is:

```
SELECT CUSTNUM, CUSTNAME, HQCITY
FROM CUSTOMER WHERE HQCITY='New York' OR
(CUSTNUM>1500 AND HQCITY='Atlanta')
```

The result of this query is:

CUSTNUM	CUSTNAME	HQCIT
0121	Main St. Hardware	New York
1525	Fred's Tool Stores	Atlanta
1826	City Hardware	New York
2198	Western Hardware	New York
2267	Central Stores	New York

Notice that since the AND is considered first, one way for a row to qualify being in the result is if its customer number is greater than 1500 and its headquarter city is Atlanta. With the AND taken first, it's that combination or the headquarters city has to be New York. If the OR operator was considered first, it would change the whole complexion of the statement. The best way to deal with this, especially if there are several ANDs and ORs in a WHERE clause, is to use parentheses. The rule is that anything in parentheses is done first. If the

Table 6-4: LIKE Wildcard Characters

Character	Description
%	Matches any string of zero or more characters.
_ (underscore)	Matches any single character within a string.
[ ]	Matches any single character within the specified range or set of characters. This wildcard is unique to Microsoft SQL Server.
[^]	Matches any single character NOT within specified range or set of characters, and also supported by SQL Server only.

parentheses are nested, then whatever is in the innermost parentheses is done first and then the system works from there toward the outermost parentheses. The rule regarding parentheses also applies to arithmetic operators, with operations contained in the innermost parentheses evaluated first.

The LIKE operator needs special consideration. Operator LIKE belongs to the "fuzzy logic" domain. It is used any time criteria in the WHERE clause of the SELECT query are only partially known. It utilizes a variety of wildcard characters, listed in Table 6-4, to specify the missing parts of the value. The pattern must follow the LIKE keyword.

Suppose that you want to find the customer records for those customers whose names begin with the letter A. You can accomplish this with the LIKE operator and the % character used as a wildcard to represent any string of characters. Thus, "A%" means the letter A followed by any string of characters, which is the same thing as saying any word that begins with A:

```
SELECT * FROM CUSTOMER WHERE CUSTNAME LIKE 'A%'
```

The result would be:

CUSTNUM	CUSTNAME	SPNUM	HQCIT
0933	ABC Home Stores	137	Los Angeles
1047	Acme Hardware Store	137	Los Angeles

6.3.3 Standard SQL Functions

SQL functions exist to make your life easier when you need to manipulate data. Think of the SQL functions as tools designed to accomplish a single well-defined task—for example, calculating square root or converting lowercase letters into uppercase. You invoke a function within SQL query by name (usually a single keyword). Some functions accept arguments, some do not, but they always return a value.

All functions could be divided into two broad categories: deterministic functions and nondeterministic functions. **Deterministic functions** always return the same result if you pass in the same arguments; **nondeterministic functions** might return different results, even if they are called with exactly the same arguments. For example, ABS, which returns the absolute value of a number passed to it as an argument, is a deterministic function. No matter how many times you call it with, say argument –5, it will always return 5 as a result. The Microsoft SQL Server function GETDATE() accepts no arguments and returns only the current date and time, and so is an example of a nondeterministic function. Each time you call it a new date and time is returned, even if the difference is less than one second.

One reason this is important is that some DBMSs restrict use of the nondeterministic functions in database objects such as indexes or views. For example, SQL Server disallows use of such functions for indexed computed columns and indexed views.

The list of functions changes slightly with each new release of the ANSI SQL standards. However, the functions supported by the various DBMS providers vary widely from the standard function list and from each other. As an example, the functions specified in the SQL-99 standard (as well as earlier standard versions) are described in Table 6-5. The SQL-99 standard refers to a version of the SQL standard released in 1999. New SQL standard versions are released every few years.

Rather than expecting a standard implementation of any of these functions, you should refer to the documentation specific to your DBMS for available functions. Limit use of functions to statements, procedures, and other executables to be used with a specific SQL implementation.

6.3.4 Function Variations

Rather than try to cover all of the function variations you might see, or even all of the functions supported by a particular vendor, the goal here is to provide a general overview of the types of functions you might see and focus on a few key

Table 6-5: SQL-99 Standard Functions

SQL Function	Description
BIT_LENGTH (expression)	Returns the length of the expression, usually string, in bits.
CAST (value AS data type)	Converts supplied value from one data type into another compatible data type.

Table 6-5 (*Continued*)

CHAR_LENGTH (expression)	Returns the length of the expression, usually string, in characters.
CONVERT (expression USING conversion)	Returns a string converted according to the rules specified in the conversion parameter.
CURRENT_DATE	Returns current date of the system.
CURRENT_TIME (precision)	Returns current time of the system, of the specified precision.
CURRENT_TIMESTAMP (precision)	Returns current time and the current date of the system, of the specified precision.
EXTRACT (part FROM expression)	Extracts specified named part of the expression.
LOWER (expression)	Converts character string from uppercase (or mixed case) into lowercase letters.
OCTET_LENGTH (expression)	Returns the length of the expression in bytes (each byte containing 8 bits).
POSITION (char expression IN source)	Returns position of the char expression in the source.
SUBSTRING (string expression,start, length)	Returns the string part of a string expression, from the start position up to specified length.
TRANSLATE (string expression USING translation rule)	Returns the string translated into another string according to specified rules.
TRIM (LEADING | TRAILING | BOTH char expression FROM string expression)	Return the string from a string expression where leading, trailing, or both char expression characters are removed.
UPPER (expression)	Converts character string from lowercase (or mixed case) into uppercase letters.

Table 6-6: General Function Categories

Function Category	Description
Numeric	Functions that operate with numbers and usually include a random number generator. These include statistical functions, such as those for finding mean and standard deviation.
Mathematical	Functions that are also used with numeric values, but to perform specific mathematic calculations, such as trigonometric functions for SIN, COS, and so forth.
Date/Time	Functions used to return current date/time information, format date and time strings, and perform calculations based on date and time, such as the number of days that have passed between two dates.
Aggregate	Used to generate aggregate values based on sets of numeric values, such as generating a total, a count, or finding an average.
String	Functions that perform string manipulations such as modifying strings, locating patterns within a string, inserting characters, concatenating strings, finding string length, and changing character case.
Conversion	Used to convert values between data types. These functions let you perform explicit conversions between otherwise incompatible types.

functions you are likely to use. Table 6-6 lists commonly accepted function category descriptions.

To give you an idea of the functions supported by a specific DBMS, let's take a quick look at the aggregate functions supported by SQL Server. An **aggregate function** operates on a set of values, returning a single result based on these values. These are listed in Table 6-7.

In the case of SQL Server, these functions are also part of the set of functions referred to as **built-in functions.** Built-in functions are simply the predefined functions that install with SQL Server. They are considered part of the general functionality of the SELECT statement as implemented by SQL Server. Aggregate functions can be used on a result set as a whole or to provide summary or intermediate values based on groups of rows within a result as specified by another SELECT statement clause, the GROUP BY clause. Let's take a look at a couple of examples based on the SALES table shown in Figure 6-5.

Table 6-7: SQL Server Aggregate Functions

Function	Return Data Type	Description
AVG	Number (real)	Calculates average for a range of numeric values.
COUNT	Int	Returns number of rows in a SELECT statement.
COUNT_BIG	Bigint	Returns number of rows in a SELECT statement based on a bigint type value.
MAX	Number (real)	Returns max value among selected values.
MIN	Number (real)	Returns min value among selected values.
SUM	Number (real)	Calculates sum of the selected values.

The SALES table shows the lifetime quantity of particular products sold by particular salespersons. For example, the first row indicates that Salesperson 137 has sold 473 units of Product Number 19440 dating back to when she joined the company or when the product was introduced.

Figure 6-5

SALES table		
SPNUM	**PRODNUM**	**QUANTITY**
137	19440	473
137	24013	170
137	26722	688
186	16386	1745
186	19440	2529
186	21765	1962
186	24013	3071
204	21765	809
204	26722	734
361	16386	3729
361	21765	3110
361	26722	2738

SALES table.

Consider the following query:

Find the average number of units of the different products that Salesperson 137 has sold (i.e., the average of the quantity values in the first three records of the SALES table).

Using the AVG operator, you would write:

```
SELECT AVG(QUANTITY) FROM SALES WHERE SPNUM=137
```

The result would be:

AVG (QUANTITY)
443.67

To find the total number of units of all products that she has sold, you would use the SUM operator and write:

```
SELECT SUM (QUANTITY) FROM SALES WHERE SPNUM=137
```

The result would be:

SUM (QUANTITY)
1331

Notice that when used with the SELECT statement, the aggregate function is used as either part of the SELECT list, or as in these examples, the entire SELECT list.

Now, let's take a look at an example that relies on grouping rows, once again using the SALES table in Figure 6-5. At some point, you might want to find the total number of units of all products that each salesperson has sold. That is, you want to group together the rows of the SALES table that belong to each salesperson and calculate a value—the sum of the Quantity attribute values in this case—for each such group. Here is the way such a query might be stated: "Find the total number of units of all products sold by each salesperson." The SQL statement, using the GROUP BY clause, would look like this:

```
SELECT SPNUM, SUM (QUANTITY) FROM SALES GROUP BY SPNUM
```

The result would be:

SPNUM	SUM(QUANTITY)
137	1331
186	9307
204	1543
361	9577

Notice that GROUP BY SPNUM specifies that the rows of the table are to be grouped together based on having the same value in their SPNUM attribute. All of the rows for Salesperson Number 137 will form one group, all of the rows for Salesperson Number 186 will form another group, and so on. The Quantity attribute values in each group will then be summed—SUM(QUANTITY)—and the results returned to the user.

FOR EXAMPLE

The Importance of Parentheses

Parentheses and their placement can play an important role in SQL expressions. Most people don't take the time to memorize operator precedence, the order in which operators are evaluated. That means that they don't necessarily know how an expression containing multiple operators, especially one containing different types of operators, is going to be evaluated. Take, for example, the following statement:

```
SELECT  2  *  2  +  6
```

This statement returns a result of 10. When evaluating the expression, the database server first multiplies 2 times 2 (for 4), then adds 6 to the product, giving you 10.

What if we turn it around, as in the following:

```
SELECT  2+6*2
```

This time, the result is 14. The multiplication operator has a higher precedence than the addition operator, so it is evaluated first as 6 times 2 (for 12), with 2 then added to the product for a result of 14.

Typically, you will want to use parentheses so you can explicitly control the order in which operators are evaluated. What if you want the database server to first add 2 and 6 then multiply the sum by 2? Here's the statement you need:

```
SELECT  2*(2+6)
```

The addition operator is evaluated first, because it is enclosed in parentheses, then the multiplication operator. As expressions become more complicated, especially when they depend on function results or scalar values returned by queries, parentheses become more important in ensuring the expressions are evaluated properly. Errors caused by operator precedence can easily go unnoticed during application design, can lead to costly mistakes, and can be very difficult to locate and correct.

SELF-CHECK

- List and describe available operator categories.
- Explain the significance of operator precedence.
- List and describe function categories.

6.4 Understanding DML Commands

Many DML commands vary in how they are implemented by various DBMSs. Rather than trying to introduce you to all of the statements you might use or focusing on the statement syntax for a particular DBMS, this section's goal is to give you a general introduction to the statements. The section includes a few ANSI standard command syntax examples as representative examples. Statement examples are based on Microsoft SQL Server.

Popular DBMS products have full product documentation readily available. For example, you can install complete product documentation, including command syntax and command use examples, when you install SQL Server. Because of the variations in how statements are implemented, you should refer to your product-specific documentation for information about statement syntax and specific functionality.

The ANSI SQL standard defines three basic DML statements: INSERT, UPDATE, and DELETE. You use the INSERT statement to add rows to a table. UPDATE lets you modify values in specified columns and rows (existing records). Run DELETE to remove rows from tables. Keep in mind with any of these statements that you might be prevented from taking actions due to constraints or other limits placed on a table. For example, you might not be allowed to delete a row that is referenced by another row in a different table through a foreign key constraint.

Our discussion is limited primarily to the ANSI SQL standard syntax of each of these DML statements and their basic use. We use the statement syntax as defined in the ANSI SQL-99 standard, the standard on which most DBMSs implementations of the statements are based. Details of how to use advanced functionality, such as using queries to pass retrieved values for use in DML statements, is beyond the scope of this chapter.

6.4.1 Using INSERT

The standard syntax for the INSERT statement is:

```
INSERT INTO table_or_view_name
[(column_list)] { {VALUES (literal | expression |
NULL,...) |
select_statement | DEFAULT VALUES
```

You must specify the table or view to which you are inserting the new row or rows. If you specify a view, it must either be based on a single table or you must create a trigger to handle the details of the INSERT process. The *column_list* is specified only if you are not providing values for all columns. In that case, you would list the columns for which values are provided.

You have several options for providing values. You can use literal values, such as numeric values or character strings, as long as the value is appropriate to the column's data type. Character strings must be enclosed in quotes to be recognized as such. You can use expressions that evaluate as an appropriate value. For columns that allow NULL values, you can specify NULL. In some cases, you can use a SELECT statement to provide the values.

When inserting a row into a table, you must provide a value for every column unless the column:

▲ Is an identity column (in those DBMSs where identity columns are supported).

▲ Has a value calculated from the values of other columns.

▲ Allows NULLs (in which case, a value of NULL is inserted if none is provided).

▲ Has a defined default value (which can be overridden by a supplied value).

SQL Server is one of the few DBMSs that currently support the DEFAULT VALUES keyword. It specifies to use all default values when inserting the row. These can include the next value of an identity column, automatically generated values such as GUID and timestamp values, default values based on literals or expressions, and, for nullable columns that don't otherwise have a default, NULL.

As an example, think back to the SALESPERSON table in Figure 6-3. Assume that the COMMPERCT column has a default value of 10. You might use the following statement to add another salesperson to the table.

```
INSERT INTO SALESPERSON (SPNUM, SPNAME, YEARHIRE,
OFFNUM)
VALUES (427, 'Smythe', 2005, 1247)
```

Notice that in this example, we didn't include COMMPERCT in the column list, and therefore, it will receive the default value when the row is added. The other columns take their values from the literal values we've provided.

6.4.2 Using UPDATE

The UPDATE statement lets you modify existing database information. Two common examples of when you need to do this include:

▲ You did not have all of the information for the row when you inserted it into the table.

▲ You need to change database information to reflect changes in the real world.

When data becomes available, or when it changes, you need to update table data as appropriate, using the UPDATE statement. The ANSI SQL-99 standard UPDATE syntax is:

```
UPDATE table_or_view_name
SET column_name = literal | expression |
(single_row_select_statement) |
NULL | DEFAULT,...
[WHERE search_condition]
```

In general, the rules and restrictions are the same as for using the INSERT statement. You must specify the destination table or view. If the view is based on more than one table, you must have a trigger that makes the update for you. You can update directly through a view only if the view is based on just one table.

Use the SET keyword, followed by the column that you want to modify and the new value. You can also specify a column list, with values provided for each column in the list. As with INSERT, you can specify a literal value, an expression, the NULL keyword, or the DEFAULT keyword to set a column to its default value (if any). If you specify an illegal value, an error is generated. This would include an invalid value, that is, one not supported by the column data type, a NULL value for a column that does not accept NULLs, or the DEFAULT keyword for a column that does not have a defined default.

If you want to modify one row or a specific set of rows, you must include the WHERE clause with a search condition to filter the rows affected by the command. Consider this situation. The salesperson you previously entered, Smythe, married and took her husband's name (Watson). She wants all company records to reflect her new last name. To make this change, run:

```
UPDATE SALESPERSON SET SPNAME = 'WATSON'
WHERE SPNUM = 427
```

One of the most common problems when using the UPDATE statement is either forgetting to include the WHERE clause (so that all rows are updated), or using inappropriate values in the WHERE clause. Either can result in the wrong rows being updated.

In this example, you didn't have to use SPNUM as the qualifying column. However, assuming that it is the primary key, it's the value you would want to use because it uniquely identifies the row. What if you had multiple salespersons with the name Smythe and ran the following:

```
UPDATE SALESPERSON SET SPNAME = 'WATSON'
WHERE SPNAME = 'Smythe'
```

This time, you would change "Smythe" to "Watson" for every salesperson with the name "Smythe". The point here is that you must be careful when defining your search conditions when updating (or, as you will see later, deleting) table information.

Here's another example that requires a logical operator in the WHERE clause. Every salesperson that currently has a COMMPERCT value of 10 hired in 2004 or later is getting an automatic increase to 11.5. To do this, you could run:

```
UPDATE SALESPERSON SET COMMPERCT = 11.5
WHERE COMMPERCT = 10 AND YEARHIRE >= 2004
```

Now, let's say you changed your mind. You decide to put any salespersons hired in or after 2006 back on the default percentage. To do this, run

```
UPDATE SALESPERSON SET COMMPERCT = DEFAULT
WHERE YEARHIRE >= 2006
```

Just as an added note, this last example could have also been run as the following with the same result:

```
UPDATE SALESPERSON SET COMMPERCT = DEFAULT
WHERE YEARHIRE > 2005
```

The difference in the search condition logic is less complicated than in the previous example. If processing a very large number of salespersons, there could be a difference in performance between the two, with the latter running faster.

6.4.3 Using DELETE

DELETE provides a way to get rid of the information that is no longer needed. Deleting database rows is usually necessary when the entity these rows correspond to becomes irrelevant or completely disappears from the real world. For example, an employee quits, a customer does not place orders any more, or shipment information is no longer needed. Perhaps order information, once it reaches a certain age, is transferred to an archive table. However, there isn't a TRANSFER or ARCHIVE command. Instead, you would run INSERT to write the orders into the archive table, and then DELETE to remove the orders from the original table, effectively transferring them.

The ANSI SQL-99 syntax for this statement, as you might guess, is relatively simple:

```
DELETE [FROM] table_or_view_name
[WHERE search_condition]
```

The command does not support any addition of optional keywords or parameters, making it very simple to use. Keep in mind, however, that constraints or other restrictions placed on a table or individual columns could still prevent you from deleting rows from the table.

The table or view name is required. The FROM keyword is optional with some DBMSs, including SQL Server, but required by others. Some DBMSs require a WHERE clause and search condition. However, SQL Server does not, which could lead to a problem. If you run DELETE without a search condition, all rows are deleted from the table. For example, consider the following statement:

```
DELETE SALESPERSON
```

That statement would delete all rows from the SALESPERSON table. Once the change is committed, permanently written to the table, the only way to retrieve the rows would be either to recover from backup or manually reenter the information. However, reentering won't work if the table has identity columns because deleting all rows does not revert the identity back to its seed value. That means that all rows would have new identity values.

It's more likely that you would want to delete one row, or a subset of the rows, from the table. In an earlier example, you added a salesperson with a SPNUM value of 427 to SALESPERSON. To delete this person, you could run:

```
DELETE SALESPERSON WHERE SPNUM=427
```

Microsoft SQL Server does support a statement that will both delete all rows and reset the table's identity column, if it has one, to its seed value. This is a nonstandard command and is not always included as a DML statement. You might find it classified as a DDL statement, or as neither. This is the TRUNCATE TABLE statement, using the syntax:

```
TRUNCATE TABLE table_name
```

The potential problem is that this runs as a **non-logged operation.** Transaction logging is beyond the scope of this chapter, but in brief, a non-logged operation provides a way of rolling back changes as if they were never run. That means that the change isn't written to the transaction log, but instead is made directly to the database. SQL Server 2005 changed the description to say that the command is **minimally logged,** which means that the fact that the operation ran is logged, but not its effect on the database or its data. Even if the command is run from within a transaction, which normally lets you roll-back your actions if caught early enough in the process, there is no way to completely reverse the result other than by restoring the table from a recent backup. TRUNCATE TABLE is not a standard ANSI SQL command.

FOR EXAMPLE

Embedding DML Statements

As you can imagine, DML statements play a major role in most database applications. One of the justifications for normalizing database tables is to optimize performance when entering and modifying data. To use the INSERT, UPDATE, and DELETE statements, you need to understand the table structure. However, knowing too much about how tables are structured could make it easier for someone looking to steal, or maliciously change, database data.

You can avoid this by using embedded DML statements. You run the statements in the context of custom procedures or your application. You design the embedded statements so that users only need to provide the data values as parameters without necessarily knowing anything about table structure, the number of columns and column names, data types, or much of anything else about the tables. You are able to ensure that updates are made accurately and consistently while protecting data against unauthorized access.

SELF-CHECK

- Explain why vendor command syntax is often different than SQL standard syntax.
- Describe the purpose of the INSERT, UPDATE, and DELETE commands.

6.5 Understanding DDL Commands

As with DML commands, DDL commands vary widely in how they are implemented by various DBMSs. Once again, this section's goal is to give you a general introduction to the statements. The section again includes a few ANSI standard command statements as representative examples.

DDL commands are used to create and manage server and database objects. Server objects, as the name implies, are objects implemented at the server level. In Microsoft SQL Server, for example, logins (used for server access) are server level objects. Database objects are those objects created as database-specific, such as tables. There are three basic commands that relate to object management. They are as follows:

▲ CREATE: used to create server and database objects, such as CREATE TABLE and CREATE INDEX.

▲ ALTER: used to modify server and database objects, such as ALTER TABLE and ALTER INDEX.

▲ DROP: used to delete server and database objects, such DROP TABLE and DROP INDEX.

6.5.1 Using CREATE

The basic syntax of a CREATE command is:

```
CREATE objecttype objectname
commandoptions_and_parameters
```

The *objectype* is simply the type of object that you want to create, such as a table, index, or view. The objectname uniquely identifies the object. The general syntax of an object's fully qualified name in SQL Server 2005 is:

```
server.database.schema.object
```

What this means is, that in a SQL Server database, you can have only one object of a particular name in a particular schema, which is used to organize database objects. For xample, you could have a table named:

```
MyServ.OpsData.Sales.Employees
```

You could also have another table named:

```
MyServ.OpsData.Operations.Employees
```

Even though this would be allowed, because the table's fully qualified name is different, it isn't recommended. It would be less confusing to create objects so that each object has a unique, easily identifiable name. In this case, better table names might be:

```
MyServ.OpsData.Sales.SalesEmployees
MyServ.OpsData.Operations.OperationsEmployees
```

Command options are somewhat command specific. Many are specified through keywords, like the optional clauses in the SELECT statement. For example, the CREATE TABLE command syntax lets you specify table columns and data types. The CREATE INDEX command syntax, on the other hand, lets you specify the source table and columns to use when creating an index. Some options are supported across multiple commands, such as options that let you specify the object's physical storage.

Each command includes both required and optional keywords and parameters. Required parameters must be specified when you run the command. For example, when you create a table, the table name is a required parameter. So is specifying at least one table column. Optional parameters are parameters that you can include, but aren't required to. Optional parameters sometimes have a default value that is used if none is specified. For example, a table's primary key is an optional parameter that does not have a default value. If you don't specify a primary key, the table is created without one. The table's storage location is also an optional parameter, but there is a default storage location if none is specified.

The ANSI SQL-99 statement syntax for the CREATE TABLE statement, for example is:

```
CREATE [{GLOBAL | LOCAL} TEMPORARY] TABLE table_name
(column_name [domain_name |
datatype [size1[,size2]]
[column_constraint,...] [DEFAULT default_value]
[COLLATE collation_name],...)
[table_constraints]
[ON COMMIT {DELETE | PRESERVE} ROWS]
```

The ANSI SQL standard uses the GLOBAL and LOCAL keywords to define **temporary tables,** tables that are often created in memory only and having a limited scope. SQL Server does not support these keywords, but instead identifies temporary tables by the table name. A # is used as the first character in a local temporary table name and ## is used to identify a global temporary table.

The basic column definition is provided by the column name and data type, both of which are required. The SQL standard lets you specify a domain as an alternate to a data type. A **domain** is an object definition that includes a standard data type, but can also include a default value, collation, and constraints. Domains are not supported by SQL Server, but SQL Server does support a similar concept, known as a **user-defined data type,** which you can use instead of a standard SQL data type. Constraints, as well as supplying a default value of the column and column collation, are optional. You can also specify optional table constraints which include the primary key, foreign keys, and unique constraints.

The ON COMMIT clause is also part of the SQL standard that is not supported by SQL Server. It is used with some DBMSs to control the actions of temporary tables.

However, you shouldn't get the idea that you are shortchanged in functionality if you are using SQL Server. Microsoft supports several options that are not supported in the SQL standard; these include options to control physical storage.

6.5.2 Using ALTER

An ALTER statement will follow a similar syntax to the CREATE statement for the same type of object. ALTER TABLE, for example, lets you manage table columns, table constraints, column constraints, and so forth. ALTER INDEX lets you change the index type (as clustered or nonclustered) and change the index's key and nonkey columns. With most object types, some actions will be restricted and changes made to one object might impact another.

The ANSI SQL-99 standard ALTER TABLE statement uses the following syntax:

```
ALTER TABLE table_name
{[ADD [COLUMN] column_definition] |
[ALTER [COLUMN] column_name
{SET DEFAULT default | DROP DEFAULT}] |
[DROP [COLUMN] column_name RESTRICT | CASCADE] |
[ADD table_constraint] |
[DROP CONSTRAINT constraint_name RESTRICT | CASCADE]}
```

Though not specifically described in the standard syntax, most DBMSs let you alter other aspects of the column definition, such as column constraints, in addition to column default values. You are limited to taking one action each time you run an ALTER statement. For example, if you want to add a column, drop anther column, and add a constraint to the table, you would need to run the ALTER TABLE statement three times.

6.5.3 Using DROP

The DROP command is used to delete objects of that type. The DROP statement is different from other statements in that you can drop multiple objects of the same type in a single statement. The syntax for the DROP TABLE command is, for example:

```
DROP TABLE table_name,...
```

Your DBMS will put restrictions on dropping objects, preventing you from creating illegal conditions. For example, most DBMSs will not let you drop a table (by default) if it is referenced by any other table's foreign key.

SELF-CHECK

- Describe the purpose of CREATE, ALTER, and DELETE statements.
- Explain the role of DDL statements in the SQL language.

SUMMARY

This chapter introduced the SQL language. We began with a general introduction to the SQL language and a comparison between interactive and embedded SQL. We spent some time working with the most basic version of the SELECT statement to retrieve values from a single table and to evaluate expressions. The chapter also introduced the concept of operators and SQL language functions. We also looked at function categories used in vendor implementations of SQL and took a relatively close look at the SQL Server aggregate functions. We ended with a discussion of DDL and DML statements, including the standard SQL syntax for selected commands.

KEY TERMS

Access path	Keyword
Aggregate function	Minimally logged operation
Batch	Non-logged operation
Binary Operator	Nondeterministic function
Built-in functions	Operator precedence
Clause	Parameters
Command operators	Parsing
Command syntax	Procedure
Data definition language (DDL)	Qualifying conditions
Data manipulation language (DML)	Query mode
Data query language (DQL)	Relational result
Declarative statement	Result set
Default database	Script
Deterministic function	Search argument
Domain	Sqlcmd
Dynamic SQL	Subquery
Embedded SQL	Temporary table
Explicit conversion	Transaction control
Function	User-defined data type
Implicit conversion	Unary operator
Interactive SQL	Working database

ASSESS YOUR UNDERSTANDING

Go to www.wiley.com/college/gillenson to evaluate your knowledge of the SQL language.
Measure your learning by comparing pre-test and post-test results.

Summary Questions

1. The ANSI SQL standard defines other commands in addition to DDL and DML command statements. True or False?

2. What is the advantage of a command-line based interface for interactive SQL?

    (a) A command-line interface is easier to use than a graphic-based interface.

    (b) A command-line interface lets you run commands from an operating system batch.

    (c) A command-line interface does NOT require you to provide connection information.

    (d) A command-line interface is more forgiving of user error than other interfaces.

3. Embedded SQL is supported by .NET Framework development language only. True or False?

4. Which of the following statements accurately describes running SQL commands?

    (a) You must specify the database context when running any SQL command.

    (b) All SQL commands require you to specify a WHERE clause.

    (c) Unless otherwise specified, commands run in the security context of the user establishing the database connection.

5. SELECT commands are considered to be declarative in nature. True or False?

6. You must always specify the FROM clause when executing the SELECT command. True or False?

7. What is the purpose of the SELECT command WHERE clause?

    (a) to provide search conditions to filter the result set

    (b) to identify the source database

    (c) to identify the source tables or views

    (d) to specify the destination for reporting the command result

8. What is the general syntax for using SELECT to evaluate a function?

   (a) `SELECT  [(parameter_list)]  FROM  function`

   (b) `SELECT  function  WHERE  (parameter_list)`

   (c) `SELECT  function  [(parameter_list)]`

   (d) `SELECT  function  [(parameter_list)]`
   `        WHERE  database_name`

9. When running the following SELECT statement, what does the asterisk (*) specify?

   `SELECT  *  FROM  CUSTOMER`

   (a) retrieve all rows

   (b) retrieve NULL values only

   (c) retrieve from all databases

   (d) retrieve all columns

10. What is determined by operator precedence?

    (a) the order in which operators must be listed

    (b) the types of operands that can be used in a single expression

    (c) whether an operator performs a unary or binary operation

    (d) the order in which operators are processed

11. Parentheses are used in an expression to explicitly determine the order in which operators are processed. True or False?

12. Which of the following is NOT a standard SQL-99 function introduced in this chapter?

    (a) CAST

    (b) AVG

    (c) CURRENT_DATE

    (d) UPPER

13. Which aggregate function returns the total of all numeric values in a column?

    (a) SUM

    (b) TOTAL

    (c) MAX

    (d) COUNT

14. When does a LIKE expression evaluate as true?

    (a) when two operands are numerically identical

    (b) when two operands are logically identical

    (c) when an operand matches a pattern

    (d) when two Boolean expressions both evaluate as true

15. Which operator is used to test for a value within a range?

    (a) LIKE

    (b) BETWEEN

    (c) <>

    (d) !

16. Which operator returns the integer remainder of a division?

    (a) ||

    (b) *

    (c) &

    (d) %

17. What are the basic DDL statement types?

    (a) CREATE

    (b) ALTER

    (c) DROP

    (d) all of the above

18. Which of the following keywords are supported in the Microsoft SQL Server version of the CREATE TABLE statement?

    (a) DEFAULT

    (b) GLOBAL

    (c) LOCAL

    (d) COMMIT

19. Vendor implementations of DML statements always support all keywords defined by the SQL standard. True or False?

20. Which command is used to remove rows matching a qualifying condition from a database table?

    (a) DROP

    (b) DELETE

    (c) TRUNCATE TABLE

    (d) none of the above

Applying This Chapter

1. You are designing a database application. You have selected the application development language, but not the DBMS. You want a DBMS that supports as broad a base of features as possible. Should you select a DBMS based strictly on the SQL language standard? Why or why not? Why is the availability of product-specific documentation a selection issue?

2. You need to design SELECT statements to retrieve data from database tables in a Microsoft SQL Server database. When would you use an asterisk in the SELECT clause? When is the FROM clause required? When is the WHERE clause required? When are neither FROM nor WHERE needed with the SELECT statement?

3. You are designing a database application that will be used to enter, retrieve, and update data in the database. You want to minimize the user's understanding of table structure, including column names and data types. In addition, many operations require calculations based on dates stored in database tables and the number of months or days between selected dates. Should you rely on interactive or embedded SQL? Why? When performing calculations, how can you ensure that operators are processed in the order you want? In this specific example, why should you choose a DBMS that extends the basic SQL language standard as your database platform?

YOU TRY IT

Using Standard SQL

You are providing command specifications for a database application. The specific DBMS product has not been chosen, so, for the initial draft you are using sample commands and functions using SQL standard syntax.

1. Why should you avoid the use of the DEFAULT VALUES keyword with draft application version INSERT commands?
2. When adding records to a table, what are the conditions under which you are NOT required to provide a value for a table column?
3. You want to create a table named Ops.Quick Check. You are not defining a primary key or any constraints at this time. The column names and data types are listed below. What statement would you run?

Validation	char(4)
EnterBy	int
CheckBy	int
Status	varchar(20)

4. You decide you may need to periodically delete and recreate Ops.QuickCheck. How would you remove the table from the database?

Data Modification Language

You are writing command statements based on the table shown in Figure 6-6, as well as other tables in the General Hardware Company database. Use standard SQL syntax for the commands unless otherwise specified.

1. If this is the full table contents and you run a SELECT statement with a select list and no WHERE clause, how many rows will it return? Explain your answer.
2. Assume that PRODNUM values are generated automatically. Write statements to add the following:

PRODNAME	UNITPRICE
Bit	1.47
Torch	211.44

Figure 6-6

(d) PRODUCT table		
PRODNUM	PRODNAME	UNITPRICE
16386	Wrench	12.95
19440	Hammer	17.50
21765	Drill	32.99
24013	Saw	26.25
26722	Pilers	11.50

PRODUCTS table.

3. You want to change the price of the hammer listed in Figure 6-6 to 18.01. Show two ways you could do this.
4. Assuming that Figure 6-6 is a partial list of the table contents, what would you run to delete all hammers from the table?

Using SQL Server

You are creating a database application that will use Microsoft SQL Server as its DBMS. You are developing command statements that will be used as embeded SQL in the application.

1. The ORDER table includes the Quantity and Price columns. You need to find the total extended prices (Price times Quantity) for all items in the ORDER table. What should you run?
2. The DAILYRUN table has six columns, including an identity column. Each evening, you need to remove all rows from DAILYRUN and reset the identity to its seed value. What should you run?
3. The CALCS table has the columns ID, C1, C2, and C3. C1 and C2 accept NULL values. C2 and C3 have defined default values. You want to add a row to the column, assign a NULL value to C1 and C2, and accept the default for C3. What should you run?

222

7

DATA ACCESS AND MANIPULATION

Starting Point

Go to www.wiley.com/college/gillenson to assess your knowledge of SQL language use.
Determine where you need to concentrate your effort.

What You'll Learn in This Chapter

▲ SELECT statement keywords and clauses
▲ The use of joins and subqueries
▲ The fundamentals of writing batches and scripts

After Studying This Chapter, You'll Be Able To

▲ Use common SELECT statement keywords
▲ Design, write, and use queries to retrieve and organize data
▲ Design, write, and use queries that group data and calculate values using aggregate functions
▲ Design, write, and use queries that join two or more tables
▲ Design, write, and use queries that use nested subqueries to retrieve data
▲ Given data requirements, choose either a join or subquery as the best data retrieval solution
▲ Design, write, and execute batches and scripts
▲ Use variables in batch execution
▲ Control batch execution based on Boolean expressions

INTRODUCTION

The primary reason for designing and deploying a database is to support a business. A production database provides support for day-to-day business activities. A decision support database provides the information needed to make strategic business decisions. With both types of databases, a large percentage of the activity is related to retrieving data. Because of this, it is important to have a good understanding of what you can do with the SELECT statement, keeping in mind that the features available to you will depend on the DBMS you select for your database solution. It also helps to understand the role that batches and scripts can play in automating recurring procedures.

7.1 Using SELECT Statement Advanced Syntax

The SELECT statement is one of the major workhorse statements of the SQL language. It is the primary statement for data retrieval, but that simple statement falls short of describing its full capabilities. The clauses available with the SELECT statement let you specify the precise information retrieved from database tables, how it is sorted and organized, and even how information is grouped to return summary information.

In its most basic form for retrieving data, the SELECT statement uses the following syntax:

```
SELECT column_list FROM source WITH search_conditions
```

The column_list specifies the columns (fields) you want to return and can include calculated values. Use an asterisk (*) as the column_list to have the statement return all columns from a table. The source can include tables, views, and table-valued **user-defined functions,** which are special functions supported by some DBMSs that you can design and create to meet specific data retrieval needs. The optional search_condition is used to filter the result so that you only get the rows (records) that you actually want in your result.

This, however, is just the starting point for the SELECT statement. In order to learn more about its features and functionality, you need to see more of the statement syntax.

7.1.1 Understanding SELECT Statement Syntax

Let's take a more complete look at the SELECT statement syntax. When you get into advanced keywords and options, the available functionality becomes somewhat DBMS-specific. For our examples, we're using the SELECT statement as implemented in Microsoft SQL Server 2005.

```
SELECT column_list [ALL | DISTINCT]
[TOP expression [PERCENT] [WITH TIES]]
[INTO table_name]
FROM source [[INNER|OUTER|CROSS] JOIN]
WHERE search_condition
[ORDER BY order_expression [ASC] | [DESC]]
[GROUP BY [ALL] group_expression]
[HAVING search_condition]
```

This is still not the complete SELECT statement syntax. There are some features and functionality supported by the SELECT statement that are beyond the scope of this text. A discussion of some of the remaining keywords and options, at this point, might do more to confuse than to enlighten.

Because of this, you might see uses of the SELECT statement that include keywords not presented here, such as the FOR XML clause that is used to return database table data formatted as an **XML document fragment,** a portion of an XML document containing data organized in a hierarchical fashion. Refer to the Books Online that install with SQL Server and the Microsoft Developer Network (MSDN) Web site for more complete information on advanced SELECT statement syntax (in SQL Server) and keywords not covered as part of this text.

Table 7-1 has a brief explanation of the additional keywords introduced here. You will get a chance to see these keywords used in this chapter.

Table 7-1: SELECT Statement Keywords

Keyword	Description
ALL	Default option, specifying that all results, including duplicate rows, are returned.
DISTINCT	Limits result set to distinct (non-duplicate) rows only.
TOP	Used to limit the result set to a set number or percentage of the rows returned.
INTO	Create the table specified as table_name based on the result.
JOIN	Combines two or more data sources in a single statement based on the values in specific joining columns.
ORDER BY	Sets the order in which rows are returned.
GROUP BY	Used to group rows by column value for generation of aggregate value results.
HAVING	Used with the GROUP BY statement to filter the result.

The easiest way to understand how these keywords work is to see them in use. For this purpose, we'll use a database based on the fictitious General Hardware Company business. Figure 7-1 is a SQL Server database diagram of General Hardware showing you the tables contained in the database.

The key icon identifies each table's primary key. The links between tables identify foreign key relationships established between the tables. These relationships are used to maintain relational integrity between the tables. If you want to retrieve data based on these relationships, you must use joining statements, which are statements that combine results from multiple tables.

7.1.2 Filtering Your Result

Let's start with options for filtering your result. You can use the comparison operators =, >, >=, <, <=, and both <> and != for "not equal to" for simple filtering. If you need to combine conditions, use the AND and OR operators:

▲ **AND:** the search condition is satisfied if both conditions are satisfied.

▲ **OR:** the search condition is satisfied if either condition is satisfied.

Using AND and OR

When using both AND and OR, AND is evaluated first. You may need to use parentheses to control operator precedence or to leave no question about how a query is evaluated. For example, the following query uses parentheses, even though operators are evaluated in default order:

```
SELECT CUSTNUM, CUSTNAME FROM CUSTOMER
WHERE HQCITY='New York' OR
(CUSTNUM>1500 AND HQCITY='Atlanta')
```

This query captures customers with an HQCITY value of New York, as well as those who meet both of the remaining conditions, CUSTNUM over 1500 and an HQCITY of Atlanta. This results in:

CUSTNUM	CUSTNAME
0121	Main St. Hardware
1525	Fred's Tool Stores
1826	City Hardware
2198	Western Hardware
2267	Central Stores

If you want the OR operator evaluated first, you would use the following query:

```
SELECT CUSTNUM, CUSTNAME FROM CUSTOMER
WHERE (HQCITY='New York' OR CUSTNUM>1500) AND
HQCITY='Atlanta'
```

Figure 7-1

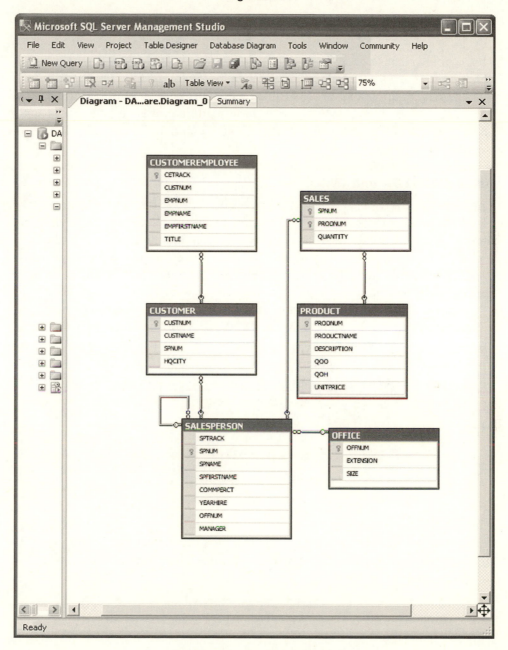

General Hardware Company.

The result changes significantly. In this case, only one row qualifies:

```
CUSTNUM              CUSTNAME
1525                 Fred's Tool Stores
```

This would mean that, with the AND outside of the parentheses, both of two conditions have to be met for a row to qualify for the results. One condition is that the headquarters city is New York or the customer number is greater than 1500. The other condition is that the headquarters city is Atlanta. Since for a given row the headquarters city can't be both Atlanta and New York, the result is extremely limited.

Using BETWEEN and IN

Another way to filter results is to use the BETWEEN and IN keywords. BETWEEN filters values in a range. You might use BETWEEN to retrieve recent orders by order number or to retrieve records from a table by date. Say that you include a date and time stamp when you enter new customer records. You could then, for example, use BETWEEN to find all customer records added between 1990 and 1999.

Suppose that you want to find the customer records for those customers whose customer numbers are between 1000 and 1700, inclusive (meaning that both 1000 and 1700, as well as all numbers in between, are included). Rather than using the AND operator, you could use BETWEEN, as in the following:

```
SELECT CUSTNUM, CUSTNAME FROM CUSTOMER
WHERE CUSTNUM BETWEEN 1000 AND 1700
```

The qualifying records are:

```
CUSTNUM              CUSTNAME
1047                 Acme Hardware Store
1525                 Fred's Tool Stores
1700                 XYZ Stores
```

Suppose that you want to find the customer records for those customers headquartered in Atlanta, Chicago, or Washington. Rather than using the OR operator, you can use the IN keyword with a list of qualifying values, as in the following query:

```
SELECT CUSTNUM, HQCITY FROM CUSTOMER
WHERE HQCITY IN ('Atlanta', 'Chicago', Washington')
```

This returns:

```
CUSTNUM              CUSTNAME
0839                 Chicago
1525                 Atlanta
1700                 Washington
```

Using LIKE

You get even more flexibility when you use the LIKE operator and its supported wildcard characters for pattern matching, so you can filter by results that match any string of characters (%), any single character (__), characters in a range or set ([]), or that don't match a specific character ([^]). Common uses of the LIKE keyword are to retrieve customers by name or geographically by the first few numbers in the customer's ZIP code. For example, you could look for all customers with a name beginning with the letter *C* using:

```
SELECT * FROM CUSTOMER WHERE CUSTNAME LIKE 'C%'
```

Or, you can reverse the logic and return those customers whose names don't begin with the letter *C*.:

```
SELECT * FROM CUSTOMER WHERE CUSTNAME LIKE '[^C]%'
```

You can combine the wildcard characters in different ways to give you control over the result. For example, consider this query:

```
SELECT CUSTNAME FROM CUSTOMER
WHERE CUSTNAME LIKE 'C_t%'
```

What will this return? You'll get customer names that have the first letter *C*, any character (including a space) in the second character position, the letter *t*, and then any other character string. The result would be:

```
CUSTNAME
City Hardware
```

When stringing together different operators and keywords to filter your result, be careful that you don't limit yourself to the point where you have conflicting criteria so that no records would ever be able to qualify. Keep the filtering logic in your search conditions as simple as possible. It will be easier to read and understand, and often will require less overhead to process.

7.1.3 Managing Your Result Set

One of the main ways you manage your result set is through the column list. You can include columns from source tables, views, and functions, computed values as computed columns, and values returned by aggregate functions. You can specify a column name as part to column list, as well. For example, suppose you want to know how much the PRODUCT inventory is worth. To find out, you might run a statement like the following:

```
SELECT PRODNUM, (QOH * UNITPRICE) AS [VALUE]
FROM PRODUCT
```

This gives you the following result:

PRODNUM	VALUE
16386	647.50
19440	175.00
19441	337.40
21765	329.90
21766	491.35
24013	367.50
26722	34.50

This gives you the calculated value based on the quantity on hand times the unit price. The resulting column is named VALUE, as specified in the query.

To limit this to returning just the first three rows, you could run the following:

```
SELECT TOP 3 PRODNUM, (QOH * UNITPRICE) AS [VALUE]
FROM PRODUCT
```

Limiting the returned rows usually makes more sense if you are also ordering the result. You'll learn how to do that a little later in this chapter.

What if you want a more permanent record of the result? You can use the INTO keyword to write the result to a table. For example:

```
SELECT PRODNUM, (QOH * UNITPRICE) AS [VALUE]
INTO PRODVAL FROM PRODUCT
```

This creates the table PRODVAL in the default database (GeneralHardware). The table has two columns, PRODNUM and VALUE, and the results you saw earlier as the table rows. When using INTO, the destination table cannot already exist. If you attempted to run the same statement again, you'd get the following error:

```
Msg 2714, Level 16, State 6, Line 1
There is already an object named 'PRODVAL' in the
database.
```

Keep in mind that error text and error message numbers are DBMS-specific. This is the error that you would see using SQL Server 2005 if you specify a table name that already exists. If you do want to recreate the same table, you must drop the table before running the query.

Next, let's take a quick look at the DISTINCT keyword. Suppose you want to find out which salespersons currently have one or more customers assigned. To do so, you might run a statement like the following:

```
SELECT SPNUM FROM CUSTOMER
```

Using the data in our sample database, the result you get is:

```
SPNUM
137
186
137
137
361
361
137
204
186
```

Notice that most of the salesperson numbers are listed more than once in the result. Supposed you don't need to know how many times the salesperson is listed, but whether or not the number appears in the list. To limit the result to unique values, you would run the query as:

```
SELECT DISTINCT SPNUM FROM CUSTOMER
```

This time, you only get four rows back. Here's the result:

```
SPNUM
137
186
204
361
```

As you can see in this example, use the DISTINCT keyword when you want to specifically limit the result to unique values only.

Here's a slightly different pair of examples:

```
SELECT SPNUM, HQCITY FROM CUSTOMER
SELECT DISTINCT SPNUM, HQCITY FROM CUSTOMER
```

Now, let's compare the results side-by-side in Table 7-2.

The entire result must be duplicated for the row to be dropped. In this case, it means the combination of SPNUM and HQCITY. This time, only two duplicates are removed from the list: one for SPNUM 137 and New York and the other for 137 and Los Angeles. The rest are all unique.

7.1.4 Sorting, Organizing, and Grouping Data

As mentioned earlier, when using the TOP keyword, it's likely that you want to retrieve records in a particular order. By default, rows are returned in **table order**, that is, the order in which the records are stored. If the table has a clustered index, table order is the same as that index order. If not, then table order is usually the order in which the rows are added to the table.

Sorting Data with ORDER BY

Here's an example of a situation where you would want rows returned in a specific order:

Table 7-2: Comparing Results

Without DISTINCT		With DISTINCT	
SPNUM	HQCITY	SPNUM	HQCITY
361	Atlanta	361	Atlanta
186	Chicago	186	Chicago
137	Los Angeles	137	Los Angeles
137	Los Angeles	137	New York
137	New York	186	New York
137	New York	204	New York
186	New York	361	Washington
204	New York		
361	Washington		

List the highest-cost products, based on UNITPRICE.

One way to get this information would be:

```
SELECT PRODNUM, PRODNAME, UNITPRICE
FROM PRODUCT
```

This gives you the following result:

```
PRODNUM            PRODUCTNAME            UNITPRICE
16386              Wrench                 12.95
19440              Hammer                 17.50
19441              Hammer                 24.10
21765              Drill                  32.99
21766              Drill                  98.27
24013              Saw                    26.25
26722              Pliers                 11.50
```

However, it's easier to see the highest cost products if you list them that way, using a query like:

```
SELECT PRODNUM, PRODNAME, UNITPRICE
FROM PRODUCT ORDER BY UNITPRICE DESC
```

The result now is:

```
PRODNUM            PRODUCTNAME            UNITPRICE
21766              Drill                  98.27
21765              Drill                  32.99
```

```
24013            Saw              26.25
19441            Hammer           24.10
19440            Hammer           17.50
16386            Wrench           12.95
26722            Pliers           11.50
```

You must include the DESC keyword to sort the results in descending order (from highest to lowest). The default is to sort the result in ascending order. You can also use the ASC keyword to explicitly specify an ascending order sort.

What if you only want the top three items? This is where you would use the TOP keyword, as in the following:

```
SELECT TOP 3 PRODNUM, PRODNAME, UNITPRICE
FROM PRODUCT ORDER BY UNITPRICE DESC
```

The result is still in the same order, but is limited to the first three rows only.

```
PRODNUM          PRODUCTNAME      UNITPRICE
21766            Drill            98.27
21765            Drill            32.99
24013            Saw              26.25
```

You can specify multiple columns in the ORDER BY clause. The result is sorted by all of the columns, with the first columns listed having the highest precedence. For example, you might want to do the following:

List the contents of the sales table sorted by PRODNUM. When there are multiple rows with the same PRODNUM value, sort them by SPNUM.

The query for this might be:

```
SELECT * FROM SALES
ORDER BY PRODNUM, SPNUM
```

This gives you the following result:

```
SPNUM            PRODNUM          QUANTITY
186              16386            1745
361              16386            3729
137              19440             473
186              19440            2529
186              21765            1962
204              21765             809
361              21765            3110
137              24013             170
186              24013            3071
137              26722             688
204              26722             734
361              26722            2738
```

If you change column order in the ORDER BY clause, the result also changes significantly. For example, the query:

```
SELECT * FROM SALES
ORDER BY SPNUM, PRODNUM
```

gives you the following result:

SPNUM	PRODNUM	QUANTITY
137	19440	473
137	24013	170
137	26722	688
186	16386	1745
186	19440	2529
186	21765	1962
186	24013	3071
204	21765	809
204	26722	734
361	16386	3729
361	21765	3110
361	26722	2738

The query still returns the same rows, but returns them in a different order.

It's important to note that the column or columns used in the ORDER BY list don't necessarily have to be part of the SELECT clause column list. For example, the following query would run without generating an error:

```
SELECT PRODNUM, PRODUCTNAME FROM PRODUCT
WHERE QOO =0 ORDER BY QOH
```

Let's break down exactly what this is requesting. The query should return the PRODNUM and PRODUCTNAME columns, limited to those columns in which the QOO (quantity on order) column has a value of 0. Sort the result in ascending order by the value in the QOH (quantity on hand) column. This gives you the following result:

PRODNUM	PRODUCTNAME
26722	Pliers
21765	Drill
24013	Saw
19441	Hammer
16386	Wrench

Notice in the SELECT statement that neither QOO or QOH is included in the SELECT column list.

Organizing Data with GROUP BY

In addition to ordering the result, you can also group the rows in the result. Many situations require calculations on several different groups of rows using the GROUP BY clause. For instance, suppose you wanted to find the total number of units of all products that each salesperson has sold. That is, you want to group together the rows of the SALES table that belong to each salesperson and calculate a value—the sum of the Quantity attribute values in this case—for each such group. Here is the way such a query might be stated:

Find the total number of units of all products sold by each salesperson.

The SQL statement, using the GROUP BY clause, would look like this:

```
SELECT SPNUM, SUM(QUANTITY) AS [SUM]
FROM SALES GROUP BY SPNUM
```

This query produces the following result:

SPNUM	SUM
137	1331
186	9307
204	1543
361	9577

Notice that GROUP BY SPNUM specifies that the rows of the table are to be grouped together based on having the same value in their SPNUM attribute. All of the rows for Salesperson Number 137 will form one group, all of the rows for Salesperson Number 186 will form another group, and so on. The Quantity attribute values in each group will then be summed—SUM(QUANTITY)— and the results returned to the user. But it is not enough to provide a list of sums:

```
1331
9307
1543
9577
```

These are the sums of the quantities for each salesperson, but because they don't identify which salesperson goes with which sum, they are meaningless! That's why the SELECT clause includes both SPNUM and SUM(QUANTITY). Including the attribute(s) specified in the GROUP BY clause in the SELECT clause allows you to properly identify the sums calculated for each group. A SQL statement with a GROUP BY clause may also include a WHERE clause. Thus the query

Find the total number of units of all products sold by each salesperson whose salesperson number is at least 150.

would look like:

```
SELECT SPNUM, SUM(QUANTITY) AS [SUM]
FROM SALES WHERE SPNUM> =150 GROUP BY SPNUM
```

The results would be:

SPNUM	SUM
186	9307
204	1543
361	9577

In addition to the SUM aggregate function, you could use GROUP BY with other aggregate functions such as AVG and COUNT. You cannot, however, use one function to evaluate the result of another function. Consider the following query:

Find the average number of units of all products sold by each salesperson.

You might want to use a query like the following:

```
SELECT SPNUM, AVG(SUM(QUANTITY)) AS [AVG]
FROM SALES GROUP BY SPNUM
```

However, this query returns the error:

```
Msg 130, Level 15, State 1, Line 1
Cannot perform an aggregate function on an expression
containing an aggregate or a subquery.
```

Combining GROUP BY, ORDER BY, and HAVING

When using GROUP BY, you are limited as to what you can include in the SELECT clause column list. All columns must either be aggregate values or be called out in the GROUP BY clause. Using the GROUP BY clause also puts an additional limit on the ORDER BY clause. When using ORDER BY with GROUP BY, the ORDER BY list is limited to either aggregates or columns included in the GROUP BY clause. The following would be a valid query:

```
SELECT SPNUM, SUM(QUANTITY) AS [SUM]
FROM SALES GROUP BY SPNUM ORDER BY SPUM
```

Or you could run:

```
SELECT SPNUM, SUM(QUANTITY) AS [SUM]
FROM SALES GROUP BY SPNUM ORDER BY SUM(QUANTITY)
```

Sometimes there is a need to limit the results of a GROUP BY based on the values calculated for each group using built-in functions. For example, take the following query:

Find the total number of units of all products sold by each salesperson whose salesperson number is at least 150.

You could modify it with an additional sentence so that it reads:

Find the total number of units of all products sold by each salesperson whose salesperson number is at least 150. Only include salespersons whose total number of units sold is at least 5000.

The query can accomplish this by adding a HAVING clause to the end of the SELECT statement, as follows:

```
SELECT SPNUM, SUM(QUANTITY) AS [SUM]
FROM SALES WHERE SPNUM>=150 GROUP BY SPNUM
HAVING SUM(QUANTITY)>=5000
```

This gives you the following result:

SPNUM	SUM
186	9307
361	9577

Salesperson Number 204, whose total is only 1543 units sold, is dropped from the results.

Notice that in this last SELECT statement, there are two limits specified. One limit, that the Salesperson Number must be at least 150, appears in the WHERE clause as filter logic. The other limit, that the sum of the number of units sold must be at least 5000, appears in the HAVING clause. It is important to understand why this is so. If the limit is based on individual attribute values that appear in the database, then the condition goes in the WHERE clause, in this example, the Salesperson Number value. If the limit is based on the group calculation performed with a built-in function, then the condition goes in the HAVING clause. In our example, this is the case with the sum of the number of product units sold.

In queries like the one used here, the order in which keywords appear in the statement is also critical. HAVING can be used only with the GROUP BY clause. The GROUP BY clause must always precede HAVING. You have the same restriction when using both GROUP BY and ORDER BY. The GROUP BY clause must always come before the ORDER BY clause.

7.1.5 Understanding Operator Precedence

Before going much further, we need to take a moment to talk about operator precedence. Expressions used in SELECT statements and filtering expressions can become quite complex. You have some control over precedence through the use of parentheses, but it may help to see commonly used operators, ranked by precedence. Table 7-3 lists operators from highest to lowest precedence. Operators at the same precedence level are evaluated from left to right. When the same symbol is used for two operations (for example the + symbol, or the = symbol), the type of operation that is being performed can be determined by the context in which the symbol is used.

This list is for operators implementing in SQL Server's Transact-SQL language. The term bitwise operator might be one you have not previously encountered. **Bitwise operations** are performed at the binary (bit-by-bit) level. The precedence can vary by DBMS implementation.

Table 7-3: Operator Precedence

Level	Operators
1	~ (bitwise not, invert bit values)
2	* (multiplication)
	/ (division)
	% (modulo division)
3	+ (set numeric to positive)
	− (negate numeric value)
	+ (add)
	− (subtract)
	+ (concatenate)
	& (bitwise AND comparison)
4	= (equality comparison)
	> (greater than comparison)
	< (less than comparison)
	>= (greater than or equal to comparison)
	<= (less than or equal to comparison)
	<> (or !=) (not equal to comparison)
	!> (not greater than)
	!< (not less than)
5	^ (bitwise exclusive OR comparison)
	| (bitwise OR comparison)
6	NOT (negate logical value)
7	AND (logical AND comparison)
8	ALL (compare all values in a set)
	ANY (compare for any value instance in a set)
	BETWEEN (test for value in a range)
	IN (test for value instance in a set)
	LIKE (compare similar values based on literal text and wildcards)
	SOME (test for one or more instance occurrences in a set)
9	= (assign value)

7.1.6 Combining Statement Results

You can combine the results from different SELECT statements using the UNION, EXCEPT, and INTERSECT keywords. In each case, both SELECT statements you are trying to combine must have:

▲ The same number of columns.

▲ Columns in the same order.

▲ Columns with compatible (but not necessarily the same) data types.

The UNION operator combines the results of two queries into one. The final result is a list of unique rows unless you also include the ALL keyword, with the syntax UNION ALL. UNION ALL returns all rows, including duplicate rows.

First, let's look at a sample query:

```
SELECT HQCITY FROM CUSTOMER WHERE SPNUM = 137
```

This gives you the following result:

```
HQCITY
New York
Los Angeles
Los Angeles
New York
```

The next query is:

```
SELECT HQCITY FROM CUSTOMER WHERE SPNUM = 186
```

The result is:

```
HQCITY
Chicago
New York
```

Finally, combining the two with UNION, as in:

```
SELECT HQCITY FROM CUSTOMER WHERE SPNUM = 137
UNION
SELECT HQCITY FROM CUSTOMER WHERE SPNUM = 186
```

gives you, as a final result:

```
HQCITY
Chicago
Los Angeles
New York
```

As you can see, the result lists all three unique cities, listing each one only once.

The EXCEPT keyword returns results in the first query that do not appear in the second. In this case, we're going to use a different second query to get some different values for comparison. This time, the query is:

```
SELECT HQCITY FROM CUSTOMER WHERE SPNUM = 186
```

The result is:

```
                    HQCITY
                    Chicago
                    New York
```

Now combine the two with the EXCEPT keyword:

```
SELECT HQCITY FROM CUSTOMER WHERE SPNUM = 137
EXCEPT
SELECT HQCITY FROM CUSTOMER WHERE SPNUM = 186
```

The result is:

```
                    HQCITY
                    Los Angeles
```

This is because the second query returned Chicago and New York. New York was returned by both queries, and therefore is excluded when you combine the queries with EXCEPT. You get the opposite result when you use the INTERSECT keyword. It returns the values that appear in both queries. For example:

```
SELECT HQCITY FROM CUSTOMER WHERE SPNUM = 137
INTERSECT
SELECT HQCITY FROM CUSTOMER WHERE SPNUM = 186
```

gives you the following result:

```
                    HQCITY
                    New York
```

This is because New York is the only city that was included in the result set of both queries.

7.1.7 Using SELECT with Other Commands

You can also use SELECT as the value source with other statements. To see this, we'll use a couple of examples using the INSERT and UPDATE statements.

You can use a SELECT statement to replace the values clause when using INSERT. For example, suppose you have a table named EmpCopy with three columns: EmployeeNumber, FirstName, and LastName. You want to use values from SALESPERSON as your source. You might use a statement like the following:

```
INSERT EmpCopy SELECT SPNUM, SPNAME, SPFIRSTNAME
FROM SALESPERSON
```

In this example, SELECT is used as a clause of the INSERT statement. Notice that you do not enclose the SELECT clause in parentheses in this statement. The only result returned by the command is a message specifying how many rows are inserted by the operation.

You can also use SELECT in situations where a scalar input value is expected. Consider the following:

Restructure the salesperson commission program as an interim measure while the new program is finalized. Reset everyone's commission to an average of all current commissions.

FOR EXAMPLE

Combining Keywords

One of the real strengths of the SELECT queries lies in what you can do by combining keywords in different ways to get the exact results that you want. GROUP BY, for example, is useful in generating all types of summary result reports. For example, you might want to generate a report that provides a daily sales report by salesperson over a month. You would use the GROUP BY clause with two grouping conditions, grouping first by day and then by salesperson. Suppose you have an ORDER_HEAD table from which you can get this information. You might use:

```
SELECT SPNUM, SPNAME, SUM(ORDER_TOT)
FROM ORDER_HEAD
GROUP BY DAY_DATE, SPNUM, SPNAME
```

This would return a result grouped first by day, and then within that group, by salesperson. The SPNUM and SPNAME groupings are identical. The reason you need to have both in the GROUP BY clause is so that you can have both in the SELECT list. Otherwise, either one could be used by itself to define the grouping. This particular query, however, might not give you the information in the format in which you need it. It would probably be easier to review the result if you return the result in SPNUM order, by adding an ORDER BY clause, as in:

```
SELECT SPNUM, SPNAME, SUM(ORDER_TOT)
FROM ORDER_HEAD
GROUP BY DAY_DATE, SPNUM, SPNAME
ORDER BY SPNUM
```

In this situation, you couldn't order the result by SPNAME. Why not? Because it isn't an aggregate and it doesn't appear in the GROUP BY clause. If you wanted, to sort by SPNAME, you might change the query to read:

```
SELECT SPNUM, SPNAME, SUM(ORDER_TOT)
FROM ORDER_HEAD
GROUP BY DAY_DATE, SPNAME, SPNUM
ORDER BY SPNAME
```

The statement needed to do this is actually rather simple.

```
UPDATE SALESPERSON SET COMMPERCT =
(SELECT AVG(COMMPERCT) FROM SALESPERSON)
```

The result only tells you how many rows are updated. To see the effect of the change, you would need to retrieve the row data from the SALESPERSON table and be sure and include the COMMPERCT column.

SELF-CHECK

- Describe the purpose of the TOP, DISTINCT, GROUP BY, ORDER BY, and HAVING keywords.
- Describe the limits on the ORDER BY clause when used with the GROUP BY clause.
- Compare and contrast the use of UNION, EXCEPT, and INTERSECT.

7.2 Using Joins and Subqueries

More advanced queries are possible using joins and subqueries. A **join** is a query that combines columns from two or more sources. Effectively, you are reversing the non-loss decomposition process used to normalize the database, pulling the related data back together in a combined result. Technically, you can only join two sources, such as two tables. When you need to join more sources, you do it in twos. You join two tables, then join that result to a third table, and so on. A **subquery** is another variation that uses multiple SELECT statements in a single query. A subquery is a nested query, and can include several layers of nestings, with the innermost query executed first.

A complete discussion of joins and subqueries is beyond the scope of this text. Instead of trying to make you a query expert, the goal is to introduce you to their use. This will give you the tools you need to meet the vast majority of your data recovery needs.

7.2.1 Understanding Joins

Up to this point, all of the SELECT features that we have looked at have been shown in the context of retrieving data from a single table. The time has come to look at how the SELECT command combines (joins) columns from two or more tables. To make a join work, two specifications must be made in the SELECT statement. The tables to be joined must be listed in the FROM clause and the join attributes in the tables being joined must be declared and matched to each other in the WHERE clause. Since two or more tables are involved in a join, the same column (field) name may appear in more than one of the tables. When this happens, the column names must be qualified with a table name when used in the SELECT statement. All of this is best illustrated by an example. Consider the following request:

Find the name of the salesperson responsible for Customer Number 1525.

A SELECT statement that will satisfy this query is:

```
SELECT SPNAME FROM SALESPERSON, CUSTOMER
WHERE SALESPERSON.SPNUM=CUSTOMER.SPNUM
AND CUSTNUM=1525
```

This returns, as you should expect, a single row:

```
SPNAME
Carlyle
```

In brief, the query uses filtering logic to limit the result to customer 1525 in the CUSTOMER table. The tables are joined on the SPNUM column to locate the correct salesperson name. We'll take a closer look at this in a moment.

It's common to use a **table alias**, where a different value is used to represent the table name, to reduce your typing when using joins. For example, you might rewrite the previous example as:

```
SELECT SPNAME FROM SALESPERSON s, CUSTOMER c
WHERE s.SPNUM=c.SPNUM AND CUSTNUM=1525
```

The result would be the same because you haven't made any changes to what the SELECT statement is doing. You've just changed how you identify the tables so you don't have to retype the full table name each time.

Let's break that SELECT statement down so that we can see exactly what's going on. Notice that the two tables involved in the join, SALESPERSON and CUSTOMER, are listed in the FROM clause. Also notice that the first line of the WHERE clause links the two join columns: SPNUM in the SALESPERSON table (SALESPERSON.SPNUM) and SPNUM in the CUSTOMER table (CUSTOMER.SPNUM).

```
SALESPERSON.SPNUM=CUSTOMER.SPNUM
```

The notational device of having the table name, then a period, and then the column name is known as qualifying the column name. This qualification is necessary when the same name is used in two or more tables in a SELECT statement, resulting in an ambiguous column reference. SPNAME and CUSTNUM don't have to be qualified because each appears in only one of the tables included in the SELECT statement, so there is no question as to which column you want.

Here is an example of a join involving three tables, assuming for the moment that salesperson names are unique:

List the names of the products of which salesperson Adams has sold more than 2,000 units.

The salesperson name data appears only in the SALESPERSON table, and the product name data appears only in the PRODUCT table. The SALES table shows the linkage between the two, including the quantities sold. And so the SELECT statement is:

```
SELECT PRODNAME FROM SALESPERSON, PRODUCT, SALES
WHERE SALESPERSON.SPNUM=SALES.SPNUM
AND SALES.PRODNUM=PRODUCT.PRODNUM
AND SPNAME='Adams' AND QUANTITY>2000
```

As described earlier, the SELECT statement joins two tables, SALESPERSON and SALES, then joins this result to a third table, PRODUCT. The result is:

```
PRODUCTNAME
Hammer
Saw
```

Both of these are examples of inner joins. In an **inner join,** only qualifying results are returned from the joined tables. There are two other types of joins you can run: outer joins and cross joins. An **outer join** returns qualifying rows from one table and all rows from the other (outer) table. A **cross join** returns all possible rows, whether or not they meet the qualifying join logic, in every possible combination. This is known as a **Cartesian product**. However, before we show these, we need to introduce a different join syntax.

7.2.2 Using Different Join Syntaxes

Let's look at a variation on our first join example.

```
SELECT SPNAME, CUSTNAME FROM SALESPERSON, CUSTOMER
WHERE SALESPERSON.SPNUM=CUSTOMER.SPNUM
```

This is an inner join. The result is limited to rows where the SPNUM meets the qualifying logic in both tables, giving you the following result:

```
SPNAME        CUSTNAME
Baker         Main St. Hardware
Adams         Jane's Stores
Baker         ABC Home Stores
Baker         Acme Hardware Store
Carlyle       Fred's Tool Stores
Carlyle       XYZ Stores
Baker         City Hardware
```

```
Dickens       Western Hardware
Adams         Central Stores
```

The syntax used here, though supported by many DBMSs (including SQL Server), is not the ANSI standard syntax for specifying a join. For that, you would need to run:

```
SELECT SPNAME, CUSTNAME
FROM SALESPERSON JOIN CUSTOMER
ON (SALESPERSON.SPNUM=CUSTOMER.SPNUM)
```

The JOIN keyword identifies the joined table with the joining logic going in the ON clause. You could have specified INNER JOIN instead of just JOIN, but the INNER keyword is assumed. If you wanted to include additional qualifying logic, you would add a WHERE clause and include the search argument there, such as:

```
SELECT SPNAME, CUSTNAME
FROM SALESPERSON JOIN CUSTOMER
ON (SALESPERSON.SPNUM=CUSTOMER.SPNUM)
WHERE SALESPERSON.SPNUM=1525
```

To turn our initial example into an outer join, you might write it as:

```
SELECT SPNAME, CUSTNAME
FROM SALESPERSON LEFT OUTER JOIN CUSTOMER
ON (SALESPERSON.SPNUM=CUSTOMER.SPNUM)
```

In this query, rows from the SALESPERSON table are returned whether or not they qualify. We know this because we specify a LEFT OUTER join. The LEFT is in reference to the join logic, and as you can see, the SALESPERSON table is on the left side of the equality operator. These are matched to NULL values for columns in the right (CUSTOMER) table. This SELECT statement returns:

```
SPNAME        CUSTNAME
Smith         NULL
Potter        NULL
Baker         Main St. Hardware
Baker         ABC Home Stores
Baker         Acme Hardware Store
Baker         City Hardware
Adams         Jane's Stores
Adams         Central Stores
Dickens       Western Hardware
Carlyle       Fred's Tool Stores
Carlyle       XYZ Stores
```

This returns two additional SPNAME values, Smith and Potter. These salespersons are not assigned any customers, so they are not included in the CUSTOMER table. If you ran this as a RIGHT OUTER JOIN, the difference is that unqualified rows in the RIGHT table (if any) would be returned by the query.

To return all rows and every possible column combination from both tables, use a cross join. In this case, you would write the SELECT statement as:

```
SELECT SPNAME, CUSTNAME FROM SALESPERSON CROSS JOIN
CUSTOMER
```

Notice that there is no qualifying logic when you run a cross join. Rather than qualifying the rows, you are returning all rows. Because the SALESPERSON table has 6 rows and the CUSTOMER table has 9 rows, this query's result set would return a total of 54 rows, every possible combination. Let's limit the result a bit so we can see this a little easier. We're going to limit our query to the first three customers and the first three salespersons. The query becomes:

```
SELECT SPNAME, CUSTNAME
FROM SALESPERSON CROSS JOIN CUSTOMER
WHERE SALESPERSON.SPNUM < 140 AND CUSTNUM < 1000
```

From what you just learned, you would expect the result to return nine rows, every combination of three customers with three salespersons. When you check the result, you find that to be true:

```
SPNAME           CUSTNAME
Smith            Main St. Hardware
Smith            Jane's Stores
Smith            ABC Home Stores
Potter           Main St. Hardware
Potter           Jane's Stores
Potter           ABC Home Stores
Baker            Main St. Hardware
Baker            Jane's Stores
Baker            ABC Home Stores
```

There are seldom many valid opportunities to use a cross join, especially in a production database, though it is sometimes used as part of your analysis in decision support databases.

7.2.3 Using Basic Subqueries

Subqueries, as mentioned earlier, are nested queries. This can occur through several levels of SELECT statements, with each successive SELECT statement contained in a pair of parentheses. We're going to limit ourselves to the easiest type of subquery to understand, where the nested (inner) query is used to retrieve a value that is passed up to the outer query and used as input to the SELECT statement. This is known as a **noncorrelated subquery,** because the inner query does not depend on the outer query.

There is another type of query, known as a **correlated subquery,** where the inner query depends on values passed to it by the outer query. This is a more advanced type of subquery and is beyond the scope of this chapter's discussion.

In a noncorrelated subquery, the nested query is used in the qualifying logic in the WHERE clause. When you have multiple layers of nesting, the execution rule is that the innermost SELECT statement is executed first, and its results are then provided as input to the SELECT statement at the next level up. This procedure can be used as an alternative to the join.

Consider the following query:

Find the name of the salesperson responsible for Customer Number 1525.

You've already seen how you can do this as a join. When you have the option of using either a join or a subquery, you should usually use the join because it typically requires fewer resources to resolve. However, let's look at resolving this as a subquery to illustrate how a subquery works.

If you methodically weave through the database tables to solve this query, you start at the CUSTOMER table, find the record for Customer Number 1525, and discover in that record that the salesperson responsible for this customer is Salesperson Number 361. You then take that information to the SALESPERSON table where you look up the record for Salesperson Number 361 and discover in it that the salesperson's name is Carlyle. Writing this as a subquery, you can build this logic into an SQL statement as:

```
SELECT SPNAME FROM SALESPERSON
WHERE SPNUM=
(SELECT SPNUM FROM CUSTOMER WHERE CUSTNUM=1525)*
```

Just as when you used a join to retrieve this information, the query returns a single row, as follows:

```
SPNAME
Carlyle
```

Let's break down this query statement and take a closer look at what it's doing. Because the innermost SELECT (the indented one), which constitutes the subquery, is considered first, the CUSTOMER table is queried first. The record for Customer Number 1525 is found and 361 is returned as the SPNUM result. How do you know that only one salesperson number will be found as the result of the query? Because CUSTNUM contains unique values, Customer Number 1525 can only appear in one record, and that one record only has room for one salesperson number! Moving along, Salesperson Number 361 is then fed to the outer SELECT statement, which, in effect, makes the main query, that is, the outer SELECT, look like:

```
SELECT SPNAME
FROM SALESPERSON
WHERE SPNUM=361
```

The result, as you already know from the previous result, is:

```
SPNAME
Carlyle
```

As already stated, the preferred method (when possible) is to use a join to retrieve data. However, this is not always possible. There is a very interesting circumstance in which a subquery is required. This situation is best explained with an example. Consider the following query:

Which salespersons with salesperson numbers greater than 200 have the lowest commission percentage of any such salesperson, with salespersons identified by salesperson number?

This appears to be a reasonable request, but turns out to be deceptively difficult to fill. This is because the query really has two very different parts to it. First, the system has to determine what the lowest commission percentage is for salespersons with a salesperson number greater than 200. Second, it has to see which of these salespersons is assigned that lowest percentage. It's really tempting to try to satisfy this type of query with an SQL SELECT statement like:

```
SELECT SPNUM, MIN(COMMPERCT)
FROM SALESPERSON WHERE SPNUM>200
```

Another possibility you might consider is:

```
SELECT SPNUM FROM SALESPERSON
WHERE SPNUM>200 AND COMMPERCT=MIN(COMMPERCT)
```

The problem is that neither of these will give you the result you want. It's like asking SQL to perform two separate operations and somehow apply one to the other in the correct sequence. This turns out to be asking too much. But there is a way to accomplish the query, and it involves subqueries. You need to ask the system to determine the minimum commission percentage first, in a subquery, and then use that information in the main query to determine which salespersons have that value in the COMMPERCT column:

```
SELECT SPNUM FROM SALESPERSON
WHERE SPNUM>200 AND COMMPERCT=
(SELECT MIN(COMMPERCT)
FROM SALESPERSON WHERE SPNUM>200)
```

This gives you the result:

```
SPNUM
204
```

FOR EXAMPLE

Practical Joins

Most database applications make extensive use of joins. In fact, the closer you come to the 3NF goal, the greater the need for joins when retrieving data. Sometimes, joins can become quite complicated. Consider this situation. You structure customer orders so that they use two tables, ORDER_HEAD and ORDER_DETAIL. When you print a copy of the order for the customer, you want it to include the order number, customer name, the employee who wrote the order, the date, and the detail line items with descriptions. In a properly normalized database, you won't store the customer or employee names in the ORDER_HEAD table, just the identifying values so you can retrieve the information from the appropriate related tables.

Internally, your application would use a SELECT statement to retrieve the data. Actually, it would probably use two SELECT statements: one to retrieve the header information and a second to get the detail line times. In the application, you would probably use a replaceable parameter for the order number, so we'll do the same in our example. If you use @ordnum for the order number, the first SELECT statement might look like:

```
SELECT C.COMPANYNAME, E.FIRSTNAME + ' ' + E.LASTNAME,
O.ORDERNUM, O.ORDERDATE
FROM ORDER_HEAD O, CUSTOMER C, EMPLOYEE E
WHERE C.CUSTID = O.CUSTID AND E.EMPID = O.EMPID
AND
O.ORDERNUMBER = @ORDNUM
```

In this statement, you join the ORDER_HEAD table to the CUSTOMER table on CustID and then join the result to EMPLOYEE on EmpID.

Now, to get the detail line item information, you might use:

```
SELECT D.ITEMNUM, P.DESCRIPTION, D.QUANTITY,
D.SELLPRICE, (D.QUANTITY*D.SELLPRICE)
FROM ORDER_DETAIL D, PRODUCT P
WHERE P.PRODUCTID = D.SKUNUM AND D.ORDERNUM = @ORDNUM
```

There are a couple of additional things you should notice about these statements. In each case, the joining column is not part of the result set. It's used to retrieve the result, but doesn't need to appear anywhere in the result. Also, in the second query, notice that the linking column has different names in the ORDER_DETAIL and PRODUCT tables. The columns don't have to have the same names, just contain the same data. Also, as a final note, you will typically use all of the join columns as index key columns in the source tables if performance during data retrieval is a concern.

The minimum commission percentage across all of the salespersons with salesperson numbers greater than 200 is determined first in the subquery and the result is 10. The main query, then, in effect looks like:

```
SELECT SPNUM FROM SALESPERSON
WHERE SPNUM>200 AND COMMPERCT=10
```

This yields the result of salesperson number 204. Actually, this is a very interesting example of a required subquery. What makes it really interesting is why the predicate, SPNUM>200, appears in both the main query and the subquery. Clearly it has to be in the subquery because you must first find the lowest commission percentage among the salespersons with salesperson numbers greater than 200. But then why does it have to be in the main query, too? The answer is that the only thing that the subquery returns to the main query is a single number, specifically a commission percentage. There is no memory passed on to the main query of how the subquery arrived at that value. If you remove SPNUM>200 from the main query so that it now looks like:

```
SELECT SPNUM FROM SALESPERSON
WHERE COMMPERCT=
(SELECT MIN(COMMPERCT) FROM SALESPERSON)
WHERE SPNUM>200)
```

this query returns every salesperson (without regard for salesperson number) whose commission percentage is equal to the lowest commission percentage of the salespersons with salesperson numbers greater than 200. Of course, if for some reason you do want to find all of the salespersons, regardless of their salesperson number, who have the same commission percentage as the salesperson who has the lowest commission percentage of the salespersons with salesperson numbers greater than 200, then this last SELECT statement is exactly what you should write.

SELF-CHECK

- Compare and contrast joins and subqueries.
- Explain why it is typically preferred to use a join instead of a subquery when either will work.
- Describe the three basic join types.

7.3 Using Batches and Scripts

You can probably already think of several situations where you will need to periodically run the same statements exactly the same way. One way of automating this is to use batches and scripts. A batch is a set of SQL commands that run as a group. A script is one or more batches saved as a file.

Scripts are a commonly used tool for automating periodic procedures. For example, you might have a script you run each month that uses current sales information to recalculate stocking levels and order points. A video rental company could use a script to send remainder emails to customers who have overdue videos. One drawback is the fact that scripts don't give you a way to pass parameters when the script runs, so you can't control execution through replaceable parameters. Because of this, scripts are well suited to situations where you need to run multiple steps the same way each time.

7.3.1 Writing Batches and Scripts

A batch is simply a set of statements that you want to execute and can include one or more statements. For example, the following is a batch:

```
SELECT * INTO ECOPY FROM EMPLOYEES
```

This following is also a batch, but this time a multi-statement batch:

```
SELECT * INTO ECOPY FROM EMPLOYEES
SELECT * FROM ECOPY
```

You can write a batch ad hoc in a query window or using any text editor, such as Windows Notepad. When you save the batch to an operating system file, it becomes a script. When saving a script for SQL Server, you should use the extension.sql so that SQL Server will recognize it as a script file. Because the dividing line between the two is so fine, the terms batch and script are often used interchangeably.

A script can contain multiple batches. In SQL Server, the keyword GO is used to identify when one batch ends and the next one starts. For example:

```
USE GENERALHARDWARE
GO
SELECT * INTO #SALESTEMP FROM SALESPERSON
UPDATE #SALESTEMP SET COMMPERCT = 10
GO
```

The query processor executes all of the statements up to the GO as one batch. The query processor parses all of the statements in the batch as a set, checking for syntax and other errors. The statements are also optimized and compiled for execution as a group. This is more efficient than running individual statements because they must each be parsed, optimized, compiled, and then executed individually.

A result is returned when the entire batch (up to the GO) finishes executing. If an error occurs anywhere in the batch, batch execution stops at that point and the remaining statements are not executed. Unless running in the context of a transaction, any statements completed before the error are not affected. If you are running a script that contains multiple batches, execution will continue (if possible) with the start of the next batch.

There are a few things you should keep in mind when using scripts. You don't know the context under which the script will run, so you should run a USE statement as the first statement in the script to set the default database. You can't add a column to a table as part of a batch and then reference that column in the same batch (but you can reference it in the same script). Also, if an object (such as a table) is dropped in the context of a batch, it cannot be recreated in the same batch.

Let's look at a script that creates a table and then adds data to that table:

```
USE GeneralHardware
GO
CREATE TABLE EmpTest
(SPNUM CHAR(3), SPNAME VARCHAR(20))
GO
INSERT EmpTest SELECT SPNUM, SPNAME
FROM SALESPERSON
```

This script contains three batches. The first sets the default database. The second creates a table with two columns. The third batch inserts rows from the SALESPERSON table into the newly created EmpTest table.

7.3.2 Understanding Basic Programming Concepts

The ANSI SQL standard includes support for batches and scripts, but at a very limited level. Something that is supported, and commonly used, is variables. A **variable** is a way of temporarily storing a value in memory. Another common programming feature, although not included in the ANSI standard, is **control statements,** also called **control-of-flow statements.** These are statements that let your batch make decisions based on values, control the order in which statements are executed, or repeatedly loop through statements. Most DBMSs include at least some control statements in their proprietary implementation of the SQL language. However, the statements supported and statement syntax is vendor specific. We'll take a brief look at selected control statements that are supported by Transact-SQL, but a complete discussion of available statements and their use is beyond the scope of this text.

Using Variables

There are two things common to every variable. Each variable will have an **identifier,** which is a name unique within the scope in which is used, and each variable will have a data type. Data types can be standard system data tables or user-defined database.

To create a **local variable,** which exists only in the context of the batch in which it is defined, you use a commercial *at* symbol (**@**) as the first character in the variable name. The syntax for defining, or declaring, a local variable is:

```
DECLARE @name data_type
```

You can specify a static (constant) value or an expression, as long as the value is compatible with the data type. Whenever possible, SQL Server will implicitly convert the value if it is not of the same type, but is of a compatible type. Use either SET or SELECT to assign a value to a variable. Here's an example of declaring a variable and assigning a value:

```
DECLARE @num int
SET @num = 5
```

Here's the same example, using SELECT:

```
DECLARE @num int
SELECT @num = 5
```

For comparison, here's an example where an expression is used to supply the value:

```
DECLARE @right_now datetime
SET @right_now = GETDATE()
```

Now, let's take a look at a batch that declares a variable, sets its value, then uses the variable in a DML statement:

```
DECLARE @avgpct REAL
SELECT @avgpct = (SELECT AVG(COMMPERCT) FROM SALESPERSON)
UPDATE SALESPERSON SET COMMPERCT = @avgpct
```

This is functionally the same as an example you saw earlier. You declare a REAL type variable named @avgpct and set it equal to the average of all commission percentages. Then, you use the variable in an UPDATE statement to set COMM-PERCT to that value for all salespersons.

Using Control Statements

We're going to limit our discussion to some simple control statements. These are some of the statements that you are most likely to encounter, plus a way of adding statements that don't execute so you can document your script. For more information about control language and its use with SQL Server, refer to the Books Online that install with SQL Server and the Microsoft MSDN Web site for "Control-of-flow language" and follow the links provided.

We'll start with a pair of keywords: BEGIN and END. You use BEGIN and END to group a set of statements as a block. They are typically used together with other control statements to set the context for execution. You'll see how this is done in a moment.

There are several situations where your batch might need to make a decision on what to do next based on current conditions or values. You do this with IF . . . ELSE. The basic syntax is:

```
IF boolean_expression
[BEGIN]
  statement_block
[END]
[ELSE
[BEGIN]
  statement_block
[END]]
```

This is one of the places where you used statement blocks to identify sets of SQL statements, so you can identify which statements are associated with IF and which are associated with ELSE. It's easiest to understand how this works by looking at an example. Consider the following:

If there are no items currently on order, run ORDERPROC to generate restocking orders. If there are items shown as on order, first run RECPROC to receive any pending orders that have been posted and then run ORDERPROC().

There is a decision to be made based on whether or not there are any items on order. This is the basis of your **Boolean expression,** which must evaluate as True or False. Here's what the batch might look like:

```
IF (SELECT COUNT() FROM PRODUCT WHERE QOO = 0) = 0
   BEGIN
   ORDERPROC
   END
ELSE
   BEGIN
   RECPROC
   ORDERPROC
END
```

The statements are indented to make the batch easier to read. The indentations have no effect on execution. If the count of items with a QOO (quantity on order column) value of 0 is equal to zero, then there is nothing on order and you need to run ORDERPROC. If you get any value other than zero, execution skips to the statements following the ELSE clause and you run RECPROC and ORDERPROC. Technically, you are not required to use BEGIN and END when executing a single statement, like the statement after the IF clause, but it's good to get in the habit of using them in case you need to go back and make changes later, such as adding more statements.

It's a good idea to document everything you do when writing scripts. It acts as a reminder of what you did and why in case there are problems or a need to modify the script later. You can embed nonexecuting statements in a batch or scripts as comments as a way of providing in-line documentation. Comments start with /* and end with */. Everything in between these, even if it runs on for several lines, is treated as a comment. You can also use -- (a double hyphen) to create a single line comment.

Let's add some comments to an earlier script example so you can see how this is done.

```
/* This batch gives everyone the
same default percentage
as their commission percentage. This is stored in the
COMMPERCT column*/
DECLARE @avgpct REAL —This declares a variable.
/*The next statement sets the variable value*/
SELECT @avgpct = (
SELECT AVG(COMMPERCT) FROM SALESPERSON)
—This does the real work
UPDATE SALESPERSON SET COMMPERCT = @avgpct
```

FOR EXAMPLE

Using Scripts

Here's a common situation. You have several procedures that have to run at the end of each month to do periodic cleanup and to prepare data for transfer to a decision support database. You want to ensure that it is run the same way each time, but you also want to minimize the time and effort required. This is a situation made for scripting.

You can include all of the procedures that you want to run as batches inside a script. You might want to use multiple batches. Group procedures that are dependent on each other to run in the same batch so that if one fails, the other doesn't try to run. Also, if one part of the process fails because of an error, it doesn't prevent procedures that aren't dependent on that operation from running. You can use control language if you have any situations where processing decisions have to be made based on current conditions. For example, the way that you process records for transfer could depend on the total number of rows in a table. If they exceed a set threshold level, you could segment processing to minimize the impact on other activities.

SQL Server also has the ability to create scripts based on any and all objects in a database. You can automatically generate scripts that can be used to create duplicate objects in another database or at another location, drop objects, and (in some cases) modify objects. You can even generate table and view scripts for running standardized INSERT, UDPATE, and DELETE statements. That way, you let SQL Server do a big part of the work for you and you then modify the scripts generated to meet your particular needs.

In the preceding example, you see both syntaxes used for adding comments. The batch begins with a multi-line comment enclosed in /* */. The DECLARE statement is followed by a short comment on the same line. Execution stops before the identifying --. The remaining two comments are both single-line comments, one using -- and the other using /* */.

SELF-CHECK

- Describe the purpose of batches and scripts.
- Explain the role of variables.
- Explain the basic role of control language.

Summary

In this chapter, you learned about data access and data manipulation. You learned how to use the SELECT statement to run data retrieval queries and how to build queries with SELECT statement keywords. You also learned about various methods for filtering your result set and organizing the data returned by a query. You learned how to use joins and subqueries to combine the results from multiple tables into a single result. You also learned the basics of using batches and scripts to execute sets of statements as a group and to save these so that they can be retrieved and executed later, including the use of control statement to enable the command processor to control execution by making decisions based on current data and conditions.

KEY TERMS

AND	Local variable
Bitwise operations	Noncorrelated subquery
Boolean expression	OR
Cartesian product	Outer join
Control statement	Subquery
Control-of-flow statement	Table alias
Correlated subquery	Table order
Cross join	User-defined function
Identifier	Variable
Inner join	XML document fragment
Join	

ASSESS YOUR UNDERSTANDING

Go to www.wiley.com/college/gillenson to assess your knowledge of SQL language use.
Measure your learning by comparing pre-test and post-test results.

Summary Questions

1. You can only use tables as your data source in the FROM clause of a SELECT statement. True or False?

2. The HAVING keyword must be used with what other keyword?
   (a) GROUP BY
   (b) ORDER BY
   (c) JOIN
   (d) DISTINCT

3. When using UNION to combine the results of two SELECT statements, the column lists must have columns with identical data types. True or False?

4. What keyword is used to return only those rows with identical values from two different SELECT statements?
   (a) UNION
   (b) EXCEPT
   (c) INTERSECT
   (d) DISTINCT

5. A SELECT statement includes a GROUP BY clause. In what clause is sort order for the groups specified?
   (a) HAVING
   (b) GROUP BY
   (c) WHERE
   (d) ORDER BY

6. Which statement will return only the first three rows from the PRODUCT table?
   (a) SELECT * FROM PRODUCT WHERE TOP 3
   (b) SELECT TOP 3 * FROM PRODUCT
   (c) SELECT * FROM PRODUCT TOP 3
   (d) SELECT * TOP 3 FROM PRODUCT

7. When would you use the INTO keyword in a SELECT statement?
   (a) when creating a view based on the result.
   (b) when creating a table based on the result.

(c) when adding rows to the source table.

(d) when filtering the result by a range

8. Which keyword is used to filter query results by a range of values?

(a) GROUP BY

(b) IN

(c) BETWEEN

(d) INTO

9. By default, a query will return duplicate rows in the result set. True or False?

10. A WHERE clause includes both AND and OR operators. Which statement best describes how they are processed?

(a) AND operators are processed first by default.

(b) OR operators are processed first by default.

(c) Operators are processed left to right by default without regard for the operator type.

(d) Operators are processed right to left by default without regard for the operator type.

11. A cross join of two tables, each with six rows, would contain how many rows in the result set?

(a) none

(b) 6

(c) 12

(d) 36

12. An inner join returns only those rows that qualify from both joined tables. True or False?

13. A SELECT statement used to join tables can include no more than two tables. True or False?

14. An operation can be performed as a join or subquery. Which typically makes best use of available resources?

(a) join

(b) subquery

(c) Both make equal use of available resources.

15. Where is the join operator specified when joining two tables?

(a) in the FROM clause, as an ON statement

(b) in the WHERE clause, using a comparative operator

(c) in either a or b

(d) in neither a nor b

16. How is the nested query identified in a subquery?
    (a) The nested query is enclosed in square brackets.
    (b) The nested query is enclosed in angle brackets.
    (c) The nested query is enclosed in quotes.
    (d) The nested query is enclosed in parentheses.
17. Which of the following is a valid local variable name?
    (a) TempVal
    (b) #TempVal
    (c) @TempVal
    (d) *TempVal
18. Control-of-flow statements are defined as part of the ANSI SQL standard. True or false?
19. Which must you specify when declaring a local variable?
    (a) data type
    (b) initial value
    (c) default value
    (d) related column
20. A Boolean expression is one that evaluates as true or false. True or False?

Applying This Chapter

The questions in this section are all in reference to the tables shown in Figure 7-2. Assume that the values shown in the sample SALESPERSON, CUSTOMER, and CUSTOMER EMPLOYEE tables represent the full table content.

1. How many rows would you expect to be returned by the following query?

   SELECT * FROM SALESPERSON WHERE COMMPERCT=10

2. You want a list of cities in the CUSTOMER table and the number of customers in each headquarters city (HQCITY). What query should you use?
3. Modify the query in question 2 to order the list by count, lowest to highest. What query should you use?
4. You want a count of customers assigned to salespersons, by salesperson, in salesperson number order. The query should return the salesperson number, name, and customer count.
5. You need a list of customers in the CUSTOMER EMPLOYEE table and the number of employees on file for each. Label the columns Customer and Employee Count.
   Tip: Enclose the table name in square brackets.

Figure 7-2

(a) SALESPERSON table

SPNUM	SPNAME	COMMPERCT	YEARHIRE	OFFNUM
137	Baker	10	1995	1284
186	Adams	15	2001	1253
204	Dickens	10	1998	1209
361	Carlyle	20	2001	1227

(b) CUSTOMER table

CUSTNUM	CUSTNAME	SPNUM	HQCITY
0121	Main St. Hardware	137	New York
0839	Jane's Stores	186	Chicago
0933	ABC Home Stores	137	Los Angeles
1047	Acme Hardware Store	137	Los Angeles
1525	Fred's Tool Stores	361	Atlanta
1700	XYZ Stores	361	Washington
1826	City Hardware	137	New York
2198	Western Hardware	204	New York
2267	Central Stores	186	New York

(c) CUSTOMER EMPLOYEE table

CUSTNUM	EMPNUM	EMPNAME	TITLE
0121	27498	Smith	Co-Owner
0121	30441	Garcia	Co-Owner
0933	25270	Chen	VP Sales
0933	30441	Levy	Sales Manager
0933	48285	Morton	President
1525	33779	Baker	Sales Manager
2198	27470	Smith	President
2198	30441	Jones	VP Sales
2198	33779	Garcia	VP Personnel
2198	35268	Kaplan	Senior Accountant

(Continues)

Sample tables.

6. Return a list of customer names and employee names from the
CUSTOMER EMPLOYEE table. Include the Customer name in the list,
and whether or not the customer has any employees in the CUSTOMER
EMPLOYEE table. Label the columns Customer and Employee. Order the
result so that customers who do not have employees listed are grouped
together in the result.

7. Write a script that creates a table named EmpCount. The table will have two columns, one with data type CHAR(4) and the other with data type INT. Name the columns Customer and Count. After creating the table, insert rows into the table using the query in Question 5 as your source. Before doing anything, the script should make sure that GeneralHardware is the default database.

8. How can you verify that the batch in Question 7 worked correctly? What specific statements should you use?

YOU TRY IT

Using SELECT Statements

You design a database for a video rental company. The database is normalized to 3NF. Whenever a customer rents a title, a rental invoice is generated. This is stored in two tables, RHead and RTail. RHead contains information on the invoice as a whole, including the CustNum to identify the customer, and RTail contains information for each detailed item in the invoice.

Three tables are used to track customer information. CustInfo contains general information about the customer. CustSec contains more sensitve information, such as telephone number and address. CustRentals has information about current and past rentals. The table has two rental columns, one for VHS and one for DVD. The CustNum column is used to establish the relationship between the tables.

There are two tables for videos. One contains titles on VHS tape and the other DVDs. You are preparing to add a third table for games, which you plan to call Games. Each title has a unique tracking number that is generated internally. The data type for the tracking number is the same in both tables, NCHAR(10). Each value is unique, so that none of the numbers are duplicated between the VHS table and the DVD table.

1. Describe how you would generate a list of invoices that include the Customer's name and address? Include tables and specific columns required by the solution.

2. You need a fast way of checking to make sure that none of the numbers in VHS are duplicated in DVD. How can you do this? (Minimize the size of the result set needed by your solution and the result that you would expect to see.)

3. You want to be able to run a monthly rental history report by customer. The report would include the Customer number and name, but not include any senstive information about the customer. List videos by both tracking number and title.

(a) What tables would be needed?
(b) What values would you use to retrieve the information you need?
(c) How would this solution need to be modified if you start renting games?

Using Batches and Scripts

You have several activities that must be completed at the end of each month and at the end of each quarter. These include reporting and data manipulation operations. You need to automate as many of these operations as possible. You also want to simplify them so that you can delegate some of the periodic requirements to someone else.

There are two databases involved, both of which are hosted on the SQL Server 2005 database server OURDATA. The databases are named SalesData and OpsData. End-of-period activities include both databases, but all of the activities run separately on each. There are no requirements for combining data from the databases or transfering data between the databases.

1. Assuming that the end-of-quarter activites can run sequentially, first for one database and then for the other, what is the minimum number of scripts required? Explain your answer.

2. When you create your scripts, what extension should you use and why?

3. Some operations must run as a set because they are dependent on each other. Each set of operations is independent of other sets. You want to minimize the potential impact of errors on script execution. How should you do this? How does your solution help?

4. There are several either/or decisions that must be made while the scripts are running. How can this functionality be implemented? What is the possible restriction on the decision logic used?

8

IMPROVING DATA ACCESS

Starting Point

Go to www.wiley.com/college/gillenson to assess your knowledge of ways to improve data access.
Determine where you need to concentrate your effort.

What You'll Learn in This Chapter

▲ Basic procedures for diagnosing performance problems
▲ The use of indexes and views to improve data access
▲ The use of procedures and functions to improve data access

After Studying This Chapter, You'll Be Able To

▲ Identify the most common hardware bottlenecks
▲ Identify common sources of database performance bottlenecks
▲ Identify tools and utilities that measure performance
▲ Design and create indexes to improve data retrieval
▲ Design and create views that filter table data returned to a user by column and row
▲ Design and create user-stored procedures to automate periodic tasks
▲ Design and create user-defined functions (UDFs) that return scalar or table values

INTRODUCTION

Data access is a broad subject, so any discussion of ways to improve data access performance will range across various topics. This chapter covers some of the issues that you are most likely to encounter, which includes providing a look at several database objects and providing general guidelines for their use. You will learn about performance bottlenecks, including what they are, the types of symptoms they are likely to cause, and the most likely solutions to correct performance problems. You will learn how to design indexes and views to support data access and help improve query response. You will also learn about the potential role of user-stored procedures and user-defined functions in your database design.

8.1 Understanding Performance Roadblocks

Improving database access includes efforts to make it easier to access the data and to improve performance during data access. Database performance is often a critical issue. Users won't care how well you've designed the database if they have to wait for the information they need. Time, in nearly all business environments, is money, and delays have a real-world cost. Performance can make or break a database application and, in some cases, a business.

Not convinced that performance can be a critical business issue? Think for a moment about designing a database to support an Internet-based business such as an audio download site. Users connect to the Web site, search for the music that they want, enter their payment information and download the songs. Simple enough, except that to be successful you need a huge library of available music. Also, you're not the only business offering this service. Users are going to rate your business based on whether or not you have the music they want and on how long it takes to search the music database. Take too long, and they're off to another site, one with better performance.

One key to faster performance is identifying and correcting performance bottlenecks. A **bottleneck** is anything that stands in the way of optimum performance. There are three major potential sources of performance bottlenecks:

▲ Hardware platform: primarily the database server, but in some cases, can also include the network.
▲ Database: performance during data reads and writes directly impacts application performance.
▲ Application: a poorly written, inefficient application can result in poor performance even if the hardware and database server are working at optimum levels.

We'll keep our look at performance focused on familiar territory. We're limiting our discussion of database performance to hardware and database performance issues. Many application performance issues are specific to the application framework in which you are working and the programming language used to create the application and are beyond the scope of this chapter.

8.1.1 Recognizing Potential Bottlenecks

Before you can try to optimize database and server performance, you need to understand potential sources of performance problems. Most problems are caused by one or more of a small group of likely suspects. When you suspect a performance problem, that is where you'll want to start your investigation and focus your corrective actions.

All DBMSs, by their nature, are resource-intensive applications. Because of this, hardware is usually the initial suspect when you have performance problems. Hardware is not the only potential source, however. The problem can be in the database design. Normalization, while often critical to write performance, can sometimes impair read performance. Indexes, which can be a great benefit during data reads, add to the resource requirements when writing data. You must consider the database and its hardware platform as a whole when looking at performance issues.

8.1.2 Understanding Hardware Performance

Most hardware performance issues are caused by either disk performance, system memory, or the system processor. It can get especially complicated because these are closely interrelated. A memory problem, for example, can sometimes give you symptoms that initially look like a hard disk bottleneck. Let's take a look at each of these areas and some types of problems you might see.

Understanding Disk Drive Issues

When considering disk storage, the key performance issues relate to disk access. These issues include how quickly the hard disk can process read and write requests and the time required to locate and transfer the data. The **disk queue**, the number of requests waiting to be resolved, can tell you whether or not the hard disk can keep up with requests. Data read and write statistics tell you how much data is being transferred into and out of the hard disk. If either of these becomes excessive, you could have a problem.

There are two basic ways to resolve hard disk issues. One is to upgrade the hardware. The other is to reduce the load. Often, the best solution is a combination of the two.

Installing more or faster hard disks can sometimes resolve the problem, but at a cost. Most DBMS manufacturers recommend using RAID (redundant array of inexpensive, or independent, disks) disk systems, both because most RAID

Figure 8-1

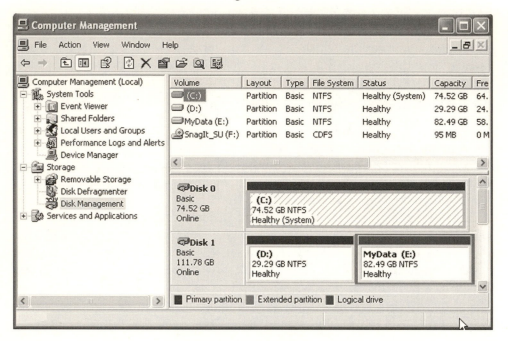

Hard disk configuration.

systems provide fault-tolerant storage and because many configurations are optimized for read and write performance. However, this isn't always the best corrective action. If there is a fundamental flaw in your design or if the disk problem is masking another hardware bottleneck, like memory, upgrading the disk subsystem is a temporary fix at best.

There are different ways that you can reduce the load on disk subsystem. One way is splitting the load between multiple hard disks when you find that disk requests are interfering with each other. Keep in mind that you split the load across multiple physical hard disks. As you can see in Figure 8-1, a physical hard disk can be partitioned into one or more logical hard disks, so you need to understand the system configuration. Saving database objects to different logical hard disks lets you manage disk space use, but does nothing to improve disk performance.

Another way you can reduce the load is by increasing system memory so that more data can be cached. Most DBMSs cache data. A **cache** is a data storage area in memory, a common feature in most database systems. Caching involves storing data and servicing read and write requests through system memory, reducing the need for immediate disk access.

Finally, you can reduce the load by using a **dedicated server.** This means that SQL Server is the only server application running on the server. Some companies will have one server supporting multiple services, such as acting as both a database and application server. This puts an added load on all resources, including the hard disk.

Disk fragmentation can impair disk performance, though it usually isn't considered a bottleneck in itself and often isn't a serious issue in database systems. Fragmentation occurs when files are broken up into smaller pieces to use available disk space. The more you delete and create files, the faster the drive fragments. Most computers create and delete more files than you would suspect, many of them temporary files used by applications and deleted when no longer needed.

Disk fragmentation is less of an issue for database servers than for computers operating in other roles. In a well-designed database system, the database files are kept somewhat segregated from other files, often on their own drive. Because you are protecting the database files, they are more likely to remain contiguous, minimizing the potential impact if other files become fragmented.

Microsoft Windows ships with Defrag.exe, a disk defragmentation utility, which physically moves the file segments so that they form contiguous files. You can also launch the disk defragmenter via the Computer Management console, as shown in Figure 8-2.

Figure 8-2

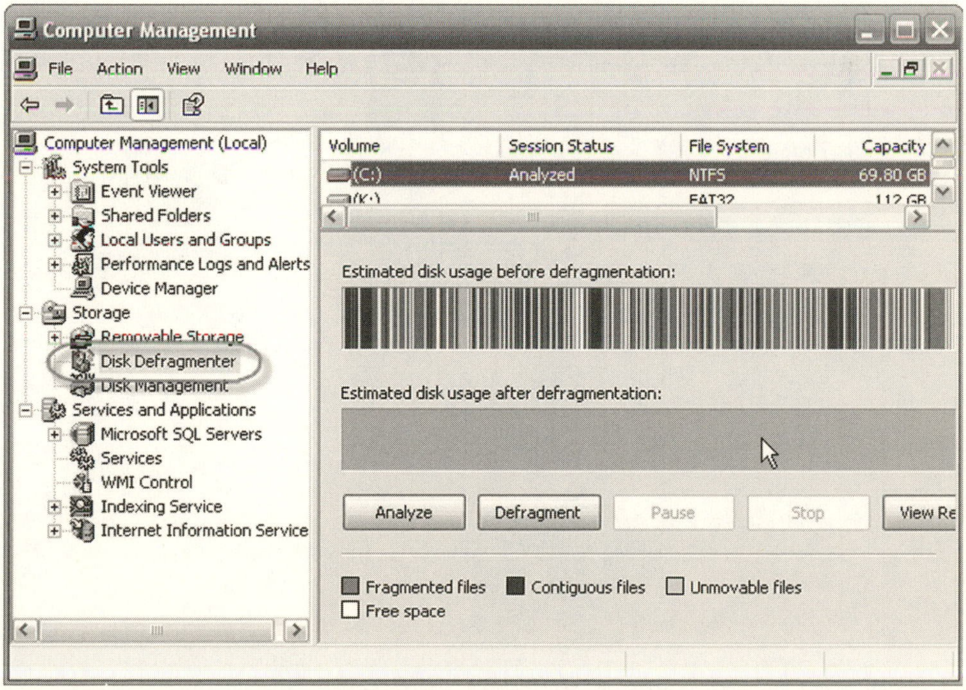

Disk defragmenter.

The best way to avoid problems is to periodically check for fragmentation and defragment the disk, if necessary. You can configure Windows to do this for you automatically on a regular schedule.

Understanding Memory Issues

Databases use a lot of memory. Most DBMSs will set aside memory to cache data. When there is a data read request, the DBMS checks memory first before going to the physical hard disk. When data is written, it writes to memory first until the hard disk can be updated (Figure 8-3). Many DBMSs also cache queries and other executables, depending on available space, in case they are needed again. These requirements are in addition to the memory needed just to run the operating system, DBMS, and any other service running on the server.

If memory becomes as issue, you can either reduce the load on system memory or you can increase the amount of memory installed in the computer. In most cases, other than reconfiguring the computer as a dedicated server, there

Figure 8-3

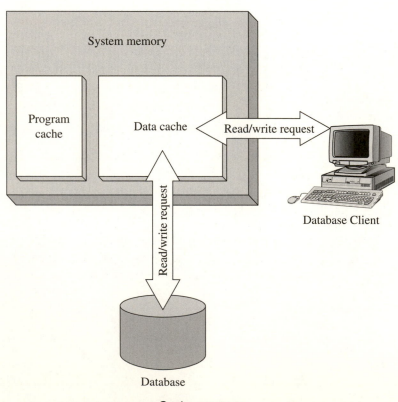

Cache memory.

is little you can do to reduce memory requirements. That leaves increasing memory, typically installing more system memory.

Before installing memory, however, check the database and operating system configuration to see how memory is being used. With some DBMSs, such as SQL Server, you can specify the amount of memory made available to database operations. This could place an artificial limit on memory, causing a memory bottleneck, even though there is more physical memory available.

As mentioned before, memory directly impacts disk use. Modern operating systems increase available memory through use of a virtual memory **paging file.** This is hard disk space that is set aside and used like system memory. Paging is the process of moving data between system memory and the paging file, as shown in Figure 8-4. When physical RAM memory doesn't meet your memory requirements, paging increases, interfering with other disk operations and making the hard disk look like your bottleneck.

Understanding Processor Issues

Every program that runs, every query that is executed, every module called from your application—all these put an additional load on the system processor. To

Figure 8-4

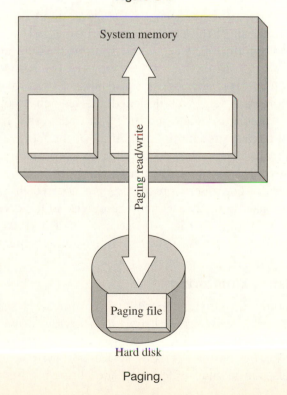

Paging.

determine if the processor is the bottleneck, look at the processor free and busy time. The higher the percentage of busy time, the greater the load in the processor. When this averages over 90 percent of total time, then processor performance is likely a bottleneck.

The only ways to correct a processor bottleneck are to reduce the processor load, install a faster processor, or install one or more additional processors. You need to be aware that there are a couple of possible problems with using a multiple processor computer. Different DBMSs have different support options, some limiting the number of processors supported. A few lower-end database products cannot recognize or use multiple processors, which means that an additional processor would be a waste of money.

Many DBMSs, including SQL Server, let you configure **processor affinity.** This controls how, or even if, the database server makes use of multiple processors. The problem might not be with the processors, but that the database has been configured to ignore any additional processors.

8.1.3 Understanding Database Performance

Database performance issues relate to database object design and use. One of the goals of data normalization is to improve write performance by reducing the amount of data that must be written during updates. However, normalization can impact read performance because data retrieval often means having to join multiple tables to get all of the data you need. In the real world, you typically work toward a compromise between "perfect" normalization and database read performance.

Database objects, especially indexes, also impact performance. Indexes are used to sort and organize data. Well-designed indexes help to optimize data read performance. The problem is that each time you update the data in a table, the database server must also update the data in all of the table indexes. The more indexes you have, the more overhead required to keep them updated.

The problem can be that you don't have the right indexes to support your application's queries. The query processor may not recognize or use poorly designed indexes, making them a waste of resources. SQL Server 2005 provides utilities and reporting tools that let you see how, or if, indexes are used by the query processor and that can even suggest design improvements.

8.1.4 Performance Monitoring

Performance monitoring tools are specific to the operating system and DBMS. Some DBMSs provide a wide array of tools to help you locate and correct performance problems while others leave you effectively on your own. In every case, the DBMS relies heavily on the operating system and system resources, so operating system tools can be vital to detecting and correcting problems.

Figure 8-5

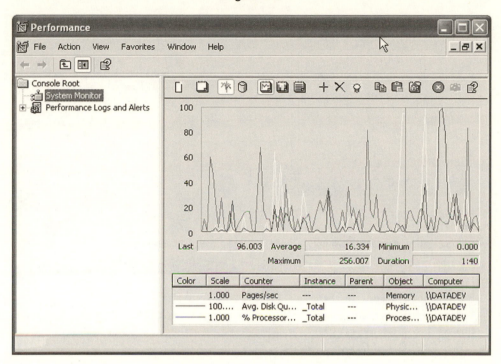

System monitor graph view.

The primary tool in Windows operating systems is the Performance Monitor, called System Monitor in Windows XP and Windows Server 2003. The System Monitor can provide you with real-time performance information and can also collect and log performance data to give you a performance baseline and for detailed analysis. A **performance baseline** is performance data you collect to use for comparison later when performance problems are suspected. The Windows XP System Monitor graph view is shown in Figure 8-5. The graph view is the default view for observing real time performance data.

Performance data is collected through **performance counters**, which are programs that monitor specific system activity. Performance counters are organized into related groups, known as **performance objects.** Performance counters are designed to let you collect detailed performance information. A selection of counters available for the PhysicalDisk performance object are shown in Figure 8-6. You can see the counters for monitoring the disk queue length and read and write data transfers. Hardware-related performance counters are installed with Windows by default. When you install SQL Server, it also installs a large set of SQL Server-specific performance objects and counters.

Figure 8-6

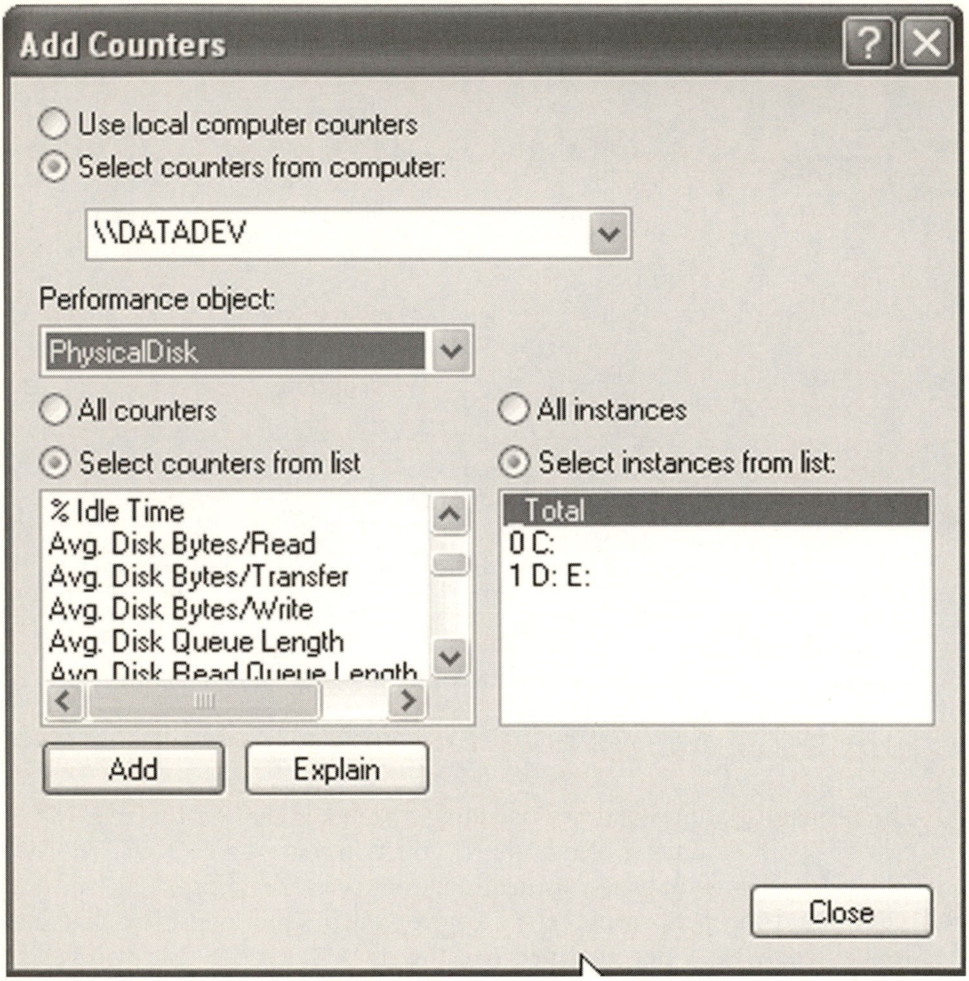

Performance counters.

The Windows XP and Windows Server 2003 Performance utility also lets you create alerts. An **alert** monitors one or more specified performance counters. When you create an alert, you specify the counters that it monitors and the threshold value at which the alert is activated, or fires. A **threshold value** is a specified minimum or maximum value that, when exceeded, indicates a potential problem. For example, you might suspect an intermittent processor bottleneck. You could create an alert configured to fire when the %Processor Time, which monitors processor activity, exceeds 95 percent. You can have the alert notify you each time this threshold is exceeded.

SQL Server also provides tools for monitoring database server activity. A complete discussion of the available tools and utilities is beyond the scope of this chapter, but it's worth the time to take a brief look at some examples.

There are two utilities specifically identified by SQL Server 2005 as performance tools. These are SQL Server Profiler and Database Engine Tuning Advisor. Profiler lets you capture database activity for analysis. You can even capture sample activity to use for automated testing and then replay the activity on a development server to observe the effect of configuration changes. Database Engine Tuning Advisor, which was introduced with SQL Server 2005, analyzes system activity and reports on index use. It can suggest improvements to table indexes and even automatically create the indexes for you.

Another way of monitoring database activity, specifically query activity, is by reviewing execution plans. SQL Server provides options for both textual and graphical execution plans. An example of a graphical execution plan is shown in Figure 8-7.

The execution plan identifies how the query processor resolves the query, the specific steps involved and resources required. One way that this can help monitor performance is that it shows you not only what indexes are used by the query, but how they are used by the query. SQL Server Books Online provides

Figure 8-7

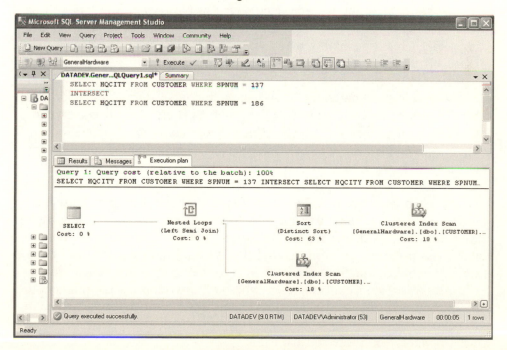

Execution plan.

detailed documentation about how to collect and read information about query execution plans.

8.1.5 Knowing What to Use

How do you know which tools you need? It depends on the information that you need to collect. First, determine whether the problem is related to the operating system or the DBMS. System hardware is controlled by the operating

---

FOR EXAMPLE

Database Optimization

Over time, users have started complaining about database performance. You tried to write it off with the idea that no application is ever fast enough to please all users, but the complaints become louder and more frequent. You finally have to face facts—you have a problem.

You go through all the right steps. You monitor performance and compare it against your performance baseline. You identify the most likely causes of the performance bottleneck and take corrective action. You document what you did and you're finished, right?

Wrong! Any time you are trying to correct a performance problem, you have to test and verify that you've corrected it. Otherwise, how can you be sure that the changes you made had any impact at all, let alone a positive impact? There's a possibility that you've actually made the problem worse, especially if your corrective action included changing database or server configuration settings.

Monitoring and evaluation is at least as important during resolution and correction as it is when diagnosing the problem. Don't forget that everything is closely related to everything else. This includes hardware resources, operating system configuration, and database server configuration. Changes to any one almost always have some impact on others, and not always for the better.

After you've taken your corrective action, run the same tests as you did before when you were trying to diagnose the problem. Compare these both to that data and to your baseline data to see where you stand. Only then, when you have evidence that you've corrected the situation, should you tentatively consider the problem solved. But you still are not completely finished. Spot check performance over time to make sure the problem doesn't reappear. Also, go back to the users who originally reported the problem to see if they think it's fixed. Only then should you consider yourself to be in the clear.

Until the next problem, that is.

system, so you would use operating systems utilities to monitor system hardware and to look for bottlenecks. Database performance monitoring is a function of the DBMS, so to monitor database performance you would use database utilities, either supplied with the DBMS or through a third-party developer. Keep in mind that performance tuning isn't an either/or proposition. You need to tune both the database server and the hardware platform (and operating system) on which it is deployed.

The tools you have available will depend on your operating system and DBMS. Even though we have used Windows and SQL Server utilities as examples, the specific utilities we've discussed are vendor-specific and apply to these products only. With any vendor's products, refer to the documentation provided with the product or on the manufacturer's Web site for information about available utilities. With that in mind, let's take another quick look at your options.

The primary Windows utilities for anything to do with performance are the Performance utility and the various hardware property dialog boxes, which are where the majority of the hardware configuration settings are found. The database tuning process starts with two utilities, SQL Server Profiler and Database Engine Tuning Advisor. Together, they can point out weak points in your database design. Once located, how you fix them is up to you.

SELF-CHECK

- Explain how server performance relates to improving data access.
- List the most common hardware bottlenecks.
- Describe the potential impact of indexes on both read and write performance.

8.2 Using Indexes and Views

We've already talked about server performance as it relates to data access. Indexes can and do directly impact performance. Because of this, you need to carefully consider index design as part of the database design process and be ready to revise your design as indicated by its impact on live server activity.

Another data access consideration is deciding what information you want to make available and how you want to make it available to your users. Most often, this is more directly an issue of what data you are going to make available to application programmers, who in turn make it available to the users. In many cases you will want to avoid revealing too much about the internal structure of your database because of potential security concerns. Also, nearly any database is going to have sensitive data that must be protected against unauthorized access. This is where views come into the picture as one of your primary tools for managing data access.

We're going to take a little closer look at both indexes and views in this chapter. We'll look at some additional guidelines and options for creating each, and give you some ideas for how they might fit into your database design.

8.2.1 Working with Indexes

Indexes have a direct impact on query performance. Clustered indexes impose a physical organization on a table, sorting the table rows in index order. Non-clustered indexes provide logical organization, organizing data based on key columns, but not affecting physical table order. Because of this, a DBMS that supports clustered indexes limits you to one clustered index. After all, data can only be stored in one order. The number of nonclustered indexes allowed is DBMS-specific.

Designing Indexes

During database design, you need to consider whether or not an index is needed and, if so, how many indexes and what columns you should include as **key columns.** Index key columns are the columns that set the index sort order.

Indexes are not always appropriate. Smaller tables don't derive any benefit from indexing because it's faster to scan the table than to retrieve rows from the index. Also, columns with low selectivity, those with few unique values, don't benefit from indexing. For example, a column tracking sex as either male or female wouldn't benefit from indexing, nor would a column storing state information for a customer if most of your customers are located in the same state.

Then what columns do benefit from indexing? Primary key columns are one candidate. In fact, most DBMSs, including SQL Server, require an index on primary key columns and create the index automatically when you set the primary key. SQL Server also creates an index automatically when you apply a unique constraint on a column. Foreign key columns are another candidate, especially because they're the column that you're most likely to use in queries that join tables. Finally, columns that are commonly referenced in queries, either in WHERE clause search logic, or in the GROUP BY or ORDER BY clauses are usually prime index candidates. Columns used in SELECT column lists are also good candidates for inclusion as included (nonkey) columns in nonclustered indexes.

Index design is an area where you will probably need to work closely with the application designers. Application designers can help you understand the queries that they are going to need, including the columns used by those queries. This is your basis for index design.

Unfortunately, indexes are not something that you can fix once and ignore. As the table sizes change, so does the effectiveness of some of your indexes. Application requirements also can change over time, so that some indexes are seldom used and others that would be used by application queries don't exist. You need to periodically monitor index use to determine their effectiveness, especially if users report degraded performance.

Considering their effect on data retrieval, you might be tempted to just create indexes for all table columns. There are two potential problems with this. One is disk space. Each index row requires space based on its key columns. The more indexes you create, and the more columns you include, the more space required. Some DBMSs also limit the number and size of index key columns, restricting your index design. You might also be limited in the types of columns you can include in an index. SQL Server, for example, doesn't let you use large object (LOB) data types as index key columns.

You also have to consider the effect of indexes on write performance. Each time you add a row to a table, you add a row to each table index. If you change a key column value, the same change must be made to all indexes that use that key. As you add more indexes, you increase write requirements.

There is one thing you can do to help improve performance when working with very large tables in SQL Server. You should organize your physical storage so that the table is located on a different physical hard disk than its nonclustered indexes. This allows the database to split read and write activity across multiple hard disks, reducing the load on any one. Clustered indexes, by design, must be stored with the table because they are physically part of the table structure.

Creating Indexes

The CREATE INDEX command is used to create table indexes. The basic syntax for this command in SQL Server Transact-SQL is as follows:

```
CREATE [CLUSTERED] | [NONCLUSTERED] [UNIQUE]
INDEX name
ON object (column_list)
INCLUDE (column_list)
```

As you can see here, you can create an index as clustered or nonclustered, defaulting to nonclustered indexes. Specify UNIQUE if you want the index to act as a unique constraint on the key columns. This requires that each row of combined values for the key columns be unique. For example, take a look at Figure 8-8.

You could not create a unique index on the CUSTNUM column in CUSTOMER EMPLOYEE because the column contains duplicate values. However, you could create a unique index that includes both CUSTNUM and EMPNUM as key columns.

Figure 8-8

CUSTOMER EMPLOYEE table			
CUSTNUM	EMPNUM	EMPNAME	TITLE
0121	27498	Smith	Co-Owner
0121	30441	Garcia	Co-Owner
0933	25270	Chen	VP Sales
0933	30441	Levy	Sales Manager
0933	48285	Morton	President
1525	33779	Baker	Sales Manager
2198	27470	Smith	President
2198	30441	Jones	VP Sales
2198	33779	Garcia	VP Personnel
2198	35268	Kaplan	Senior Accountant

CUSTOMER EMPLOYEE table.

The *object* on which the index is based is typically a table. In some DBMSs, and with some restrictions, you can also create an index on a view. The INCLUDED keyword is specific to SQL Server 2005. Columns specified as included columns through the INCLUDED keyword benefit from improved access through indexes, but do not impact index sort order like the key columns.

The CREATE INDEX statement supports additional options that are beyond the scope of this chapter, but are fully documented in SQL Server Books Online. These include options that let you manage how much free space is left for inserting new rows when you create an index and whether or not users will be able to access the table on which the index is based during index creation. There is also an option that lets you drop and then recreate an index in the same operation.

To create the index described earlier for the CUSTOMER EMPLOYEE table, you could run:

```
CREATE UNIQUE INDEX ix_CE_NUMS
   ON [CUSTOMER EMPLOYEE] (CUSTNUM, EMPNUM)
```

You should try to give your indexes descriptive names. This will be helpful in identifying the index you want if you need to modify indexes in the future.

Additional commands are also available to manage existing indexes. ALTER INDEX lets you manage an index and DROP INDEX lets you delete indexes. However, you cannot use ALTER INDEX to change the index key and nonkey columns. If you want to change the index columns, you must drop and then recreate the index.

Understanding How Queries Use Indexes

When the SQL query optimizer is presented with a new SELECT statement to evaluate, it seeks out information about the tables named in the FROM clause. This information includes:

▲ Which columns are used as index keys.

▲ Which columns have unique values.

▲ How many rows each table has.

The query optimizer finds this information in the database metadata. The query optimizer uses the information about the tables, together with the various components of the SELECT statement itself, to try to find an efficient way to retrieve the data required by the query. For example, in the General Hardware Company SELECT statement:

```
SELECT SPNUM, SPNAME
FROM SALESPERSON
WHERE COMMPERCT=10
```

the query optimizer might check on whether the COMMPERCT is used as an index key. If this attribute does have an index, the query optimizer might decide to use the index to find the rows with a commission percentage of 10. However, if the number of rows of the SALESPERSON table is small enough, the query optimizer might decide to read the entire table into main memory and scan it for the rows with a commission percentage of 10.

Another important decision that the query optimizer makes is how to satisfy a join. Consider the following General Hardware Company example:

```
SELECT SPNAME FROM SALESPERSON, CUSTOMER
WHERE SALESPERSON.SPNUM=CUSTOMER.SPNUM
AND CUSTNUM=1525
```

In this case, the query optimizer should be able to recognize that since CUSTNUM is the CUSTOMER table primary key and only one customer number is specified in the SELECT statement, only a single record from the CUSTOMER table, the one for customer number 1525, will be involved in the join. Once it finds this CUSTOMER record (in an index), it can match the SPNUM value found in it against the SPNUM values in the SALESPERSON records. If you've identified SPNUM unique through a unique index, all it has to do is find the single SALES-PERSON record (preferably through an index) that has that salesperson number and pull the salesperson name (SPNAME) out of it to satisfy the query. Thus, in this case, an exhaustive join can be completely avoided.

When a more extensive join operation can't be avoided, the query optimizer can choose from one of several join algorithms. The most basic way of resolving a join, which runs using a Cartesian product of the tables involved, is known as a **nested-loop join.** However, this is a relatively inefficient way of joining tables. One of the two tables is selected for the outer loop and the other for the inner loop. Each of the records of the outer loop is chosen in succession, and, for each, the inner loop table is scanned for matches on the join column. If the query optimizer can determine that only a subset of the rows of the outer or inner tables is needed, then only those rows need be included in the comparisons.

A more efficient join algorithm than the nested-loop join is called the **merge-scan join,** but it can only be used if certain conditions are met. The principle is that for the merge-scan join to work, each of the two join columns either has to be in sorted order or has to be indexed (which also makes it a sorted column). If this condition is met, then comparing every record of one table to every record of the other table as in a nested-loop join is unnecessary. The system can simply start at the top of each table or index, as the case may be, and move downward through the columns.

8.2.2 Working with Views

Views provide access to selected data. A view is based on a SELECT statement and can have one or more base tables. Though limited, a view can also be based on other views. This is easy to see when you look at the syntax for creating a view.

Creating Views

The basic syntax for creating a view in SQL Server is:

```
CREATE VIEW name AS select_statement
```

SQL Server also supports additional options that control how the view is created. These options are beyond the scope of this chapter, but are documented in SQL Server Book Online.

Because the view is based on a SELECT statement, you can join tables through a view. This provides easy access to denormalized data without changing the structure of the database. You can also use views to limit access by filtering tables. You can filter the base tables vertically, limiting the columns included, or horizontally, limiting the rows included. You can also include computed columns in your view to support queries that need values based on values computed from table columns or function results.

SQL Server does put some limits on the SELECT statement. For example, you can't use the INTO keyword. Also, you can't have an ORDER BY clause in the statement unless you also include the TOP keyword. You can't base the SELECT statement on temporary objects, like a temporary table, because they might not be there when you try to retrieve data from the view. That's because SQL Server, in most cases, doesn't persist the contents to the view. It generates the view result set each time you call the view. That way, changes to the view's base objects are automatically included.

You also have the ALTER VIEW and DROP VIEW commands available to manage existing views. ALTER VIEW lets you modify the view definition, which includes letting you specify a different SELECT statement for the view. Use DROP VIEW to delete existing views.

Using Views

Views are most often used to provide restricted access to the underlying base objects. In SQL Server, views can also simplify security management because you can give users (or an application) access to a view without granting them access to the underlying objects. This helps prevent unauthorized access or modifications to the base data.

Let's look at an example using the CUSTOMER table in Figure 8-9. There is a requirement for operations that are performed on a city-by-city basis.

You've been asked to create a view based on CUSTOMER with the data filtered by city. Here's the statement you might use to create the view for New York customers:

```
CREATE VIEW v_ny_cust AS SELECT * FROM CUSTOMERS
WHERE HQCITY = 'New York'
```

To retrieve data from this view, you could use

```
SELECT * FROM v_ny_cust
```

Here's a view based on a join that lets you retrieve customer employee information with the customer name rather than CUSTNUM value:

```
CREATE VIEW v_custemp_name AS
SELECT CUSTNAME, EMPNUM, EMPNAME
FROM CUSTOMER C, [CUSTOMER EMPLOYEE] E
WHERE C.CUSTNUM=E.CUSTNUM
```

Figure 8-9

CUSTOMER table			
CUSTNUM	CUSTNAME	SPNUM	HQCITY
0121	Main St. Hardware	137	New York
0839	Jane's Stores	186	Chicago
0933	ABC Home Stores	137	Los Angeles
1047	Acme Hardware Store	137	Los Angeles
1525	Fred's Tool Stores	361	Atlanta
1700	XYZ Stores	361	Washington
1826	City Hardware	137	New York
2198	Western Hardware	204	New York
2267	Central Stores	186	New York

CUSTOMER table.

To View, or Not to View

Any business database is going to contain sensitive data, data to which you need to limit access. In some cases, you are required by law to protect the data. The more direct a user's access is to the data, the greater the possibility that something can go wrong and that the wrong person will see or even modify what should be secure data.

One solution is to manage table security at the column level, defining column by column who can view what data. The biggest potential problem with this solution is that it is easy to make mistakes. A better solution is to avoid direct access to the data completely and instead give users indirect access through views. You can create views as necessary to meet different users' access requirements.

Consider the types of data that you might have in employee records and related tables. Database administrators will likely have access to all of that data, simply because someone has to have complete access for management and maintenance purposes. If you can't trust your database administrators, you likely have a lot more serious problems than someone taking an unauthorized peek at employee records.

What about other departments? Human resource managers would probably need access to most, if not all, of the employee data. Keeping with our plan to use indirect access, you would create a view that includes most, or all, of the employee data. The person doing your payroll, however, needs much more limited access. You might create a view for them, and your payroll application, that gives access to information needed to create a paycheck, such as time cards, pay rate, tax ID, and similar information. The benefits advisor needs to know about things like which health plan the employee has chosen, but the access needed is limited and easily defined.

What about the employee's manager? Most of the time, there is very little information to which the manager needs access, which is the guideline to use when designing any views. Access is probably limited to things like contact information, accrued and used vacation, performance reviews, and the information you need to write performance reviews. As to the rest of the information available, if you can't justify a need for it, leave it out. Other managers, if given any access at all, should have even less, which means another view.

Throughout the design process, keep this in mind: if you don't give people the information they need to do their jobs, they will let you know. If you give them more access than they need, you may not find out until after the damage has been done.

Does creating all of these views take time and effort? Obviously, but the benefits in simplifying access and managing data security far outweigh the costs. Also, most views are objects that you can create once and forget. Unless access needs change or you have to restructure the objects on which they are based, there is seldom any reason to modify views after you create them.

The view returns the customer name, employee number, and employee name. Keep in mind, however, that by default the database server must execute the join each time the view is called, with the associated overhead. Access is simplified though, because the user or application programmer only needs to know what view to specify in the SELECT statement's FROM clause, not the full syntax for the join. While not that significant in this example, it can make a big difference with working with complicated joins and subqueries.

You can also specify a view as your destination when running INSERT or UPDATE, but with restrictions. When inserting rows through a view, any columns not included in the view must either have default values or be generated automatically by the database server, or an error will be returned. These include columns such as identity columns, columns with defined default values, and columns that allow NULL values.

When modifying tables through a view, the view must either be based on a single table or you must define a trigger that executes in place of your modification statement. In that case, the trigger will take the data passed by your statement and use it to modify the underlying tables.

Before leaving the subject of views, we need to mention one special type of view supported by SQL Server, the **indexed view.** An indexed view is a view for which you have created a clustered index. When you do this, the view result is persisted through the index structure. The advantages are easy to see. The view acts like a denormalized table, giving you easier access to the joined table data. Also, the persisted index improves access performance because SQL Server doesn't have to execute the SELECT statement and recreate the result set each time you access the view.

There are three major disadvantages to using indexed views that tend to limit their use in database solutions. First is that there are several restrictions on the SELECT statement and base tables used to define the view, so indexed views aren't always a viable solution. Second is that, as part of the process of creating the view, you bind the schema on the underlying tables. **Schema binding** prevents you from making any changes to the structure of the base tables, such as adding columns or changing column data types. Finally, indexed views come with measurable resource overhead. When you add or modify data in any of the view's base tables, SQL Server must also update the view's index.

SELF-CHECK

- Describe the role of indexes in improving data access.
- Describe the role of views in improving data access.

8.3 Using Programmable Objects

Programmable objects are just what the name implies, database objects that you create and program yourself. These are objects based on SQL language commands, variables, and, if supported by your DBMS, control-of-flow statements. The types of programmable objects supported and the level of support provided will vary by DBMS. We're going to use SQL Server 2005 as our example platform for this discussion.

The two most common programmable objects are procedures and functions. Both are similar in that they are based on a set of executable statements. In some ways, you can think of them as a named batch that you've designed to perform a specific task. **Procedures** are sets of executable statements that support input and output parameters. **Input parameters** let you provide data to be used by the procedure. If the procedure needs to return a value, it uses an **output parameter** for that purpose. **Functions** that you can create are similar to system functions in that they can accept input parameters and return a specific type of value. Depending on the type of function, it will return either a scalar or table value. Another type of programmable object, a trigger, is effectively a specialized procedure that is associated with specific objects and events. SQL Server also supports a few other types of programmable objects, but we're limiting our discussion to procedures and functions. These are the objects you are most likely to encounter and use.

Our goal in this chapter is not to make you an expert is designing and creating procedures and functions. Instead, the goal is to give you a brief introduction to give you an idea of their roles in your overall design, along with a few simple examples.

8.3.1 Understanding Procedures

Most DBMSs, including SQL Server, come with an assortment of predefined system procedures. In SQL Server, they are called **system stored procedures** and are easily identified by their name, which begins with sp_. Their purpose is to make it easier and faster to perform periodic or complicated procedures, and to ensure that they are performed consistently. You create procedures for the same reason, to make the database easier to use and to ensure consistent operations. Like views, procedures also aid system security by placing a level of isolation between the users and the database.

With procedures, users might know what they do, but not how they do it. Let's start with a system stored procedure as an example. The sp_helpdb system stored procedure returns information about a specified database or all system databases. It has one optional input parameter, @dbname, which lets you specify the database name. Otherwise, it returns information about all of the databases on the server. Figure 8-10 shows a sample result from using sp_helpdb to get information about all system databases.

Figure 8-10

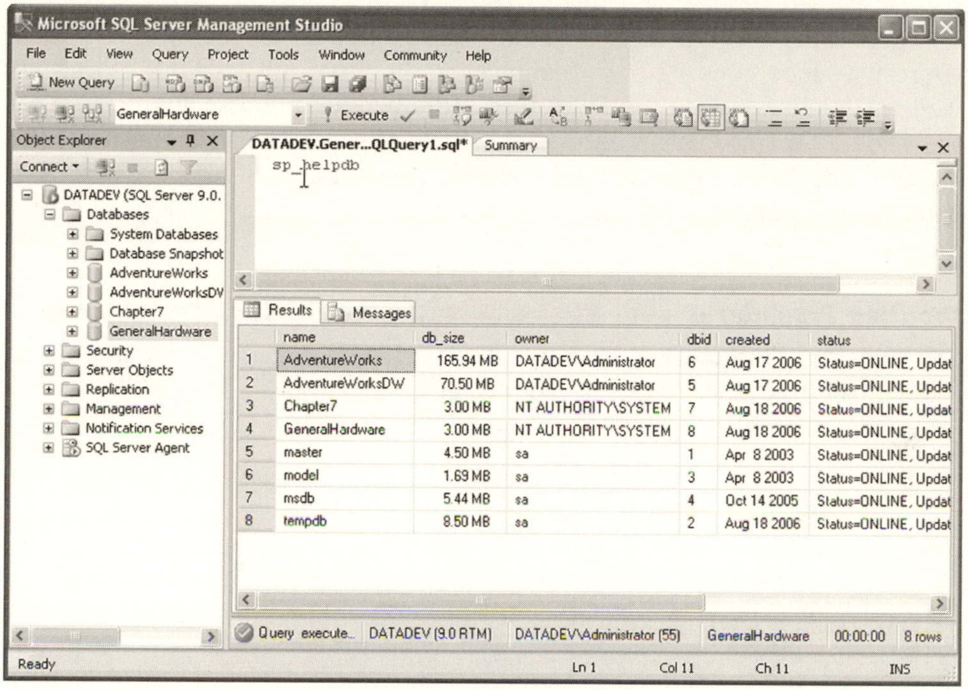

Sample database information.

SQL Server documentation tells you how to run the procedure and the information it returns. You can see the results. However, you have no idea what SQL Server went through to collect that information. Users will run procedures you create the same way. They'll know the parameters required and what (if anything) it returns, but not the details of how the result is accomplished. This lets you hide the details of the database and database objects.

Designing Procedures

Most DBMSs let you create custom procedures, sometimes referred to as user stored procedures. Procedures let you automate periodic or complex activities and ensure that operations are run consistently. It doesn't take long to find several candidates for procedures. In addition, because of how they are compiled and run, procedures are more efficient than running ad hoc queries that perform the same operations. The need for user intervention is reduced and direct access to database tables is avoided.

One common use of procedures is data entry. Rather than having the user (or application) run an INSERT command to enter data rows, you create a procedure that runs INSERT for you, passing the column values as input parameters.

The INSERT is performed the same way each time, and the only information you've revealed about table structure is the column values needed to add a row.

More complicated processes are also good candidates for procedures. Because you can include control-of-flow commands, the procedure can make decisions while it is running based on the values and other conditions it finds. However, you should design your procedures so that each procedure accomplishes a single task. You can also include error handling code that will let your procedure detect and respond appropriately to errors, rather than simply failing and reporting the problem.

Creating Procedures

You run CREATE PROCEDURE (or CREATE PROC) to create a user stored procedure. The basic syntax for this command is as follows:

```
CREATE PROC[EDURE] procedure name
[parameter_list]
AS
Sql_statements
```

The parameter list includes input and output parameters, both of which are optional. When defining a parameter, you must supply a parameter name and data type. Optionally, you can specify a default value to be used if the user doesn't specify a value for the parameter, and you can identify the parameter as an OUTPUT parameter. The SQL statement list can include most SQL commands and control-of-flow statements. You can also call other procedures as **nested procedures,** which is a procedure called and executed by another procedure. When the nested procedure finishes running, control is returned to the calling procedure.

Let's look at a simple example with four input parameters:

```
CREATE PROC proc_enter_cust
@CUSTNUM CHAR(4), @CUSTNAME VARCHAR(40),
@SPNUM CHAR(3), @HQCITY VARCHAR(20)
AS
INSERT CUSTOMER VALUES (@CUSTNUM, @CUSTNAME,
@SPNUM, @HQCITY)
```

When you run the procedure, specify values for each of the input parameters. If you wanted to add Home Town Supply as a new customer, you might run:

```
proc_enter_cust '4554', 'Home Town Supply', '361', 'Chicago'
```

Notice that the parameters are entered in the same order as they are specified. If you also include the parameter names, you can pass the parameters in any order, as in the next example:

```
proc_enter_cust @CUSTNUM='4554', @SPNUM='361',
@HQCITY='Chicago', @CUSTNAME='Home Town Supply'
```

If you want to have the procedure return a value, you need to specify an output parameter. Here's an example that returns a count of customers for a specified salesperson number:

```
CREATE PROC usp_count_cust
@SPNUM CHAR(3), @CUSTCOUNT INT OUTPUT
AS
SET @CUSTCOUNT = (SELECT COUNT(*) FROM CUSTOMER WHERE
SPNUM=@SPNUM)
RETURN @CUSTCOUNT
```

When you run the stored procedure, you have to first declare a variable to accept the output parameter value from the stored procedure. When the stored procedure includes an output parameter, you must use the EXECUTE command to run the procedure. In the next example, we use two variables, one for the input parameter and one to receive the value from the output parameter.

```
DECLARE @NUM CHAR(3)
DECLARE @RETCOUNT INT
SET @NUM = '137'
EXECUTE usp_count_cust @NUM, @RETCOUNT OUTPUT
SELECT 'The count for salesperson' + @NUM + 'is'
+ CAST( @RETCOUNT AS CHAR(2)
```

Let's talk through this batch so you can see what's going on. We start by declaring to local variables, @NUM, which will hold the salesperson number, and @RETCOUNT, which will receive the value from the output parameter. The variable receiving the output parameter variable must be of a compatible type. We set @NUM equal to 137, then use it to run the procedure. We pass @NUM as the input parameter and specify @RETCOUNT as the output parameter with the OUTPUT keyword. Finally, we use SELECT to return the value as a string result. The CAST function is used to cast the output parameter integer value as a character type to support concatenation.

The syntax for ALTER PROC, which is used to modify a procedure, is effectively the same as the CREATE PROC statement. You must include all of the same information, including parameters and the defining SQL statements, when altering a procedure as you do to create a new procedure. Use DROP PROC to delete existing procedures.

8.3.2 Understanding Functions

User defined functions (UDFs) are similar to user stored procedures in that they optimize execution and limit user intervention and direct access to database tables. When deciding whether to use a user stored procedure or UDF, the general rule of thumb is that if you need a return value, use a UDF. Otherwise, use a stored procedure. As you saw earlier, you have the option of deciding whether or not a stored procedure returns a value. A UDF, by design, must return a value.

SQL Server 2005 supports three types of functions:

▲ **Scalar function**: returns a scalar value of a specified type.
▲ **In-line table-valued function**: returns a table generated as the result of a single SELECT statement, similar to a view.
▲ **Multistatement table-valued function**: returns a table generated from multiple Transact-SQL statements.

Scalar functions can be used like system functions in expressions where a scalar value is expected. Table-valued functions can be used as a data source in the FROM clause of a SELECT statement and in other operations where a table value is required.

Designing Functions

Situations where you will use UDFs are similar to those where you would use stored procedures. You use functions where you need to automate operations, simplify them, or improve security by providing access to table data indirectly through a function. You can also use a table-valued function in most of the same situations where you might use a view. The main difference is that you can control the table returned through the value pass as an input parameter.

When you create a function, you will use one or more SQL statements to generate the value returned. Most SQL statements are allowed and can include both other UDFs and system functions.

Creating Functions

The syntax for creating a function depends on the type of function you want to create. The Transact-SQL CREATE FUNCTION command supports three slightly different syntax versions, one for each function type. The basic syntax for creating a scalar function is:

```
CREATE FUNCTION name
([parameter_list])
RETURNS data_type
[AS]
BEGIN
Sql_statements
RETURN scalar_value
END
```

The command also supports a small number of function options. These options are beyond the scope of this chapter. Functions support input parameters only. The syntax for specifying an input parameter is the same as for a user stored procedure. If you don't need any input parameters, then an empty pair of parentheses must follow the function name. The return data type is required. Place the statements used to generate the value in the BEGIN…END block. The last statement must be a RETURN statement followed by the return value. Let's rewrite the earlier procedure used to return a customer count as a UDF:

```
CREATE FUNCTION fn_CountCust
(@SPNUM CHAR(3))
RETURNS INT AS
BEGIN
DECLARE @CUST INT
SET @CUST = (SELECT COUNT(*) FROM CUSTOMER WHERE
SPNUM=@SPNUM)
RETURN @CUST
END
```

Whether or not you specify the relational schema when you create a function, as with any other database object, the relational schema is part of the fully qualified function name. With most objects, if you don't specify the schema, the default schema (typically dbo) is assumed. However, when you call a UDF, you must specify the schema. So, to use the function we just created, you might run:

```
SELECT dbo.fn_CountCust('137')
```

The results would be an integer value of 4. To get an output like the one you saw in the earlier example, you could use:

```
DECLARE @NUM CHAR(3)
DECLARE @CUSTCOUNT INT
SET @NUM = '137'
SET @CUSTCOUNT = (SELECT dbo.fn_CountCust(@NUM))
SELECT 'The count for salesperson' + @NUM + 'is'
+ CAST( @CUSTCOUNT AS CHAR(2))
```

The syntax for an in-line table-valued function is similar, except that the return type is always TABLE. Here's the basic syntax:

```
CREATE FUNCTION name
([parameter_list])
RETURNS TABLE
[AS]
RETURN (select_statement)
```

This time, let's create a UDF that doesn't require an input parameter. Functionally, this will be equivalent to a view. We want to join the CUSTOMER and

SALESPERSON tables to return the customer name, salesperson name, and head-quarters city. Here's the statement to create the function:

```
CREATE FUNCTION fn_GetCust ()
RETURNS TABLE
RETURN (SELECT SPNAME, CUSTNAME, HQCITY
FROM SALESPERSON JOIN CUSTOMER
ON (CUSTOMER.SPNUM = SALESPERSON.SPNUM))
```

Notice the empty parentheses, identifying that the function does not have any input parameters. We don't need to qualify the column names in the SELECT clause because each of the column names is unique. To use this function, we could use:

```
SELECT * FROM dbo.fn_GetCust
```

Finally, the syntax for a multistatement table-valued function is a little more complicated. As the returned value, you specify a table-type local variable. You must also include the table definition. At minimum, you must specify the table columns and data types, but the definition can include other table features such as identity columns and column constraints. The basic syntax, in this case, is

```
CREATE FUNCTION name
([parameter_list])
RETURNS @ret_variable TABLE (table_definition)
[AS]
BEGIN
Sql_statements
RETURN
END
```

Notice, that in this case, the RETURN keyword is specified on a line by itself. For our example, we're going to create a function that returns either a list of customers for a specific salesperson or, if no salesperson is specified, a list of all customers:

```
CREATE FUNCTION fn_GetBySP
(@NUM CHAR(3)=NULL)
RETURNS @custcopy TABLE (CustNum CHAR(4),
CustName VARCHAR(40), SPNum CHAR(3), HQCity VARCHAR(20))
BEGIN
If @NUM IS NULL
INSERT @custcopy SELECT custnum, custname, spnum, hqcity
FROM customer
else
INSERT @custcopy SELECT custnum, custname, spnum, hqcity
FROM customer WHERE SPNUM = @NUM
RETURN
END
```

This time, we better step through the function so you can see what's going on inside it. We declare an input parameter named @NUM and set its default value to NULL. In the RETURNS clause we declare a table variable named @cust-copy, along with the table definition. If @NUM has a value of NULL, then we insert all rows from CUSTOMERS into the table variable. Otherwise, we filter

---

FOR EXAMPLE

Replacing Views?

Remember the "For Example" box in the last section. You want to be able to retrieve data about employees, but filter the data returned by department and job requirements. The solution was to create one view for the Human Resources manager, another for payroll, another for the employee's manager, and so on. You might think that another solution would be to create a multistatement table-valued function to retrieve the data. When calling the function, you pass the appropriate user type, such as HR or manager, to filter the result.

The problem is that this isn't really a workable solution in this situation. Why not? There are two major flaws. One is that a UDF lets you filter the result by row, but the same columns are always returned. The only way around this would be to have the function return every column you might possibly need, but return NULL values for inappropriate or unnecessary data. The problem has to do with security. You would need to embed some type of security check inside the procedure, otherwise what is there to prevent the employee's manager from running the function and passing the parameter to return data for the HR manager?

There are, however, any number of possible situations for which a UDF would be well-suited. Say, for example, that you need to run sales reports by customer and salesperson each month so you can calculate commission payments. As long as the salesperson number is associated with the sales records, you could create a UDF to simplify this activity. Create a UDF that lets you pass the salesperson number and then retrieves data for just that salesperson. You could even take it a step further with a scalar function. You could have the function use the salesperson number to retrieve the commission percentage for you, calculate the percentage, and return the commission amount as a scalar value.

The same general rule of thumb applies for determining access through functions as it does for views. If you don't give people the information they need to do their jobs, they will let you know. If you give them more than they need, you may not find out until after the damage has been done.

the rows we insert into the table variable by the input parameter value. To retrieve a list of customers for salesperson 137, you could run:

```
SELECT * FROM dbo.fn_getbysp('137')
```

If you want to use the default value to retrieve all of the customers from the table, you would run:

```
SELECT * FROM dbo.fn_getbysp(DEFAULT)
```

Notice that if you want to use the default value of an input parameter, you must pass the keyword DEFAULT as the parameter value.

The syntax for ALTER FUNCTION, which is used to modify a procedure, is effectively the same as the CREATE FUNCTION statement. You must specify all parameters, just as if you were creating a new function. Use DROP FUNCTION to delete existing functions.

SELF-CHECK

- Compare and contrast user stored procedures and UDFs.
- List and describe the types of UDFs supported by SQL Server 2005.

SUMMARY

In this chapter, you learned about improving data access, which included improving access performance, simplifying access, and protecting table data from unauthorized access. You were introduced to the concept of bottlenecks and shown some of the types of bottlenecks you are most likely to encounter. You learned about the role of indexes in improving read access, as well as their possible impact on write access. You learned how to design and create views to control user access to data. You also learned about using procedures and functions both to automate database operations (including data access queries) and to control access to database data.

KEY TERMS

Alert	Dedicated server
Bottleneck	Disk queue
Cache	Function

Indexed view

Input parameter

Key column

Merged scan join

Nested loop join

Nested procedures

Output parameter

Paging file

Performance baseline

Performance counter

Performance object

Procedure

Processor affinity

Schema binding

System stored procedures

Threshold value

ASSESS YOUR UNDERSTANDING

Go to www.wiley.com/college/gillenson to assess your knowledge of ways to improve data access.

Measure your learning by comparing pre-test and post-test results.

Summary Questions

1. A perceived hardware performance problem can sometimes mask a problem with a different hardware component. True or False?

2. Normalization has no impact on data access or database performance. True or False?

3. Which of the following would you use to capture SQL Server activity?

   (a) SQL Server Profiler

   (b) System Monitor

   (c) Performance Monitor

   (d) Database Engine Tuning Advisor

4. Excessive virtual memory paging is typically caused by which of the following?

   (a) a hard disk that is too slow

   (b) an overworked hard disk

   (c) too little system memory

   (d) too slow of a processor

5. What is usually the best solution for memory bottlenecks?

   (a) install a faster hard disk

   (b) increase available disk space

   (c) install a faster processor

   (d) install more RAM memory

6. On a Windows XP computer running SQL Server 2005, which of the following would you use to observe real-time hardware performance?

   (a) SQL Profiler

   (b) Database Engine Tuning Advisor

   (c) System Monitor

   (d) alerts

7. When is the best time to collect baseline performance data?

   (a) before installing SQL Server

   (b) before the database application goes live

(c) shortly after the database application goes live

(d) when you suspect a performance issue

8. Running multiple server applications can adversely impact which of the following?

(a) disk performance

(b) memory performance

(c) processor performance

(d) all of the above

9. Views let you filter table data by column and by row. True or False?

10. Which columns should typically be used as index key columns?

(a) columns that are seldom retrieved by queries

(b) columns containing few unique values

(c) columns that are commonly used as join columns

(d) columns containing a very high percentage of NULL values

11. You are creating a view based on a single table. Which would you use for vertical filtering?

(a) the SELECT column list

(b) the FROM clause

(c) the WHERE clause

(d) the GROUP BY clause

12. Which statement best describes the results returned by a view?

(a) The results are persisted when the view is first created.

(b) The results are generated each time the view is called.

(c) The results must be immediately updated any time base tables are updated.

(d) The results are a snapshot of the data when the view as created.

13. Indexing table columns typically improves read and write performance. True or False?

14. You can use input parameters to vary view results. True or False?

15. You must specify the return data type when creating a scalar function. True or False?

16. When creating an input parameter for a stored procedure, what, in addition to the parameter name, must be specified?

(a) data type

(b) default value

(c) INPUT keyword

(d) both a and b

17. Which UDF type requires a table definition?
    (a) scalar
    (b) in-line table-valued
    (c) multistatement table-valued
    (d) both b and c
18. When calling a UDF, you must include the schema name with the function name. True or False?
19. When creating procedures or functions, input parameters are optional. True or False?
20. When are you required to use the EXECUTE command when calling a UDF?
    (a) when passing default values for input parameters
    (b) when the function returns a value
    (c) when passing input parameters by name
    (d) never

Applying This Chapter

You are designing a database solution for Good Reading Bookstores. You are using SQL Server 2005 as your DBMS running on Windows Server 2003 The tables you have defined so far are shown in Figure 8-11.

The tables have been loaded with initial data and the application is currently undergoing beta testing. The following questions refer to the Good Reading Bookstores database.

1. You are comparing potential hardware platforms. You load the database on each with sample data. How can you generate a sample load so that the same load is used on each platform?
2. Referring back to Question 1, how can you observe performance differences between the two machines?
3. When should you collect baseline performance data?
4. You plan to use functions and procedures to automate some management activities. What should you use as your general guideline for deciding whether to use a function or a procedure? How can you decide what type of function to use?
5. You will frequently need to run reports on the SALE table and include an extended total by book and customer. What type of database object can you create to simplify this?
6. During beta testing, how can you determine whether or not the indexes you've created are being used when queries are executed?

Figure 8-11

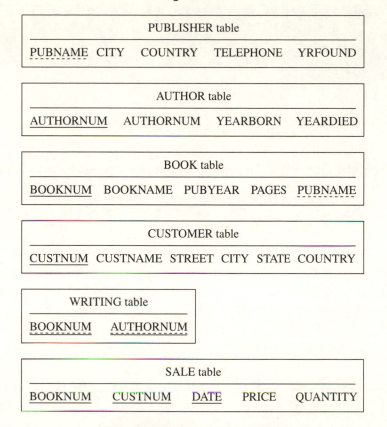

Good Reading Bookstores tables.

7. How do the table primary keys, indicated by a solid line under the column name, relate to default table indexes?

8. Several queries needed by regular operations depend on joining multiple tables. How can you simplify these queries for your users?

Video Rental Company

You design a database for a video rental company. The database is normalized to 3NF. Whenever a customer rents a title, a rental invoice is generated. This is stored in two tables, RHead and RTail. RHead contains information on the invoice as a whole, including the CustNum to identify the customer, and RTail contains information for each detail item in the invoice.

Three tables are used to track customer information. CustInfo contains general information about the customer. CustSec contains more senstive information, such as telephone number and address. CustRentals has information about current and past rentals; the table has two rental columns, one for VHS and one for DVD. The CustNum column is used to establish the relationship between the tables. It is also used as the primary key in each of the customer tables.

There are two tables for videos. One contains titles on VHS tape and the other DVDs. You are preparing to add a third table for games, which you plan to call Games. Each title has a unique tracking number that is generated internally. The data type for the tracking number is the same in both tables, NCHAR(10). Each value is unique, so that none of the numbers are duplicated between the VHS table and the DVD table. The tracking number is used as the primary key in the VHS and DVD tables.

The database is deployed on a computer running Windows XP and SQL Server 2005. The computer is also running Internet Information Services (IIS). The database application is written as a Web application, which is hosted on the same server, so employees launch a Web browser on their computers and connect to the application through the local network.

1. Users complain about poor performance when posting rentals. This has been an ongoing complaint and you suspect the server hardware. Assume you suspect memory as the problem. Go through the general steps you would use to verify and correct a memory problem. Other than SQL Server, what additional loads are there on system resources? How could you reduce these?

2. Currently, the only indexes on the database are those that SQL Server created by default. You want to optimize reports run on customer rentals. The report will include basic customer information and the titles of current rentals. How could you retrieve this information (what tables are required)? What indexes should you create to optimize performance (identity by table and column)? Justify your answer.

3. You want to be able to limit the report generated in Question 2 to a single customer. You want to ensure a consistent result, with the same columns returned the same way each time. How should you do this and keep the number of additional database objects required to a minimum? Describe the object or objects that you would create.

4. How would the solution change if you wanted to retrieve either one customer or all customers?

Periodic Activities

You have several activities that must be completed at the end of each month and at the end of each quarter. These include reporting and data manipulation operations. You need to automate as many of these operations as possible. You also want to simplify them so that you can delegate some of the periodic requirements to someone else.

There are two databases involved, both of which are hosted on the SQL Server 2005 database server OUR-DATA. The databases are named SalesData and OpsData. End-of-period activities include both databases, but all of the activities run separately on each. There are no requirements for combining data from the databases or transfering data between the databases.

The databases are normalized to 3NF. In some cases, you have included denormalized tables to support read requests. The databases are optimized for read performance. You evaluate index use and update the indexes twice a year. You document the indexes by generating creation script files for each of the indexes any time an index changes. These scripts are kept in a directory on the database server to keep them readily accessible.

Periodic updates are run over weekends to keep them from interferring with user activities.

1. You plan to create objects as necessary separately on each database. What type of database object would you create to perform the periodic acitivities? Why should you create separate objects for each activity?

2. Rather than running monthy updates, you decide to run them each quarter. When you do, you need to identify the month and year for which each monthly update is being run. How can you do this?

3. You want to be able to return the number of rows updated by the monthly update. How could you do this? How would this change your requirements for running the update?

4. You need to ensure that periodic updates run as quickly as possible so that they are finished over one weekend. What change can you make to the databases to optimize write performance instead of read performance?

5. What kind of database object can you create that will reverse this change with minimal effort on your part? Describe what it would need to do.

6. What periodic changes might you need to make to this object?

9

DATABASE ADMINISTRATION

Starting Point

Go to www.wiley.com/college/gillenson to assess your knowledge of database administration requirements.
Determine where you need to concentrate your effort.

What You'll Learn in This Chapter

▲ The reasons for data and database administration
▲ Data and database administration roles
▲ Database administration management tasks

After Studying This Chapter, You'll Be Able To

▲ Justify the need for data and database administration
▲ Identify the tasks for which data administrators are responsible
▲ Identify the tasks for which database administrators are responsible
▲ Identify where data and database administration responsibilities overlap
▲ Explain guidelines for choosing between manual and automated management procedures

INTRODUCTION

Administration includes a set of critical responsibilities that begin with database planning and continue as long as the database is in use. Considering the importance of the data contained in corporate databases, administration is definitely not an area to shortchange. In this chapter, we'll look at justifying administration roles, identify the two basic administration roles and responsibilities related to each, and talk a little about guidelines for performing administration tasks.

9.1 Understanding the Need for Administration

Administrative tasks touch on every aspect of database implementation and use. There are administrative requirements throughout the life cycle of a database application, though the specifics change depending on where you are in the cycle. To understand the requirements, it helps to understand the basic life cycle (Figure 9-1).

Figure 9-1

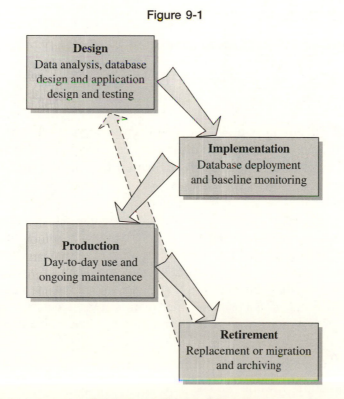

Database application life cycle.

Early in the life cycle, during database design, the tasks focus more on data requirements. As you move through the life cycle, day-to-day activities and the database server take precedence. Toward the end of the application's functional life, the focus turns back to the data, with possible data migration or data archiving requirements, merging into a new design cycle. It's important to understand administration requirements and roles played by administrators.

9.1.1 Identifying Administration Roles

There are two basic administration roles, which constitute the "people side" of database management, though the boundaries between the roles often become blurred in the real world. These two administration roles are data administration and database administration. A data administrator, sometimes called a **data analyst,** is responsible for planning and analysis, setting data policy and standards, promoting the company's data as a competitive resource, accounting for the use of data, and providing liaison support to systems analysts during application development. **Systems analysts,** in the simplest sense, are information services (IS) specialists who identify ways for computers to perform critical tasks. In a broader sense, much of this work involves analyzing complex systems and how they interact, analysis that often focuses on data flows within an organization and between an organization and outside entities (such as customers and vendors). **Data flow** refers to the path taken by data from its producer or owner to the **data consumer,** the person using the data. Communication between data administrators and systems analysts is often aided by the fact that many data administrators start out as systems analysts before focusing on relational data requirements.

The **database administrator's** function is more operationally oriented and is responsible for the day-to-day monitoring and management of the company's various active databases, as well as providing liaison support to program designers during application development. Database administrators typically carry out policies and apply standards set by data administrators.

For our purposes, we are treating data administration and database administration as separate entities with separate responsible individuals. In the real world, these jobs are often combined into a single department, group, or even individual, depending on the size of the organization and the scope of the management requirements. There has also been a recent trend toward outsourcing administration duties to an on-call consultant rather than keeping a database specialist on staff. This is usually done as a cost-saving measure, often with mixed results.

9.1.2 Justifying the Need for Administration

The initial question that arises is, why do companies need these data and database administration departments? What value do they add? Are they just additional cost centers that don't produce revenue? At one time or another, most companies have struggled with these questions, but in today's heavily data-intensive, information-dependent business environment, these functions are recognized as being more important than ever.

DBMS manufacturers have recognized the need not only for administrators, but for qualified administrators. Toward this end, most manufacturers offer certification programs. Certification candidates must take and pass one or more exams to earn certification. Certifications offered and certification exam objectives vary between different DBMS certification programs. One ongoing problem with these programs is to design them so that they test for real-world-based skills and knowledge. A parallel industry has grown up alongside the certifications, offering certification training with some giving money-back guarantees of passing.

Justifying Administration

Data as a corporate resource has taken its rightful place alongside other corporate resources. Virtually all aspects of business have become dependent on their information systems and the data flowing through them. Today's organizations could not function without their vast stores of personnel data, customer data, product data, supplier data, and so forth. Indeed, data may well be the most important corporate resource because it describes all of the others. Furthermore, the effective use of its data can give a company a significant competitive advantage.

The problem is that available personnel and other resources within a company tend to be scarce (is there ever enough money to go around?), and there is typically internal competition for them. Data is no exception. As more and more corporate functions seek the same data for their work, bottlenecks can form and the speed of accessing the data can slow. Arguments arise over who "owns" the data, who should have access to it, and, especially, who is responsible when problems arise. Without someone clearly responsible for data issues, companies respond in a variety of ways without completely understanding the problem, such as bringing in faster computers, but these solutions have their limits and often come with inherent drawbacks.

Management cannot be left to chance or performance optimization left as an afterthought. Any shared corporate resource should have a dedicated department to manage it. It makes little sense to have an important resource either not managed at all or managed part-time and half-heartedly by some group that has other responsibilities. It also makes little sense to have any one of the groups competing for the shared resource also managing it—the resource manager must be impartial when a dispute arises. The answer is to have a department, or personnel within a department, specifically dedicated to data and database management. These should be personnel whose sole purpose is taking care of corporate data.

Justifying Job Specialization

Database administration is often organized as a responsibility within the information services (or information technology, depending on your organization) department. However, this does not mean that the tasks should be handed over to the department as general responsibilities for anyone who happens to have the time to take care of them. Many of the functions involved in the management of data are highly specialized and require specific expertise. They can vary from long-range data planning to working with the idiosyncrasies of a particular database management system. This argues for a full-time staff of specialists who do nothing but manage a company's data and databases.

A good example of this is database design. To do a really good job of both logical and physical database design requires considerable education and practice. The question then becomes one of who among the information systems personnel should be responsible for designing the company's main, shared databases. The systems analysts? The application programmers? Which systems analysts or application programmers? Even though one of these choices is often the solution, it doesn't always make a lot of sense to have any of these people design the databases for at least two reasons. First, it is unreasonable to expect any of them to be as expert at designing databases unless they specialize in this area of development. Second, if any one application development group designs the shared databases, they will tend to optimize them for their own applications and not take into account the needs of the other applications. The solution is to have application-independent, full-time database specialists (i.e., data and database administration personnel), who are experts at database design and who optimize the database designs for the overall good of the company.

Justifying Operational Management

At the operational level, for the day-to-day management of the company's production databases, an independent department must be responsible for data and database management, for the reasons already mentioned. Since the data is likely to be shared among several corporate functions and users, the data should be managed by an independent group whose loyalty is to the overall company rather than to any individual function. Also, someone has to make sure that any periodic data updates take place, overseeing the application or personnel responsible for those updates. Once again, it's prudent to have an independent data administration group keep track of who is responsible for updating which tables and to monitor whether these persons have kept to the expected schedule, for the benefit of all who use the data.

Working with the databases at the operational level requires an in-depth knowledge of the DBMS in use, of the databases themselves, and of such specific skills and tasks as physical database design, database security, and backup and recovery.

Integrating External Data

In today's information systems environment, some databases are not designed by a company's own personnel but are acquired as part of purchased software packages. A prominent example is **Enterprise Resource Planning (ERP) software** like the multifunction, integrated software sold by companies such as SAP and Peoplesoft. These packages consist of application modules that manage a variety of corporate functions (personnel, accounting, etc.). They typically include a central database shared by all of the application modules. When a company decides to go the ERP route, they are making an important commitment to having a shared data resource. Once again, the only arrangement that makes sense for the management of this shared resource is to have an independent group that is tasked with managing it for the overall good of the company.

Meeting Decentralization Requirements

With the advent of personal computers, local area networks, and new user-friendly software in the 1980s, many companies decentralized at least some of their information systems work. These technologies permitted user departments all over the company to handle some or all of their information systems needs on their own, without having to rely on the central information systems organization. Although such developments as ERP software with its centralized database concept have swung the pendulum back toward the centralized IS environment to some extent, decentralization is a fact of life to a greater or lesser degree in virtually all companies.

The question then is, in terms of the advantages of data and database administration, do we need these functions more or less in the decentralized environment than we do in the centralized environment? Some people might say that we don't need them. In fact, when the move toward decentralization began, one of the stated reasons was to reduce the overhead of the central IS department, including database administration. Furthermore, many people are quite content to develop their own databases on their PCs using low-level PC-based DBMSs. Despite these trends, there is a very strong argument that data and database administration are even more important in a decentralized environment than in a centralized one.

First of all, most large companies do not have a totally decentralized IS. Most have a hybrid centralized/decentralized environment. And if nothing else, the centralized portion includes a central, shared database, which certainly requires a database administration function to manage it. Moreover, with company data present in a variety of central databases, databases associated with local area networks, and even databases on PCs, the coordinating role of data administration is crucial. This coordinating role is a key responsibility of data administration.

FOR EXAMPLE

Recognizing the Need for Administration

Lower-level DBMS products, like Microsoft Access, are specifically designed to let users design and develop their own databases and simple database applications. One reason for their popularity is that traditional corporate IS departments are often slow to respond to users' requests for changes, even changes that seem as minor as changing report options. Part of the problem is that "simple" changes often aren't that simple when dealing with older mainframe databases and applications.

The result is that you have "pools" of data throughout the company. This often results in both duplicated data and duplication of efforts, but this isn't the only reason for wanting to maintain more centralized control over corporate data. In fact, there are a wide variety of potential issues.

With individual databases, one person is typically responsible for the data and its administration, such as it is. Data inaccuracies are common, resulting in different users generating different results from the "same" data. Data updates occur in a haphazard manner, if at all, leading to business decisions being made on out-of-date information. Backups are often an afterthought, meaning that data loss is common. Also, most users don't give any thought to security, opening the door to data theft and other industrial espionage.

One answer to these potential problems is to put all data, both centralized and decentralized, under one common management umbrella. This gives you a way of setting standards for issues such as data backup and data security. It lets you identify and consolidate duplicate data, reducing the effort required to manage and maintain the data. With modern DBMSs like SQL Server, it's even possible to integrate public and private databases. You can keep a master copy of the data on a database server where it is properly managed and maintained. Individuals can still have their own copies in local Access databases, kept up-to-date from the master copy. This lets them have the impression that they are in control over their own data and lets them meet some of their own custom requirements, such as individualized reports.

SELF-CHECK

- Compare and contrast data administration and database administration roles.
- List key justifications for dedicated administration personnel.

9.2 Identifying Administration Responsibilities

There are several ways to look at administration responsibilities. One is by role, identifying and understanding the tasks for which data administrators are responsible and those for which the database administrators are responsible.

When discussing these responsibilities, always keep in mind that the two roles are closely tied to each other, will overlap, and may even be performed by the same person. Guidelines established by the data administrator directly impact how the database administrator does his or her job. Performance problems discovered by the database administrator can force the data administrator to rethink and redesign some aspect of the database, as well as work with application programmers to ensure that any necessary changes are made to the application.

It can also be easy to lose track of who is responsible for what. When assigning responsibilities, it's important that they be defined clearly and completely so that everyone understands what they should be doing. Understand that terms rely on context, and misunderstandings are easy. For example, say "database" to a data administrator and the first thing likely to come to mind is the data—defining entities, how tables are structured, and so forth. Say "database" to a database administrator and the first thing to come to mind might be the physical database file, how it's physically stored on the server hard disks, and relationships between different distributed databases.

Table 9-1 lists general duties of the data and database administration roles. However, when discussing these roles you need to keep in mind that these are not hard and fast divisions. Responsibilities often overlap, with data or database administrators working together or taking over duties traditionally assigned to the other role.

Table 9-1: Data and Database Administration Roles

Data Administration	Database Administration
Data coordination	Performance monitoring
Data planning	Security
Data standards	Metadata management
Liaison requirements	Software management
Training	Troubleshooting
Arbitration	
Publicity	
Competitive advantage	

We're going to keep our discussion of administrator responsibilities to a very general level. We'll focus on the types of things that each role needs to do, not worry about the specifics of how each is done. Even though the responsibilities are somewhat common across different DBMS platforms, the tools provided by the different DBMS products to meet the responsibilities can vary widely.

9.2.1 Understanding Data Administration Responsibilities

As information systems are used in all aspects of a company's business, data administrators find themselves playing key roles in the corporate environment. Those who understand the data a company possesses and how it flows are in the best position to understand how the company really functions. These data flows include data moving from department to department within the company, as well as between the company and its customers, suppliers, and other external entities. This is why data administrators often come from the ranks of systems analysts, but with additional training to understand requirements specific to relational databases.

But, what exactly, do data administrators do? To say that they manage data is far too simple of an explanation for our purposes. Instead, we need to take a look at what we mean by that blanket term *managing data*. At the same time, you will begin to see why the data and database administrator roles are often filled by the same person or persons because of overlapping responsibilities.

Managing Data Coordination

With data playing so prominent a role in the corporate environment, its accuracy is of the utmost importance. In the centralized/decentralized environment of most businesses, data and copies of data can be scattered among mainframe computers, local area network servers, and PCs. The more fragmented the data and storage methods, the higher the possibility of inconsistency and error. There are few things more annoying than two people making important presentations in a meeting and showing different figures that should be the same. It is up to the data administrators to keep track of the organization's data. This includes download schedules, update schedules and responsibilities, and data interchange with other companies. This is not to suggest that data administration should try to control all of the databases on all of the employees' PCs. That would be impossible. However, in attempts to avoid total data anarchy, data coordination becomes the job of the data administrators, which means that they maintain a reasonable amount of control over the company's data.

Managing Data Planning

Data planning refers to identifying data requirements, analyzing available data, and designing ways of meeting data needs. Data planning begins with determining what data will be needed for future company business efforts and the applications that will support those efforts. Data planning may be limited to data generated and used internally within the company. However, today it often means coordinating with other companies in a supply chain or acquiring external customer data for use in marketing. In either case, there is the need to plan for integrating the new data with the company's existing data. A number of methodologies have been developed to aid in data planning. These methodologies take into account the business processes that the company performs as part of its normal operations and add the data needed to support these operations. While the methodologies generally operate at a high strategic level and may not get into the details of individual attributes, they do provide a broad roadmap from which to work.

Related to **strategic data planning,** your long-term data plans and requirements, is the matter of what hardware and software will be needed to support the company's information systems operations in the future. The questions involved range from such relatively straightforward matters as how many disk drives will be needed to contain the data to broader issues of how much processing power will be needed to support the overall IS environment. While this is specifically the database administrator's responsibility, data administration must be involved so that the database administrator is not working blindly. Information like projected growth based on historical requirements or upcoming additional needs of which the data administrator might be aware provide the database administrator with critical information for planning hardware requirements. Another data planning issue is how metadata should be put to use. With some DBMSs, metadata and the data dictionary is managed separately from the operational data. This management involves what data should be stored in the data dictionary, what uses the data dictionary should be put to, who should interact with the data dictionary and how, and on what kind of schedule all of this should take place. Yet another data planning issue many companies must face is the migration of old, pre-database data and applications into the company's database environment. Related to this is the problem of migrating data from one DBMS to another as the company's software infrastructure changes.

Managing Data Standards

In order to reduce errors, improve performance, and enhance the ability of one IS worker to understand the work done by another, it is important for the data administrator to set standards regarding data and its use. One example of data standards is naming standards, which include attribute names, table names, and other server and database object names. Names must be meaningful and consistent.

For example, it could be very confusing if the human resources department uses the name Serial Number as the attribute name for employee numbers while the manufacturing department uses Serial Number for finished product serial numbers. This could be possible, though, because each would be used in a different table and would result in a unique column name. Similarly, you add unnecessary confusion if you use Serial Number in some tables and Employee Number in others to refer to the same value. An even bigger problem arises if you use different identifying values in different tables, making it difficult (if not impossible) to establish relationships between tables.

Another issue of data standards relates to data access. It's important to insist on consistency in the way that programs access the database. These include issues such as how connections are established, how data is retrieved, and how data manipulation commands are passed. Here, the data administrator must work with application programmers and the database administrator to develop standards that help minimize problems relating to performance and security. Also, well-established standards help to make application programs easier to maintain when it comes time to make changes or add functionality.

Data standards also come into play in the IS interactions between companies in supply chains, as shown in Figure 9-2. When data is exchanged using **electronic data interchange (EDI)** technology, technology used for electronic data transfer and related data standards, adjustments have to be made to account for data structure and other differences in the information systems of the two companies involved.

Many companies use non-relational data formats for passing information such as purchase orders. It's common to find XML documents based on predefined schemas as the transfer standard. The need to be able to generate messages in those formats can impact how database data is structured.

In Figure 9-2, you see a retailer sending a purchase order to the warehouse using EDI technology. The order is received automatically by the computer at

Figure 9-2

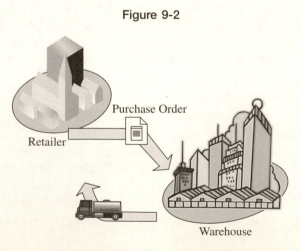

Electronic data interchange (EDI).

the warehouse, the order is filled, and the items shipped to the retailer. EDI helps automate the process, with data administrators on each end managing the data standards needed.

Handling Liaison Requirements

You've already see how liaison activities are a vital part of data administration When working with application developers, data administrators are responsible for providing support to the systems analysts and programmers in all matters concerning the data needed by an application. During the systems analysis phase of application development, the support may include help in determining what data is needed for the application and which of the data items needed for the application already exist in the active database. As already mentioned, jointly developed access standards are a critical requirement involving not just application programmers, but database administrators as well.

Another aspect of such liaison activity is database design. Data analysts are generally involved in database design at some level, but the decision of what precise level of involvement is usually dependent on a number of factors. In an IS environment in which the data administration organization is very strong and in which there is a significant amount of data sharing among different applications and different functional areas of the company, the data analysts may do all of the logical database design work themselves. Here again, they can stand as an impartial group creating the best design for the overall good of all the sharing users. The other choice is for the application developers to do the database design with either active consultation by the data analysts or approval responsibility after the fact by the data analysts. In the active consultation role, the data analysts lend their expertise to the effort, as well as determine how the new data should mesh with data in the existing database, if there is to be such a merging. In the approval role, the application developers (usually the lead programmers for this activity) design the database, which is then shown to the data analysts for discussion and approval.

Here again, we see the close relationship between data and database administration. Database administrators typically have a role in the process as well, providing an understanding of the physical capabilities and requirements of the DBMS. A "perfect" database design is useless if your DBMS can't physically implement the functionality called for in that design. For example, the database design might call for native storage of XML documents and for direct retrieval of data inside the documents using XML queries. The problem with this is that most DBMSs don't support XML data types or direct retrieval of XML data.

Managing Training

In some companies, data administrators are responsible for training all those in the company who have a reason to understand the company's data. In some cases, that training can also include the DBMS environment, though that specific need is usually better met by database administrators. Management personnel need to understand why the database approach is good for the company and for their individual functions specifically. Users must understand why the shared data must remain secure and private. Application developers must be given substantial training in how to work in the database environment, including training in database concepts, database standards, and how to write DBMS calls in their programs. These requirements might also include how to do database design, how to use the data dictionary to their advantage, and in general, what services they can expect data and database administrators to provide.

Arbitrating Disputes and Access

To introduce the concept of **arbitration,** the act of resolving disputes between disagreeing parties, we should spend a moment on the question of data ownership. Who in a company "owns" a piece of data or a database? To be technical, since data is a resource of value to the company, the data "belongs" to the company's owners or stockholders. In more practical terms, in many companies data is controlled by its primary user or users. In this case, data and database administrators act as custodians of the data in the sense of providing security, backup, performance monitoring, and other such services. Here again the roles overlap, with it being difficult determine where one set of responsibilities ends and the other begins. In some companies with an advanced level of data sharing, ownership responsibility actually falls to data administration itself.

If ownership has been established in a department other than IS and a new application requires the use of existing data, it becomes the job of data or database administration to act as an intermediary and approach the owner of the data with the request for data sharing. Similar issues can arise if one department in the company simply wants to query another department's database. If there is a dispute over such data sharing, then the data administration group acts (in theory) as an arbitrator between the disagreeing parties.

In some cases the issue isn't what you can access, but the speed and quality of access. The data administration group might find itself acting as arbitrator between two database users or groups of users who are sharing the same database server, each demanding priority access for better performance. The fundamental issue becomes determining what is best for the company. For example, marketing and sales might argue over access to the same customer sales data. In this case, it is likely that the sales department's access is more time-critical.

It's important to understand that this role belongs to data administration in theory, but not always in fact. It depends on your organization and who ultimately is responsible for decisions about data and its use. Just because the logical department to make the decision is data administration, doesn't mean it will always work that way. For example, decisions about data access might fall solely with departmental managements, leaving data administrators with an advisory role, at most.

Managing Publicity

Often, the data management group performs a **publicity** function, informing potential users of what data exists in the database. Knowing what data exists might encourage employees to think about how they can use the company's data to gain competitive advantages that did not previously exist. They may discover how to automate more of their work and to integrate their work more directly with related business processes that are already automated.

However, this publicity carries with it critical concerns about security. You must carefully consider not only what information about the database and its data you publicize, but also to whom you make this information available. Various departments might need to be involved in decisions about what to publish, depending on who is responsible for the data. For example, the amount and type of data you would make available about employees depends on the data consumer, the person or department accessing the data.

Ensuring a Competitive Advantage

Data administrators, by virtue of their knowledge of the company's data and the way it flows from one company function to another, are in a unique position to understand how the company works. This is especially true since virtually all company functions today are dependent on information systems. A very important and high-profile responsibility of the data administration function is to respond to questions about how the company's business procedures can be adjusted or modified to improve the company's efficiency. This can also extend to data administration taking the initiative and making suggestions for improvement on its own.

9.2.2 Understanding Database Administration Responsibilities

After seeing the responsibilities given data administrators, you might wonder about what's left for the database administrators. Don't worry, there's plenty of work to go around. You've already seen how the roles overlap, and that sometimes it's difficult to determine exactly which role is responsible for what. Pay attention to this overlap as we discuss database administrator responsibilities. In addition, there are several activities that belong uniquely to the database administrator.

Database administration is a technical function that is responsible for the day-to-day operations and maintenance of the DBMS environment, including such related tools as the data dictionary, if handled as a separate function. This is quite analogous to the role of the systems programmers who are responsible for maintaining the mainframe operating systems. Like operating systems, DBMSs tend to include many highly product-specific features that require a thoroughly trained individual to handle.

You might find, depending on the company, that there are responsibilities that go beyond those listed here. The database administrator's role tends to become something of a catchall. When something comes up related to the database, if it isn't specifically the responsibility of someone else, then it must belong to the database administrator.

Monitoring Performance

One of the key functions performed by database administration is performance monitoring. Using utility programs, the database administrators can gauge the performance of the running DBMS environment. This activity has a number of implications. It is important to know how fast the various applications are executing as part of ensuring that response time requirements are being met. Also, this type of performance information is pertinent to future hardware and software acquisition plans. Depending on the characteristics of the DBMS and the operating system under which it is running, the performance information may be used to redistribute the database application load among different CPUs or among different memory regions within a system. Finally, performance information can be used to ferret out inefficient applications or queries that may be candidates for redesign.

The database administrators must also interface with the IS organization's systems programming staff, who maintain the mainframe operating systems (if present). The systems programmers will also have performance and troubleshooting responsibilities, which may overlap with those of the database administrators. The net of this is that it greatly facilitates matters if the two groups get along well with each other and can work together effectively. This is less an issue than it has been in the past as PC-based databases rival (or exceed) mainframe performance and mainframe-hosted databases become the exception rather than the rule.

Keep in mind that performance depends not only on the DBMS and database, but the hardware platform, operating system, and even the network. It may be necessary to work with network administration or PC administration and help staff to complete some monitoring tasks. This is especially true if you plan to run tests that will place a heavy load on network infrastructure that could interfere with the performance of other network applications. These also may be issues relating to database administration security access. As a database administrator, you could have unlimited access to the DBMS and any hosted databases, but still have limited access to operating system resources and utilities.

Monitoring Security

Database administrators keep track of which applications are running in the database environment. They can track who is accessing the data in the database at any moment, either directly or through an application. Again, there are software utilities that enable them to perform these functions.

Monitoring the database users is done from several perspectives. One is the matter of access security, making sure that only authorized personnel access the data. This includes managing database users and authorizing user access to the database, as ordered by data administration personnel in conjunction with the data owners. Another perspective is the need to maintain records on the amount of use the various users make of the database. This can have implications in future load balancing and performance optimization work. This information can also be used in allocating system costs among the various users and applications.

A related concern is database auditing. Even assuming that only authorized users have accessed the database, reasons involving accounting and error correction require that a record be kept of who has accessed and who has modified which data items. This is also critical if you suspect unauthorized access, someone hacking into the database. This **audit trail,** the ongoing log of user activity, is a necessary tool when attempting to detect and hopefully block unauthorized access. The level of auditing supported is DBMS-specific. Some DBMSs are limited to tracking user connections only, or simply to the fact that the user accessed database data. Others can record detailed activity, including specific data modifications.

Managing Metadata

There are multiple concerns relating to managing metadata. In most cases, database administrators are the only individuals who should have direct access to metadata. This means that, except in some specific, limited instances, database administrators are the only ones who should be making changes to the metadata information. When permission to make metadata changes is delegated, it needs to be both carefully tracked and tightly controlled. You can configure SQL Server, for example, to not only block metadata changes, but to also log the attempt, including the user or application trying to make metadata changes.

The database administrator, working with the data administrator, may also need to publish some of the database structure. Users and application programmers often need to understand, at some level, how database objects are structured to enable database access. However, DBMSs give you ways of isolating the database tables from direct access, including views and user stored procedures.

The database administrator is also responsible for both documenting and protecting the database metadata. This means backing up the metadata in case of problems and documenting database and database object structure. One way of doing this is by scripting the databases, creating scripts that can be run to recreate database objects or, if necessary, to completely recreate the database.

Managing Software

Database administration personnel will be involved with a wide range of data and software maintenance activities. The degree of involvement depends on how the IS department is organized. These activities include installing new versions of the DBMS, installing fixes or patches (corrections) to the DBMS, performing backup and recovery operations, and performing any other tasks related to repairing or upgrading the DBMS or the database. One potential concern, which must be coordinated with network and system administrators, is permissions. The database administrator might not have sufficient permissions to install fixes. It may be necessary to either give the database administrator additional permissions or have a network administrator perform the installations.

Operating system patches and service packs are also an issue, but traditionally not a database administration responsibility. Operating system updates are more often the responsibility of computer support personnel or network administrators. Network administrators and database administrators usually work together to determine which updates need to be applied and scheduling the activities. Current Windows operating system versions are often configured so that most updates are applied automatically, without any administrator interaction.

One particular data maintenance activity is modifying the database structures as tables are modified and new tables are inevitably added. This is fundamentally an issue of database design, which means it also involves data administration.

Managing the Physical Database

A database administrator must understand not only how data is organized, but how the physical database (and database objects) is organized. In the mix of centralized and decentralized IS environments that exist today, there is a wide range of database administration responsibilities relating to database design. For the shared, central databases, database administrators are responsible for physical database design. They may also either be responsible for or be a participant in logical database design. Logical design, however, must be coordinated with data administrators.

Notice that responsibility for physical database design is consistent with personnel's expertise in the features (and idiosyncrasies!) of the DBMS in use and with his or her overall responsibility for the performance of the DBMS environment. For decentralized databases on LAN servers or even on PCs, the database administrator's role in database design might be that of a consultant who is called in on request.

Managing Troubleshooting

Inevitably, failures will occur for reasons ranging from a bug in the application code to a hardware or system software failure. The question is, who do the users

FOR EXAMPLE

Determining the Bottom Line

One possible point of contention when dividing work between data administration and database administration is determining not only who is responsible for what, but also who has the final word. The responsibilities listed here are guidelines based on how the roles are typically defined, but each company has to fill in the details based on its particular situation and administration needs.

The general rule of thumb is that data administrators set the standards, while database administrators apply the standards. Data administration is more of a thinking role, analyzing needs and proposing solutions. Database administration is more of a doing role, finding ways to apply solutions in the real world. The assumption is that each is a specialist in his or her area of responsibility.

Disagreements can arise. Each department addresses issues from its own frame of reference, which can result in competing solutions. Turf battles erupt, as each group wants what's best for "their" database. Though they shouldn't, the issues can become personal with the final solution becoming a matter of personal pride.

Sometimes the deciding factor is simple and direct. Can you or can't you physically implement the solution in the chosen DBMS? If not, then you have to find a different solution. If you can, then things become more complicated. Before you can settle on the best solution, you have to define *best*. What are the overriding project goals? Which is more important, read performance or write performance? Is it more important to optimize server performance or to minimize space requirements?

Before these issues arise, or at least before bridges are irreparably burned, it's important to determine who within in the company is the final arbitrator between data and database administration. The final decision should go back at some point to the data consumers, or more likely, the manager responsible for the data consumers. Early in the design process, you need to think about design issues that might arise and make decisions then about priorities. Then, identify one person (or a very small group) that both data and database administration can agree on as having the final say. This makes it possible to resolve these issues more quickly when they arise (and they will) and to get back to the job of getting and keeping the database running.

call when a failure occurs? In most organizations, the database administrators are the direct contact for troubleshooting. The key to the troubleshooting operation is to make an assessment of what went wrong and to coordinate the appropriate personnel needed to fix it, including systems programmers, application programmers, and the data administrators themselves.

It is important to understand that the database administrator's role is to coordinate troubleshooting and problem correction, but not necessarily to do the actual troubleshooting and repair. The database administrator typically, but not always, is responsible for handling problems relating to the database. For example, if the problem turns out to be inherent in the data design, it then becomes primarily the data administrator's responsibility.

However, database server problems aren't necessary related to the database or DBMS. Hardware problems can occur as easily on a database server as on any other type of computer. Connection problems could result from network failures or problems with the client computer. Even problems that might, at first glance, appear to be data related could have a different source, such as the database application.

An important, but often overlooked, part of the troubleshooting process is complete and accurate documentation. While troubleshooting a problem, you should document the steps taken and their results, as well as the final resolution. Documenting the steps taken helps keep you from duplicating your efforts. Documenting the final resolution provide a handy reference should you see the same problem again in the future.

SELF-CHECK

- List the responsibilities usually delegated to data administration.
- List the responsibilities usually delegated to database administration.

9.3 Understanding Management Tasks

Up to now we have focused on what administrators must do without any consideration for specific tasks, when they are required, or how they are accomplished. The closer we focus on specific task details, the more we have to concern ourselves with DBMS-specific issues. While some tasks are common to all DBMSs, such as backing up and restoring data, the commands used and features supported can vary widely between DBMS implementations.

The goal of this chapter is not to make you a data or database administration expert, but instead to give you an insight into what is involved with each responsibility. You've been introduced to the responsibilities of each role, but a look at some specific management tasks, along with how and when they are performed will help you have a better understanding. Because of their more directly hands-on nature, we'll focus on database administration tasks. We'll also look at some issues relating to specific management tasks. Where there are DBMS-specific differences, we'll be focusing on the tools and utilities provided with Microsoft SQL Server 2005.

9.3.1 Considering "What" and "When"

In Figure 9-1, you saw the database application life cycle represented as four phases: design, implementation, production, and retirement. Let's continue by revisiting that life cycle and how these phases relate to administrator responsibilities.

The design phase of the life cycle includes database and application design. The majority of the work falls on the data administrator to perform the data analysis, prepare the database design, and design database objects (including those needed for data access). The data administrator must also work with application programmers to ensure they understand the database design and to develop data access standards. Keep in mind that even though these activities are considered part of data administration, some of the design activities are handed off to the programming staff, especially when there are experienced database programmers. Much of the work might also be done by an outside consultant.

With implementation, responsibilities begin to shift more toward database administration with the requirements to create the physical database and database objects, to deploy the database, and to perform baseline monitoring. However, there is still a significant amount of work for the data administrators. Not only are you deploying the database, you are also deploying the data. There are going to be significant requirements for data entry, data migration from other sources, or (as it is in most cases) both. It may also be necessary to revisit the design phase to correct problems or performance issues discovered during implementation.

Most of the issues that arise during the production phase, those relating to day-to-day use and to ongoing maintenance, are database administrator responsibilities. Issues relating to maintaining and securing the database require ongoing monitoring and management. However, there are still issues that might arise that are traditionally considered data administration issues, such as issues relating to arbitrating data access, the acquisition and integration of new data, or requirements to modify the database design as business needs change.

You might be tempted to think that retirement, with its requirements for archiving and protecting historical data, fall entirely on database administration. However, as one database application phases out, a new one typically phases in, and often the existing data is the foundation on which the new database and application are built. Determining what data needs to be migrated is a data administration requirement. Of course, determining the actual methodology used to migrate the data and performing the data migration more often than not puts the responsibility right back on the database administrator.

9.3.2 Considering "When" and "How"

We need to think about how different activities are performed. There are some key, and closely related, considerations here. One consideration is the specific processes required to perform different administration tasks. Another consideration is determining whether the tasks should be performed manually or should be automated. **Manual tasks** are tasks that require operator intervention. In order words, you must initiate the task each time it is performed. **Automated tasks** run without direct operator intervention, either on a periodic basis or in response to an alert or other triggering event.

Additionally, there is the issue of what utilities to use. Often, you have the choice of using either a command-line interface or graphical interface utility. Sometimes, the choice is simply one of personal preference, but there can be important differences. The functionality and specific features supported can sometimes vary between graphical-user-interface (GUI)-based and command-line utilities, with the command-line utility usually being the more powerful of the two. It may be an issue of automation, because some GUI-based utilities aren't designed for automated use.

Picking the Right Utility

When deciding what utility to use to perform a task, you must consider several factors, including the following:

▲ **Available Utilities:** sometimes, there's only one way to perform a task, so the decision is made for you.

▲ **Functionality:** you must determine which utility is able to perform all of the aspects of the task that you require.

▲ **Reporting Options:** there is often an issue, especially during performance monitoring and troubleshooting, of how much information is provided by the utility and in what form.

▲ **Interaction and Conflict:** some utilities have a more pronounced impact on database performance while running, meaning that you might want to either use an alternate utility or run the procedure after hours (hopefully as an automated process).

In all cases, pick the tool or utility that is able to complete the task you need done. Take SQL Server for example. You can perform some common tasks, like backup and restore, using either a command-line command or SQL Server Management Studio. Other tasks, such as setting up a data protection mechanism known as database mirroring, are supported through command-line utilities only, so there's no choice to make.

After considering your requirements, if you still have multiple options available, and other factors are more-or-less equally balanced, consider ease of use. There is no reason to make your job more difficult than necessary. Consider, again, running a data backup. Most database administrators find it easier to use SQL Server Management Studio to set up backups, especially when different types of backups running under different schedules must be included, because of the graphical scheduling interface.

Deciding on Automation

How do you determine whether or not you should automate a task? There are a few simple guidelines you should consider. First, how often do you perform the task and under what circumstances? If it's something that you'll be doing once, like creating a specific database table or adding a specific user to the database, then you will usually want to do the job and be done with it. The same is true for procedures that are rarely performed, or performed intermittently with no set schedule.

The opposite is true for periodic procedures that are performed on a regular basis. Once again, let's consider database backups. Backups are an ongoing, periodic activity, usually occurring on a set schedule. How often you back up your database depends on factors such as how quickly the data changes, how much data you can afford to lose (or repost), and what other mechanisms you have in place to protect your data. At least part of the data in most databases is backed up at least once a day and, in many cases, even more often than that. Trying to run those backups manually would be a waste of effort, especially when you consider that backups are usually run after hours whenever possible.

As is usually the case, there is an important exception to these automation guidelines. It's sometimes better to automate the execution of a procedure, even when setting up the automation takes longer than it would to just run it. This is most often the case when running procedures that either interfere with user access to the database or severely degrade server performance while they are running. Another possibility is that you are supporting multiple locations and you want to ensure that a change is made to all of the locations, the same way, and at the same time. If one database is updated and the others are not, you have a consistency problem. You can avoid this by scheduling the change to happen the same way and at the same time, in all locations.

As an example, think about table indexes. They can become fragmented over time. **Fragmentation** is a condition in which the data is randomly spaced in small pieces all over the hard disk rather than being located in one place. This happens over time as data is added to and removed from a table. When fragmentation becomes severe enough, performance starts to degrade and you have to rebuild the indexes to correct the problem. However, rebuilding indexes is a resource-intensive process and can result in tables becoming temporarily unavailable. Often, the best solution is to schedule the rebuild to occur automatically after hours when the impact on other operations is minimized.

9.3.3 Considering Ongoing Management Tasks

Automating some tasks requires more work than others. When you need to automate a task that requires multiple steps, you might want to create a script or even a stored procedure that includes all of the steps. One advantage of creating a procedure is that it lets you pass parameters to control the process. With SQL Server 2005, you can also create maintenance plans that define the tasks to perform, task options, and even the execution schedule.

Understanding Maintenance Requirements

An important consideration is what ongoing management tasks must be performed on a periodic basis. These tasks will vary depending on how the database is used, how active it is, and so forth.

One key to meeting maintenance requirements is to clearly identify the requirements. Once you've done this, you can determine the most appropriate schedule, or even if a periodic schedule is appropriate. Some activities, especially those that require taking the server offline or otherwise making it unavailable, might be limited to running on an as-needed basis only.

Regular backups are generally accepted as a periodic requirement for any database. No matter how well you protect the database, no matter what redundancies you put in place, recovery after a failure often comes down to whether or not you have a good backup.

Other maintenance requirements will depend on your database. You may need to defragment tables and indexes each month. You might want to check for data and file inconsistencies at the same time. You could have special requirements related specifically to your database application and special procedures that need to run weekly or monthly to meet those requirements.

Using Maintenance Plans

Every database is different, as are its specific management requirements. That said, there are several tasks that can and should be performed on a regular basis. SQL Server lets you define sets of scheduled management tasks as **maintenance plans.** SQL Server Management Studio includes predefined task templates for common tasks, as well as a task that lets you specify the SQL Server statements to be executed. An example of a maintenance plan in progress is shown in Figure 9-3.

The connections between the tasks are known as **precedence constraints.** They let SQL Server make decisions about the next step to take (the next tasks to execute), depending on the success, failure, or completion of the previous task. You can even have it notify you that the tasks have run and whether or not any errors occurred.

For the most common tasks, Microsoft simplifies the process ever further through the Maintenance Plan Wizard. This wizard steps you through the process of designing a maintenance plan, including the tasks that it should perform, any task options (such as identifying specific databases), and the execution schedule. The task list from which you make your Maintenance Plan Wizard task selections is shown in Figure 9-4.

Figure 9-3

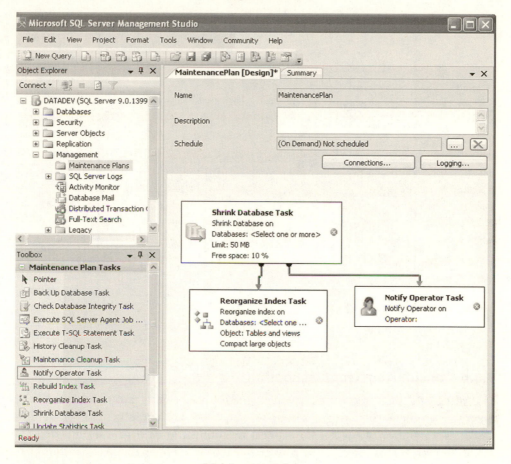

Maintenance plan.

Once created, either manually or through the Maintenance Plan Wizard, you can modify your maintenance plan. You can change, for example, the tasks to run, task options, precedence constraints, and the task schedule. You can also delete a maintenance plan when no longer needed.

This ability to create scheduled maintenance plans is not unique to SQL Server, but SQL Server has automated the process more than most other DBMSs. This is also not your only option for automating process execution in SQL Server. You can also define SQL Server Agent jobs, which can include operating system commands as well as SQL command statements, with periodic schedules. You can define alerts, both through SQL Server and through the Windows operating system, that execute in response to different conditions. However, these options for automated execution are beyond the scope of this chapter.

Figure 9-4

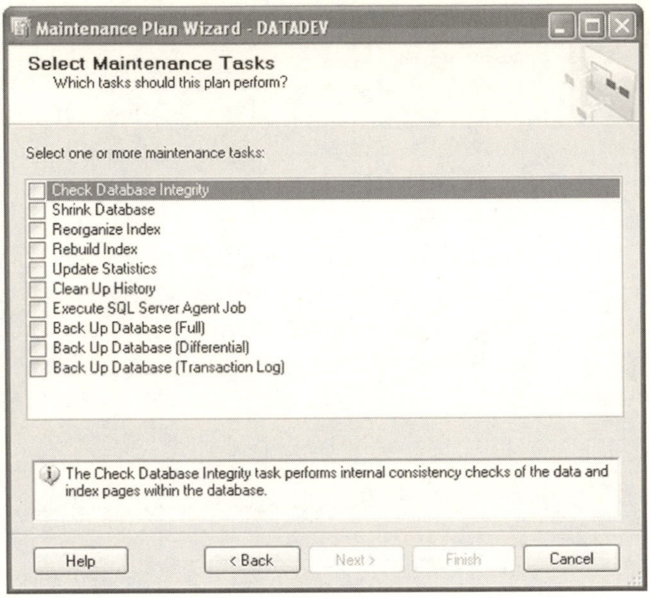

Available tasks.

9.3.4 Considering Troubleshooting

The processes and procedures involved in troubleshooting are as varied as the potential problems you might see. However, there are some general guidelines we should mention while on the subject of administrator responsibilities.

When problems arise, your primary goal as a data or database administrator is to correct the **business problem,** which refers to anything that prevents the business from operating as it should. This means that you do what is necessary to get or keep the business up and running as quickly as possible. Downtime, when the server is unavailable to database users or applications, is not only an annoyance, it's expensive. Depending on the type of business and how heavily it relies on the database, it can be measured in as much as thousands of dollars per minute. The actions you initially take to make the data available do not always represent a complete correction of the problem, sometimes just a correction of the immediate symptoms.

Once you have things up and running, it's your responsibility to either fix the problem permanently, or ensure that the problem is fixed. Not all problems are your direct responsibility, but if they impact the database server, the data it hosts, or the ability to get to that data, making sure that they are corrected is. This includes going beyond fixing the symptoms and identifying and correcting the underlying cause. Otherwise, you might leave a problem that's going to show

FOR EXAMPLE

Simplifying Your Life

Here's the situation. A company has just implemented a database that will contain all of the corporate data. You've been hired to fill both the data and database administration roles. Any time the company is open for business, you're on call. How can you possibly do this job and have any hope of maintaining a life outside of work?

The key is proper use of automation. Identify all of the tasks that need to be performed on a periodic basis. This includes what tasks you need to perform, when, and how they should run (what databases, tables, and so forth are involved). Create and schedule automated procedures to do these for you, and have the database server log the results. That way, as long as there aren't any problems, you just need to check the logs every so often and make sure that everything ran right.

Want to make your life even easier? Few things are more frustrating than an unexpected page at an inopportune moment. What if you could head off some of these in advance? By carefully reviewing the database design and monitoring database activities, it is often possible to identify potential problem areas and put an automated solution in place. For example, some modules within the database application create working tables in the database. It is supposed to drop those tables when finished, but that part doesn't always happen. The application programmer is (supposedly) working on a solution, but for now, it's your problem. The tables build up and eventually you run out of hard disk space. When that happens, no new data can be entered into the database.

The fix is easy. The tables are named so that they are easy to identify and isolate, so you just need to drop the tables and shrink the database. In fact, you've even already create a procedure that does that for you. Now you need to take the next logical step. You can create an alert that monitors available hard disk space. Before available space reaches a critical point, say when 10 percent remains, you have the alert run the procedure for you.

up again when least expected or convenient. Fixing the underlying problem also includes verifying the correction. This doesn't mean that you will always find the cause, especially when dealing with data errors or corrupted records. These are sometimes caused by transient problems, by one-time glitches like a momentary power surge. In that case, it's unlikely that you will find a root cause, but that doesn't mean you shouldn't try.

Here's an example. A user complains that the application reports a data error when trying to access a specific data row. You verify that you can duplicate the problem, find that the problem is consistently with that one table, and correct by restoring the data from backups. Problem fixed, right? Not necessarily, because the underlying cause could be that the hard disk is beginning to fail and that the data error is an early warning sign. In this example, you need to make your best effort to try to discover the cause of the error, which in this case might include running disk utilities or diagnostic programs to check the hard disk.

SELF-CHECK

- Explain, in general terms, how application life cycle phases relate to administration responsibilities.
- List and describe the factors to consider when choosing a tool or utility to perform a management task.

SUMMARY

In this chapter, you learned about administration roles and responsibilities. You learned how you can justify the need for dedicated administrators. Next, you learned about the responsibilities of data administrators and database administrators. Finally, you learned about issues relating to administration tasks, such as choosing the proper utilities and using automation appropriately.

KEY TERMS

Arbitration

Audit trail

Automated tasks

Business problem

Data administrator

Data analyst

Database administrator

Data consumer

Data flow

Data planning

Electronic data interchange (EDI)

Enterprise resource planning (ERP) software

Fragmentation

Maintenance plan

Manual task

Precedence constraint

Publicity

Strategic data planning

Systems analyst

ASSESS YOUR UNDERSTANDING

Go to www.wiley.com/college/gillenson to assess your knowledge of database administration requirements.

Measure your learning by comparing pre-test and post-test results.

Summary Questions

1. Which of the following is another term for data administrator?
   (a) data analyst
   (b) system analyst
   (c) database administrator
   (d) systems programmer

2. Why is it important to have an administrator dedicated to day-to-day operational tasks?
   (a) to ensure that the tasks are done properly and on time
   (b) because of the level of technical expertise required to perform management tasks
   (c) to ensure that decisions are made based on requirements of the business as a whole
   (d) all of the above

3. Database administration is not needed in a decentralized data environment. True or false?

4. Data administrators and database administrators perform identical job functions. True or false?

5. Which of the following is not a phase of the database application life cycle?
   (a) design
   (b) evaluation
   (c) implementation
   (d) production

6. Which of the following is primarily a database administrator responsibility?
   (a) arbitration
   (c) security monitoring
   (d) setting data standards
   (e) data coordination

7. Which of the following is primarily a data administrator responsibility?
   (a) physical database design
   (b) performance monitoring

    (c) publicity

    (d) security monitoring

8. The database administrator should be the primary point of contact when database failures occur. True or False?

9. Which of the following statements best describe data standards management?

    (a) The database administrator has sole responsibility for setting data standards.

    (b) How connections are made for data access should be left up to the individual application programmers.

    (c) Data standards include naming and data access standards.

    (d) none of the above

10. Who should have unlimited access to database metadata?

    (a) users

    (b) application programmers

    (c) data administrators

    (d) database administrators

11. The database administrator should be the only person involved when troubleshooting database problems. True or False?

12. Training should be primarily delegated to data administration. True or False?

13. Automated tasks should be limited only to tasks running on a periodic schedule. True or False?

14. During which phase of a database application's life cycle do most of the responsibilities fall on the data administrator?

    (a) design

    (b) implementation

    (c) production

    (d) none of the above

15. A manual task is one that requires operator intervention. True or False?

16. GUI-based utilities can be used with manual tasks only. True or False?

17. Which of the following would most likely be set up as a recurring task executing on a set periodic schedule?

    (a) database table creation

    (b) index rebuild

    (c) database backup

    (d) adding login accounts

18. In SQL Server, what is a maintenance plan?
    (a) a set of maintenance tasks scheduled for execution
    (b) a list of required maintenance activities
    (c) tasks that execute based on an event threshold
    (c) tasks schedules created automatically for you during database creation

Applying This Chapter

1. You are hired as the database administrator for a mid-sized company that has recently deployed a centralized database. A data administrator is already on staff, hired when they first started designing the database. You will be working with the data administrator on an ongoing basis.
    (a) In general, how should you expect your responsibilities to relate to the data administrator's responsibilities?
    (b) Briefly describe your expected role and responsibilities?
    (c) What are your responsibilities in setting and implementing data access standards?
    (d) Who is more likely to have direct contact with database users? Why?
    (e) There are rumors about potential downsizing. You have heard that the data administrator WILL NOT be laid off. Why should you also be kept on staff, instead of keeping just the data administrator?

2. In each of the following, suggest a way of resolving the situation.
    (a) A user has a personal database that is based on analysis of over a year's worth of sales records locally stored on a PC. Other users want access to the data. The data's owner wants to keep a local copy of the data. What should you do?
    (b) Several maintenance tasks must be completed each weekend. The tasks do not require operator intervention when they run. How should you implement this?
    (c) You suspect users are gaining access to and changing sensitive data. You need to document this. What should you do?
    (d) You've designed procedures that should run when specific performance thresholds are met or exceeded. How can you do this?

Delegating Responsibilities

The left column of Table 9-2 lists specific data and database requirements. For each of these, identify whether the primary responsibility is that of the data administrator or database adminstrator. Write "Data" for data administrator tasks and "Database" for database administrator tasks. When the responsibility is shared, identify which role has the greater responsibility.

Table 9-2: Tasks and Responsibilities

Requirements	Primary responsibility
Manager wants access to payroll history in the Human Resources database. The Human Resources department does not want to give them access. This needs to be resolved.	
Backups must run nightly and each weekend.	
A hard disk was added to the database server. The data needs to be split between the old and new hard disks.	
Application programmers need to know how to retrieve customer information from the Customers table and what information is available in the table.	
Direct access to the Employees table is limited to a defined group of users.	
All logon and logoff activity must be recorded and a permanent record maintained.	
Standards must be set for creating new attribute names as additional data is added to the database.	

Table 9-2: (Continued)

Microsoft has released a service pack for SQL Server 2005 that must be applied as soon as possible.
Columns must be added to existing tables to hold additional data now being tracked.
A vendor has released a new schema for XML purchase orders. Application programmers are not sure how the purchase order data relates to this new schema.

10

TRANSACTIONS AND LOCKING

Starting Point

Go to www.wiley.com/college/gillenson to assess your knowledge of transaction and locking support.

Determine where you need to concentrate your effort.

What You'll Learn in This Chapter

▲ Transaction features and properties
▲ Concurrency control methods
▲ SQL Server 2005 transaction processing

After Studying This Chapter, You'll Be Able To

▲ Describe the features of an ACID transaction
▲ Use BEGIN TRAN, COMMIT TRAN, and ROLLBACK TRAN to manage transaction processing
▲ Compare and contrast implicit and explicit transactions
▲ Identify possible concurrency errors and their causes
▲ Design transactions to minimize concurrency errors
▲ Identify concurrency methods used by various DBMSs
▲ Use transactions to modify SQL Server data
▲ Find and clear blocking transactions

INTRODUCTION

Transactions are a key part of nearly any database application. Transactions provide a means of helping to ensure that you maintain database integrity and consistency by requiring that either all dependent changes are made to the database data or none of the changes are made. In this chapter, you will learn about transaction processing, including transaction properties and transaction scope. You will also learn about potential concurrency errors that can occur and methods different DBMSs use to avoid these. You'll also see how to apply transactions in a real-world environment, using examples based on SQL Server 2005.

10.1 Understanding Transaction Basics

As you learned in Chapter 2, the term transaction refers to one or more statements that execute as a group. Sound like a batch? The concept is similar, but there is one key difference when running statements in the context of a transaction. All of the statement must either complete as a group, meaning that all of the updates are made, or must be rolled back, meaning that any changes made by the statements are reversed as if the statement never ran. The basic purpose of transactions is to ensure consistency and data integrity during database updates.

10.1.1 Understanding Transaction Processing

When you think about the database systems that support businesses like airlines, banking, finance, or retail sales, you can look at them as large transaction processing systems. Each business generates transactions in the tens of thousands that interact in the process of doing business. Even though some of these transactions just read the database and display data, most perform some type of updating. Such critical database systems must be available at all times and must provide fast response times for hundreds of concurrent users.

Systems of this type are especially susceptible to two major types of problems. The first is concurrent transactions attempting to update the same data item. **Concurrent transactions** are transactions being processed simultaneously by the database. The transactions can affect one another adversely, producing incorrect and inconsistent results. The second problem is hardware or software malfunctions. These could cause database failures with resulting data loss or corruption. Concurrency control, which is the process of managing concurrent transactions, and failure recovery are key to maintaining data integrity. Because interference between transactions can cause errors during both read and write operations, concurrency control is critical for both.

Understanding Key Points

A transaction is a single unit of work for the database. A well-designed transaction should accomplish one thing, and all of the statements in that transaction should be related to that one thing only. For example, suppose a bank customer wants to transfer money from a savings account to a checking account. This requires two actions: extracting the money from savings and adding the money to checking. Both actions should take place in the context of a single transaction.

With nearly all DBMSs, these changes are initially made to copies of the table data stored in memory. The changes are written to memory. The transaction processor also writes "before and after" versions of the data to the transaction log. If the transaction completes without error, updating both tables, the database is instructed to **commit** the transaction. This means that the changes can be written permanently to the hard disk, and the transaction is identified as committed in the transaction log. If there is an error while the transaction is running, the DBMS is instructed to roll back the transaction. A **rollback** is the reversal of the changes made by the transaction. It's as if the statements in the transaction never ran.

Who or what instructs the database to commit or roll back the transaction? The batch, application, or connection that initiated the transaction is responsible for either committing or rolling back the completed transaction. Committing or rolling back the transaction are your only options for completing a transaction. Statements executed in the context of a transaction must either commit as a group or roll back as a group. **Partial updates,** when some of the tables involved in an operation are updated, but not all, are normally not allowed.

As with most standards, there are exceptions. Some DBMSs give you the ability to identify groups of statements within the transactions and manage the commit and rollback process by group. This is a more advanced feature of transaction management and beyond the scope of this chapter. Another way to manage partial transactions is nesting transactions, having a transaction executing inside another transaction, which is covered later in this chapter.

Understanding the Need for Transactions

Let's consider a specific example. Your database supports an application that supports automatic purchase order processing. After the order is filled, final processing involves five tables, shown in Figure 10-1.

Inventory quantity on hand is reduced by the items sold and shipped. The Sales table, which tracks sales history for order point calculations, is increased by the same amounts. Also, an order is created, which adds rows to the Order-Head and OrderTail tables. Finally, the CustomerBalance table is increased by the amount of the order. If any of these updates are not made, not only is the data inaccurate, it is inconsistent. If either Inventory or Sales don't get updated,

Figure 10-1

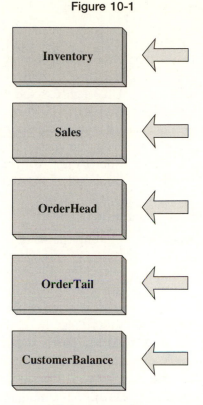

Order processing.

they're no longer consistent with each other. Their balances are no longer based on the same information. The same is true with the order tables and CustomerBalance. One of the goals of transactions is to prevent such inconsistencies from happening.

Understanding the Transaction Log Role

For DBMSs that support a transaction log, transaction statements write to memory and to the log file. At some point, the changes in memory are used to update the database tables on the hard disk. Typically, this occurs when the database server issues a **checkpoint.** The checkpoint writes to the log and is used to divide the log and manage log processing and recovery. When the checkpoint is issued, changes relating to committed transactions that are still buffered in memory are written to the hard disk. With some DBMSs and in some configurations, committed and completed transactions are deleted from the transaction log when the checkpoint is issued. This is done to minimize log file size. However, it's more common to leave the transactions in the transaction log until a backup of the log is run, and then delete the completed transactions at that time.

What if a hardware error occurs before the changes can be written permanently to the hard disk? That is where the transaction log becomes a critical part of transaction management, through a process know as **recovery.** After you restart the DBMS after a failure, the DBMS checks the transaction log for completed, which is to say committed, transactions. These transactions are **rolled forward,** which means that the database table updates are made from the changes recorded in the transaction log. Otherwise, the change might be lost. Uncommitted transactions are treated as if they don't exist, with no changes made to the database.

10.1.2 Using Transaction Commands

The basic commands defined for controlling transactions are:

▲ **BEGIN TRAN[SACTION]:** this identifies the starting point of the transaction. Statements executed after this command are treated as part of the transaction.

▲ **COMMIT TRAN[SACTION]:** this is used to identify successful completion of the transaction. Run COMMIT TRAN when you are sure that all updates have been made and that no errors have occurred. This can also be run as COMMIT WORK.

▲ **ROLLBACK TRAN[SACTION]:** run this command when an error occurs. All statements executed since the BEGIN TRAN statement are rolled back. This can also be run as ROLLBACK WORK.

Some DBMSs support additional statements that let you name a transaction or let you set points within the transaction that let you perform a **partial rollback,** which is when changes are reversed back to a specified point within the transaction, but we're limiting our discussion to these basic transaction commands.

Many programming languages provide direct support for transaction management. For those that don't, you control transactions by passing the transaction commands to the database server. Either way, it is strongly suggested that database applications be designed so that all modifications to the database are performed in the context of a transaction.

When run in a batch or as part of an application, logic must be included to test for or respond to errors, so that the program can correctly commit or roll back the transaction. When using transactions from the command line, you need to manually commit or roll back the transaction. One way of doing this, demonstrated in Figure 10-2, is having a decision point after each statement is executed to determine whether or not an error occurred. Figure 10-2 represents

Figure 10-2

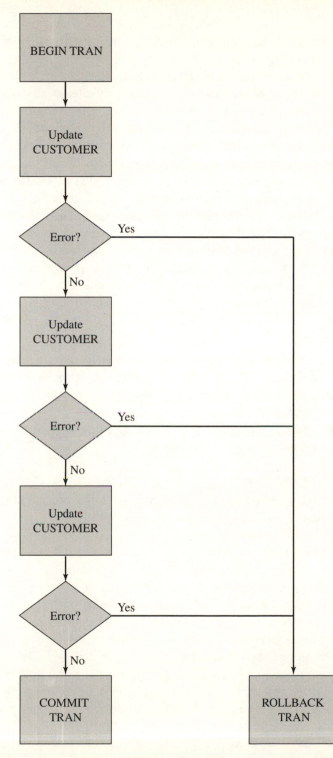

Transaction flow.

a transaction that is updating individual rows in the CUSTOMER table, with a check made after each update.

This is admittedly an inefficient way of testing for and responding to errors. However, it is the one method that is supported by nearly all DBMSs. Some DBMSs, including SQL Server, give you a second option. You can identify a block of statements within a transaction. You also identify a separate block of error handling code. If an error is detected while the statement block executes, execution is redirected to the error handling code. This is shown in Figure 10-3, with the same operations as in Figure 10-2, but managed in a different fashion:

You place the statements necessary to respond to the error in the error handing code block. Somewhere within that error handling code will be a ROLLBACK TRAN statement. The drawing in Figure 10-3 is not a completely accurate depiction of how this works because it implies that the check is made after all of the statements execute. What actually happens is that as soon as an error occurs, processing switches immediately from the statement block to the error handling code block without attempting to execute any additional statements.

Using Transactions

Exactly when, then, do you use transactions? The short answer is that you should use transactions any time you could need to roll back your changes in case of an error. This includes all critical or sensitive database activities, or activities that need to reference multiple data sources.

Think about what happens when a warehouse sale is posted as a customer order. When the order is posted, it needs to:

▲ Update the inventory records for each of the order line items.
▲ Update the customer's outstanding balance with the order amount.
▲ Create a customer order record documenting the sale.

The order would then be forwarded to the warehouse for filling and shipment. Now what happens if there is a problem with one of the steps, such as a problem with creating the customer order record? Both the inventory and customer records would be updated, but because the order isn't created, it doesn't go to the warehouse for fulfillment. The items never get pulled and shipped. The data in the database is inconsistent. The inventory records show fewer items on hand than are actually there and the customer is charged for items never received. A problem like this could be very difficult to isolate and correct.

If the order were run in the context of a transaction, when there was an error creating the customer order, the changes to the customer records and inventory records would be rolled back. The customer still doesn't receive the order, but the inventory and customer records remain consistent. The customer is never charged for the order.

Figure 10-3

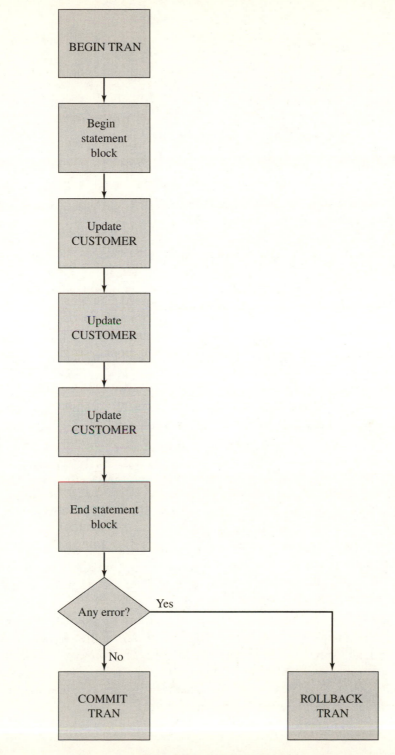

Catching transaction errors.

FOR EXAMPLE

Automatic Recovery

Let's take a moment to consider the importance of the transaction log in maintaining database consistency and integrity. During normal operations, at any point, you will likely have several updated data pages in the cache (in cache memory) waiting to write to the hard disk. This helps improve overall performance because the writes can be delayed until the disk and processor are less active. But what happens if you have an unexpected failure. A UPS fails suddenly, shutting off the server without shutting down. Someone accidentally (or maliciously) unplugs the server. In short, something happens.

What does that mean from a data standpoint? It means that you likely have inconsistencies in the database. Some, but not all, of your updates have been written to the hard disk. Even worse, you don't know which updates have been made, so you don't even have a starting point for recovery.

Maybe you don't have a starting point, but the database server does. The database server has the transaction log. Remember that when a checkpoint is issued, it causes all **dirty pages** (pages that have been modified in memory) to write to the hard disk *immediately*. When the server starts back up, it knows where to start the recovery process, from the most recent checkpoint. Starting at that point, it applies all of the committed changes it finds. The committed change is saved as a data page, so even if the update had already been made, the server is just overwriting the page with the same current data. The important point is that any dirty pages that weren't written to the hard disk before the failure are written during the recovery.

Unfortunately, there's nothing the server can do about recovering uncommitted transactions because it has no way of knowing whether or not they completed successfully. Any pages relating to uncommitted transactions are *not* written to the hard disk and are, in fact, removed from the transaction log because they are no longer needed.

This doesn't mean that there isn't some level of manual recovery required. You still need to check any data that was recently posted to the database to make sure that these changes were made. If not, you will have to repost them manually. Why? Even though you might have completed the operation, depending on when the error occurred, the application might not have committed the transaction before the failure.

10.1.3 Understanding Transaction Properties

An abbreviation that you will commonly see when discussing transactions is **ACID.** This stands for atomicity, consistency, isolation, and durability. Let's look at each of these separately.

▲ **Atomicity:** either all of the statements in the transaction are executed, or none of the statements are executed. An atomic transaction represents a complete unit of work.

▲ **Consistency:** the transaction preserves database consistency. If a transaction executes successfully and performs its database updates properly, the database is transformed from one consistent state to another consistent state.

▲ **Isolation:** a transaction must appear as though it executed by itself without interference from any other concurrent transaction. In practice, however, many concurrent database transactions execute simultaneously.

▲ **Durability:** changes made to the database must be permanent. Even if and when there are subsequent failures, the effects must persist in the database. One way this is ensured is through the transaction log and the recovery process after a failure, as discussed earlier.

Factors relating to isolation deserve a closer look. To ensure complete isolation, the DBMS would not be able to process any other transactions while the current transaction is running. This could have disastrous effects on performance while transactions build up in a queue, waiting for other transactions to complete. For this reason, operations of one transaction are interleaved with operations of other transactions. However, the database system must guarantee the effects of database updates for every pair of concurrent transactions to be as though one transaction executed from beginning to end and then the second started, or vice versa. Transactions must execute independently, and intermediary or partial results of incomplete transactions must be transparent to other transactions.

10.1.4 Understanding Transaction Scope

Transaction scope support and scope options are somewhat DBMS-specific. Two scope options, implicit and explicit transactions, are supported by most DBMSs to varying degrees. Another scope supported by some SQL management systems, including SQL Server, is autocommit transactions.

Explicit Transactions

We'll start with explicit transactions because they're the easiest to understand. With an **explicit transaction,** the entire transaction life cycle is controlled through transaction commands. Transactions start when BEGIN TRAN is issued and complete with either COMMIT TRAN or ROLLBACK TRAN.

Explicit transaction control, where supported, is recommended for new application development because you have complete control over the transaction. There is no question as to when a statement is executing in the context of a transaction, and the application defines the entry and exit point for all transactions. Applications written to use the OLE DB or ODBC API support explicit transactions, as do Microsoft ADO and ADO.NET. **Data application programming interfaces**, or **data APIs,** provide the interface through which the programming language accesses the database. One consideration when choosing a data API is transaction support. Another is programming language and development platform support. Most languages support ODBC and OLE DB. Microsoft languages support ADO and ADO.NET, with ADO.NET support limited to the.NET Framework.

Data APIs provide an interface by providing the commands necessary to access, retrieve, and manipulate database data. These include commands that let the application establish a connection to the database, pass authentication information if necessary, and then close the connection (disconnect) when finished. Some APIs include commands that directly retrieve and manipulate data, but the exact functionality is API-specific. In all cases, and at the very least, the APIs let you pass SQL commands to the database server and receive data from the database.

Implicit Transactions

Implicit transactions start automatically when a query or modification statement that initiates a transaction is executed. The transaction continues until you explicitly execute either COMMIT TRAN or ROLLBACK TRAN. After issuing either command, another transaction starts as soon as another transaction statement is run. Under SQL Server operating in implicit transaction mode, a transaction begins when you execute any of the following statements:

- ▲ ALTER TABLE
- ▲ Any CREATE statement
- ▲ DELETE
- ▲ Any DROP statement
- ▲ FETCH
- ▲ GRANT
- ▲ INSERT
- ▲ OPEN
- ▲ REVOKE
- ▲ SELECT
- ▲ TRUNCATE TABLE
- ▲ UPDATE

Some of these statements might not be familiar to you. The FETCH and OPEN statements are used with server-side **cursors,** which provide a way of processing individual rows within a result set. GRANT and REVOKE are used with security management to allow and remove permissions. Cursor use and security management are beyond the scope of this chapter.

The biggest drawback of using implicit transactions is that you don't control the start of the transaction, but you must identify the end of the transaction. This can lead to very long running transactions which, in turn, can result in access problems and impair performance.

The main reason for enabling implicit transactions is that they are required by some legacy applications. You should not develop new applications to use implicit transactions. The ODBC API even includes commands to place the database in implicit transaction mode. The OLE DB API can be used with implicit transactions, but does not include a way of putting the database into implicit transaction mode. It can, however, issue commands that disable implicit transactions. The ADO and ADO.NET APIs do not support implicit transactions.

Autocommit Transactions

With **autocommit transactions,** which is the default state for SQL Server and many other DBMSs, each statement is treated as an individual transaction. If you want a statement to run and, if no errors occur, commit—there's no need to do anything special when you execute the statement.

When operating in an autocommit mode, explicit transactions are still supported. It's not uncommon to have some statements, like data retrieval queries, run as stand-alone transactions in autocommit mode, while using explicit transactions when multiple dependent statements are used.

Nested Transactions

Most DBMSs support nested transactions. A **nested transaction** occurs when you explicitly start a new transaction while already operating within the scope of a transaction. Nested transactions can be used with both explicit and implicit transactions.

Here's an example. The line numbers are included for reference only. The indents are included to make the nested transaction easier to see.

```
1  BEGIN TRAN
2  INSERT CUSTOMER VALUES ('1442', 'Get it here', '137','Memphis')
3    BEGIN TRAN
4    INSERT CUSTOMEREMPLOYEE VALUES
5    ('1442', '3221', 'Thomas', 'Jane', 'Owner')
6    IF @@ERROR = 0
7          COMMIT TRAN
8    ELSE
```

```
9              ROLLBACK TRAN
10 —More processing statements here
11 —Commit or rollback transaction
```

The BEGIN TRAN in statement 1 is the start of the outer transaction. You add a row to the CUSTOMER table. The BEGIN TRAN statement in line 3 starts the inner transaction, which adds a row to the CUSTOMEREMPLOYEE table. Depending on the value of @@ERROR, which identifies whether or not an error occurred when the most recent statement executed, you either commit or rollback the inner transaction. This does not commit the statement in line 2. The ROLLBACK TRAN statement acts differently however. If you execute the ROLLBACK TRAN in line 9, everything rolls back to the initial BEGIN TRAN statement.

Even though you run the COMMIT TRAN statement in line 7, it doesn't mean that the change will write to disk. This change is still controlled in the context of the outer transaction. If, after the statements shown here, you run COMMIT TRAN, both added rows would write to their respective tables. If you run ROLLBACK TRAN, all changes, including those in the inner transaction, are rolled back.

You should try to avoid the use of explicit nested transactions like the previous example. That's because a transaction should represent a single unit of work, that is, it should accomplish a single task. Also, as you can see in that example, there really isn't much benefit to including a nested transaction. So why even bring them up? Because you might end up using a nested transaction without ever realizing it. You can end up with a nested transaction when calling procedures that include transactions. For example:

```
BEGIN TRAN
DECLARE @TestVal int
EXEC p_GenSummary @TestVal OUTPUT
IF @TestVal = 0
COMMIT TRAN
ELSE
ROLLBACK TRAN
```

If the procedure, p_GenSummary, includes a transaction as part of its steps, that transaction runs as a nested transaction. Even if you commit the changes inside the procedure, you still need to commit them in the calling batch. If you roll the changes back in the calling batch, it rolls back the changes made inside the procedure.

With nested transactions, it's possible to lose track of whether or not you have any **open transactions,** those that you need to either commit or roll back, at any point. In SQL Server, you can use @@TRANCOUNT to get a count of open, or pending, transactions. If @@TRANCOUNT returns zero, then you don't have any open transactions. If you do have open transactions, it returns a count of transactions. It's a good idea to check before closing an open connection, when using a query window in SQL Server Management Studio, for example. If you close a connection that contains open transactions, those transactions are rolled back.

10.1.5 Recognizing and Resolving Potential Problems

We've already discussed one potential problem with transactions, an error occurring during the transaction so that only some of the statements are executed. This can lead to inconsistent, incorrect, and invalid data if you commit the transaction at that point. Another potential problem is that it's possible that a transaction is just poorly written and attempts an illegal or inappropriate action. Integrity functions in the database management system work to preserve the integrity of the database by performing the following actions:

▲ Monitor and scrutinize all transactions, especially those with database updates.
▲ Detect any data integrity violations by transactions.
▲ If a violation is detected, take appropriate action such as:
  ▲ Rejection of the operation.
  ▲ Reporting of the violation.
  ▲ Correction of error condition, if possible.

While it would be convenient if the DBMS could handle all of these functions by itself and completely in the background, this isn't the case. Management systems include various tools and implement functionality to assist, but some of the logic involved needs to be built into the application. Consistency and integrity are insured by having the management system and application work together.

Consider a situation where you have an application that automatically processes customer orders. It uses a transaction to update the inventory quantities, generate an order, and update the customer's outstanding balance. The transaction creates an order in the OrderHead and OrderTail tables. Let's add some business rule conditions, as follows:

▲ Each order must have a unique order number.
▲ Each detail item must be related to a valid order.
▲ Each order must have at least one detail item.

Okay, so how do you handle these? Let's take the last item first, because it's potentially the trickiest one of the set. This isn't something that the database can easily check through table constraints, so it's an issue better resolved by the application. The application needs to verify that there is at least one valid detail item before committing the transaction. An even better solution would be using that as a decision point for whether or not it even starts the transaction. If you never start it, then you don't have to roll it back because the order doesn't qualify.

The other two conditions are easier to enforce because they can be handled by table constraints. You could use a unique constraint to enforce uniqueness on the order number and a foreign key constraint to enforce the relationship. If either is violated, the database server generates an error. However, instead of just having the transaction fail and roll back, you could include logic

FOR EXAMPLE

Transactions from the Command Line

Let's talk about explicit transactions from the command line. When using SQL Server 2005, considering that it defaults to autocommit transactions, you might wonder why you would need, or even want, to use explicit transactions.

One possible reason is simple. We all sometimes make mistakes. When connected to a database server with administrator permissions and making direct changes to table data, the consequences of our mistakes could be far-reaching. Say you're doing some cleanup work in the database and you're deleting some old customer records. You run:

```
delete customer where custid = 'AJA1244'
delete customer where custid = 'BX54T4'
delete customer
```

At some point, immediately after you press F5, you realize your mistake. You immediately run:

```
ROLLBACK TRAN
```

The query window responds with:

Msg 3903, Level 16, State 1, Line 1
The ROLLBACK TRANSACTION request has no corresponding BEGIN TRANSACTION.

You've lost all of the data in the customer table. The situation isn't hopeless. You have backups (hopefully) and you can restore the customer table from the most recent backup. That means an interruption to user operations, lost time, lost money, and possibly a lost job (yours).

What if you ran the following, instead:

```
begin tran
delete customer where custid = 'AJA1244'
delete customer where custid = 'BX54T4'
delete customer
```

This would give you a chance to verify your changes before committing the transaction and if you do have a mistake, like the typo in the last DELETE statement, you can roll the changes back and start again. Now, if you still end up committing the changes without first verifying, you're on your own.

in the application to correct the error and resubmit the rows for insertion into the appropriate tables.

Another potential problem is concurrent access of the same data. What if another transaction is updating the same tables at the same time? Here's what might happen. Both transactions read the balance from CustomerBalance at the same time. Each transaction calculates a new balance based on the order being processed. One transaction updates CustomerBalance, then the other. The change made by the second transaction overwrites the change made by the first, so that the first change is lost. CustomerBalance no longer matches up with the customer orders. This is an issue of concurrency, which we'll discuss in more detail later in this chapter.

SELF-CHECK

- Describe the properties of an ACID transaction.
- Compare and contrast implicit and explicit transactions.

10.2 Managing Concurrency Control

The database environment supports processing of transactions, several of which may interact with the database at the same time. This can lead to problems resulting from two or more transactions trying to access and update the same tables at the same time. You could line the transactions up, one after another, so that each one is effectively the only thing happening in the database server, but keep in mind that you could be looking at thousands of transactions.

Remember that a database system, in essence, is a transaction-processing environment. Every effort to accelerate transaction processing deserves top priority. Each transaction consists of central processing unit (CPU) processing and input/output (I/O) operations. Transaction processing is interleaved so that while one transaction waits for I/O, the CPU can process another transaction. This is the primary motivation for concurrent transactions. Benefits to concurrent processing include:

▲ Overall increase in system throughput.
▲ Improved response times.
▲ Simultaneous data access.
▲ Shorter transactions finishing quickly without waiting for longer transactions to end.
▲ Unpredictable response delays being minimized.

Put simply, concurrent transaction processing is a functional requirement of any DBMS. That means you need a way of managing concurrency control.

Figure 10-4

Transaction T1	Warehouse Database	Transaction T2

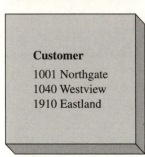

Transaction T1

Check on hand for item 120
Check credit for customer 1001
Reduce on hand for 120 by 350
Generate order
Commit transaction

Warehouse Database

TextBookInventory

100 Chemistry
120 Physics
310 Intro. To Literature

Transaction T2

Check on hand for item 120
Check credit for customer 1040
Generate order
Reduce on hand for 120 by 500
Commit transaction

Customer

1001 Northgate
1040 Westview
1910 Eastland

Sample transactions.

10.2.1 The Need for Concurrency Management

The easiest way to see the need for concurrency management is with an example. Take a look at Figure 10-4.

Textbook 120 (Physics) has a quantity on hand of 1100. Transaction T1 starts processing first, then T2. T1 reads the quantity on hand from TextBookInventory, goes through the processing steps listed in the figure, sets the remaining quantity at 750, and commits the transaction. Now, consider what happens if T2 reads the quantity on hand after T1, but before T1 reduces the amount by 350 books. T2 does processing based on a quantity of 1100. When it makes its update to TextBookInventory, it overwrites the value assigned by T1, setting the quantity at 600, and commits the transaction. You're left with a data error. The quantity is off, showing 350 more books than are actually there. This is one of the most common concurrency problems, known as a lost update, which occurs when one transaction overwrites another transaction's changes.

10.2.2 Recognizing Concurrency Problems

There are four types of concurrency problems that can result from processing concurrent transactions. You can end up with lost updates, dirty reads, non-repeatable reads, and phantom reads. If concurrency has to be allowed in transaction processing, then these problems must be resolved. Before considering solution options, you need a clear understanding of the nature of these problems.

In a **lost update,** an apparently successful database update by one transaction can be overwritten by another transaction. This is one aspect of the problem you saw in Figure 10-4. T1 updated the database to show 750 books left in inventory, then T2 updated the same record, changing the number in inventory to 600. This leaves us with an inaccuracy in the TextBookInventory table. The other problem is that T2 is working with inaccurate data, because the data changed after it was read, but more on that problem next.

A **dirty read,** also called an **uncommitted dependency** (or dependency on an uncommitted update), is the result of one transaction reading data that is being modified by a second transaction. For this example, you need to look at Figure 10-5.

In Figure 10-5, the transaction is filling a customer order. The general flow for processing the order is as follows:

▲ Locate the items being ordered.
▲ Reduce the quantity on hand for each item.

Figure 10-5

Transaction T1	Warehouse Database	Transaction T2
Check on hand for item 120		Check on hand for item 120
Reduce on hand for 120 by 1000	**TextBookInventory**	Reduce on hand for 120 by 600
Check credit for customer 1001		Check credit for customer 1040
Generate order	100 Chemistry	Generate order
Commit transaction	120 Physics	Commit transaction
	310 Intro. To Literature	

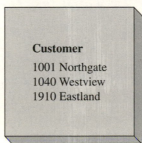

Customer

1001 Northgate
1040 Westview
1910 Eastland

Dirty read example.

▲ Verify customer credit.

▲ Finalize the order and commit the transaction.

Item 120 has 1100 units on hand before transactions T1 and T2 start processing. Textbook quantities are reduced by the amount ordered by customer 1001. For item 120, it is reduced by 1000 copies, leaving 100 on hand. In T2, the application checks inventory levels for customer 1040's order and finds that there are insufficient copies to fill the order. This is a dirty read because the change made by T1 has not been committed. The line item for item 120 is canceled out due to insufficient quantity to fill the order. After this happens, in T1, it is determined that customer 1001 has insufficient credit, so all of the changes to TextBookInventory made by T1 are rolled back. However, this happens too late to fill those items for customer 1040. The customer doesn't get the books, and the company possibly loses a sale, because of a dirty read.

A **nonrepeatable read** is also referred to as **inconsistent analysis.** This occurs when one transaction is reading a table multiple times while another transaction is modifying the same table. Take a look in Figure 10-6.

Figure 10-6

Transaction T1	Warehouse Database	Transaction T2
Read all TextBookInventory	**TextBookInventory**	Order more copies of 120
Check processing criteria	100 Chemistry	Order more copies of 200
Identify qualifying rows	120 Physics	Commit transaction
Read qualifying rows	131 Physical Science	
Process rows and modify values	200 Social Studies	
Commit transaction	310 Inro. To Literature	

Customer

1001 Northgate
1040 Westview
1910 Eastland

Nonrepeatable read example.

Figure 10-7

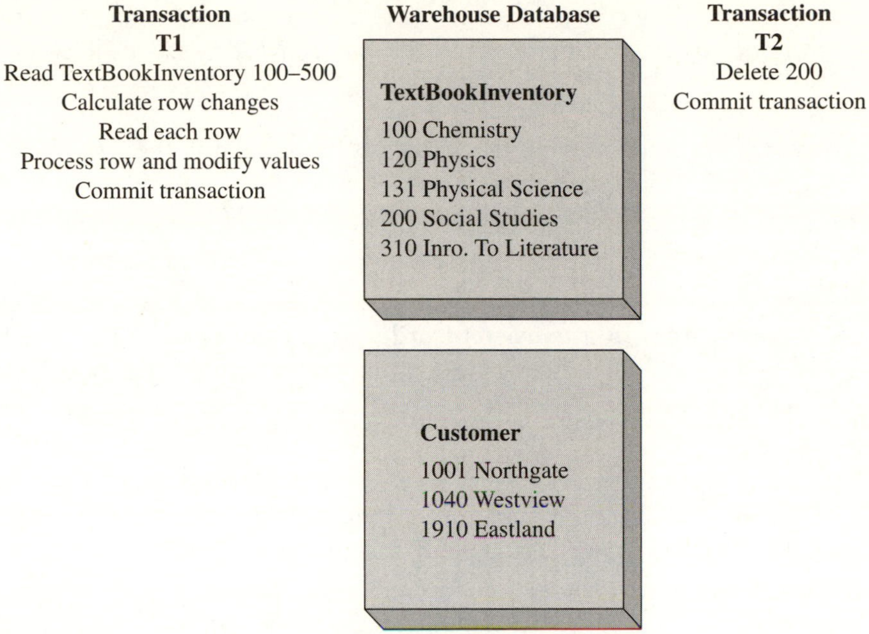

Transaction T1	Warehouse Database	Transaction T2
Read TextBookInventory 100–500	**TextBookInventory**	Delete 200
Calculate row changes		Commit transaction
Read each row	100 Chemistry	
Process row and modify values	120 Physics	
Commit transaction	131 Physical Science	
	200 Social Studies	
	310 Inro. To Literature	
	Customer	
	1001 Northgate	
	1040 Westview	
	1910 Eastland	

Phantom read example.

In this example, T1 reads selected columns from the TextBookInventory table to determine if they meet a set of criteria for further processing. In this example, the criteria include the suggested order point and the quantity on hand. When it determines which rows meet the criteria, it goes back and reads selected rows from the table, this time extracting all columns, before making updates. In the interim, T2 has made changes to rows in TextBookInventory. When T1 reads the rows a second time, it might discover that items 120 and 200 no longer qualify, resulting in an error.

The last error type is the **phantom read** error. This happens when a transaction reads a range of rows, but when it goes back to read the same rows again, either one or more are missing or rows have been added. The missing rows or added rows are referred to as **phantoms**. Take a look at Figure 10-7.

In Figure 10-7, T1 reads a range of rows from TextBookInventory. It calculates changes to be made to the rows. While it is making those calculations, T2 deletes one of the rows. As a way of helping to ensure data integrity, T1 goes back and reads each row again before writing the changes. When it does, it will discover that one of the rows is a phantom—it no longer exists.

10.2.3 Designing for Concurrency

One way of minimizing concurrency errors is by designing your database application with concurrency in mind. Some specific things you can do include the following:

▲ **Minimize transaction size:** the smaller a transaction is the less likely it is to interact with other transactions.

▲ **Limit transaction operations:** the transaction should accomplish one task and should include only those statements needed to accomplish that task.

▲ **Access resources in a consistent order:** you can minimize the possibility of two transactions interfering with or mutually blocking each other if, whenever possible, you write transactions to access resources in the same order.

▲ **Minimize resource access time:** keep the time that you hold a resource open for access to a minimum by going in, doing what you need to do, and then getting back out as quickly as possible.

▲ **Watch when you run resource-intensive operations:** whenever possible, schedule operations that include long-running transactions to run after hours or during off-peak times.

Database normalization can also impact concurrency management. The normalization process tends to break a table down into smaller, more tightly focused tables. Because of how the data is split during normalization, a transaction that updates user address information doesn't necessarily access the same table as one that updates user payables information.

10.2.4 Concurrency Methods

Methods for managing concurrency vary by DBMS. Methods include scheduling and serialization, locking, timestamp ordering, and optimistic processing. There is some overlap between these methods, and most management systems allow for optimistic processing in addition to other concurrency methods. The goal is to allow concurrent processing while ensuring **transaction isolation,** that is, making sure one transaction doesn't interfere with another transaction.

Though not often used, you need to understand transaction scheduling and serialization first because the concept is important to the other concurrency methods. **Transaction scheduling** manages concurrency fundamentally by avoiding it. Processing is scheduled so that as one transaction begins commit or rollback, the next transaction in the queue begins processing. **Serialization** refers to the transactions running serially, one after the other, rather than concurrently. More advanced schedule algorithms base the schedules on serial use of resources rather than simply on serializing the transactions. This allows for concurrent transactions, as long at the transactions do not require the same resources.

There are a couple of problems inherent in transaction scheduling. One is the performance loss because of the serialized transactions. The other problem is the overhead required to schedule the transactions and to manage transaction processing.

Timestamp ordering is another schedule-based concurrency management method that preserves the transaction order. It uses a timestamp protocol that manages transaction processing to ensure that the transaction order is preserved. As each transaction is entered for execution, it is given a timestamp value. This is typically taken down to the level of the individual statements, with each statement given either a read timestamp or write timestamp, as appropriate. Access to individual resources is serialized, based on timestamp order.

The potential problems are similar to those described earlier for transaction scheduling. Delays caused by serialization are less pronounced because serialization is managed at the statement level rather than the transaction level, but longer running transactions can still delay completion of shorter transactions. Also, scheduling and management carry a significant amount of processor resource overhead.

Locking is the method most commonly used by current DBMS versions. While one transaction is accessing a resource it places a **lock,** an access restriction, on the resource, controlling the level of access allowed by another transaction. There are two basic types of locks. A **shared lock** is used to manage read access. When one transaction places a shared lock on a resource, other transactions can access the same resource, but only for read access. An **exclusive lock** is used with write access. When a transaction places an exclusive lock on a resource, no other transaction is able to access the resource. Many DBMSs set a default **transaction isolation level,** which sets the locking level automatically during transaction processing.

You also have control over the **lock scope** or **locking level.** This refers to the specific resource that is locked. Most DBMSs support different locking levels, letting you lock the database, a table, or even an individual row. The more granular the locking level, the smaller the scope of the lock, the less interference with other transactions.

The use of exclusive locks effectively serializes the transactions during write operations, blocking other transactions' access until the write operation is complete. This is also the biggest potential drawback to this method, that a transaction's access to resources it needs can be blocked. If the blocking transaction is also a long-running transaction or is delayed for some reason, it could cause the **blocked transaction** to time out, resulting in an error. A blocked transaction is one that cannot continue because it cannot access the resources it needs.

With **optimistic processing** techniques, the transaction processor doesn't check for potential conflicts, like with scheduling or locking methods. Instead, it assumes that there is little, or no, possibility of conflict between the transactions. If an error is detected during transaction processing, it's necessary to abort and roll back, then restart the transaction. Most database systems let you use optimistic processing on an ad hoc basis in addition to other concurrency management methods. The current trend in database management system and database application design is toward more optimistic methods of transaction management. This is an area that is continuing to evolve as manufacturers release new versions of the DBMS products.

FOR EXAMPLE

Why Concurrency Matters

Most businesses have the same basic goal, to make money. That means that they are looking for ways to either make more money, or reduce their expenses, the cost of making money. Some expenses are obvious, such as building, inventory, and salaries. Others are hidden and not always noticed. That leads us to concurrency errors.

Many experts agree that cutting costs pays off better in profits, dollar-for-dollar, than increasing revenues. Errors cost, including concurrency errors. Think about the examples in this chapter, and you can start to see some of the hidden costs, such as the following:

- Lost sales due to inaccurate inventory and dirty reads.
- Data inaccuracies that have to be corrected, such as through a costly, time-consuming physical inventory.
- Lost time, which costs more in employee wages, for the time required to repost orders because of errors.
- Lost administrator time troubleshooting problems that might or might not really exist.

Administrators can lose a lot of time, and possibly have to cause additional server down time, looking for the source of intermittent problems. Some of these problems could be caused by transient concurrency errors. Because of the brief error duration and mixed symptoms, problems like this can be especially hard to isolate and correct.

The cost of any one of these (except possibly the lost order) is minimal when taken by itself. Over time, and over multiple occurrences, they can add up to a measurable expense.

SELF-CHECK

- What are the benefits of concurrent processing?
- List design considerations that can help minimize concurrency errors.
- List methods used by various DBMSs to minimize concurrency errors.

10.3 SQL Server Transaction Management

So far, most of our discussion has been about DBMS transaction support in general. However, databases are not deployed on a general DBMS. They are hosted by a specific database server, each with its own way of managing transactions and resolving potential problems. In order to look at transaction processing and management in any detail, you need to focus on a specific DBMS. For our purposes, we'll use SQL Server 2005 as our example.

10.3.1 Understanding Transaction Processing

SQL Server 2005 uses lock-based concurrency management as its primary management method. The transaction isolation setting, which in turn defines locking defaults, is specified for the connection. Those defaults apply to any transaction initiated through that connection. You also have locking hints available. These are specified at the statement level and let you acquire a specific type of lock and specify the scope of the lock (the resource locked).

When you execute a transaction, SQL Server determines the resources needed and the types of locks that should be acquired. It writes the statements to the transaction log, acquires the locks it needs, retrieves the data into memory, and processes the data. Changes are made to the cached copy in memory. Changes are made managed at the page level, that is, in 8KB blocks. As you've already learned, a page that has been modified in memory is referred to as a dirty page. Dirty pages remain in memory only until the transaction is committed, at which point they can be written to the hard disk. The term dirty page refers simply to fact that the data has changed, not the state of the transaction. Both committed and uncommitted pages are referred to as dirty pages.

SQL Server controls the transaction log through checkpoints, a concept introduced earlier in this chapter. SQL Server uses an internal schedule to periodically issue checkpoints. There are also database server events and conditions that will cause a checkpoint to be issued, including the following:

▲ The active portion of the log is larger than can be efficiently recovered after an error.
▲ An ALTER DATABASE statement is executed.
▲ The database is backed up.
▲ The server is stopped or shut down.

This is a partial list, but it gives you a good idea of the types of events that cause a checkpoint to be issued. Transact-SQL also includes a CHECKPOINT command that manually issues a checkpoint when run. When the checkpoint is issued, it forces a write of all committed dirty pages to the hard disk.

10.3.2 Managing Locks, Locking, and Transaction Isolation

Lock management through transaction isolation is not unique to SQL Server, but it is the primary concurrency control method used by SQL Server. SQL Server 2005 supports the four transaction isolation levels defined by the SQL-99 standard. These are, from least to most restrictive:

▲ Read uncommitted
▲ Read committed
▲ Repeatable read
▲ Serializable

SQL Server supports one additional level that is not part of the SQL-99 standard, snapshot isolation. The level is set for a connection using the SET TRANSACTION ISOLATION LEVEL statement.

The **read uncommitted** isolation level is the least restrictive, but also provides the least protection against possible concurrency errors. When running under this isolation level, transactions do not acquire a shared lock when reading data. Transactions also ignore exclusive locks, meaning that they can read data that has been locked for modification. Because of this, your transactions can be affected by dirty reads, nonrepeatable reads, and phantoms.

The **read committed** transaction isolation level is the default database level. This level prevents a transaction from reading uncommitted changes made by other transactions. This means that dirty reads are prevented, but nonrepeatable reads and phantoms are both still possible. That is because it is possible for another transaction to make changes to the data and commit the changes between reads.

The **repeatable read** transaction isolation level prevents both dirty reads and nonrepeatable reads. This is because it prevents the current transaction from reading uncommitted data and also prevents other transactions from modifying data being read by the current transaction until after the transaction completes.

It doesn't completely protect you against concurrency errors, however, because phantoms can still occur. Even though another transaction can't modify table rows, it could insert new rows to a table. This isolation level is not commonly used.

Snapshot is a special transaction isolation level, specific to SQL Server 2005. Data used by the transaction is cached in memory at the start of the transaction. The transaction uses this snapshot, rather than the table data, so it is not affected by changes made by other transactions. You need to exercise caution, however, because the transaction results will be based on this snapshot and the state of the data at the beginning of the transaction. That means that the results might not be consistent with the current data. Snapshot isolation is useful in several situations, though, such as when generating data for a long running report. It ensures that the report remains internally consistent and consistent with the point in time on which it is based.

The **serializable** transaction isolation level is the most restrictive and gives the highest level of protection against concurrency errors. When running under this level of isolation, a transaction cannot read uncommitted data, other transactions cannot modify data read by this transaction, and other transactions cannot insert rows or key values into a range read by this transaction. Because of this, dirty reads, nonrepeatable reads, and phantoms are prevented.

The potential problem is that all other transactions are blocked from modifying any resources that this transaction needs to access. In most cases, the delay is minimal and likely to go unnoticed. However, it can become a problem when dealing with long-running transactions or in a very active system. One potential consequence is that two transactions could **deadlock.** This is a condition that results when each transaction is blocking the other, like in Figure 10-8.

Figure 10-8

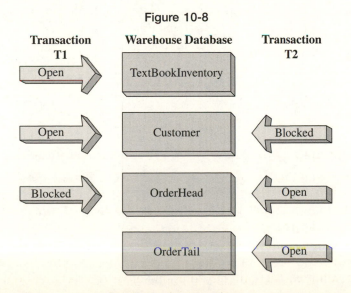

Deadlocked transactions.

FOR EXAMPLE

Lower Level—Better Performance?

SQL Server 2005 defaults to the read committed transaction isolation level, but is that always the best choice? The fact that SQL Server offers choices for setting the transaction isolation level in itself tells you that this is not always the case. Not only can you set the transaction isolation level when you open a command line connection, like a query window, but you can also specify the transaction isolation level when establishing a connection from a database application. But how do you choose?

Choosing the right transaction isolation level depends on several factors. The time you take to make the right choices can pay off, though, in better data integrity and possibly in better performance. The data integrity is easy to see. The higher the isolation level, the better protected the transaction from interference from other transactions. Performance issues might not be as obvious.

In the simplest terms, the less restrictive the isolation level, the less likely that your application might need to wait for resources. Does this mean that a lower level always means better performance, though? Not necessarily. Performance includes both database and application performance. Any performance gains from lowering the transaction isolation level could be lost if the application has to do additional verification testing or has to correct errors that it has detected.

T1 accesses the TextBookInventory, Customer, OrderHead and OrderTail tables, in that order. T2 accesses OrderHead, OrderTail, and then Customer. Each transaction acquires a lock on each table it accesses. In this situation, T1 is holding Customer open and trying to access OrderHead. T2 is holding OrderHead and OrderTail open and trying to access Customer. Neither one can continue because its access is blocked by the other. This situation will continue until one of the transactions times out.

10.3.3 Recognizing, Clearing, and Preventing Deadlocks

Blocked transactions and deadlocks are perhaps your biggest potential concerns in a transaction processing environment. These conditions can cause performance to grind to a halt and lead to transaction processing errors and time-outs, resulting in critical data updates not being made.

The first thing you have to do is accept that in almost any transaction processing environment, intermittent occurrences of blocked transactions are going to be a fact of life. Your database application must be able to account for these and respond appropriately. The most common error, as with the situation in Figure 10-8, is that one transaction eventually times out. As a response, this means recognizing that an update has timed out, rolling back the transaction, and then resubmitting the changes in the context of a new transaction.

Avoiding Blocked Transactions

The best solution, whenever possible, is to avoid blocked transactions and deadlocks in the first place. Earlier in the chapter you were given guidelines for designing transactions that minimize concurrency errors. These same guidelines apply to avoiding blocks and deadlocks.

Two key considerations are the transaction length and the order in which transactions access resources. In Figure 10-8, if both transactions accessed resources in the same order you would have had one temporarily blocking the other, but could have avoided the deadlock. Of course, this would depend on an ideal development environment where developers, even those working on different applications, keep in close contact with each other to ensure that this standard is met. Each developer will probably have his or her idea as to the best order. The order will also be influenced by the application's specific requirements. In the real word, the best you can usually hope for is to have the transactions within a single application access resources in a consistent order.

You can also minimize the occurrence of blocked transactions and deadlocks by using appropriate locking levels. You might have avoided the deadlock if the transactions acquired locks at the row level instead of the table level. As long as the transactions don't need access to the same rows within a table, neither is blocked by the other.

You need to avoid holding a transaction open any longer than necessary. As soon as the transaction completes its processing, you should either commit or roll back as appropriate. Either action will cause the transaction to release any locks it has acquired. Leaving a transaction open is sometimes an unexpected consequence of nested transactions.

One way that database management systems detect blocked transactions is through time-outs. A **time-out** occurs when a transaction is unable to complete processing within a specified time. You can configure the maximum time allowed, typically in milliseconds, or configure the DBMS to allow the transaction to run indefinitely until it finishes (usually not recommended because of the potential adverse affect on performance).

The most common reason for a transaction to time-out is that it can't access the resources it needs and waits for those resources until they either become available or the transaction times out. Time-outs can sometimes result because there is an excessive load on the database server, especially if the time-out periods are set too short for the operational environment. They can also occur as the result of an error.

Figure 10-9

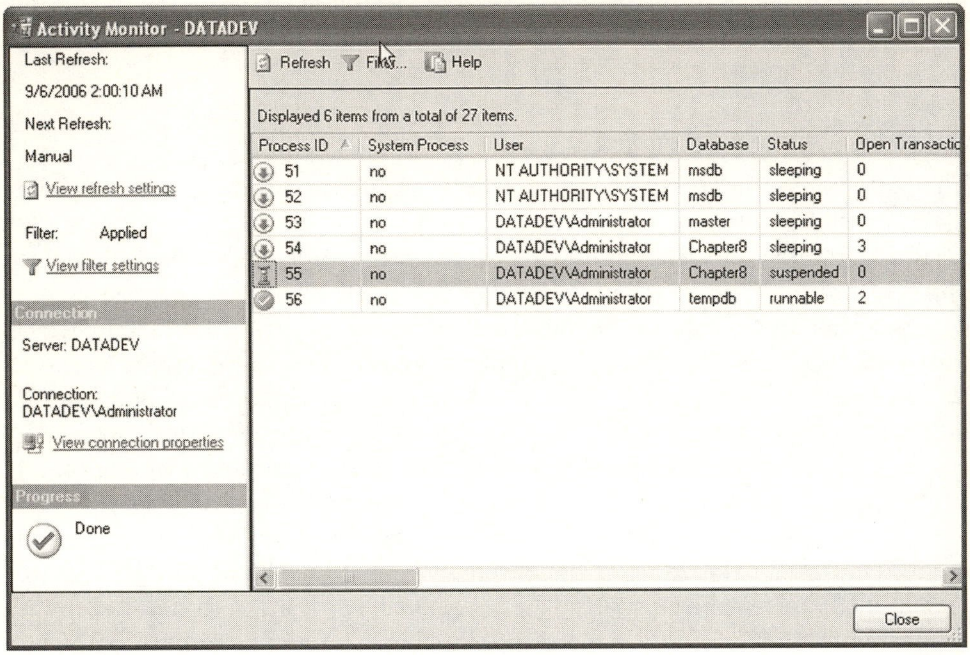

Suspended transaction.

Detecting and Clearing Blocks

Sometimes it becomes necessary to clear a blocking transaction. The steps involved in doing this programmatically are somewhat advanced and beyond the scope of this chapter, but we'll take a look at the manual procedure for clearing a blocking transaction. To see this, you need to go back to SQL Server Management Studio, specifically, the Activity Monitor, shown in Figure 10-9.

Process ID 55 is shown as suspended. This means that it is in a wait state and something is preventing it from continuing. To see what that something is, scroll across, as shown in Figure 10-10, until the blocking column is visible. You see that Process ID 54 is blocking Process ID 55 from continuing.

To clear the block, you need to do one of the following:

▲ Complete the transaction running in the connection for Process ID 54.

▲ Close the connection.

▲ Kill the process.

When you **kill** a process, you exit it without completing any open transactions. You can do this by running the KILL command followed by the process

FOR EXAMPLE

Could It Be—Deadlocks?

One area where many database applications fall short is in error reporting. The application receives errors from the database server, but either isn't designed to evaluate the error's cause or it doesn't pass the errors along to the user. Instead the applications just report some type of generic database error.

If database activity increases with time, it's not unusual that database errors will also increase. It's not that the rate of errors is increasing, but as the overall work volume increases, the number of errors increase. In some cases it could be that you're pushing the limits of the hardware, or that there is some inherent flaw in the database design that doesn't become significant until activity reaches a threshold point. However, a likely culprit for increased errors as database activity increases is deadlocks. Because deadlocks are caused by competition for database resources, as you have more requests for those same resources, deadlocks will also increase, even in a well-designed database. The problem is, if your application isn't telling you that deadlocks are occurring, how will you know?

If you start experiencing increased problems with time-outs or with applications hanging without good reason, especially if the server load has increased at the same time, you should suspect deadlocks as a potential suspect. SQL Server gives you the tools you need to verify whether or not they are the problem. Start with the SQL Server error logs. Deadlocks and transaction time-outs are reported to the error log, and you can easily view the error log through SQL Server Management Studio. Once you know that deadlocks are occurring, you can use SQL Server Profiler to help you pinpoint the transactions that are the most common culprits.

Your next step from there depends on what you find. If the problem is poorly designed transactions, then your first step is setting them right. Use the tips already recommended in this chapter, like keeping the transactions short, making the transaction locks more granular, and accessing resources in a consistent order. You might also consider lowering the transaction isolation level. Most transactions don't need to be run under the serializable, or even repeatable read, isolation levels. However, you probably don't want to drop to read uncommitted or use an optimistic isolation method. Why not? You already know that transactions are interfering with each other. Why take a chance on replacing errors that you know are occurring with the possibility of introducing data errors that are even harder to detect and resolve?

Figure 10-10

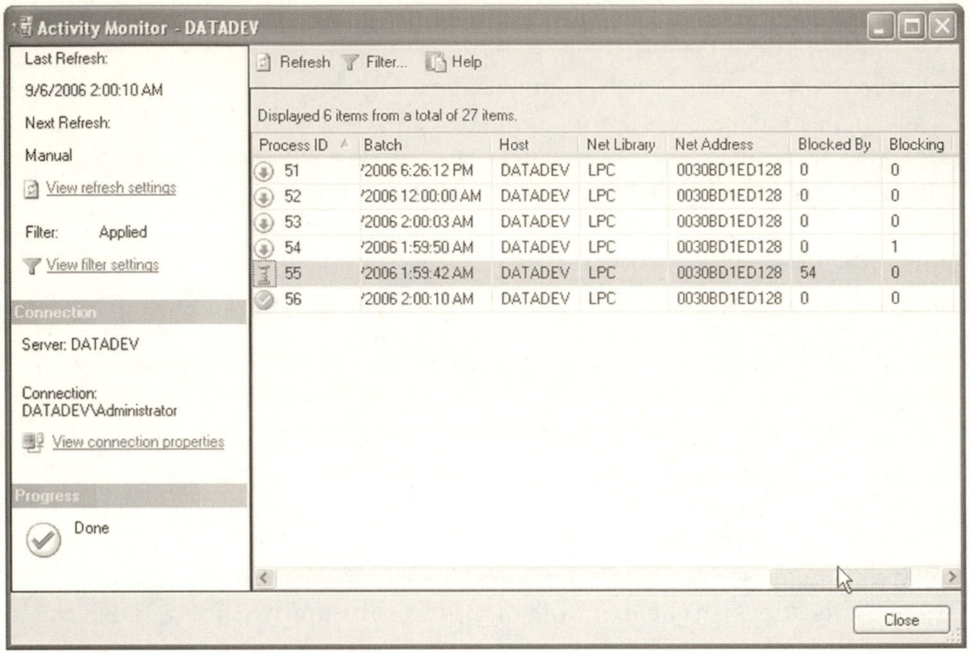

Blocked and blocking transaction.

ID number or through Activity Monitor. To kill the process in Activity Monitor, right-click the blocking process and run Kill process. You will be prompted to verify your action.

SELF-CHECK

- Describe when SQL Server issues a checkpoint.
- List the transaction isolation levels supported by SQL Server.
- Describe the circumstances under which a deadlock occurs.

SUMMARY

Transactions are a key part of nearly all database applications. During this chapter, you learned about transaction basics, including ACID properties and transaction commands. You also learned the differences between implicit and explicit transactions. You learned about possible concurrency problems and methods used by various DBMSs to avoid the problems. You also learned about SQL Server transaction support, including isolation level support and methods for detecting and clearing deadlocks.

KEY TERMS

ACID

Atomicity

Autocommit transaction

Blocked transaction

Checkpoint

Commit

Concurrent transactions

Consistency

Cursor

Data API

Deadlock

Dirty page

Dirty read

Durability

Exclusive lock

Explicit transaction

Implicit transaction

Inconsistent analysis

Isolation

Kill

Lock

Lock level

Lock scope

Lost update

Nested transaction

Nonrepeatable read

Open transaction

Optimistic processing

Partial rollback

Partial update

Phantom

Phantom read

Read committed

Read uncommitted

Recovery

Repeatable read

Rollback

Roll forward

Serializable

Serialization

Shared lock

Snapshot

Time-out

Timestamp ordering

Transaction isolation

Transaction isolation level

Transaction scheduling

Uncommitted dependency

ASSESS YOUR UNDERSTANDING

Go to www.wiley.com/college/gillenson to evaluate your knowledge of transaction and locking support.
Measure your learning by comparing pre-test and post-test results.

Summary Questions

1. Rolling back a transaction reverses all changes made by that transaction. True or False?

2. What does the acronym ACID stand for?

    (a) atomicity, concurrency, isolation, and durability

    (b) atomicity, consistency, isolation, and durability

    (c) automation, concurrency, isolation, and durability

    (d) automation, consistency, isolation, and durability

3. When SQL Server 2005 is operating in implicit transaction mode, which statement will initiate a new transaction?

    (a) INSERT

    (b) CREATE TABLE

    (c) SELECT

    (d) All of the above

4. When a database server is configured for autocommit transactions, you must run either COMMIT TRAN or ROLLBACK TRAN after each statement. True or False?

5. Which function returns a list of open transactions?

    (a) @@TRANCOUNT

    (b) @@COUNT

    (c) @@TRANSACTIONS

    (d) none of the above

6. What happens when you close a connection that has an open transaction?

    (a) A checkpoint is immediately issued.

    (b) The transaction is committed.

    (c) The transaction is rolled back.

    (d) There is no way to know in advance what will happen.

7. A dirty page is one that has been updated in memory, but not written to the hard disk. True or False?

8. An uncommitted read is also known as which of the following?
   (a) dirty read
   (b) phantom read
   (c) nonrepeatable read
   (d) inconsistent analysis
9. What is a phantom read?
   (a) reading data that is changed, but not committed
   (b) reading data that is committed, but not written to the hard disk
   (c) reading a range of rows, with one or more rows missing on a subsequent read
   (d) data that is changed after it is read by a transaction
10. Which of the following is NOT a method for minimizing the occurrence of concurrency errors?
    (a) Keep transaction size to a minimum.
    (b) Segregate additional operations as nested transactions.
    (c) Have all transactions access resources in the same order.
    (d) Keep resources open for as short a time as possible.
11. Which concurrency method assumes that transaction interaction is unlikely, so the transaction processor does not check for potential conflicts?
    (a) locking
    (b) timestamp ordering
    (c) Optimistic processing
    (d) transaction scheduling
12. Which locking level is less likely to cause a blocked transaction?
    (a) server
    (b) database
    (c) table
    (d) row
13. A transaction will acquire a shared locked before modifying data to prevent other transactions from accessing the same data. True or False?
14. Database servers use concurrent transaction processing to improve performance and optimize processor use. True or False?
15. SQL Server 2005 transaction isolation support is limited to isolation levels specified in the SQL-99 standard. True or False?
16. Which transaction isolation level is the least restrictive?
    (a) read uncommitted

(b) read committed

(c) repeatable read

(d) serializable

17. The read committed transaction isolation level ignores exclusive locks during read operations. True or False?

18. A deadlock occurs when two transactions mutually block each other's access to resources. True or False?

Applying This Chapter

1. An application is designed to process queries by passing individual query statements to the server for execution. You want to modify the application to use transactions to group related statements. The database used is hosted on a SQL Server 2005 database server.

   (a) What logic should you include when completing the transactions?

   (b) How can you ensure that the statements are executed in the context of a transaction?

   (c) You want to ensure that you avoid lost updates and direct reads. What is the minimum transaction isolation level you should use? What types of concurrency errors are NOT prevented?

   (d) Should a transaction become blocked, how can you use SQL Server Management Studio to identify the blocking transaction? How can you removing the blocking processes through SQL Server Management Studio?

2. You determine that many of the problems that users are reporting are related to application transactions. The application is written with many of the statements specifying locking hints to control the type of lock acquired and locking level. The application includes three long transactions. You cannot rewrite the queries, so you have to learn to live with them.

   (a) When would you want to acquire an exclusive lock? Why?

   (b) When updating individual rows, what locking level is most appropriate? Why?

   (c) Changes made by transactions should not be able to change relationships between tables. What is the easiest way to enforce this?

   (d) What should you check about the long-running transactions to minimize the chance of deadlocks? How does this help you prevent deadlocks?

YOU TRY IT

Transaction Management

You are a database administrator for a company whose core busiess is retail sales. Users access the database through various, relatively small, database applications. There are also times when you or another administrator need to run ad hoc statements and queries from a command line. The database supports hundreds of users, most of whom are working and potentially accessing the database at the same time. The number of users is expected to increase significantly over the next year.

1. Explain the potential impact of the usage changes to blocked transactions.
2. How does having the transactions used by applications access resources in the same order help to prevent deadlocks? What is the possible impact on blocked transactions?
3. Why is concurrent transaction processing important in this environment?
4. What one action can you take to increase the relative isolation between transactions? What are the potential benefits of this, if any? Potential disadvantages?

Concurrent Transactions

A small Midwestern savings and loan provides three basic types of services to its customers—various types of savings accounts, various checking account options, and loans. Most of the internal account functions

use a third-party account application that uses SQL Server as its data store. It also has a custom Web application that enables customers to access account information, transfer account balances, and make loan payments online.

A procedure runs each morning and checks payment due dates for loans. For customers who have opted to do so, it will deduct the payment amount from a savings or checking account and make the customer's payment automatically. Information about the payment is written to a tracking table for verification.

1. Why are transactions necessary when transferring money between accounts?
2. You need to ensure maximum transaction isolation during automated loan payments. How can you do this? Under what conditions might automatic payments become blocked?
3. Some of the savings and loan's reporting requirements built into the Web application are summary reports based on the specific moment in time when the report is run. How can you ensure this?
4. The reporting module of the third-party accounting application defaults to the read committed transaction isolation level. Reporting is considered a low-priority function. Some reports must make multiple reads of the source tables to collect the information needed. How can you justify not using a higher isolation level?

11

DATA ACCESS AND SECURITY

Starting Point

Go to www.wiley.com/college/gillenson to assess your knowledge of data access and security.
Determine where you need to concentrate your effort.

What You'll Learn in This Chapter

▲ Database connectivity concepts and requirements
▲ Server and database access control
▲ How to protect data against unauthorized access and modification or data loss

After Studying This Chapter, You'll Be Able To

▲ Design a database solution that meets connectivity requirements
▲ Select appropriate client and application interface options
▲ Design a database solution that includes multitier connectivity
▲ Create and manage server and database security principals
▲ Control server and database access
▲ Manage and monitor the connection process and active connections
▲ Incorporate access permissions into a database design
▲ Select appropriate physical data storage options
▲ Design a backup plan that addresses the what, when, where, and how of data backups

INTRODUCTION

Data access is critical to any database design. This means ensuring that users can get to the data they need and that the data is protected against mistakes, malicious actions, and equipment failures. This chapter begins by introducing data server and database connectivity concepts and requirements. From there, it moves on to including server and database access requirements in your database design and implementation. Finally, it introduces access permissions and data protection methods.

It is important to note that you cannot guarantee a completely secure database or server. No matter what safeguards you implement, given enough time, patience, and technical expertise, someone can eventually find a way to compromise your database server and data. Because of this, it is important that your security plans focus not just on protection, but also on detecting and recovering from security breaches.

11.1 Understanding Database Connections

Data is useless if your users can't access it. There are two basic access methods, direct access like you have with a Sqlcmd prompt or query window, and indirect access through a database application. There is one common factor with either access method—you must make a connection to the database server before you can access any data.

You can see this when you launch SQL Server Management Studio. Before you are allowed to do anything else, you are prompted for connection information so you can establish a connection with the server. Each time you launch Management Studio, you are prompted with a dialog box like the one shown in Figure 11-1, requesting the server name and login credentials. The **login credentials** are used to identify you to the server and set your level of access. The server uses the information provided to validate your access permissions and establish the connection.

Even though you never see a connection dialog box, the process is similar when an application connects to a database server. The application passes its connection criteria to the database server and the server allows (or denies, depending on the credentials), the connection.

11.1.1 Understanding Connectivity Concepts

The client/server model is the most basic connectivity model. Most advanced, multitier connection models still have, somewhere at their core, an aspect of the client/server model. Let's begin our look at connectivity and connectivity issues with a look at the classic client/server model as a way of introducing connectivity concepts.

Figure 11-1

Connect to server dialog box.

A **connection,** in the simplest terms, is a communication path. Whenever you use the telephone you establish a connection, a communication path between you and another person that enables you to talk. You also establish a connection when you use your browser to visit a Web site, or when you talk to someone through **instant messaging (IM),** which is a type of communication application enabling conversations between users over the Internet. The same is true when you connect to a database server; you establish a communication path between the client and the server.

In the classic client/server model, like the one shown in Figure 11-2, end-user PCs are the clients connecting to a database server. The server contains the application programs, the DBMS, and the database, which all of the clients share. When an end user wants to run an application or retrieve data from the shared database, the client computers handle the initial processing of the request. The request is sent on to the server for processing by the application code, including data retrieval from the shared database, as necessary. The server returns the results to the client PC where the client is responsible for formatting the screen display.

Figure 11-2

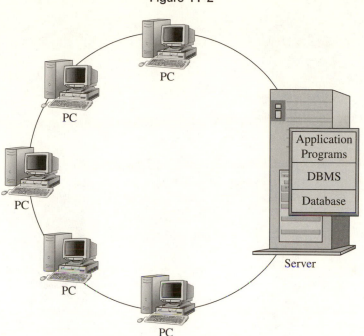

Local area network (LAN) client/server model.

Although the term client/server system is usually associated with a system built on a local area network, in a broad sense the World Wide Web (the Web) can be considered to be a massive client/server system built on the Internet. As shown in Figure 11-3, the clients are PCs used to connect to the Internet. The browser software running on the PCs handles the client side screen presentation duties. The servers are the Web servers with which the PCs communicate. With this expansion of the idea of a client/server system, the World Wide Web, built on the Internet, qualifies as the world's largest client/server system!

Direct connections to a database server over the Internet, though possible, are rarely used. A primary reason for this is the potential security risk of directly exposing a database server to the Internet. The Internet is full of individuals who make it their life's work to steal or wreak havoc upon other peoples' data. A more realistic configuration is shown in Figure 11-4, which you could consider as a multitier configuration made up of two overlapping client/server models. PCs, the end-user client computers, connect to the Web server. The Web server, though acting as a server, can also be considered a client. It connects to the database server, passing end-user client requests to the database and returning its responses to the clients' PCs.

Figure 11-3

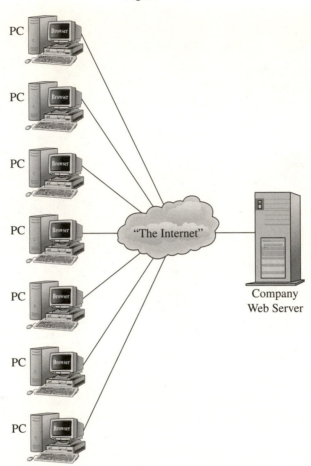

Internet client/server model.

Now that you see what a connection is, and how it relates to the client/server model, we can now focus on the components that make up that connection.

Investigating the "Hard" Components

Common to each of these illustrations is the **connection path,** which is the physical pathway through which the data travels. In Figure 11-2, the connection path is the network cable. In Figure 11-3, the connection path is the Internet. In Figure 11-4 you have both, the Internet between PCs and the Web server, and the LAN cable between the Web server and database server. Of course, the connection path doesn't have to be a physical cable. Ever been to a coffee shop that offers WiFi connectivity for your laptop? **WiFi** is a term used to refer to the most commonly used wireless communication technologies for PCs.

Figure 11-4

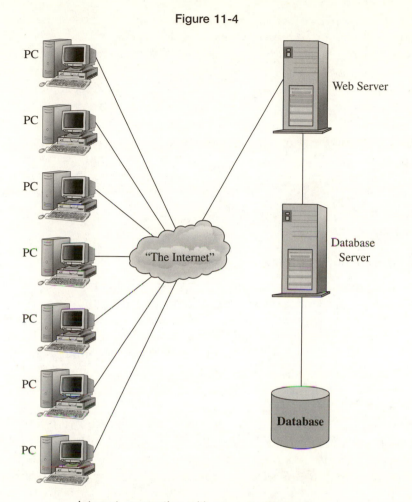

Internet connection with separate Web server.

With WiFi, the connection path is the radio frequency transmissions between the computers.

The other part of this hardware connection is the physical network adapter your computer uses to communicate. For traditional wired networks, this means a network interface card (NIC), sometimes called a network adapter. This provides the computer's physical connection to the network and handles the low-level communication functions. Wireless networks use a network adapter that is functionally a wireless transmitter/receiver that supports WiFi connectivity.

The connection could also be made through a dial-up modem, cable modem, or other connection device for remote connectivity. A **modem** is a device that converts digital data to an analog signal for transmission and then back to digital before passing the data to the computer. Currently, the most commonly used path for remote connectivity is the Internet. Many companies support connections over the Internet through a **virtual private network (VPN).** A VPN provides a secure, reliable communication path. VPNs can be used over the Internet, or over a private LAN or WAN. In either implementation, the VPN acts as a network inside a network, with a protected communication path deployed through a public pathway. Other than the details of how it is implemented, a VPN is operationally like any other network. Technically, a VPN is a network built out of "soft" components. It uses special software at each of the nodes (connection points) and special protocols known as tunneling protocols. The name of the protocols comes from the fact that the VPN "tunnels" through the public media pathway, effectively isolating VPN traffic from the rest of the network traffic.

Investigating the "Soft" Components

Connectivity requires more than just the physical path. Each end of the connection needs communication software that manages the process. Today's operating systems come with multiple types of communication software embedded, each for a specific use. The computers also need a protocol in common, which is effectively the language that the computers use to communicate. A **protocol** defines the rules the computers use for data format and transmission. It determines, among other things, how the data is packaged for transmission and the maximum size of data packets.

There are still more requirements. Look at the instant message (IM) communication session shown in Figure 11-5. You need to have a way of identifying the person (and/or computer) at the other end. There also has to be a way of making sure that the message gets routed to the appropriate person, or more accurately the appropriate computer, and their response gets routed back to you.

The requirements are similar for database connectivity. There's a lot going on in the background that you probably aren't aware of when you connect to a database server. Your computer and the database server need:

▲ A way to identify each other.
▲ A common language.
▲ A way of ensuring that the information gets to the correct destination.

Think about that last point. It's more complicated than you might think. A database might have hundreds, even thousands, of concurrent connections it must manage and maintain. It has to keep track of each of these, including the client computer, user, and any data associated with the connection. Even at the client end there's a lot happening. Not only does the data have to arrive

Figure 11-5

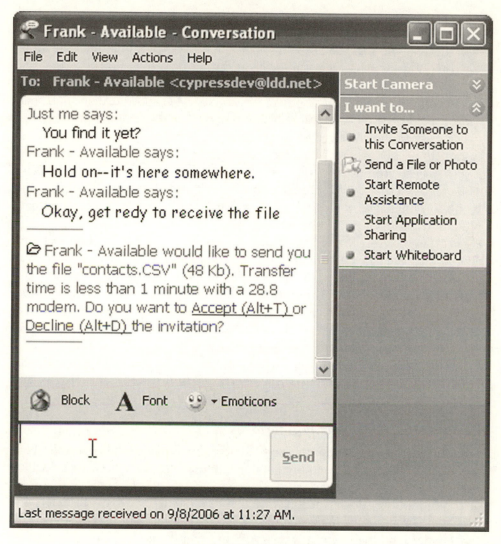

Sample IM conversation.

at the correct PC, once there, it must be routed to the right application inside the PC.

A detailed discussion of all of the ins and outs of PC communications would be a course in itself and is far beyond the scope of this chapter. It's enough that you know the basics of what's going on and what needs to be managed at the PC and server ends. We do, however, need to talk a little about the high-level software components required and the database and server objects you need to design, create, and manage in order to enable communication with the database server.

11.1.2 Understanding Client/Server Connectivity

In the traditional client/server model, you have two computer types involved. These are the client that provides the interface with the user and the server that stores and maintains the database. Though the traditional model puts the application on the database server, realistically it can reside just as easily on the client computers. In fact, that's the model used in most small-scale database applications. A copy of the application runs on each client PC and the client PCs share the database stored on a central database server.

The basic foundation for connectivity, including the communication path, physical connection, and the basic communication protocol, are provided by the network. These are primarily the responsibility of network administrators (or a similar role) within your company. That doesn't mean that you don't have your own responsibilities as well. You might have protocol options available and have to configure protocol use at the server.

Most discussions about database design focus almost exclusively (at least initially) on the data. However, the data is useless if you don't have a way to access it. Database connectivity, built on the foundation provided by the network, is a necessary part of your final design and a required component during implementation. The requirements for designing and configuring connectivity requirements are somewhat DBMS-specific, but there are some common factors that should be discussed. When looking at requirements specific to DBMS implementations, we'll use SQL Server 2005 as our example. Though the implementation details may be different with other DBMSs, the general concepts and requirements will be similar.

Understanding Connectivity Interfaces

During database design and implementation, you will make final decisions about the communication path. Even though this is a function of the network on which the clients and server are deployed, there are DBMS-specific options that control communication flow. After making these decisions, you have to determine which data application programming interface (API) you will use.

To understand the role of the data API, imagine yourself as a bicycle courier. You've been called by one of General Hardware Company's customers. You need to pick up a package and deliver it to the customer. You arrive at General Hardware Company, identify yourself, identify the customer, and request the package. Package in hand, you ride across town and deliver it to the customer.

That's not unlike what happens in a communication session between a client and a server. The requirements for that session are also similar to the physical transfer. The client needs to identify itself to the server. In some configurations, the server must also identify itself to the client through a process known as **mutual authentication.** The client needs to pass commands to the server and receive a response. Your first thought might be that this is all handled by the application software, or maybe at the command prompt, but we need to take things down a level. This functionality is provided by the data API. This decision lies more with the application developer in most cases, but it's likely that you might be called on to make recommendations.

There are several options available, depending on your database server, whether you plan to connect directly or through an application, and the application programming language that you select. You may already be familiar with two APIs: Open Database Connectivity (ODBC) and OLE DB. **ODBC** is an industry standard API that provides connectivity with a wide variety of data sources. **OLE DB** is a Microsoft data access API that also supports a wide variety of sources. One advantage of OLE DB is that Microsoft has provided versions that are optimized for specific DBMSs, including OLE DB for Oracle and OLE DB for SQL Server. Microsoft has also released a new data access technology that is OLE DB-based and is specific to SQL Server 2005, called **SQL Native Client.**

Each of these options provides the same basic functionality. They let a client (or client application) identify itself to the server and establish a connection. They let the client prepare commands and pass them to the server for execution. They also provide various means for receiving a response back from the server. The differences are in the details.

If you are writing an application and aren't sure as to the final database platform, or perhaps want to leave a level of flexibility built in, it's likely that you would want to use ODBC or a generic version of OLE DB. If you are using a Microsoft programming language and want to provide better performance and more options, then a product-specific version of OLE DB might be more appropriate. If you are working with SQL Server 2005 and want to use newly released features like XML data types, then you need SQL Native Client or the .NET Framework SQL Client object library.

Meeting Client Interface Requirements

Let's step away from database applications for a moment. Data and database administrators often find it necessary to access a server directly through management utilities to make changes or fix problems. However, sitting down at the server isn't always an option, or even a good idea. You need a way to set up a client with the necessary connectivity software and management tools.

Luckily, most manufacturers have provided a way to do just that. In the case of SQL Server, the Setup program gives you the option of installing just the client tools, which includes all of the necessary drivers, data APIs, and management utilities. You might be worried that this could be a security risk, but it's not if you've set up security properly on your database server and as long as you log off or lock your computer when you leave your desk. Someone trying to hack into the database through your PC, assuming they could get access to it, would still need login credentials that provide a high enough level of access to enable them to do any damage.

Meeting Application Interface Requirements

Administrators have more of an advisory and assistance role in meeting application interface requirements. Connection requirements are met through functionality built into or added on to the programming environment and language. The interface choice will depend on the specifics of the project requirements, DBMS support requirements, and the capabilities of the development platform.

FOR EXAMPLE

What about ADO.NET?

You may be familiar with ADO.NET, objects providing the functionality that lets you connect to a data source and manipulate data in the .NET Framework. If so, you might be wondering where it fits in as part of the access model we've been discussing.

ADO.NET is a collection of data object libraries that let you connect to various data sources, send requests, and receive and manipulate data. For example, there are object libraries that contain objects designed for working directly with operating systems files, such as XML document files. More closely related to our discussion are the object libraries that let you work with database servers. These include generic libraries based on ODBC and OLE DB, as well as product-specific libraries designed for use with products such as Oracle and SQL Server.

When using a .NET Framework language, the question becomes not what technology to use in your database application, but which data object library to use. The choices are somewhat language dependent, but the most commonly used languages (Visual Basic and C#) support the same object libraries. The differences between the two are in details such as command syntax, but other than that, the choices are essentially the same.

The choice comes down to picking the object library best suited to your requirements. When writing a custom application for a specific DBMS, the best choice is usually to pick a server-specific interface option, like OLE DB for Oracle or the SQL Client library. This is only possible if the decision has been made about the database server platform, but realistically, that decision should be made relatively early in the design process. That's because several data design decisions, such as data types, are also somewhat DBMS-specific. Along with your data object recommendation, you might have other responsibilities in the application development process. You could, and probably will, be called on to provide information about the database and connection requirements, such as the minimum requirements for connecting to the server, the database object structure, and the availability of custom functions and procedures.

Current development environments provide interface options, letting the developer choose the option best suited to the database server. The database designer/implementer may be asked to make recommendations, but not the final decision.

11.1.3 Understanding Multitier Connectivity

As you move into a multitier environment, the difference is one of scale and distribution rather than basic functionality. Different functions are delegated to different specialized servers. Typically, the database server becomes more focused on that single task.

Let's take a look at an example of this type of environment so you can see something of the delegation involved between the servers. In this example, there is a multi-tiered Web application; however this is not the only type of configuration you might see. Most Web applications are multi-tier applications, but multi-tiered applications are not necessarily Web applications.

Suppose that Good Reading Bookstores develops a Web site to sell books to consumers online and that you are about to become one of its customers. The browser software in your PC sends a message to Good Reading's Web server and establishes a connection with it. The Web server sends your browser Good Reading's home page which your browser displays. From here, you can make requests of the application running on Good Reading's Web server. This application sends commands to the relational DBMS on Good Reading's database server, ordering it to perform requested operations and returning the information to your browser. This continues with other requests as necessary. Every time the database must be accessed, the application in the Web server passes a command to the database server, which queries the database and returns the result.

Figure 11-6 shows this process in some detail, introducing some of the specialized software involved. When your browser sends a message to the Web server (and vice versa), the message follows the rules of the **Transmission Control Protocol/Internet Protocol (TCP/IP)**, the protocol on which the Internet and most other networks are based, and the **Hypertext Transfer Protocol (HTTP)**, which is an additional protocol layer supporting World Wide Web traffic on the Internet.

There is a potential problem in that there can be different kinds of hardware between the Web server and the database server, different kinds of application software languages, different browsers on the client side, and a variety of different kinds of data. These are tied together using specialized interfaces and specialized software known as **middleware.** Because of the importance of connecting the applications in the Web server with the databases in the database server, various companies have developed specialized middleware with a variety of broad features, capabilities, and connectivity options. Among the products of this type

Figure 11-6

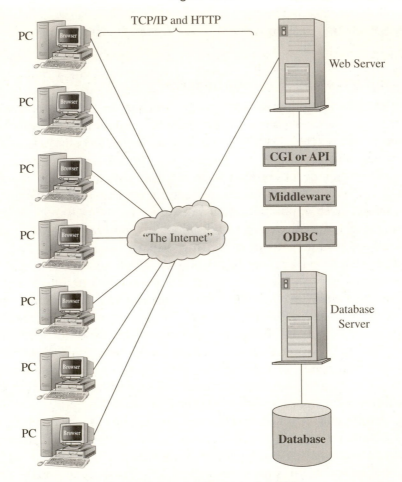

Accessing a database via the Web.

on the market are Cold Fusion, Oracle Application Server, Microsoft Active Server Pages (ASP), ASP .NET, and others.

In order for the application software running on the Web server to connect with software outside of the Web server, there must be agreed upon interfaces. Web applications use **Common Gateway Interface (CGI)** or various APIs. CGI is a standard way for passing requests and data between a Web server and an application. These interfaces have software scripts associated with them that allow them to exchange data between the application and the database server. The connection to the database server could be made directly at this point, but more likely the connection is made using a standard interface, such as ODBC.

FOR EXAMPLE

Multitier Application Design

Designing a multitier database application doesn't necessarily mean designing a Web application for use on the Internet. Larger companies often find it appropriate to design enterprise applications that use a multi-tier design, but the concepts involved are similar to those already discussed for a Web application.

Suppose you have completed the database design and implemented a preliminary version on a development server. Several applications will use this database, including the one in this example, a data entry application. Let's start with a little background and a few requirements. The database will be used in a nationwide medical study. Study candidates fill out a ten-page questionnaire. The answers are entered into a tracking database that will also track other medical information.

The application you're designing is a data entry application that will enter the survey results. Because of security requirements, end-user client computers cannot connect directly with the database server. The client computer will do initial data validation, with more advanced checks handled by a server application and, where appropriate, table and row constraints used as a final line of defense. After normalization, you have four tables involved, each holding part of the data. To understand your responsibilities, look at the application as having three distinct, but related components. These components are the client running on end-user computers, a middle component running on an application server, and a server component on the database server.

The client component performs initial validation before sending the data to the middle component and receives results or error information back from the middle component. You need to provide data requirements such as the types of data needed by the database and any limits such as field length or maximum and minimum values.

The middle component accepts data from the client and uses it to pass commands to the database server. In this example, assume that you've created user stored procedures on the server to perform the data entry, one procedure for each of the four tables. The middle component connects to the database server and calls these procedures, passing the data from the client as input parameters. It will receive back any response, such as possible errors, from the database server. As you get closer to the server, your responsibilities increase. You probably need to provide guidelines for connecting to the database server, connection parameters, the procedure names, and procedure syntax which is probably limited to the order in which you must pass the input parameters. You may also need to provide assistance and guidelines relating to decoding and responding to server errors.

Continued

The server component is primarily the application data but also includes other database objects you create to support the application. The responsibilities at this level fall almost exclusively on you and include providing an appropriate data design and database tables. You'll design, create, and (hopefully) document the procedures used for data entry. You'll also configure other requirements such as primary key constraints, foreign key constraints used to relate the four tables, and constraints enforcing value limits.

SELF-CHECK

- What does the term **mutual authentication** refer to?
- When do you need to use SQL Native Client?
- How does a multitier database application design differ from a client/server database application design?

11.2 Managing Access Control

An important issue that we have not yet addressed is security. Different DBMSs have different ways of managing security and data access, most of them based on login names and passwords to prove the identity of security principals. A **security principal** is an entity, a server object in this case, that can be identified through a process known as authentication, The security principal sets the connection's **security context,** the default security base for the connection determining default permissions. **Authentication** is the process by which the principal is identified and allowed access.

Many management systems, including SQL Server, take a multitiered approach to security, with server access managed separately from database access. Access is based on two security objects: logins and users. As a brief introduction, **logins** are used to manage server-level security and **users** are used to manage database-level security. Some manufacturers have a single-tiered security structure that does not make this distinction and uses the terms interchangeably.

In a two-tier security system like the one used by SQL Server, logins typically have the following in common across manufacturers:

▲ Login name
▲ Password
▲ Default database
▲ Server-level permissions

Because validation is based on the login, two-tier systems typically do not associate passwords with users. Common features of users typically include:

▲ User name
▲ Associated login
▲ Database access permissions
▲ Object-level permissions

It's common to have several data users associated with a single login, one user for each database to which you want to give the login access. Be careful to create only those logins and users you actually need in order to help minimize the possibility of unauthorized access.

In a single-tier system, you have one account acting as the security principal for both server and database access. In this type of system, the account will have an associated password, server-level permissions, and database-level permissions, including permissions assigned at the database object level.

Because of the differences you will find between the various manufacturers' solutions to security requirements, we will focus on SQL Server 2005 as a representative example of one manufacturer's choices. Throughout this discussion, keep in mind that SQL Server security is based on both logins and users, and that logins and users are distinctly different security objects with different security management roles.

11.2.1 Controlling Server Access

One of the decisions you make during SQL Server installation is the authentication type, choosing either **Windows authentication** (with Windows user accounts used for authentication) or **mixed authentication** (supporting SQL Server authentication and Windows authentication). **SQL Server authentication** is based on logins and passwords stored with the database server and authenticated by the database server. What you are choosing is the type of logins that your server will support. You can change your selection at any time through the server properties, as shown in Figure 11-7.

Windows authentication support is not unique to SQL Server. Windows authentication integrates database server security (or other server application security) with Windows and Active Directory domain security. **Active Directory** is a Microsoft directory service that supports a full-featured network security environment organized around security boundaries known as **domains.** Login to the server is granted to Windows and domain user accounts and groups. Authorization is based on the user account you used when you logged in at your computer. In order to log in at the database server, either your Windows user account must be authorized as a login account or the account must belong to a Windows group that is authorized as a login account. When creating the account, you specify the

Figure 11-7

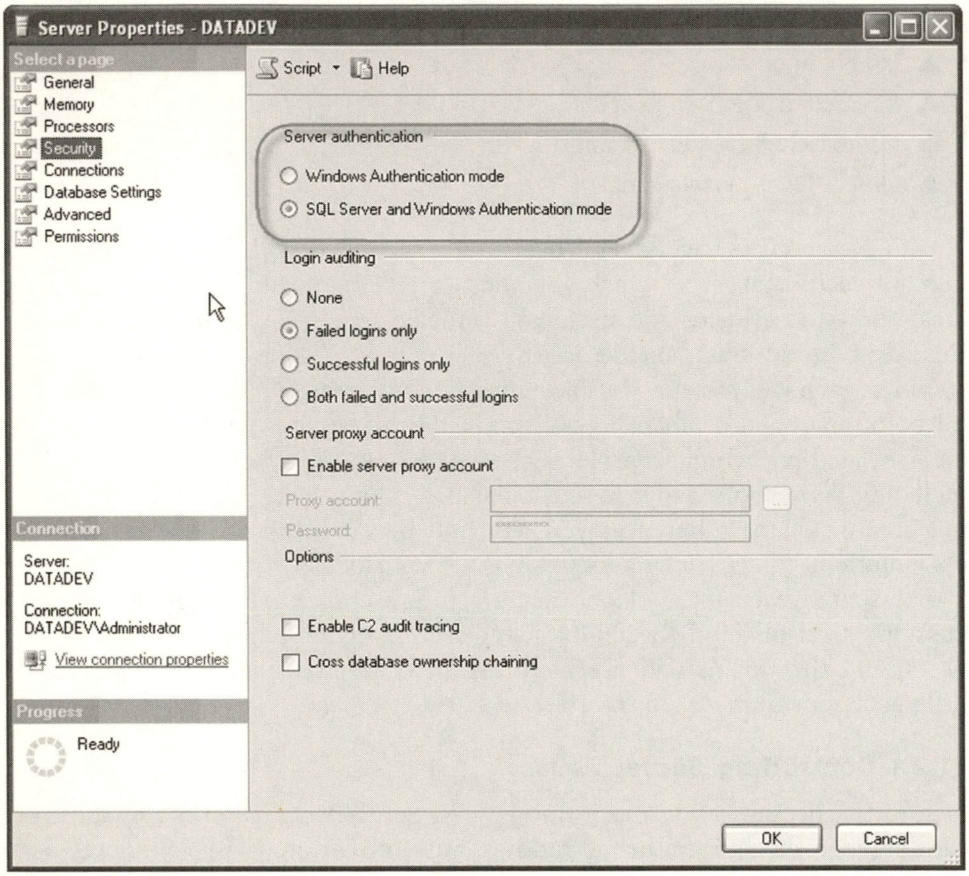

Authentication options.

account name, default database, and server access permissions. User accounts, passwords, and group membership are managed through Windows and Active Directory management utilities.

In SQL Server, members of the Administrators group as the default administrator account are granted login privileges during installation. Any additional login accounts must be configured manually. When you attempt to connect using Windows authentication, the user is passed to Windows for authentication and the status (whether or not you are authenticated as a valid user) and group membership are passed back to SQL Server.

If you choose mixed authentication, you can also create SQL Server logins. These are managed separately from Windows, with the accounts and passwords authenticated by the database server. The only SQL Server login account created by default is the **sa account,** which is a system administrator account with

Figure 11-8

Management Studio Logins folder.

unlimited access permissions to the server and its databases. It should go without saying that you want to protect access to the sa account with a **strong password,** one that includes mixed letters, numbers, and characters that would be difficult to guess.

SQL Server provides command-line commands for login management, as well as lets you create, manage, and delete logins through the SQL Server Management Studio Logins folder, shown in Figure 11-8.

What you can do after logging in depends on the permissions assigned to your login account. SQL Server primarily assigns permissions through **roles,** which are roughly analogous to groups and are assigned different rights and permissions. Other DBMSs use a similar management concept, but use different terms to refer to groups of logins. You assign permissions to a login by granting the login membership in the role containing the permissions you want that login to have. There is also a limited set of permissions that can be managed explicitly by user and server object. Most DBMSs have similar methods for managing permissions. As you will see later in this chapter, database permissions are handled in a similar manner, but with users instead of logins as the security principal.

11.2.2 Controlling Database Access

In a multitiered system, database access is managed through database users. Each database's users are managed separately from those associated with other databases. That means that after logging in you might have access to some databases on the server, but not others. SQL Server also includes a **Guest** account that allows for anonymous access. The Guest account is disabled by default and Microsoft recommends that you leave the account disabled unless you have a specific need for supporting anonymous access.

SQL Server lets you manage users through command-line commands and the SQL Server Management Studio. Each database has a Users folder like the one shown in Figure 11-9, for user management. When you create a user you will typically associate it with a login, though SQL Server does support other creation options. These additional options are beyond the scope of this chapter, but are explained in SQL Server's online documentation.

The recommended method for managing permissions is again through roles, this time groups of users rather than logins, which have assigned permissions. In SQL Server, all database users are members of the **Public** role for that database, so any permissions you want to assign everyone would be given to this role.

Figure 11-9

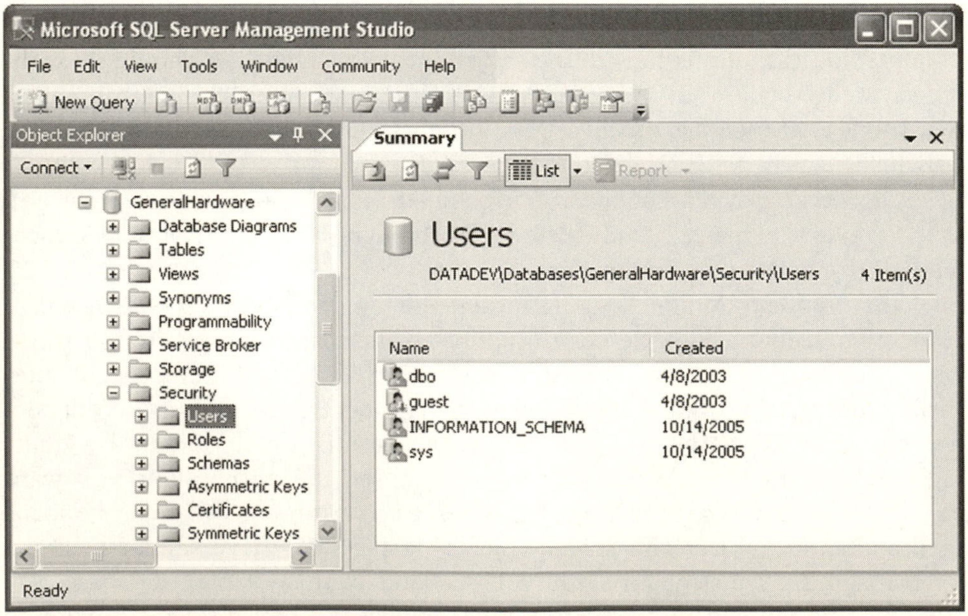

Database Users folder.

You can also manage permissions through explicit assignments to individual users, but this is discouraged because of the added management overhead involved in handling permissions at that level. Permission management is discussed in more detail later in this chapter.

11.2.3 Understanding the Connection Process

Now that you have an understanding of the security objects involved, we can take a closer look at the connection process from the context of SQL Server. The process for most other high-level DBMS products is similar. We'll start with the connection dialog box, only this time we'll look at advanced connection properties.

In Figure 11-10, you're logging in to the database engine, the database server, using Windows authentication. This is also referred to as connecting with **integrated security,** referring to SQL Server security integrated with Windows security, or a **trusted connection,** meaning that the user is trusted to connect to SQL Server. If you choose SQL Server authentication, you must provide a valid SQL Server login name and password.

The Connection Properties tab in the Connect to Server dialog box is shown in Figure 11-11. Here, you can specify the database for the connection, overriding the login's default database. You can specify network communication parameters, in this case the network protocol to use for communication and the network packet size. The **packet size** controls how much data is sent at a time. Additional connection properties let you set the connection and command execution time-outs, with a value of 0 used for no time-out, meaning that the client will wait indefinitely for the server's response.

When you connect, the login criteria are either passed to Windows for authentication or authenticated by SQL Server. The connection to the server is established and a process ID value assigned for the connection. The login's default database is set as the connection's current database, unless a different database is specified.

When connecting with a connection that opens a command-line prompt, like the Sqlcmd command, connection parameters are passed as command options. For example, the following command line connects to a server named Datadev using the login sa, a password of P*ssword, and sets GeneralHardware as the current database:

```
sqlcmd -sDatadev -Usa -PP*ssword -dGeneralHardware
```

Command options are case-sensitive, so you have to be careful when typing the command. For example, the capital –U option is used to specify the login, but the lower case -u option specifies the command to output Unicode characters instead of ASCII characters.

If you wanted to connect as a trusted connection, you would use the following:

```
sqlcmd -sDatadev -E -dGeneralHardware
```

Figure 11-10

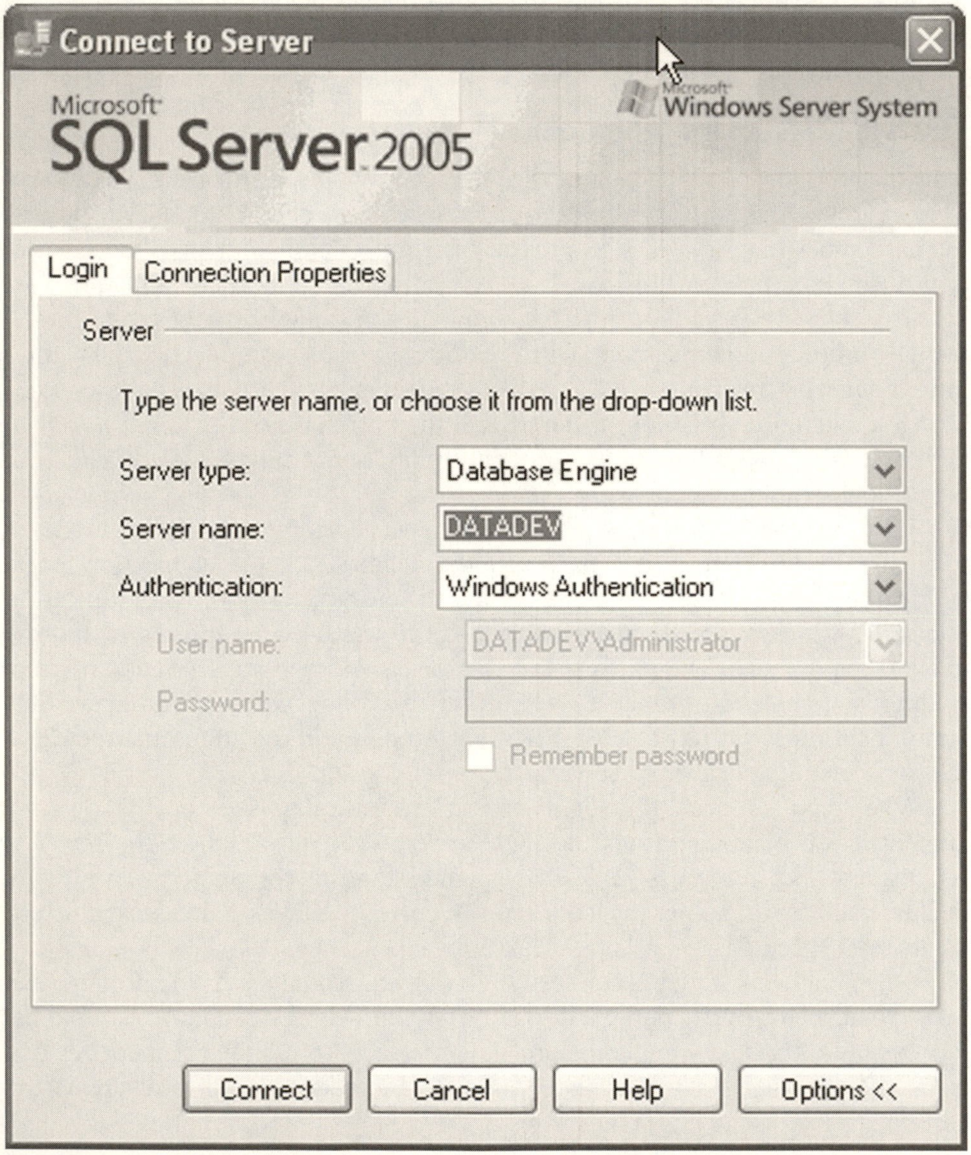

The Login tab in the Connect to Server dialog box.

Notice that when connecting as a trusted connection you don't need a password. SQL Server 2005 also supports other commands that open a command-line interface, but Sqlcmd is the only one that supports SQL Server 2005-specific features. All of these commands have the same potential shortcoming though, in that passwords are passed in clear text. That makes it easy for someone to

Figure 11-11

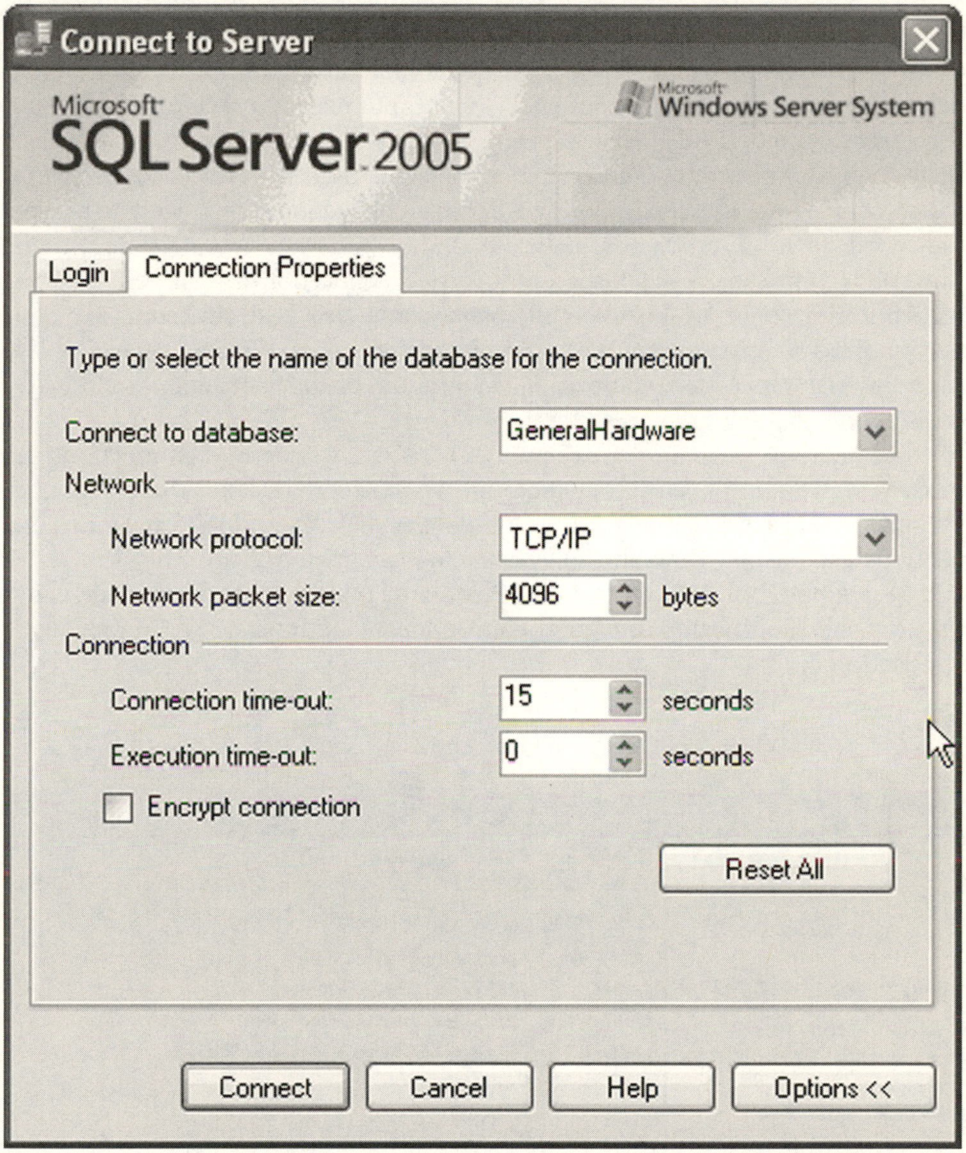

The Connection Properties tab in the Connect to Server dialog box.

intercept them or, if run from a batch, read the passwords from the batch file. The process for establishing the connection is the same as discussed earlier for the connection dialog box.

The same connection information is needed when using a data API to connect to a database server from an application. For example, Microsoft Visual Studio supports a SQL Client command library based on a SQL Server-specific OLE DB provider. The command library contains a set of objects built around the OLE DB provider, making the functionality of the provider API available for easier use to the programmer. Because the command library is based on a SQL Server-specific version of the provider, it is optimized for working with SQL Server and supports SQL Server-specific features and functionality.

An object known as a SqlConnection object is used to connect to the server. When connecting, the application must pass a connection string, which specifies the server, login criteria, initial database, and, if you want, connection options. The connection can be established as a trusted connection or using SQL Server authentication, once again passing the password in clear text. As before, the connection process is the same. Once opened, the connection remains opened unless closed by the application, you exit the application, or the connection is closed by the server by killing its process ID.

The Activity Monitor in Figure 11-12 shows active connections as processes. Notice not only that there are several connections active, but that various connection methods are used. Process IDs 56 and 59 are both connections established through SQL Server Management Studio. Process IDs 57 and 58 are both Sqlcmd connections. Process ID 60 is a connection made using the .Net SqlClient Data Provider, a connection made from a .NET Framework application.

Figure 11-12

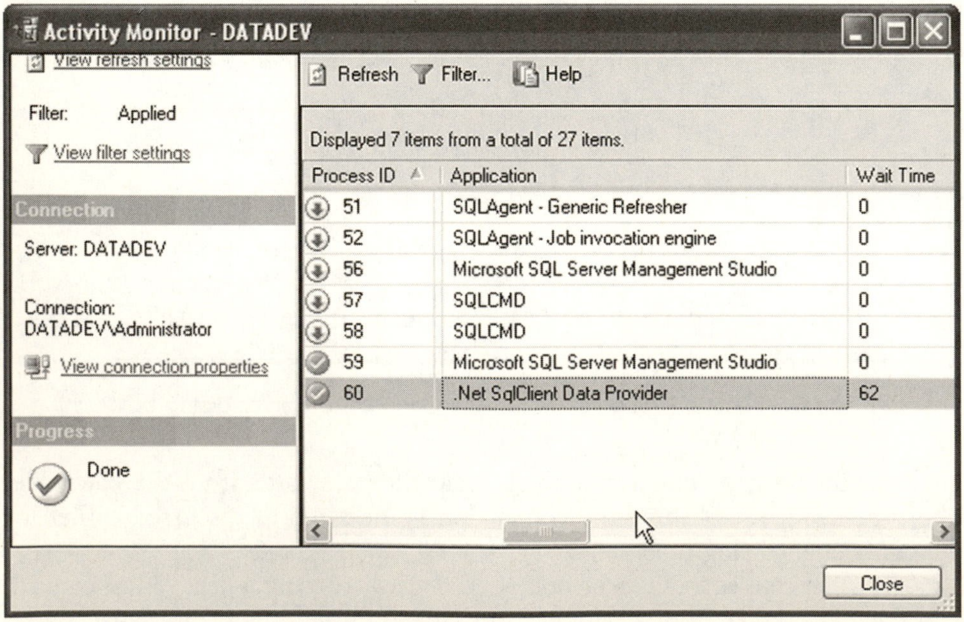

Activity Monitor.

FOR EXAMPLE

Implementing SQL Server Authentication

Microsoft recommends using Windows authentication with SQL Server whenever possible. From an administration standpoint, it's typically easier to set up and manage. From a database administrator's standpoint, it means you get to pass part of the management duties off to a network administrator. All this brings us to the question, why ever use SQL Server authentication? The answer, quite simply, is that it depends.

Like so many other design decisions, you have to consider your network environment and application requirements as a whole when deciding on an authentication method. If all of the database users are part of the same network, then Windows authentication probably is the only authentication method that you need. However, there are other possibilities that must be considered.

The biggest advantage to Windows authentication is also its biggest weakness, that users are authenticated based on the currently logged on user. This assumes that the client computer is running some version of Windows and that it is part of your network. These aren't always good assumptions.

Many established networks, and even some newer networks, are heterogeneous network environments supporting a mix of operating systems. That means you have computers running operating systems other than Windows and possibly not fully compatible with a Windows networking environment. This is especially true if you are migrating from a legacy database to SQL Server. Those unsupported clients may still need access to the data hosted on the SQL Server database, which often means providing access through SQL Server authentication.

In a world where electronic communication is often the key to a successful business and where an immeasurable amount of buying and selling occurs across the Internet, some clients who need access to your data aren't necessarily members of your network, nor do you want them to be, even if they're accessing your servers. A concern in this interconnected environment is the potential theft or destruction of data. Companies spend a lot of time, effort, and money isolating their networks from the internet. Though some exposure is often necessary, the less exposure, the better.

Consider a situation where you're deploying Web servers running an e-commerce application so you can sell on the Internet. The Web servers need access to the data stored on your network database servers, but you don't want to expose anything more about your internal network than absolutely necessary. Because of this, the Web servers are not members of your Active Directory domain, but they still need access to the data. In many cases, the easiest way to configure that access is to configure the database servers to support SQL Server authentication.

Continued

One final point on that last example: you will rarely, if ever, want to directly expose your database servers (and data) to the internet. That means burying the servers, along with the rest of the network, behind a firewall, and maybe even behind multiple layers of firewalls. Then, you configure the firewalls to support the minimum possible amount of traffic into and out of the network. One trick that some network and database administrators use is to configure SQL Server, which is inside the firewall, and its clients outside of the firewall so that they use nonstandard configuration settings. This makes it harder for someone to slip in through the hole you've opened for that purpose.

SELF-CHECK

- Are the terms login and user interchangeable in a multitier access configuration?
- When using SQL Server configured for Windows authentication, how do you create and manage users and passwords?
- Are database users managed separately for each database?
- When connecting to a database server using a data API, what does the connection string specify?
- Does SQL Server authentication give you a way of configuring connectivity for non-Windows client computers?
- Can you monitor active connections to a SQL Server database through SQL Server Management Studio?

Activity Monitor provides useful information about connections, such as the login name used to connect, when the connection was made, the current database, active command (if any), the client's network address, and information about blocked and blocking processes. The client network address can be helpful when trying to identify a database client or troubleshoot a connection problem. Auditing can also be helpful. If you enable auditing on the server, you create a record of who logs into the server, when, and from what client.

11.3 Protecting Your Data

Protecting data is a broad subject. It includes wide-ranging issues relating to data access, data security, and data integrity. A detailed discussion of data protection issues and methods for protecting your data is beyond the scope of this chapter.

Instead, we'll discuss a few key topics relating to data. We're focusing on two areas: securing data against unauthorized access and protecting data against loss. You've already learned something about access security and a little about permission management, at least management through roles on SQL Server.

Why is this important when learning about databases and database design? You might think that security is a more advanced topic, as aspects of it are, but security concerns must be considered during database design and implementation. Basic security needs directly impact database design and database design impacts how you can meet security needs.

One reason for concern about data security is simple: it's your data, and you want to protect it. Data loss or corruption could interfere with business operations. Errors resulting from corrupted data and the time and effort required to correct the data result in real-world costs to your business. Less obvious, but just as damaging, is the possibility that you could lose credibility with your customers.

There are also potential legal concerns about data security. If your database contains sensitive data, such as personal identifying information (PII), credit card numbers, medical records, and so forth, you may be required by law to protect that data. Accidental or malicious disclosure of the data could result in fines and other penalties. You could also be found responsible for collateral problems. For example, if data stolen from your database is used for identity theft, you could be held at least partially responsible for the results of that theft if it is found that you didn't do everything you could to protect the data.

Your legal responsibilities relating to security vary with your geographic location, the industry in which your business operates, and the type of data involved. If you do maintain sensitive data in your database, it is well worth investigating the legal requirements to protect that data, and the actions you are required to take by law if you discover that security has been compromised, such as notifying the persons to whom the data relates.

11.3.1 Implementing Data Permissions

Most PC-based DBMSs are designed to give you granular control over database security. You can control what database users can access, down to specific access permissions. This means you can control security for the database and individual database objects, such as:

▲ Tables
▲ Views
▲ Functions
▲ Stored procedures
▲ Users
▲ Roles

The complete list of **securables,** the server and database objects over which you have control of permissions, depends on the DBMS and the types of database objects it supports. The types of permissions depend on the type of object. For example, at the database level, you can control whether or not a user can manage database properties or create, modify, and delete database objects. With tables, you can determine if a user is limited to retrieving data from a table or if the user can also insert and modify table data.

The detail of control varies by DBMS. The requirements vary by database and by user. Even with all of these possibilities, there are some general guidelines about security that you should keep in mind in all instances, including:

▲ Minimize the number of objects managed.
▲ Grant the least possible permissions.
▲ Audit changes whenever possible.

Let's take a closer look at these guidelines.

Minimizing Managed Objects

The greater the number of objects that you are managing, the greater the chance that you will lose track of permission assignments and make mistakes. Let's start with database users. While it is possible to manage permissions individually for each user, most DBMSs let you organize users into groups or roles. The preferred management method is to assign permissions to the group or role, and then control user permission by controlling the user's membership to these groups of users. You need to change a user's permissions? Instead of having to change the assignments made to the user, you simply change the user's memberships.

Let's look at how SQL Server handles this. Each database has a set of predefined roles. If the permissions you need are granted through one of these roles, simply add the user as a role member and the permissions are passed through to the user. Any permissions you want to grant to all users you simply grant to the Public role because all users are and must remain members of this role. A user can belong to any number of roles.

If you need custom permissions, SQL Server lets you create custom roles. Take a look at Figure 11-13. There are three custom roles. We're going to keep the permissions in general terms. The Managers role assigns permission to view and modify the CUSTOMER, CUSTOMEREMPLOYEE, and SALESPERSON tables. The Sales role grants permission to view CUSTOMER and modify ORDERHEAD and ORDERDETAIL. The SalesManagers role can view and modify CUSTOMER, ODERHEAD, ORDERDETAIL, and SALES. Sam is a member of both Managers and SalesManagers, so he can view and modify any of the tables listed in either role. If you want to take away his permissions to view and modify ORDERHEAD, ORDERDETAIL, and SALES, you would remove him from the SalesManager role.

Figure 11-13

Managers can view and modify:
CUSTOMER
CUSTOMEREMPLOYEE
SALESPERSON

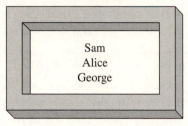

> Sam
> Alice
> George

SalesManagers can view and modify:
CUSTOMER
ORDERHEAD
ORDERDETAIL
SALES

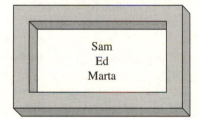

> Sam
> Ed
> Marta

Sales can view:
CUSTOMER
Sales can modify:
ORDERHEAD
ORDERDETAIL

> Marta
> Jack
> Andy

Sample roles.

Notice that Marta is a member of the Sales and SalesManagers roles. The permissions granted through roles are additive, so that means she can view and modify CUSTOMER, ORDERHEAD, ORDERDETAIL, and SALES. She would have the same permission if she belonged to SalesManagers only.

Not only can you allow access, you can block access by explicitly denying permissions to a user or role. This overrides any permissions allowed. The use of denied permissions should be limited because they can make it difficult to identify and correct access problems. When possible, simply do not allow access as a way of preventing access to a resource.

When setting object permissions, you can set the permissions by individual object or by object type. Whenever possible, keep assignments as general as possible. For example, if a role needs to be able to view the contents of all tables, assign the permission through the type (table) rather than individually for each table. SQL Server 2005 also organizes objects as belonging to an organizational schema. Each object belongs to one and only one schema. However, a schema can contain any number of objects. You have the option of assigning permissions at the schema level and having the permissions apply to all objects contained in that schema.

Minimizing Permissions

This guideline's relatively easy to understand. Don't give users a greater level of permission than they need to do their jobs. Users who need to only view data should be allowed to run SELECT statements, and only SELECT statements, against data sources. Data entry personnel will need to be able to insert, and possibly modify, as well as view data.

You need to identify database users and their access permission requirements during the design phase. Use this to make permission assignments during implementation. If you don't give the users, or applications, the permission they need you will find out almost immediately. If you give them more permission than they need, it's likely that someone will eventually figure that out. You, however, might not find out until after the user has done damage to the data.

Auditing Changes

It's a good idea to log changes made to users and permissions through auditing. This gives you a trail to follow should you have problems in the future. It also gives you a way of finding out if someone is granting permissions without authorization.

Consider this possibility. A worker in the warehouse slips items out the back without anyone knowing and sells them. In order to hide this activity, the worker needs to be able to directly change inventory quantities so the thefts are less likely to be noticed during a physical inventory. The worker finds an administrator willing to work with him or her for a percentage of the profits. The administrator, looking to cover his or her own tracks, gives the worker permission to make the changes. The administrator is trying to keep as far out of the direct loop as possible. If you are auditing permission changes, you're more likely to discover the scheme through the permission change, or at least discover it more quickly, than through the unexplained changes in inventory quantities.

11.3.2 Minimizing Table Access

Some database administrators will tell you that their jobs would be a lot easier if they didn't have to let the users into the database. Unfortunately, that's not realistic, but it's not without a grain of truth. Each access point you open into the database is a potential security hole. The greater the access, the greater the risk.

You can't lock the users out of the database, but you can isolate them from the data tables. You don't have to give your users access rights to the data tables. Instead, you can create views and user defined functions (UDFs) to support user access requirements and not allow permissions to the tables themselves. It may seem like a minor point, but the key is not granting direct access to the tables rather than denying access to the tables. Blocking table access by explicitly denying permissions can have unexpected consequences and can prevent users from getting to the data they need.

Most access requirements and, likely, many of your data modification requirements can be met through views. UDFs are an option when views don't quite meet your needs. You can design UDFs to let users pass parameters that can in turn be used as selection or filtering criteria.

11.3.3 Keeping Data Safe

You have two fundamental goals related to protecting database data. One is keeping the data safe. The other is having a way to recover the data in case of problems. The first is a key part of many database designs, but the second is critical to all database systems.

The most common method for keeping data safe is to use fault-tolerant storage. **Fault-tolerant** storage means that your data is protected against loss in case of a disk failure. Most database service manufacturers recommend keeping data files on fault-tolerant RAID (redundant array of inexpensive, or independent, disks) subsystems that support variations of either disk mirroring or striping with parity.

You provide a means of recovery through backups. Data backups should never be considered an option, but must be included as a necessary part of any database design.

Protecting your data includes protecting the hardware platform on which it is hosted. For instance, unexpected power outages that shut off the computer without following proper shutdown procedures, can result in data errors and inconsistencies. Hardware failures can sometimes cause data corruption. That is one of the reasons why hardware platform design and selection is considered an important part of database system design.

11.3.4 Understanding RAID Configurations

Windows Server operating systems support RAID configurations implemented through software. You can also buy hardware-based RAID disk subsystems.

Figure 11-14

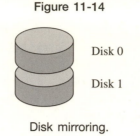

Disk 0

Disk 1

Disk mirroring.

Hardware RAID is more expensive than configuring RAID through the operating system, but can provide better disk read and write performance. Hardware RAID systems, depending on their design, can either connect as a local hard disk or can be accessed as network storage through a high-speed, high-bandwidth network connection.

Disk Mirroring

Figure 11-14 shows two hard disks configured for **disk mirroring**. Disk 0 and Disk 1 contain the same data. During each write, the same data is written to Disk 0 and Disk 1. If either hard disk fails, you still have a full set of the data on the other hard disk. Write performance can suffer slightly because of the duplicate writes, but read performance improves because the configuration supports **split reads**, reading from either hard disk.

A variation of disk mirroring is **disk duplexing**, which uses hard disks connected to different disk controllers. In this configuration, you are protected against failure of either hard disk or disk controller.

Disk Striping with Parity

Figure 11-15 shows three hard disks configured for **disk striping with parity**, three being the minimum number of drives required for this configuration. The maximum number of disks varies depending on whether you are using hardware or software RAID and, for software RAID configurations, the operating sys-

Figure 11-15

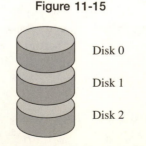

Disk 0

Disk 1

Disk 2

Disk striping with parity.

tem. In this configuration data is spread across the hard disks along with parity information. Because read and write operations split across multiple drives, you will typically see a performance improvement in both, though some of this improvement is lost in software configurations because of the overhead required to generate parity information. This isn't a problem with hardware RAID systems.

If any one hard disk is lost, the parity information is used to reg enerate the missing data. If more than one hard disk is lost, then the data is lost. In a software RAID configuration, read performance falls off sharply when one of the hard disks fails. Hardware-based systems don't suffer from this performance loss because the hardware is optimized for data recovery.

Using Backup Servers

Some management systems take data protection one step further with the option of having backup, standby, or mirrored servers. The methods supported by different manufacturers vary widely, with some manufacturers supporting multiple mirroring solutions. The basic idea is the same in each configuration: you have a complete copy of the server (software and data) standing by in case of failure, as shown in Figure 11-16.

Variations include options for both manual and automatic failover. With **automatic failover,** the backup server takes over automatically without any intervention. With **manual failover,** as the name implies, administrator intervention is required to complete the changeover between the servers. Some configurations

Figure 11-16

Client computers

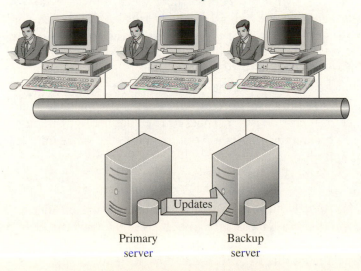

Primary server   Backup server

Sample backup server configuration.

include support for duplicate live servers so that operations can be split between the servers, improving performance.

Why not use server mirroring all the time? After all, it protects against a wider range of potential problems. There are two potential problems with server mirroring. The first is that not all DBMSs support a backup server or failover option. The other is that these solutions are relatively expensive, requiring duplicate hardware and, in many configurations, multiple software licenses (one for each server).

If the solutions are so expensive, what's the justification for using them? Backup servers, especially configurations that provide for automatic failover, give you a way of designing a database system with a guarantee of near-zero down time. Imagine, for a moment, a database system that supports a stock brokerage. Clients need the ability to post trades and have them recorded and executed immediately any time, day or night. Any outage, no matter how brief, means delayed or lost trades. Not only does this mean lost revenue, it would probably mean losing any customers that were affected. If word gets out, it could means losing even more customers, and possibly your business.

11.3.5 Using Data Backups

The surest way to recover from a failure is to have reliable backups. Data backups let you recover from the most catastrophic failures, even the loss of the entire server. Backup features vary by DBMS, but in every case, regular backups are a critical requirement, not an option.

Backup design must be part of your overall database design solution. You should be ready to implement your backup plan as you implement the database. You can judge how complete your backup plan is by whether or not it answers four key questions: "what," "when," "where," and "how." "Who" would also be a question, except that the "who" ultimately falls on the database administrator, who either runs the backups, or makes sure that they are run on a regular basis.

Answering the "What" of Backups

What do you back up? That's the easiest question. You back up everything at least once. You need to have a backup copy of all of your data, including lookup and reference data that doesn't change, to facilitate recovery in case of data loss.

The more critical the data is to your business, the more important that it be backed up, and all data is important. If not, then why is it taking up space on your server? Of course, more volatile data needs to be backed up more frequently, but make sure you have a copy of everything.

Everything literally means everything, including database metadata. The need to back up production data is easy to see, but that's not the only data in your database. If your DBMS includes system databases that store information about databases and their contents, you need to back these up also. The same is true of the data dictionary, if maintained as a separate component in your DBMS.

Answering the "When" of Backups

Answering the "when" is a little more difficult. The easy answer is that you need to back up the data after it changes. Configurations that constantly back up the production databases throughout the day are possible, but are expensive and often difficult to implement.

The important question here is, "How much data can you afford to reenter after a failure?" The answer tells you the maximum interval between backups. For some companies, once a day is often enough. For others, you might need to run backups at a much shorter interval, such as once an hour. The potential impact on other operations can influence your decision, possibly forcing you to run backups during off-peak times. Scheduling can be a definite problem if your DBMS makes the database unavailable during backups. However, most current management systems, including SQL Server, allow user access and support most database operations while a backup is running.

Consider the earlier example of a stock brokerage. Data changes rapidly in this type of environment. If data is lost, it can be difficult (if not impossible) to accurately repost or re-create the data. In this environment you need to back up the data as often as possible, but with minimal impact to database operations. One way of doing this is to run backups that back up large amounts of data infrequently, probably no more than once a week. You would then supplement this by backing up changes only. These could run as often as every minute, backing up just the changes that were committed during that period.

Backup frequency, as well as the amount of overhead you can allow for backups, will also help determine the "How" part of the question.

Answering the "How" of Backups

With that lead-in, let's go ahead and talk about "how" before we talk about "where." Most database systems support multiple backup options. All systems include some method for a **full backup** of all database data. This can be through a special backup utility, or in some cases, can be done by backing up the database and object files through the operating system. Some systems require you to back up the entire database when you run a full backup, but others let you back up the full content of separate database files individually. It is strongly recommended that you run a periodic full backup as a base for recovery with most companies running one at least once a week. Most manufacturers recommend an interval of no longer than once a month.

Most DBMSs provide an option for backing up changed data only between full backups so that the backups run faster. These can be run as incremental or differential backups. An **incremental backup** backs up only those changes made since the last backup. This means that the backups take very little time to run, but when recovering data, you must restore each of the incremental backups in the order in which they were made. **Differential backups** back up all changes since the last base or full backup. That means that each successive differential backup takes longer to run, but after restoring the base backup, you only need to restore from the most recent differential backup.

DBMSs that use a transaction log for tracking changes to the backup support **transaction log backups.** When you back up the transaction log, you back up the **inactive portion** of the log only. That means that you back up only those transactions that have been completed, either committed or rolled back. The inactive portion is then deleted, freeing up the space and helping to keep the transaction log a manageable size. Because of their small size and because they usually run quickly and with minimal interference to user operations, transaction log backups are typically used to support backup plans that require frequent (such as hourly) backups. During recovery, you first restore the base data and any change (incremental and differential) backups. Then, you restore all transaction log backups, starting at that point, in the order in which they were taken.

Usually, if your DBMS supports multiple backup options, it also lets you mix and match those options to meet your needs. Let's say that General Hardware Supply, a fictitious company, determines that they can run backups after hours only. This means running backups between 9:00 p.m. and 6:00 a.m. Monday through Saturday and any time on Sunday. Because there are other automated operations occurring at night, they want the backups run during the week to run as quickly as possible. They also want a full backup to run at least once a week. You could meet this requirement by configuring the backups to run automatically, scheduling a full backup to run on Sunday and incremental backups to run each of the remaining evenings.

Looking back at the brokerage example again, you would run infrequent full backups, no more than once a week and possibly once a month or less. If you were to cut full backups back to once a month, you would probably want to run differential or incremental backups at least once a week, and more often if your schedule and server activity allows. For the very frequent backups, such as those that run as often as every minute, you would probably use transaction log backups. Where this solution becomes a problem is in recovery after a failure. You could find yourself having to recover from the full backup, the most recent differential backup, and potentially thousands of transaction log backups. This is one situation where you might strongly consider the added expensive of a duplicate server as an appropriate investment.

Answering the "Where" of Backups

Now, to our last question. "Where" refers to the backup destination, with most backups running to one of two places: to a shared network drive or to removable media. Let's look at each of these options.

Figure 11-17 illustrates one option for backing up to a shared network drive. The backup runs on the database server and is written to a shared folder on another computer, typically a secure file server dedicated to this purpose somewhere on the network.

Figure 11-17

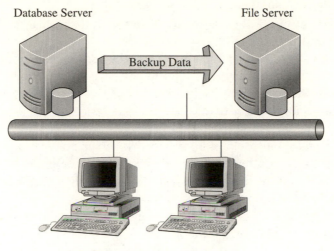

Shared network destination.

One of the biggest advantages of this method is its ease of use. Backups can run fully automated, as long as the network remains available and the destination server doesn't run out of space. Backups can run very fast, depending on your network bandwidth. It also leaves the data readily available for recovery should there be a problem. Some companies, after moving most of their production data to PC-based platforms now use some of the extra storage space on mainframe or minicomputers as a backup destination.

The disadvantage is that the destination computer is a potential point of failure. Some events, such as fire or flood, could take out both the database server and the backup file server unless they are kept well separated in different locations. There is also a potential security concern. You need to ensure that the destination server is protected against unauthorized access.

The other option used to be more common, backing up to **removable media,** which is storage media that can be physically removed from the hard disk. Most often, this means backing up to some kind of magnetic tape, but can sometimes include optical media such as DVD. One problem with this method is that the media capacity is often relatively less than the size of the database, meaning that you need a backup device with a data carousel, or someone has to physically change the media. This is also why media selections are usually limited to magnetic tape or DVD. The storage capacity of diskettes and even writeable CDs is too small for them to be considered for use except in some very limited situations requiring selected backup of a subset of the database data. A **data carousel** is a backup device that has multiple live media bays, which writes to several tapes at once, for example, or changes the media for you automatically. Another concern is that magnetic media has a limited lifespan and must be replaced after a set number of uses. Magnetic tapes are also susceptible to magnetic fields that can degrade or even erase the data.

The biggest advantage of using removable media is that is makes it easy to keep a copy off-site and protected. Companies that use removable media often have multiple sets, rotating one set off-site on a regular schedule, such as once a week.

You can also combine methods. You might have some data backed up to a network server and other data backed up to removable media. Another option is to run most backups to a network location, but periodically back up to removable media to create a copy for off-site storage. Some companies combine the methods by running all backups to a network server and periodically backing up the network server to removable media. Because these backups don't impact the database in any way, they can be run at a convenient time without worrying about the impact on performance.

Taking a final look at our brokerage example, it's likely that you would run all of the backups to a network location because this would be the easiest configuration to fully automate. With as many backups as are required, automation would be a critical concern. Then, as added security, you would back up the server used as the backup destination on a regular basis. A daily backup schedule would probably be appropriate, backing up all of the database backup files each time.

11.3.6 Protecting Your Server

One of the ways that database servers optimize performance is by keeping recently accessed and changed data in memory. Even though servers are designed to recover after hardware failures, a sudden power loss often means that recent changes are lost and can result in data inconsistencies. Also, sudden power loss and power fluctuations can cause hardware to act in an unexpected manner. For example, loss of power might cause the hard disk to perform a random write, corrupting disk data.

The best way of protecting against hardware failures is to insist on high-quality hardware designed for use as a server, preferably for use specifically as a database server. You also need to ensure that preventative maintenance is performed on the computer hardware on a regular schedule based on the manufacturer's recommendations.

However, just because you select high-quality hardware, that doesn't mean that it's necessarily appropriate for use as a database server. One example is caching disk controllers. The disk controller is the interface between the computer and the hard disk drive. A caching control has onboard memory that enables it to cache data during read and write operations, helping to optimize disk performance. However, if the disk controller is not designed to be database-aware, the additional cache can result in data errors if power is lost. Unless the disk controller is designed for use with your DBMS, it's recommended that you disable the onboard caching.

The issue of power keeps coming up when discussing possible hardware problems. The best way of protecting against power problems is to use an uninterruptible power supply (UPS). A UPS has an internal battery. AC power is used to charge the battery, and electricity from the battery is then converted back to AC to power the computer. This isolates the computer from the incoming AC power, protecting it from power surges and sags (high and low power events). It also powers the computer is case AC power is lost. Most UPS systems are designed to work with the operating system to initiate a proper shutdown before its battery completely discharges, helping prevent data loss or corruption.

FOR EXAMPLE

The Need for Backups

The importance of backups cannot be overemphasized. Good, reliable backups can mean the difference between an annoying interruption and a catastrophic and unrecoverable loss. Backups are your best, last line of defense against problems that threaten your data.

When making your design decisions, keep in mind that recovery after a hardware or software failure isn't the only possible use of database backups. They may also be needed to recover from other possible problems. Consider this situation. Everyone is gone and you're working late, cleaning up some problems that resulted from using some inexperienced temporary employees to do data entry. You know what you're doing, so you work directly from a command line in a query window. A few minutes into your cleanup, you accidentally delete the ORDERS table, six months' worth of customer orders that include all of the open orders waiting to be filled and shipped. Rather than writing up your letter of resignation and leaving quietly through a side door, you can recover the lost table, and just the lost table, from backups.

SELF-CHECK

- How many hard disks does a disk mirroring configuration require?
- What guideline should you use when assigning user permissions in SQL Server 2005?
- What is the preferred method for limiting user access to database tables?
- You want to minimize the time required to run daily backups and have backups run completely unattended. Which is the best solution?
- What is a benefit of running backups to removable media?

SUMMARY

This chapter looked at concepts and activities relating to data access and data access security. The chapter first looked at server connectivity and designing to meet connectivity requirements. It then looked at security principals, focusing on a two-tier security system with separate server-level and database-level principals, including their role in the connection process. Finally, the chapter discussed managing data access through access security and methods for protecting against and recovering from data loss.

KEY TERMS

Active Directory	Mixed authentication
ADO.NET	Modem
Authentication	Mutual authentication
Automatic failover	Open Database Connectivity (ODBC)
Common gateway interface (CGI)	OLE DB
Connection	Packet size
Connection path	Protocol
Data carousel	Public
Differential backup	Removable media
Disk duplexing	Role
Disk mirroring	Sa account
Disk striping with parity	Securable
Domain	Security context
Fault-tolerant storage	Security principal
Full backup	Split read
Guest	SQL Native Client
Hypertext Transfer Protocol (HTTP)	SQL Server authentication
Instant messaging (IM)	Strong password
Inactive portion	Transmission Control Protocol/ Internet Protocol (TCP/IP)
Incremental backup	Transaction log backup
Integrated security	Trusted connection
Login	User
Login credentials	Virtual private network (VPN)
Manual failover	WiFi
Middleware	Windows authentication

ASSESS YOUR UNDERSTANDING

Go to www.wiley.com/college/gillenson to evaluate your knowledge of data access and security.
Measure your learning by comparing pre-test and post-test results.

Summary Questions

1. You are designing a client/server database application that will run on your local network. The network is a heterogeneous environment that includes Windows and non-Windows client computers that will require direct access to the database server. The network is not configured as an Active Directory domain. How should you configure authentication?

   (a) Windows Windows authentication only.

   (b) SQL Server authentication only

   (c) mixed Windows and SQL Server authentication

   (d) none of the above

2. Your company's programmers are developing a point-of-sale application. The customer will have the option of choosing from various data platform options. What is the most appropriate data interface to use in this situation?

   (a) ODBC

   (b) SQL Native Client

   (c) OLE DB for SQL Server

   (d) you don't have enough information to choose

3. During database design and implementation, the database administrator is directly responsible for which of the following?

   (a) client and server communication path

   (b) server security principals

   (c) application data interface API

   (d) All all of the above

4. In a multitier application environment, middleware refers to the specialized software used to integrate the various application components. True or False?

5. You deploy a database server running SQL Server 2005. Which of the following client configurations would require SQL Native Client?

   (a) a multitier application client that needs to access a web application through a PC browser

   (b) a client/server application client that needs to access the server through a local Windows application that performs data retrieval and modification

(c) a client computer used to update data after hours that runs scripts that call user stored procedures to modify data through a Sqlcmd interface

(d) a client computer that is used by the database administrator to remotely manage the server

6. You are configuring logins on a database server configured for Windows authentication. What information do you provide?

   (a) account name

   (b) password

   (c) default database

   (d) both a and b

   (e) both a and c

7. When using mixed authentication in SQL Server, after creating a SQL Server login, what must you do to enable access to databases hosted on the server other than the login's default database?

   (a) configure login access permissions

   (b) configure database access permissions

   (c) add the login to the Public role

   (d) Create create database users associated with the login.

8. What is the biggest potential security concern when using Sqlcmd to connect to a database with a SQL Server login?

   (a) The login name might be compromised.

   (b) The password might be compromised.

   (c) The server name might be compromised.

   (d) The initial database name might be compromised.

9. You run the following to open a connection from a Windows client computer:

```
sqlcmd -sDataSrc -E
```

   What will be used as the initial database?

   (a) the default database associated with the logged in Windows user

   (b) the default database associated with the sa account

   (c) DataSrc

   (d) there is no way to know from the information provided

10. When connecting to a database server from a Windows client using integrated security, you create a trusted connection. True or false?

11. Under what circumstance would it be possible to use the terms *login* and *user* interchangeably when discussing database server security?

    (a) when the database server is configured to use an integrated security configuration

   (b) when database server security is based on a single-tier security principal design

   (c) when the server hosts only one user database

   (d) when using SQL Server 2005

12. What is the justification for using a fault-tolerant disk subsystem for server data storage?

   (a) to ensure data integrity during transaction processing

   (b) to protect against malicious acts

   (c) to guard against the failure of a single physical hard disk

   (d) to facilitate data recovery after a catastrophic failure

13. You want your database design to facilitate recovery after malicious acts that destroy data. What action should you take?

   (a) Use table constraints to define data integrity requirements.

   (b) Run regular backups.

   (c) Use RAID storage systems configured for disk mirroring.

   (d) Deny user access to base tables.

14. You are designing a database solution that uses SQL Server 2005. The solution requirements call for all users to have permission to run SELECT on any database table. What is the best way to configure this?

   (a) Grant the permission on each table explicitly to each database user.

   (b) Grant the permission on each table to a custom role and add all database users as role members.

   (c) Grant the permission on the table object type to a custom role and add all database users as role members.

   (d) Grant the permission on the table object type to the Public role.

15. How can views be used to enhance database security?

   (a) by filtering the columns to which users have access

   (b) by filtering the rows to which users have access

   (c) by avoiding granting direct access to tables

   (d) all of the above

Applying This Chapter

1. You are designing the access requirements for a database application. The application will use a client/server configuration with the application software running individually on each client computer. The network is configured as an Active Directory domain with the database server and all clients configured as domain members.

(a) Who has responsibility for maintaining the connection path and physical connection components?

(b) Describe the software requirements on the client side for connectivity.

(c) Explain how security principals for connecting to the database server should be configured and managed. Include specific requirements and responsible administrative roles.

(d) Describe the role of database users in this configuration.

(e) You want to keep the configuration for data backup and recovery as simple as possible and allow for quick recovery after a failure. Full backups can be run no more than once a week. Periodic backups should run no more than twice a day. Describe and justify the configuration including backup types and destinations.

2. You are designing a multi-tier database application that provides its user interface through a Web application. The Web server connects to the database server through a separate application server. Clients connect to the Web server using any current Web browser. The Web server allows for public access. The SQL Server database server used as the data source is configured for Windows authentication. The network on which the database server is deployed is configured as an Active Directory domain with the database server configured as a domain member.

(a) Except for the database server, identify which computers, if any, must be domain members. For each computer type, explain why or why not.

(b) Briefly describe how the application server would connect to the database server.

(c) Summarize the database access permission requirements to support the application.

3. A database server is deployed in a highly secure environment. Data access must be tightly controlled. Data must be protected against loss or accidental disclosure through unauthorized access.

(a) Explain at least two ways your design could allow for off-site storage of backups.

(b) Describe hard disk configuration options that would meet the data security requirements.

(c) Assuming that the database server uses a two-tier security system, briefly compare and contrast the roles of the different security principals.

Planning a Client/Server Data Environment

You are planning the database server for a client/server database solution. The solution includes two production databases and one decision support database, all running on the same database server host. The databases will support multiple client applications, each running on the appropriate client machine, as well as direct access through scripts, procedures, and ad hoc queries run from command line interfaces. The database server and all clients are members of an Active Directory domain. Server and database access must be managed separately.

The design should be as easy to maintain as possible with minimal database administrator requirements for managing access and security. Data access requirements are determined by users' job requirements. Users often make lateral shifts, changing jobs within the company based on seasonal requirements.

The design must minimize downtime and ensure that you have the server back up and running as soon as possible after a failure. The wording in the requirements document calls for "near zero downtime" for the database server. A copy of all data must be physically stored in a secure location, specifically a safe deposit box leased for that purpose, with the copy refreshed on a weekly basis. At any time, there must be at least one copy at that location.

In planning the client connection requirements, you need to identify the features that the DBMS must support and design the server side of the access requirements. Be as specific as possible.

1. Plan the data access requirements and how they will be met, including server features necessary to meet the specifications.
2. Also, develop a plan for managing database access security, based on user access requirements, that minimizes management overhead. Database security can allow for direct access of database tables.

3. Develop a plan that minimizes downtime and the features required for DBMS support. Explain how the backup storage requirements will be met.

Planning a Secure Multitier Environment

You are desiging the database solution portion of a multitier application. The solution must support both direct client access through the local network and indirect access through an application server. There will be two management clients that need server access only. The application server requires encrypted communications with both the database server and its clients. You need to know who has been connected to the database server, and when, at any time.

Backups must be designed to minimize the amount of time required to back up data during the day for backups run between 7:00 a.m. and 6:00 p.m., when the last of these periodic backups are run. An additional backup should run each night at midnight and a full backup run each weekend. All backups must run without any operator interaction. The backup system must be set up so that no more than 30 minutes' worth of work is at risk at any time and based around full, differential, and transaction log backups. Recovery should not require transaction log backups taken over multiple days. Backups should be immediately available for recovery.

1. Develop a plan to meet the access requirements. Identify security principals involved for direct access to data and software requirements to facilitate connectivity. Compare and contrast how the data access design will vary depending on whether the database server supports a one-tier or two-tier security system.
2. Design a backup system that meets all of the specified requirements. Describe what backups will run, when, and to what destination(s). Compare design requirements when using permanent or removable storage media.

12
SUPPORTING DATABASE APPLICATIONS

Starting Point

Go to www.wiley.com/college/gillenson to assess your knowledge of data application support.
Determine where you need to concentrate your effort.

What You'll Learn in This Chapter

▲ Centralized database support
▲ Distributed database support
▲ Internet-based application support

After Studying This Chapter, You'll Be Able To

▲ Include LAN configuration requirements in database planning
▲ Design two-tier and three-tier data configurations
▲ Design multi-purposed server and consolidated data configurations
▲ Design distributed data configurations.
▲ Identify replication and table partitioning design requirements.
▲ Develop solutions to meet distributed transaction, distributed query, and distributed management requirements.
▲ Manage Internet performance issues.
▲ Manage Internet availability and scalability issues.
▲ Manage Internet security and privacy issues

INTRODUCTION

One of the strengths of PC-based database management systems (DBMSs) is their flexibility. You can deploy them in various configurations, supporting all sorts of applications, as part of a small network or to be published on the Internet. This chapter looks at the three most common database configurations for application support. We start with a look at centralized database configurations and variations on the traditional client/server model. Then, we'll look at distributed database configurations that you might use to support enterprise applications. We finish with a quick look at issues related to supporting Internet-based applications.

12.1 Supporting a Centralized Database

When PC-based DBMS products were first introduced they were considered an option for small or specialty database applications. PC hardware capabilities and the ability of DBMSs to take advantage of that hardware have grown rapidly over the years to where PC-based DBMSs are usually the first choice when deploying mission-critical applications.

One important design decision in many database applications is the number and placement of database servers. Over the years, two basic arrangements for locating data hosted in database servers have been developed. One, known as a client/server database, is for personal computers connected together on a local area network, and is our current focus. This **centralized data environment** is a configuration based on a single, centralized database. The other, known as a distributed database, is for larger, geographically dispersed computers located on a wide area network and using multiple physical databases.

12.1.1 Understanding Local Area Networks (LANs)

A **local area network (LAN)** is an arrangement of personal computers connected together by communications lines. It is local in the sense that the PCs must be located fairly close to each other, within a building or within several nearby buildings. Additional components of the LAN that can be utilized or shared by the PCs can be other, often more powerful server computers and peripheral devices such as printers. The PCs on a LAN can certainly operate independently, but they can also communicate with each other. Finally, a **gateway computer** on the LAN can link the LAN and its PCs to other LANs, to one or more mainframe computers, or to the Internet.

One of the primary justifications for a LAN is the ability to share resources. One of the most important resources in any business is information. A key part of nearly any LAN is one or more file servers that provide central file storage and let users share data files. Another component that you will commonly see is a database server.

12.1.2 Understanding Data Configurations

The configuration that first comes to mind when discussing database applications is the traditional client/server configuration. Data is located on the database server supporting applications running on the client or, in a multitier application, an application server. However, this is not the only data configuration you might encounter, and even in a client/server configuration, you may have data in locations other than the database server.

In a client/server configuration, there are two computer types involved, the client and the server. Processing requirements are split between the computers, and components of the database application are often running on each. Data flow is easy to track. Say that someone at a client computer wants to query the database at the server. The query is entered at the client, and the client computer performs the initial keyboard and screen interaction processing, as well as initial syntax checking of the query. The system then ships the query over the LAN to the server where the query is actually run against the database. Only the results are shipped back to the client.

This becomes a **two-tier approach** when you not only have applications at the client but also locally stored data, as shown in Figure 12-1. Software has been developed that makes the location of the data transparent to the user at the client. In fact, this functionality can be built into your database applications. In this configuration, the user issues a query at the client, and the software first checks to see if the required data is on the PC's own hard drive. If it is, it is retrieved from the hard drive, and that is the end of the story. If it is not there, then the software automatically looks for the data on the database server.

This two-tiered model is typically discouraged for several reasons. Data located on the local hard disk is often difficult to share in an environment likely implemented to promote data sharing. The data is also more difficult to secure, maintain, and recover in case of errors. Administration and maintenance falls on the user and often never gets done. You might use this model as an interim solution while migrating to a centralized database, but it should not be considered a long term solution.

In an even more sophisticated **three-tier approach,** shown in Figure 12-2, if the software doesn't find the data on the client PC's hard drive or on the LAN server, it can leave the LAN through a gateway computer and look for the data on, for example, a large, mainframe computer that may be reachable from many LANs. As with the two-tier approach, this is often considered a transitional configuration. It could also be used as a way of justifying the continued existence and support of a mainframe computer as a very large, very fast (and very expensive) data store supporting the PC database.

Figure 12-1

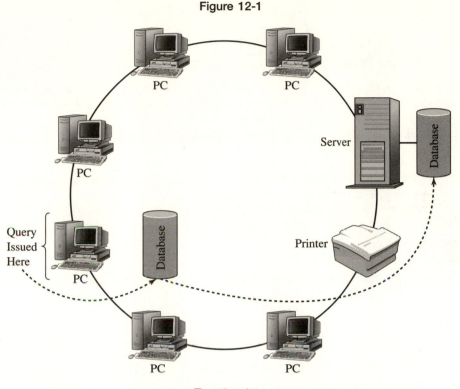

Two-tier data.

How these multiple data sources are handled depends on your DBMS and client application. Some DBMSs support a flexible data dictionary that can make the process transparent to the database application. With other DBMSs, including SQL Server, the DBMS tracks data hosted in its own databases only. Multi-tiered data environments like those discussed here are treated as **distributed data environments** because of the heterogeneous data sources, even though all data sources are physically located on the local network.

As is often the case, you must be careful how you use terms relating to database applications and make sure that you understand the context in which they are used. When discussing a three-tier configuration, you need to specify whether you are talking about the data locations or the database application configuration. The same term, *three-tier,* is sometimes used when discussing a multitiered application, referring to the database server, application servers, and client computers as the three application tiers. The middle tier could involve multiple computers, such as an application server and a Web server. You can easily have a single-tiered approach to data storage, with all of the data stored on the database server, supporting a multi-tier (or three-tier) database application.

Figure 12-2

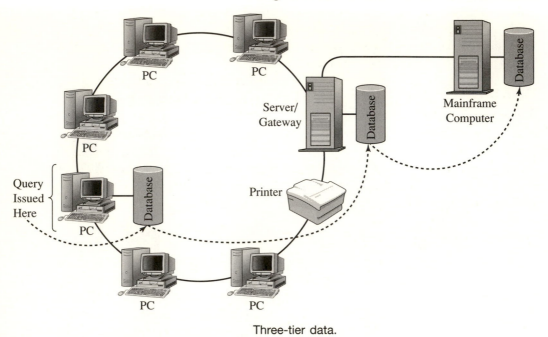

Three-tier data.

12.1.3 Understanding Server Configurations

There is a potential configuration concern when you look closely at the PC database server in Figure 12-2. Notice that it is identified as a server/gateway, which means that the computer is serving double duty and running two different server applications. While this is possible, it must be carefully monitored. SQL Server is a resource-intensive application, relying heavily on the physical server's hard disk(s), memory, and processor(s). Any other server applications running on the same computer must share those same resources. If there is contention between the applications for resources, the performance of one, or even both, can suffer.

However, careful planning and ongoing management can overcome these potential problems. There is often a tendency to "over buy" when purchasing a database server, getting more hardware than you actually need. This has become even more common as the cost of computer hardware has dropped, with processing power and storage capacity increasing at the same time. If you do deploy a **multi-purposed server,** one server running multiple server applications, you need to monitor resource use by each of the applications and total resource use. You may reach a point where it becomes necessary to either scale up the hardware platform or scale out, putting the different server applications on different computers.

Another server configuration you might see is having different copies of your database server, or separate **server instances,** running on the same computer.

These can be different instances of the same DBMS, or could even be different DBMSs, such as having SQL Server and My SQL running on the same computer. Each instance, though running on the same hardware, is treated as a completely separate database server. Each is managed separately, with separate configurations, and using computer resources separately.

Using separate server instances should almost always be limited to a development environment as a way of minimizing hardware when testing different database servers or different server configuration parameters. However, there are rare instances when you might use this configuration in a production environment. For example, you might need multiple database servers that need different security configurations, but the resources requirements are such that they can share a hardware platform without interfering with each other. As with running different server applications, this configuration needs to be carefully monitored.

12.1.4 Consolidating Data Sources

Most database management systems are designed to support multiple user databases. There are usually a specified maximum number of supported databases, but this is usually large enough not to be a concern, allowing for hundreds, thousands, or even more databases. The realistic limiting factors are available disk space and memory. Each database will require a minimum amount of space, and, even if the database is not currently being used, the DBMS will typically set aside a portion of its dedicated memory for database support.

It's common to see a database server hosting multiple databases. It might be that different databases are required for different divisions or departments within a company. Your company's security guidelines may require that sensitive or confidential data be stored on a database separate from other data. When supporting a decision support system (DSS) based on a data warehouse, you will often keep the DSS data and the production data on which it is based on the same database server. As you've already learned, the term data warehouse refers to a shared database containing accumulated data that is used to support management decisions.

In a strictly centralized data environment, one where all of an application's data resides on a single database, the assumption is that each database is essentially a stand-alone data store supporting its own unique application or set of applications. At most, you need to support periodic data transfers, such as loading a decision support data warehouse with data from a production database. However, there is little or no direct interaction between the databases, at least between the data in the databases, during normal operations.

When you do have interaction between the databases, you move into a distributed data environment. Because the data is spread across multiple databases, even though they are located on the same physical server, you have many of the same data support issues you would have if using **distributed database servers** (a multiple server configuration supporting related data).

FOR EXAMPLE

Data in Transition

You might wonder about the justification for two- and three-tier data when a centralized environment with a single database and a single server is obviously easier to manage and maintain. The decision to use a multitiered data environment is usually one made more out of necessity than out of choice.

It's easy to think of the transition from PCs hosting their own data, data stashed away in different applications such as spreadsheets, or from a traditional mainframe, to a PC-based DBMS as something almost surgical in nature. One day, you're operating with all of these different sources and manually compiling the results, and the next, everything is sitting in the database server ready for use. The reality is often very different. The transition is often more of a gradual migration than a sudden switch.

There are several issues that must be considered and real-world factors that must be included when migrating to a new data environment. Even though you are moving data from PCs to the database, the data is continually changing. It may be necessary to run different systems in parallel until the changeover is complete. The transition could be made in phases, putting the most critical data or data needed by the largest number of users onto the database first and then gradually moving the rest of the data as time and resources allow.

There are special issues that can arise when dealing with an existing mainframe or minicomputer. A company's options are often limited by long-term lease or service agreements. Maybe when you acquired another company and its assets, the mainframe contract came along as an unavoidable part of the deal. You might not need the mainframe as your primary data source after you've extracted the data from it, but you have to keep paying for it, so you might as well get some use out of it. In other cases there are practical reasons why you can't move the data to a PC-based database server. The transition might be too expensive to make it cost effective, or the mainframe data is a required source for a proprietary or third-party application that runs on the mainframe only. It might be that communication with customers or clients is mainframe-based and it is either too difficult to move to a different method or there are licensing, patent, or copyright issues that prevent it.

The reason really doesn't matter. The bottom line is that there are often valid, unavoidable justifications for maintaining data in a two-tier or three-tier configuration, even if just temporarily "during the migration." It's important to understand, however, that "during the migration" has become a permanent way of life for some companies.

SELF-CHECK

- Can a traditional centralized data environment have multiple database servers as long as they are all deployed on the same LAN?
- What does a three-tier data environment include?
- What is a data warehouse used to support?
- What is a multi-purposed server?

12.2 Supporting a Distributed Database

In today's world of universal dependence on information systems, all sorts of people need access to a company's databases. These people include a company's own employees, its customers, potential customers, suppliers, and vendors of all types. It is possible for a company to have all of its databases concentrated at one mainframe computer site with worldwide access provided by telecommunications networks. However, even though a centralized system like this can be advantageous, it poses some problems as well. For example, if the single site goes down, then everyone is blocked from accessing the company's database. Also the communications costs from the many far-flung PCs and terminals to the central site can be prohibitive.

As an example, we're going to use a large multinational company with major sites in Los Angeles, Memphis, New York (corporate headquarters), Paris, and Tokyo. Let's say that the company has a transactional relational database that is actively used by all five sites. There are six tables, named A, B, C, D, E, and F, and response time regarding queries made to the databases is an important factor. Figure 12-3 shows a centralized configuration with all of the tables hosted on the database physically located in New York.

While we are discussing distributed databases and related support issues, we'll use this example to see options available to distribute and maintain the data.

12.2.1 Understanding Distributed Data

The reasons for implementing distributed data environments can vary as much as the companies using those environments to meet their data requirements. The reasons and justifications for using a distributed data environment, however, usually come down to one or more of the following (in no particular order):

▲ Reduce costs.
▲ Make the data universally available.

Figure 12-3

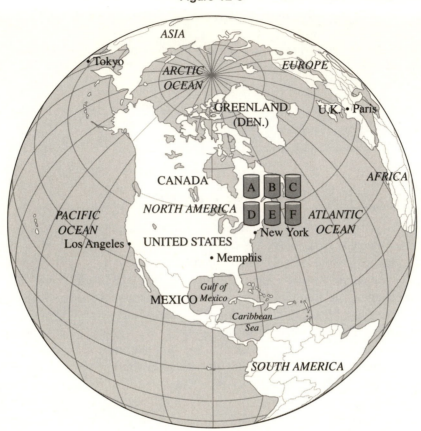

Centrally located data.

▲ Reduce data communication requirements.

▲ Improve performance during data operations.

▲ Keep data physically near its primary consumers.

▲ Have the data owner and primary consumer take some responsibility for upkeep.

Before distributing the data, or even considering a distributed data environment, you need to plan how you would divide the data, how it would be maintained, and the potential impact on data operations. If migrating from a centralized to a distributed environment, you must think about how the change will affect access requirements, database applications, security configurations, and any number of other design considerations. You must accept that the issue is not *if* these design characteristics will change in the new environment, but *how* they will change. A

Figure 12-4

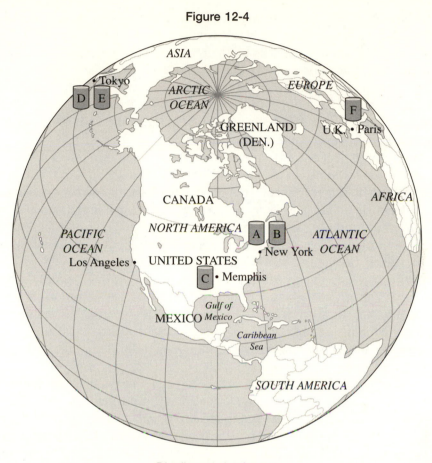

Distributed databases.

clear understanding will help you balance the costs and drawbacks against the benefits. Sometimes the best solution is to keep your centralized design and improve your communication infrastructure rather than changing your data design.

The simplest solution, in most cases, is to locate the data near its primary consumer. In our example, that means deploying databases and placing the tables physically near the offices that most frequently use them. Figure 12-4 shows how you might do this: Tables A and B are located in New York, while Table C is moved to Memphis, Tables D and E to Tokyo, and Table F to Paris. Let's take a look at what this means from a support and management standpoint. With Table F in Paris, for example, the people there can use it as much as they want without running up any telecommunications costs. Furthermore, the Paris employees can exercise **local autonomy** over the data, taking responsibility for its security, backup and recovery, and concurrency control.

Is this a workable solution? Possibly, but you don't know enough about data needs yet to know definitely. Does this solution have possible drawbacks? Definitely, including some drawbacks that carry over from the centralized database and some new ones introduced by the distributed environment.

The main problem that is carried over from the centralized approach is availability. If New York went down in the original configuration, Table F (as well as the rest of them) is unavailable. In our new design, if the Paris site goes down, Table F is equally unavailable to the other sites.

One new problem relates to data access. What if an office issues a query that joins data from multiple tables? In the dispersed approach, a join might require tables located at different sites! Though not an insurmountable problem, this would obviously add some major complexity. Another possible issue is security. Although you can make the argument that local autonomy is good for issues like security control, an argument can also be made that security for the overall database can better be handled at a single, central location.

Moving the data to be near its primary consumer is one possible solution, but is by far not the only solution, nor is it often the best solution. It's doubtful that any one location will need access to only one database table. However, you do have several different configuration options available, though they may be limited somewhat by the functionality and features provided by your DBMS.

Another possibility is to keep a full copy of the database at every location, as shown in Figure 12-5. As you can see, this involves maintaining a database with all six tables physically located in each office location. An obvious advantage to this configuration is availability. If a table is replicated at two or more sites and one of those sites goes down, everyone everywhere else on the network can still access the table at the other site(s). Telecommunication requirements to support client access are minimized. Joins are run using local tables rather than distributed copies, making them easier to manage as well. Before you create this distribution environment, however, you need to make a couple of key decisions. You need to determine which copies of the database will support data updates and how those updates will get distributed to the other copies. You also need to consider possible problems inherent in this design.

One of the biggest potential concerns with a distributed data design that duplicates data between locations is disk space. You need sufficient disk space at each location to support the database copies. Security is another possible concern. If a table is replicated at several sites, it becomes more of a security risk by the mere fact that there are more copies in more locations and more opportunities for a dedicated hacker or data thief. Security management overhead, though possibly (but not necessarily) distributed, increases because there are more servers and databases to secure.

Figure 12-5

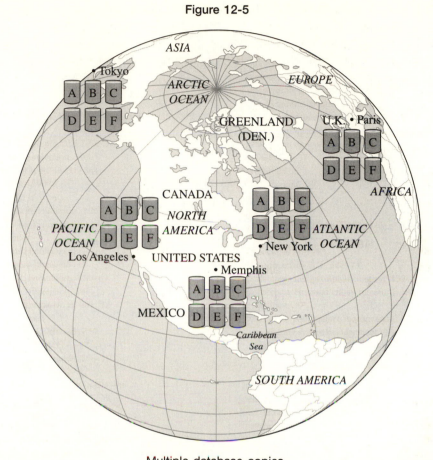

Multiple database copies.

Possibly the biggest problem that data replication introduces is that of data updates and concurrency control. If you allow updates to only one master copy of the database that contains a consolidated data set, say the copy on New York, you cut down significantly on the possibility of concurrency errors, but you lose any benefits relating to telecommunication and improved access any time you need to make a data update. If you allow updates to all of the databases, the possibility of concurrency errors increases significantly. With either, you have the issue of getting the updates made to all of the database copies.

12.2.2 Understanding Replicated Data

An important part of most distributed database environments is **replication.** This is the means used by the database server to update multiple destination databases with data from a central source database. The terminology used to describe replication concepts, as well as the specifics of how replication is implemented, varies by manufacturer.

Basically, replication is the process of copying changes from one table to one or more other tables. The way this is accomplished varies, with different DBMSs supporting one or more of the following options for replication type:

▲ **Snapshot replication:** a copy is made of the entire table and written as a whole to the destination, overwriting any data currently in the table, or creating the table for initial load of a remote database.

▲ **Change replication:** also known as **merge replication.** Changed rows in the source table are written to the destination, overwriting or inserting data as appropriate, which can result in update conflicts.

▲ **Transactional replication:** completed transactions are copied from the source database's transaction log to the destination transaction logs, where they are applied to the database tables.

With some replication configurations, you have a single consolidated database with a full set of all rows. This leaves three options for managing updates. This design decision is made somewhat independent of the replication type. One option for managing updates is that changes are made to the consolidated database only, and then distributed out to the other copies. This option has the fewest issues relating to concurrency, but requires access to the consolidated database to make changes. The next option is to allow changes at the consolidated copy and the replicated copies. The copies send their changes to the consolidated database where the changes are consolidated and sent back out to the copies. This allows for local updates but has a somewhat higher risk of concurrency errors and requires careful management. The third option allows updates at the consolidated database and at any copy, but the copies are able to directly update each other. This method has the highest risk of concurrency errors and the longest **latency,** the time between when the update is made and when it is replicated throughout the system. However, this third method is sometimes the only workable solution when you have intermittent or unreliable connections between the database locations.

The final replication design combines the type and update method. For example, you might have an environment that uses change replication that permits updates at the copies only, consolidating the changes at the consolidated database. However, it might be more appropriate to permit updates at the copies, but then allow the copies to use change replication to update each other (especially if there is no one consolidated master copy). You can also mix and match methods. For example, you might use snapshot replication once a month to send fresh copies out to all of the remote locations to ensure consistency with the source database.

Figure 12-6

Data partitioned by table.

12.2.3 Understanding Partitioned Data

So far, we've looked at working with complete tables or the complete database, but these are not your only configuration options. You could have a situation where remote locations need to frequently access some, but not all, of the database tables. Using replication to keep the tables updated and manage data changes, you could have a situation like the one shown in Figure 12-6, with a consolidated copy of the database in New York, and, in Los Angeles, copies of Table A and Table E only. That gives users in Los Angeles local access to those tables. They also have access to the other database tables, but through remote connections. Because A and E are the tables that users in Los Angeles most often need to access, communication requirements are reduced while keeping the storage requirements somewhat less than what is needed for the whole database.

Figure 12-7

Distributed tables with no consolidated database.

The principle behind making this concept work is flexibility in placing replicated tables where they will do the most good. You want to

▲ Place copies of tables at the sites that use the tables most heavily in order to minimize telecommunications costs.

▲ Ensure that there are at least two copies of important or frequently used tables to realize the gains in availability.

▲ Limit the number of copies of any one table to control the security and concurrency issues.

▲ Avoid any one site becoming a bottleneck.

Though used in Figure 12-6, this configuration doesn't necessary require a master or consolidated copy of the database containing all of the tables in any one location. Another option is shown in Figure 12-7, with tables distributed around the world and no one consolidated database. Some database administrators don't feel comfortable with a configuration like this and prefer to have one central consolidated copy to ensure that all database data is secured and backed up on a regular basis.

Figure 12-7 shows an arrangement of replicated tables based on the principles mentioned. There are two copies each of Tables A, B, E, and F, and three copies of Table D. Apparently, Table C is relatively unimportant or infrequently used, and it is located solely in Los Angeles.

You can take this partitioning of table data down to an even lower level. Most manufacturers' replication schemes support horizontal and vertical data partitioning. With **horizontal partitioning,** you filter the rows so that a subset of the available rows is replicated to the remote site. This is used when you want a local copy of some, but not all, of the rows. With **vertical partitioning,** you filter the columns so that only selected columns are replicated. This is typically done as a security measure, giving the remote locations only the data they need to do their jobs without generating multiple copies of more sensitive data. You can combine the two types of partitioning and filter a table both horizontally and vertically.

You can see an example of partitioning, which is sometimes referred to as table **fragmentation,** in Figure 12-8. This figure shows the same network we've been using, but with Table G added. Table G might be, for example, the company's employee table: the records of the employees who work in a given city are stored in that city's computer. G1 is the subset of records of Table G with the records of the employees who work in Memphis, G2 is the subset of records for the employees who work in Los Angeles, and so forth. This makes sense when one considers that most of the query and access activity on a particular employee's record will take place at his or her work location.

The drawback of partitioning is that when one of the sites, say the New York headquarters location, occasionally needs to run an application that requires accessing the employee records of everyone in the company, it must collect the records from every one of the five sites. One way to minimize this problem would be to keep a consolidated copy of Table G with all employee records in New York.

FOR EXAMPLE

Distributed Data

As you can see, there is no one best distributed data configuration. The design, like any database design solution, must be matched to the company, its data, and the way it does business. There are some general guidelines that apply in most situations, such as minimizing the exposure of sensitive data and keeping data communication requirements to a minimum, but even with strict adherence to these guidelines the available configurations vary widely.

Continued

For example, consider the requirements for a nationwide automotive aftermarket parts retailer. It keeps a consolidated inventory, as well as consolidated copies of customer and customer order records in the home office. It wants to deploy databases at each retail sales location to support local point-of-sale operations. How might you design a solution to meet their needs?

Start with a look at the data requirements at each location. What does each location need for point-of-sale support? Most likely, it needs the local customers, its own local physical inventory, and copies of its customer orders. Point-of-sale applications need to respond to query requests and complete customer orders as quickly as possible, so you would want all of this information stored on the local database server. What each location doesn't need is a full set of inventory and order data for all locations. This could drastically increase the local storage requirements and the additional table rows could impact performance.

In this scenario, you also don't keep a full copy of the customers at each location. This saves storage space, but isn't necessarily the best configuration. Customers might buy from more than one store location. The logic to handle searching for the customer data if it isn't found locally makes the application a little more complex. The number of distributed transactions can also increase because of the distributed customer records, so performance could suffer when posting customer orders. However, keeping a full copy at each location isn't without its possible problems. The biggest problem is the possibility of conflicts and concurrency errors when updating multiple copies of the table and having to reconcile the changes between the copies. These issues have to be balanced out, and a best compromise chosen, when designing a distributed database.

This is a situation where you would use horizontally partitioned tables at each of the sales locations with a master copy of each of the tables located in the home office. Assuming that each location handles its own ordering and restocking, you could post all activity relating to the location to the local database. You still have the issue of keeping the consolidated database updated, but this could be done using either a change-based or transaction-based replication method. If you restrict changes to the local database only and include an identifier for the local retail sales location as part of the primary key in each of the tables, you can minimize the possibility of conflicts during updates.

It's likely in this situation that you would have tables in the consolidated database that are not replicated to the remote locations. The sales locations would likely not need copies of any tables that contain data relating to home office operational requirements. There are a few more issues you need to resolve, but we will come back to those later.

Figure 12-8

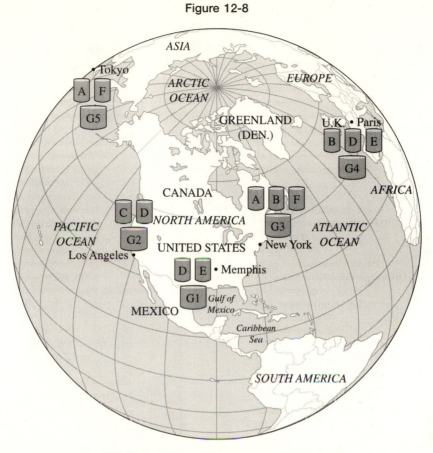

Distributed data with partitioned Table G.

12.2.4 Distributed Data Support Issues

The possible issues that can result from a distributed data environment are more varied and numerous than could possibly be covered in this chapter. The possibilities vary widely depending on the particular data configuration, the application configuration (client/server or multitiered), the DBMS used, access requirements, security requirements, and so on. The closer you look at the environment, the longer and more varied the list becomes. That doesn't mean you have to ignore the subject completely. Some issues apply across the various manufacturers' products and can occur in different configurations. The following discussion focuses on some of the common issues you are most likely to encounter.

Managing Transactions and Concurrency

Most production databases act primarily as a transaction processing environment. This means that issues relating to transactions and concurrency are critical in any configuration. The configuration does, however, affect the types of issues you might see.

The simplest example to see and understand is probably a configuration where you have a master consolidated database and all changes are made to that database. The concurrency issues, such as lost updates or dirty reads, are the same as in a centralized environment and addressed in much the same way. The same is true, at the local database, for changes that are made to a local copy of the data using local tables only. In this case there is an added issue in that the updates must also be made to the consolidated database and other replicated copies.

The easiest way to minimize potential conflicts that can arise is to use a transactional replication design so that changes are made incrementally to the databases. This helps to ensure that all changes are made, and are made in a proper order. This isn't appropriate for all environments, though, because it requires reliable, relatively high-bandwidth connections between sites. If transactional replication isn't possible and you are replicating changed rows, the replication management system has an added responsibility: resolving data conflicts. When changes are made to the same row at the same time in two different tables, a conflict that is likely to cause a lost update will result. There is logic designed into the replication management component of the DBMS that resolves the issue based on several parameters, such as when the updates were made and which copy of the database is considered most **authoritative,** that is, is the "correct" copy of the data.

What if a transaction involves multiple tables? This can be a problem, because either all changes to all tables, even those in different locations, must either be made or rolled back as a group. Because the nature of the data and of the applications that use it require that all of the data in the replicated tables worldwide always be consistent, accurate, and up-to-date, a more complex synchronous procedure must be used to process transactions. Although there are variations on this theme, the basic process for accomplishing this is known as the **two-phase commit,** so called because of how the transactions are processed using a prepare phase and a commit phase. In the **prepare phase,** the database gets everything ready for the update. If no errors occur, the **commit phase** is entered and the transaction is committed at each database server. The specifics of how this is implemented vary by manufacturer, but the general process flow for a successful transaction is similar to the following:

1. The transaction processor starts the prepare phase and locates the databases hosting the affected tables.
2. The changes are written to the database transaction logs.

3. Depending on the transaction isolation settings, the database locks the affected tables (or individual rows) for update.

4. The databases send messages that they are ready to commit.

5. Transaction process control enters the commit phase and issues a commit instruction to each affected database.

This process requires **well-connected** servers, meaning that there is a full-time, reliable, high-bandwidth connection. If there is a problem anywhere at any step in the process or if the connection to any involved server is lost, the transaction is rolled back on all servers.

Microsoft has a component (separate from SQL Server) that is designed specifically to manage distributed transactions, called the **Microsoft Distributed Transaction Coordinator (MS DTC).** Because it is separate from SQL Server, MS DTC can manage distributed transactions when using data sources in addition to SQL Server (in a heterogeneous environment), or even when processing transactions that don't include SQL Server as a data source.

When initiating an explicit distributed transaction through SQL Server, you run BEGIN DISTRIBUTED TRAN to identify it as such. To complete the transaction, run COMMIT TRAN or ROLLBACK TRAN from the command line, script, or application. When you execute BEGIN DISTRIBUTED TRAN, the MS DTC takes over management of the process, enlisting the servers involved and ensuring that all servers are ready before committing the transactions.

One reason that the process is similar for many other manufacturers is because they also use calls to MS DTC to manage distributed transactions when the database server is deployed in a Windows networking environment. Those manufacturers who don't often embed a distributed transaction management component into the database server. Watch carefully, though, if you know that you'll be deploying in a distributed data environment. Some manufacturers provide no direct support for distributed transactions, leaving it up to you to build these controls into your data application.

Managing Distributed Queries

A **distributed query** is one that retrieves data from different databases. In most cases, it includes a **distributed join,** which is one that joins data from the different databases. This doesn't necessarily mean a physically distributed environment, because the process of joining data between different databases hosted on the same database server is also considered a distributed join. As with distributed transactions, methods for handling distributed queries vary between different manufacturers, but there are similarities. The easiest way to understand the process is through an example. We'll use SQL Server 2005 as our sample database server, but even when initiating the join from a SQL Server database server, the joined tables can include tables hosted on other DBMSs.

You do not do anything to identify a distributed query as different in the SELECT statement. The difference is that you specify data sources located on different database servers. Data sources must be fully qualified, at least to the point that the database server can uniquely identify and locate the source. However, depending on the remote sources, special clauses or functions may be needed to access the remote servers and retrieve the necessary data.

The server executing the query is also the controlling server. It issues the commands necessary to retrieve the data from the remote databases. The specifics of this process are somewhat transparent to the user. Once the controlling server has all of the data that it needs cached in local memory, it completes the process as if running a local query.

As with distributed transactions, this process depends on well-connected servers to keep performance at an acceptable level. It is also suggested that you filter the results at the source servers to minimize the amount of data transferred. This is another situation where views and UDFs can be helpful in managing and optimizing the process. The queries may also require special security configurations to enable connectivity between the servers involved in the query.

Some DBMSs, like SQL Server, require you to fully qualify each data source so that it is uniquely identified. Other DBMSs do not require you to fully qualify the tables and columns used in a distributed join, instead relying on a distributed data dictionary to locate the table data. Even then, using fully qualified object names is still an option and is the preferred way of running the join. One potential problem with this is that if there are any variations in the data in the different tables, such as might occur because of replication latency, you might not get the results you expect from your query.

Managing Management Issues

Managing and administering a distributed data environment often requires a balancing act between local autonomy and company standards. In order to prevent complete chaos, it is necessary for someone to have final say over the data environment as a whole, even if various administrative duties are delegated to local administrators.

The two most common management models are a centralized management model and a localized management with central oversight model. The **centralized management** model is the easiest one to understand and is the least likely to result in administrative errors. In this model, all database servers, no matter where they are physically located, are administered from a central location using remote management tools. This is possible because most modern DBMSs ship with embedded remote management utilities. SQL Server Management Studio, for example, lets you register any number of local and remote servers for management and administration purposes. The primary advantage of this model is that one person, or one administration group, has total control. There is no question

FOR EXAMPLE

The Need for Distributed Operations

Let's revisit our nationwide auto parts chain store. Previously, it had set up the local stores with the data each store needs for point-of-sale operations. Now we're going to throw in another likely design requirement as a business rule.

Each customer must be listed once, and only once, in the consolidated database.

There are others requirements you might add, such as checking other nearby locations if you don't have something in stock or letting customers return items to any location, but this is enough for now. You can think about how to handle those problems on your own, later.

Life has definitely gotten more complicated, possibly more complicated than you realize at first glance. Each customer is tracked separately in the system. You want to make sure that all sales are tracked for sales analysis and marketing purposes (all this data feeds a data warehouse at the home office). Let's say that you track customers by telephone number, and, by definition in your data design document, each telephone number represents a unique customer.

The customer steps up to check out with a purchase, gives the employee a telephone number, and the application does a search of the local customer table. The number comes up not in file, so you need to enter a new customer into the system, right? Not necessarily. What if this person purchased items from a different location before? The application would do a second search, as a distributed query, just to make sure. It could issue a query against all of the other locations, but this is where the master copy comes in. The most efficient way to check is to run a query against the master customer table in the home office.

Now, let's assume that the customer was found in the master table. All updates must be made to the local databases, so now you have another problem, updating the customer record with this sale. We mentioned embedding the location as part of the primary key, and now that information becomes important. The application would use that code location to identify the remote database. It would have to create the order as a distributed transaction that updates the local inventory, employee (for sales bonus), and order tables while also updating a remote customer table.

Would it be easier to code the application so that updates that affect other locations are made directly to the master table? Possibly, but this would add two additional problems. One, the design requirement is that all updates be made to the local database. The other is that you set up replication so that the remote copies update the master copy, not the other way around. If you start allowing updates at both, the possibility of concurrency errors (such as lost updates) and replication conflicts increases.

as to the rights and responsibilities to make changes to the servers and databases. Though not an absolute requirement, this model works best when all of the database servers are well-connected.

Centralized management is not always appropriate or even possible. **Localized management with central oversight** delegates some or all of the administrative duties to local administrators. The general idea is that a local administrator would know his or her server, network, and user requirements better than someone off in a remote location. Unfortunately, there are several potential problems inherent in this model. There is a possibility of inconsistency in how servers are managed or in how well administrators adhere to company guidelines. It can be difficult to coordinate changes that have to be made to multiple servers at the same time. Some local administrators might resist controls imposed by company guidelines or changes made from a central location.

There are some special requirements at the central management point in either of these models. The requirements aren't special in terms of what is expected of administrators so much as they are a matter of scope. For example, administrators working in the central role need to understand server configurations and data stores at each of the locations. They also need a thorough understanding of data requirements at each location and data flows between the locations. They need to not only understand company guidelines regarding data management, but how they apply to each location.

SELF-CHECK

- What are some reasons for implementing a distributed data environment?
- Which replication type supports the lowest level of granularity for incremental updates?
- What is latency?
- What replication options are available in most DBMSs?
- What is the advantage of permitting local autonomy when determining how a distributed data environment is managed?

12.3 Understanding Internet Issues

Today most systems are either directly connected to the Internet or are connected to systems that are. Managing an Internet database environment presents several unique challenges in comparison to managing a database environment in a system that is specifically not connected to the Internet. In the Internet database environment, the general public potentially has access (planned or unplanned access by hackers) to the company's company's databases. The public responses to the applications that involve the Internet are often unpredictable, meaning that the load on the system and access to the databases can change rapidly. The environment requires constant monitoring and management, with administrators having to react quickly when the situation changes.

12.3.1 Managing Performance Issues

Most Web users experience widely different performance levels when interacting with the Web. Sometimes, the performance varies on visits to the same Web site. **Response time,** the elapsed time from pressing the Enter key or clicking on a "Go" icon to having the Web server's response as a new Web page fully displayed on your monitor, can vary greatly. Response, or perceived response (how quickly the Web server seems to respond), can be critical. Competition for customers continues to increase with ever more companies offering ever more services. A consumer's lack of patience with poor performance at one Web site can easily mean that the customer will leave for a competitor's site. The complexity of the Internet and Web environment means that there are many potential reasons for poor performance. Performance varies depending on whether your connection to the Internet is through a dial-up (56K) modem or a broadband connection, the level of hardware at your Internet service provider, traffic levels with which you're competing, Web server response speed, and so forth.

From the point of view of the Web site, a major factor is the amount of traffic coming in from the Internet. Internet traffic to a Web site, the number of people or companies trying to access it simultaneously, can vary greatly because of a variety of factors such as the following:

▲ The time of day (which must be considered on a worldwide basis).
▲ The season of the year (e.g., the Christmas shopping season).
▲ The changing popularity of a Web site.
▲ A major new product release (or product rumors).
▲ A major event (with an overwhelming spike in traffic possibly overloading the server).

These spikes (some huge) in Internet traffic require predictive capacity planning. Companies want to be able to maintain reasonable response times during spikes without spending large amounts of money to buy a lot of extra computer equipment that will sit idle much or most of the time. Accomplishing this takes planning and significant expertise.

Of course, system performance is also affected by software design and, in particular for our interest here, by database design. Physical database design is of particular interest in the Internet database environment. Various performance-boosting physical design techniques are applicable, such as careful index design, selective denormalization, and so forth.

In addition, we will mention two performance-boosting techniques that are of particular interest in the Web database environment. Both are very similar in how they improve performance. One is specific to the Internet environment and Internet technologies. The other is common to any user data requests made of the database server.

When a query comes in from a PC and is passed from the Web server to the database server to the database, often someone will want the retrieved data again fairly soon. If a copy of that data can be held on a temporary basis (cached in memory) to fill the next request, you can gain two benefits: not only is the response time for future retrievals of the same data improved, but the amount of traffic between the Web server and the database server can be decreased. Reducing the load on the database helps improve performance servicing in other data requests. This concept of holding data temporarily cached in memory, called **database persistence,** can be accomplished with a **query cache** which is a special area of dedicated memory associated with the Web server. The cache could also be located, and often is, on a **proxy server** used with the Web server; the proxy server provides additional support that includes holding a temporary copy of retrieved data. Cached data can include the results of database queries, but also can include other data that might be needed to serve other requests, including full Web pages.

The other performance-boosting technique is used when accessing data over the Internet (or over an internal Intranet) through ad hoc queries. Repetitive queries can be stored or "canned" in the database server cache (just like queries made over the local network) and recalled when needed. This way, the system avoids going through query optimization and coming up with an efficient access path every time the query is run.

12.3.2 Managing Availability Issues

A company's Web site and the databases that it accesses need to be available to the public at all times. This is especially true if the company is expecting to receive traffic to the site on a worldwide basis, which, after all, is one of the hallmarks of e-commerce. Three o'clock in the morning in one part of the world is the middle of the day in another, and so the system really has to be up all of the time. An information system may be unavailable due to any of the following reasons:

▲ System or telecommunications failure.
▲ Failure of a support system, such as an electrical outage.

▲ Planned down period for system maintenance.
▲ Excessive traffic that clogs the system.

The challenge is to make the information systems and their databases available "24/7" without going overboard in terms of cost. How do you handle system failures, electrical outages, or planned maintenance time? You can meet these needs with redundant computer hardware and such accessories as electrical generators, UPSs, and batteries, but are these all cost-effective solutions? The trick, and the concern during planning and design, is to find ways to prepare for such eventualities at a reasonable cost. Excessive traffic is another issue. It can be caused by legitimate traffic spikes, which can certainly reduce availability, but can be planned and accounted for. Unexpected problems like computer viruses that reproduce many copies of themselves, automated "robots" searching Web sites for information, or dedicated attacks can clog systems, too.

Attacks that target Web sites, such as Denial of Service (DoS) attacks that flood the Web site with traffic, can have multiple effects. Not only do these attacks tie up the Web site so that legitimate traffic can't get through, but the added load could crash any Web applications running on the server. If the application happened to be accessing the database server at the same time, you could end up with lost or corrupted data.

Virus attacks and malicious attacks must be prevented whenever possible. You can reduce the attack surface and minimize their effects through your design and the security measures that you implement. These measures alone, however, are usually not enough. Another key is constant monitoring by software that watches for such conditions.

Other actions you take depend on your level of concern, the possibility of attack, planned user loads, predictable traffic spikes, and so forth. Balanced against these possible actions is your budget. You can only take the actions that you can afford to take. Some of the most effective configurations for ensuring availability are also some of the most expensive. Solutions such as clustering, fault-tolerant storage subsystems, and mirrored or standby servers, require duplicate hardware and software.

Growth also impacts availability, though it's somewhat easier to project and plan for its effects. Some electronic commerce efforts, in both "pure" e-commerce startup companies and established companies, have experienced rapid growth. In one case, the growth rate of traffic to the Web site was estimated at 1,000 to 4,000 percent per year in the early years. This is certainly good news for any company that experiences it! However, this means that the information system that supports this Web site must be scalable; that is, it must be capable of growing in size without adversely affecting the operations of the site. It is thus imperative that hardware and software be chosen that is capable of rapid and major expansion. Check that your chosen DBMS, as well as other components, have the ability to scale up and scale out as necessary.

12.3.3 Managing Security and Privacy Issues

An Internet database environment is one in which all of the traditional data security concerns are present, but in addition, the information system is exposed to the whole world through its Web site! This is not an exaggeration. In the e-commerce environment the company wants as many people as possible to visit its Web site and buy its products. This also opens a door to hackers, data thieves, virus writers, and anyone else with mischief on their minds. Your Web site is an openly published entry point into your company's information system. Obviously, this openness requires security measures such as the following:

▲ Separating the different parts of the information system so that they run on different computers. The Web server and the database server should be different computers. Furthermore, these servers should be separated from the rest of the company's information system by being on a separate LAN.

▲ Making use of firewalls. **Firewalls** provide a layer of protection between your network and the Internet. Firewalls can be hardware-based, software-based or both. They can provide different types of protection such as limiting open data paths or checking incoming messages for viruses and other suspicious code. Firewalls can be dedicated hardware devices designed specifically for that purpose or can also be implemented through specialized server software. Hardware firewalls are usually more efficient and a better choice in high volume environments. Software-based firewalls are often more cost-effective and can frequently be deployed on multi-purposed servers.

Take a look at Figure 12-9. This is a basic multi-tier, Web-based application, but also includes a firewall. Additional firewalls can be placed between the Web server and the database server to catch any malicious code that gets through the initial firewall. Firewalls can also be placed between the Web server and the rest of the company's information systems.

Understanding Data Privacy Issues

Closely related to the issue of security is the issue of privacy. Companies have long held personal data about their customers in their databases. What is different in the Internet database environment is, first, that the companies are communicating digitally with their customers through their Web sites, including passing their personal data, over the Internet. This requires the use of encryption so that the data cannot be intercepted and read while in transit over the Internet. Second, the collected personal data in the company's database makes a tempting target for someone out to steal such data. And, again, the database is potentially accessible through the company's public Web site, which brings us back to the discussion about firewalls and other security devices.

Figure 12-9

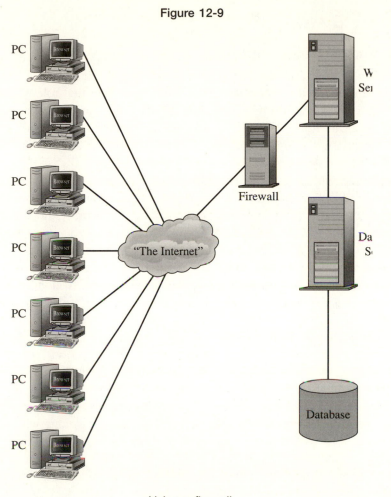

Using a firewall.

Ensuring the protection and privacy of data requires a multifaceted approach. Firewalls are part of the answer, but just part. Not only do you need to limit traffic into and out of the database, you have to limit what users can do while they are there. That means limiting database users to only those persons and applications that need access, as well as setting access permissions to no more than what is necessary. Another tool available to you with some DBMSs, including SQL Server 2005, is data encryption. Not only can you encrypt the data coming into and going out of the server, you can also encrypt data on the hard disk. Because of the resource overhead required by data encryption, it should be limited to sensitive or personal data. SQL Server makes it easy for you to choose what you encrypt, though, because it supports encryption at the table level and at the individual data column level.

FOR EXAMPLE

What Are We Getting Into?

Good Reading Bookstores, a fictitious bookseller, decides to move into the e-commerce age with a Web site. You, working in the dual role of data and database administrator, are responsible for the data tier of this new multi-tiered application. That means getting the database ready, as well as being there to advise and assist the programmers, network administrators, and newly hired Webmaster.

Let's start with your direct responsibilities. For a data administrator, data is always a good place to begin. The good news is that most of the basic framework required, things like inventory, customer, and order tracking components, are already in place. You still need to go through the whole data design process, though, to identify what new data requirements you have, if any. For example, if you aren't already tracking email addresses for your customers, you need to start doing so now. You might need to add a large object data column to the inventory table so you can include pictures of book covers and other items that you stock. If the bookstore has not done any shipping in the past, you need to add appropriate columns and tables to track shippers and shipping information.

Switch over to your database administrator hat now. Your security concerns and the possibility of attack have just increased significantly. You need to review database security to see what changes you need to make there. You also need to provide for connectivity for the application that will feed data to and process transactions for the Web server. This means working with the programmers, both to determine their requirements and to provide information about data structures. You need to work with network administrators to see what protections they are putting in place and what impact they might have on how you configured communication parameters at the database server.

You also have a new set of performance concerns. You need to see what is being done from the context of the Web server and network support components to optimize performance, but you may need to make some changes at your end, too. The server load is going to increase, but how much? That is going to be difficult to predict. It depends on how long it takes people to find the Web site and what kind of interest it generates. That doesn't mean you can't do anything to prepare. Specific actions you can take include:

- Updating the baseline performance statistics.
- Reviewing current queries and query performance.
- Reviewing any new query requirements, watching for potential problems like transactions likely to deadlock.
- Testing and tuning the database using queries needed by the new Web application and creating additional indexes as necessary.

Continued

- Implementing security auditing.
- Creating alerts to monitor key server resources.
- Crossing your fingers.

It's important to realize that when you move into a completely new situation you can't plan for every eventuality. This is especially true when dealing with the Internet. Monitor, maintain, and be ready to make changes quickly, as the situation requires.

And just in case, keep your fingers crossed, just for luck.

Understanding Data Theft

Despite companies' best efforts, data theft still occurs. Industrial theft and espionage is big business. Part of the problem is that the theft often goes undetected until it is too late to do much to minimize the effect.

One of the most common factors in data theft is that someone violated or bypassed security, leaving the data at risk. This is what happened, for instance, at the United States Department of Veterans Affairs (VA). An employee at the VA copied personally identifying information about hundreds of veterans to a laptop computer, bypassing network and database security. Later, when the laptop was stolen, so was the data. In this particular case, the thief initially wasn't even aware of what he had stolen.

Data theft more often occurs as the result of careful planning than by accident. A common trick is to get a job in a company's mail room, janitorial staff, or other position that gives you open access to the company, including employee cubicles. Then it becomes a matter of watching and waiting. A computer left logged on at the end of the day, a password written down and thrown away, along with other information picked up along the way... before long someone could have nearly unlimited access. The thief could copy the data to a writable CD, and then leave long before the theft can ever be discovered. Some thieves have even emailed the data to themselves.

SELF-CHECK

- What does response time refers to?
- What are some of the factors that affect Web site performance?
- What can cause problems with availability of a Web site?
- What is a justification for placing a firewall between a Web server and database server?

SUMMARY

This chapter looked at different database configuration options and how they can be used to support database applications. The chapter began with a close look at a centralized data environment, including the possibility of two- and three-tier data requirements in that environment. It looked at several options for implementing a distributed data environment and the role of replication in maintaining distributed data. Finally, it looked at some key issues related to supporting Internet-based applications.

KEY TERMS

Authoritative

Centralized data environment

Centralized management

Change replication

Commit phase

Database persistence

Distributed database servers

Distributed data environment

Distributed join

Distributed query

Firewall

Fragmentation

Gateway computer

Horizontal partitioning

Local area network (LAN)

Latency

Local autonomy

Localized management with central oversight

Merge replication

Microsoft Distributed Transaction Coordinator (MS DTC)

Multi-purposed server

Prepare phase

Proxy server

Query cache

Replication

Response time

Server instances

Snapshot replication

Three-tier approach

Transaction replication

Two-phase commit

Two-tier approach

Vertical partitioning

Well-connected

ASSESS YOUR UNDERSTANDING

Go to www.wiley.com/college/gillenson to evaluate your knowledge of data application support.

Measure your learning by comparing pre-test and post-test results.

Summary Questions

1. A collection of PCs connected by communication lines in a relatively small geographic area is known as a local area network (LAN). True or False?

2. Which of the following is an example of a three-tier centralized data approach?
   (a) the application includes a database server, application server, and Web server, with clients accessing data through a browser
   (b) source data located on a database server, on the local PCs running the client application, and on a mainframe computer
   (c) source data is spread across three database servers deployed on the same network
   (d) source data is deployed on three database servers deployed in different geographic locations

3. Which statement best describes the data stored in a data warehouse?
   (a) operational data needed to support day-to-day activities
   (b) archive data that is no longer applicable but kept available in case it is needed in the future
   (c) accumulated current and historical data used by decision support applications
   (d) external data waiting to be evaluated and integrated with production data

4. What is the biggest concern when deploying a database server instance on a multi-purposed server?
   (a) The requirement to share resources with other server applications could lead to less than optimal performance.
   (b) Security configuration settings must be the same for all servers hosted on the same computer.
   (c) Other server applications might overwrite data stored in the database server's databases.
   (d) It makes it more difficult for database clients to recognize the computer as a database server.

5. Which of the following statements correctly describe running multiple database server instances on a single computer?

   (a) It provides a way to minimize hardware costs, assuming the server has sufficient resources to support the instances.

   (b) Each server instance is configured and managed separately from the other server instances.

   (c) The configuration should be used in a development environment rather than a production environment.

   (d) all of the above

6. Which of the following is an advantage of a distributed database configuration in which a full copy of the database is maintained at each location?

   (a) Communication requirements are minimized.

   (b) There is no need to replicate changes between locations.

   (c) There is no possibility of concurrency errors between locations.

   (d) Disk space requirements are minimized.

7. To help ensure data integrity and minimize concurrency problems, distributed transactions are managed using a three-phase commit process. True or false?

8. You are designing an application that uses a distributed data environment. You want to minimize communication and disk storage requirements at each location. The solution should minimize the possibility of data consistency errors when updates are made at remote locations. Which configuration best suites your needs?

   (a) Put a full copy of the entire database at each location.

   (b) Put a copy of the database with all data tables at each location. Horizontally partition the tables to filter out rows not applicable to that location.

   (c) Put a full copy of only the most frequently accessed table at each location.

   (d) Put a horizontally partitioned copy of the most frequently accessed table at each location.

9. Which replication type overwrites the complete destination table?

   (a) snapshot replication

   (b) merge replication

   (c) change replication

   (d) transactional replication

10. Which replication configuration has the highest risk of conflict?

   (a) Allow updates at a master copy of the database only.

   (b) Allow updates at the remote data copies, consolidate the changes at the master copy, and distribute the changes.

(c) Allow changes to any copy and allow any copy to directly update any other copy.

(d) You don't have enough information to determine the correct answer.

11. A distributed join is a query that consolidates data from tables located in different databases. True or false?

12. You initiate a distributed query from a database server running SQL Server. There are multiple copies of the data table located on different database servers, but with the same table name. How do you ensure that the correct copy of the data is updated?

(a) List the affected database servers when you initiate the transaction.

(b) Let SQL Server choose the most appropriate table copy.

(c) Let MS DTC choose the most appropriate table copy.

(d) Identify each table by its fully qualified name.

13. A firewall can be used to filter traffic between a network and the internet to monitor for malicious activity. True or False?

14. How is database persistence implemented?

(a) through a query cache associated with the Web server

(b) by caching the query execution plan at the database server

(c) through a query cache on the firewall

(d) none of the above

15. What actions can you take to prevent accidental disclosure of data stored on a SQL Server 2005 database?

(a) Encrypt communications into and out of the database server.

(b) Encrypt data stored in database tables.

(c) Allow access permissions on an as-needed basis only.

(d) all of the above

Applying This Chapter

1. You are implementing a centralized data environment that will support database applications on the local network and act as the data back end to a Web application. You have completed the data design process and are in the process of implementing the database and the other necessary network components.

(a) What are factors that would prevent you from configuring the database server as a multi-purposed server?

(b) Why is it difficult to estimate traffic and database access requirements?

(c) What is the defining difference between a centralized and a distributed data environment?

(d) Why might it be necessary to include a firewall in the network deployment?

(e) What connectivity requirements do you need to configure at the database server?

(f) How would your design change if you needed to include data stored locally on client computers?

(g) How would your design change if you needed to include data stored on client computers and a mainframe computer?

2. You are migrating from a centralized data environment to a distributed data environment. Each location will need to maintain its own inventory and employee records. All information, including copies of inventory and employee information, will be maintained at the main office in Seattle.

(a) You want to keep storage requirements at each location to a minimum. How should you do this?

(b) When will it be necessary to execute transactions as distributed transactions? Be specific.

(c) Assuming you choose SQL Server as your database platform, briefly describe how distributed transactions are processed and the components involved.

(d) You deploy the database servers and create the databases at the remote locations. You need to perform an initial load that creates the initial tables. How can you use replication to accomplish this?

(e) Compare the support requirements for allowing inventory updates at remote sites only or at remote sites and the master copy in Seattle.

(f) What would be necessary if you want to use centralized administration for all databases?

Planning a Centralized Environment

You have a heterogeneous network environment with data stored on local PCs and on a mainframe computer. The network links to the mainframe through a gateway computer. You want to consolidate the data on a centralized SQL database server. The transition will be accomplished in phases, first consolidating the PC data and then including the mainframe data.

The database server will support specialized custom database applications. The applications are being developed in-house by staff programmers. You provide assistance to the programmers as necessary. Most access to the database server will be limited to access via the database applications, but a small number of clients will have direct access to the server.

At the same time, you are designing a separate database that will support an online research and reference application. Most of the tables needed for the application will rarely need updating. Access to this server will be limited to a .NET Web application running on a Web server.

Your database server does not support locating external data sources unless they are explicitly identified.

1. Describe the requirements for supporting data access during the intial deployment phases.
2. You need to select the hardware platform needed to support the SQL databases. The databases will be hosted on different DBMS products. Discuss the considerations for consolidating the data requirements on a single computer. Justify your answers.

Planning a Distributed Environment

You are designing and deploying a distributed data environment that will support for-profit medical clinics. You have completed the initial data design and the data load on a database server that consolidates the records for all of the clinics. The consolidated server does not directly support any one clinic. Instead, each clinic will have its own local database server. Each office will maintain its own separate staff, equipment, and inventory records. Every clinic must have full access to all patient and treatment records. There are also a full set of medical references online.

The primary concerns are accuracy, consistency, security, and how quickly patient and treatment information can be retrieved at the local clinics. All clients need access to the medical references, but speed of access to this information is less critical. Update latency must be kept to a minimum. All communcation between locations and all patient records are encrypted.

Treatment information is related to each patient and includes information about any staff involved with the treatment, medications given during the visit to the patient, and prescriptions written for the patient. The clinics do not fill prescriptions, but do sometimes give out samples they have received from drug representatives. These are noted on the treatment record, but not tracked in any detail.

You want to minimize storage requirements, but must meet the performance expectations for data retrieval.

1. Describe the data requirements at each clinic. Include which tables, if any, would need to be partitioned. Identify data, if any, that would be stored on the consolidated data server only.
2. Describe the replication requirements needed to perform an initial load of the remote databases and to mainiain data integrity and consistency.
3. Identify situations that would call for distributed transactions. Be as specific as possible. Include the steps necessary to execute a distributed transaction using a two-phase commit process, including the specific steps involved.

GLOSSARY

Access path   A plan for what steps to take to respond to a query.

Access security   Controlling user and application access to data by allowing or disallowing different activities.

ACID   Transaction acronym standing for atomicity, consistency, isolation, and durability.

Active Directory   A Microsoft directory service that supports a full featured network security environment organized around logical entities known as domains.

ADO.NET   A collection of data object libraries that let you connect to various data sources, send requests, and receive and manipulate data.

Aggregate function   A function that operates on a set of values, returning a single result based on these values.

Alert   Performance threshold monitor.

AND   Boolean operator used to test conditions in which both must be true for the result to be true.

Application data requirements   Information that the application needs and how it will be used by the application.

Arbitration   Act of resolving disputes.

ASCII   American Standard Code for Information Interchange. An encoding standard for encoding English language characters and control characters, supporting 127 printable characters.

Associative entity   Entity designed to associate key values from two entities between which a many-to-many relationship is defined.

Atomicity   Referring to the fact that either all of the statements in the transaction are executed, or none of the statements are executed.

Attribute   Information describing a data entity.

Audit trail   Ongoing log of user access and activity.

Authentication   The process by which a security principal is identified and allowed access.

Authentication method   A way of identifying a client before authorizing access to database resources. The most common authentication methods are based on user names and associated passwords.

Authoritative   Database version considered the primary or most accurate version.

Autocommit transaction   Each statement is treated as a separate transaction with BEGIN TRAN and COMMIT TRAN implied.

Automated tasks   A task that runs without operator intervention based on a schedule or in response to an event.

Automatic failover   The process of switching control to a secondary (backup) database server without operator intervention.

Balanced tree index   Common index structure based on nodes with pointer values directing you to the desired data.

Base object   An object used as the base for creating another object.

Batch   A file containing a set of executable statements.

Binary large object (BLOB) data type   Relational data type used to store large blocks for binary data.

Binary Operator   An operator applied to two operands at the time, typically in the format operand operator operand.

Binary relationship   A relationship defined between two entities.

Binary tree index   See Balanced tree index.

Blocked transaction   A transaction that cannot continue because it cannot access resources that it needs.

Boolean expression   An expression that evaluates as either true or false.

Bottleneck   Anything that adversely impacts performance.

B-tree index   See Balanced tree index.

Built-in functions   Predefined functions that install with SQL Server.

Bulk loading   The process of loading a large amount of data into a database as a single operation.

Business problem   Anything that prevents a business from operating as it should.

Business rules   Rules used to define or limit database data and its use by a business.

Cache   Data storage area in memory.

Cardinality   Value setting the maximum number of entities that can be involved in a particular relationship.

Cartesian product   A result returning all possible combinations of joins columns.

Centralized data environment   Data configuration based on a single database server hosting all application data.

Centralized management   Management model where remote databases are managed from a central location.

Centralized model   Database deployment model characterized by a single database server in a central location and accessed by local and remote users.

Change replication   Configuration where changed rows in a source table are written to the destination, overwriting or inserting data as appropriate.

Check constraint   Constraint placed on table column to limit data values to a set range, part of a specified list, or matching a format pattern.

Checkpoint   Transaction log entry that identifies the active portion of the log and forces the database server to write dirty pages to the hard disk.

Clause   See keyword.

Clustered index   Index whose order is used to physically sort table data.

Command operators   Operator symbols and keywords used to run arithmetic, comparison, and logical operations.

Command syntax   The format used when specifying and executing a command, including any keywords, and command parameters.

Commit   The process of successfully completing a transaction and finalizing its changes.

Commit phase   Final phase of a two-phase commit process in which transactions are committed on distributed servers.

Common gateway interface (CGI)   A standard way for passing requests and data between a Web server and an application.

Conceptual design   Database design process that includes data collection and identifying data requirements.

Concurrency   Relating to supporting multiple users who need concurrent access, access to the same data at the same time

Concurrency control   Database control over data access as a way to prevent errors that can occur when multiple users try to modify the same data at the same time.

Concurrent transactions   Two or more transactions being processed at the same time.

Connection   A communication path.

Connection path   Physical communication path through which data travels.

Constraint   Limit or control placed on tables and table columns.

Consumer audience   Data consumers — the people or applications who need access to data and who use data in some manner.

Control statement   A statement used to make a decision or otherwise control batch execution.

Control-of-flow statement   See control statement.

Core business   A business' or organization's primary activity. The organization's justification for existence.

Correlated subquery   A query in which the inner query depends on values passed to it from the outer query.

CREATE INDEX   SQL command used to create an index.

CREATE TABLE   SQL command that can be used to create a table, specify columns and data tables, and set table properties and constraints, such as identifying the primary key.

CREATE VIEW   SQL command used to create a view.

Cross join   A query in which all rows are returned as a Cartesian product.

CRUD   Acronym for create, read, update, and delete, the standard data processes supported by a database.

Cursor   A database object that allows for incremental processing of rows within a result set.

Data   Any and all information. The "things" that you want to record and track.

Data abstraction   A way to look at data that breaks it down into is basic components and groups the components to support different ways of looking at the data.

Data access   The process of allowing users or applications to retrieve data from a database.

Data accuracy   Ensuring that data is accurate and correct.

Data administrator   Role that includes planning, analysis, and liaison responsibilities.

Data analyst   See data administrator.

Data application programming interface (Data API)   Interface through which the programming language accesses a database or other data source.

Data carousel   Backup device that has multiple live media bays or that changes removable media for you automatically.

Data catalog   See data dictionary.

Data consumer   Person, department, or application accessing and using data. See also consumer audience.

Data definition language (DDL)   SQL statements used to create, modify, and delete server and database objects.

Data diagram   Graphical representation of a database model.

Data dictionary   Database component that describes data structures and data locations. Also called the data catalog.

Data flow   The path taken by data from its producer or owner to the data consumer.

Data integrity   Ensuring that data values are properly entered and maintained.

Data mart   A decision support database containing a subset of the data in a data warehouse.

Data model   Logical representation of business data, typically as entities and relationships.

Data modification language (DML)   SQL statements used to enter, modify, or delete data.

Data normalization   A methodology for organizing attributes into tables so that redundancy among the nonkey attributes is eliminated.

Data planning   Identifying data requirements, analyzing available data, and designing ways to meet data needs.

Data query   Term commonly used to refer to data access.

Data repository   Refers to the data storage unit where physical data files are kept.

Data security   Processes and procedures implemented with the goal of keeping data safe. Basic data security categories are access security and physical security.

Data type   A way of describing the kind of data that can be stored in a column or a variable.

Data type   Data storage format used to specify storage characteristics for data columns and variables.

Data volatility   Referring to how often data is added to the database and how often the data changes.

Data volume assessment   The process of determining the storage space required for each database table.

Data warehouse   A decision support database used to store a large amount of (typically historical) data.

Database   An ordered collection of related data elements intended to meet the information needs of an organization and designed to be shared by multiple users.

Database administrator   Role responsible for operationally-oriented administration activities.

Database engine   Core DBMS component responsible for data retrieval and modification, coordinating other DBMS component actions, providing an interface with the data user, and interfacing with the platform operating system.

Database object   Something created as part of a database, such as a table or view.

Database persistence   Act of caching queries in an Internet-based application where data is cached at the Web server or a proxy server.

Database practitioner   Information Technology personnel responsible for designing, creating, and maintaining databases.

DDL statement   Statement used to create and manage server and database objects.

DDL trigger   Trigger that fires when database or database server objects are created or modified.

Deadlock   A condition where two transactions mutually block each other.

Decision support database   A database designed to support advanced data mining activities and provide support for strategic decision making.

Declarative statement   Statement in which you specify the data for which you are looking and let the DBMS determine the procedure for accessing that data.

Decomposition process   Another term for the data normalization process. Also called "non-loss decomposition."

Dedicated server A server dedicated to running a single application.

Default constraint Value entered when no value is provided during data entry.

Default database Database context for running SQL commands when a database is not specified.

Defining association A means of expressing that the value of one particular attribute is associated with a single, specific value of another attribute.

Denormalization Taking pairs of related, third normal form tables and combining them.

Determinant attribute The attribute in a defining association whose value determines the value of the attribute on the right side of the association.

Deterministic function A function that always return the same result if you pass it the same arguments.

Differential backup Backup of all changes made since the most recent base (full) backup.

Direct memory access (DMA) Access channel that enables devices such as disk drives and network adapters to directly access (write to and read from) the computer's main memory.

Dirty page A page that has been updated in memory, but not written to the hard disk.

Dirty read A data read that reads data that has been modified, but not committed.

Disk duplexing Fault tolerant storage method based on two hard disks with identical data, with each hard disk connected to a different disk controller.

Disk mirroring Fault tolerant storage method based on two hard disks with identical data.

Disk queue Number of hard disk requests waiting to be resolved. With most operating systems, this should average one or less.

Disk striping with parity Fault tolerant storage method using three or more hard disks with data and parity information striped across the physical disks.

Distributed data environment Data configuration based on application data stored on multiple database servers.

Distributed database servers A multiple server configuration supporting related data.

Distributed join Joins data from the different database.

Distributed model Database deployment model characterized by multiple database servers, typically deployed in different physical locations.

Distributed query A query that retrieves data from multiple databases.

DML statement Any statement used to enter or modify data.

DML trigger Trigger that fires when data is entered, updated or modified.

Domain In the context of Microsoft Active Directory, a security boundary.

Domain integrity Relating to ensuring that the values entered in specified columns are legal.

Dynamic SQL   Statements executed directly through an interactive user interface, such as a command prompt, for immediate execution on the database server.

Electronic data interchange (EDI)   Technologies and standards for electronic data transfer.

Embedded SQL   Statements executed in the context of another programming language.

Enterprise Resource Planning (ERP) software   Multi-function, integrated software based on multiple software modules used to manage common business tasks and based on a shared database.

Entity   Refers to something having a distinct existence. In the context of database technologies, refers to the items that can be described and tracked in the database.

Entity integrity   Relating to ensuring that each row is uniquely identified.

Entity-Relationship (E-R) Modeling   The process of identifying entities, attributes, and relationships for a relational database model.

Entity-Relationship Diagram (ERD)   Data diagram based on entities and relationships.

Exception conditions   Less commonly used normal forms.

Exclusive lock   A lock that, when acquired by one transaction, prevents other transactions from accessing the object.

Explicit conversion   The process of manually converting data.

Explicit transaction   Transaction in which the entire transaction is controlled through BEGIN TRAN, COMMIT TRAN, and ROLLBACK TRAN.

Fault-tolerant storage   Physical data storage method designed to avoid data loss or errors in case of hardware failures.

Fault-tolerant system   Designed to protect data in the event of a hard disk failure.

Firewall   Provide a layer of protection between your network and the Internet. Firewalls can be hardware-based, software-based or both.

First normal form   Each attribute value is atomic, that is, no attribute is multivalued.

Foreign key   Relational database object used to define and maintain relationships between tables.

Forms generator   DBMS component used to design forms. Most commonly used to design data input and data presentation forms.

Fragmentation   A condition where the data is randomly spaced in small pieces all over the hard disk rather than being located in one place.

Fragmentation   Term sometimes used to describe table partitioning.

Full backup   A backup of all data, including the transaction log, if any.

Fully qualified object name   Complete object name that defines the object as globally unique.

Function   Named set of executable steps that support input parameters and return a value.

Function   Special executable designed to operate on data and return a result.

Functional dependency   See Defining association.

Gateway computer   In the context of LAN communication support, a computer used to link a LAN with other LANs, with the Internet, or a different network type on which a mainframe computer is located.

Globally unique identifier (GUID)   Value generated in such a way that even if created for different tables or on different servers, each value is unique.

Guest   SQL Server default database user account supporting anonymous access.

Heterogeneous data environment   Operational environment characterized by having a resource mix that can include any combination of different database types, DBMS systems, operating systems, and hardware platforms.

Hierarchical database model   Database model based on a hierarchical (parent/child) data organization. This is primarily a legacy mainframe database model.

Horizontal partitioning   Filter a table by row.

Horizontal partitioning   Splitting table contents by row.

Hypertext Transfer Protocol (HTTP)   A protocol layer and part of the TCP/IP protocol suite supporting World Wide Web traffic on the Internet.

Identifier   An attribute that identifies a specific instance of an entity as unique.

Implicit conversion   The process of automatically converting data into a compatible data type.

Implicit transaction   Transactions begin automatically after the end of the previous transaction. The end of the transaction is controlled using COMMIT TRAN and ROLLBACK TRAN.

Inactive portion   The portion of the transaction log containing completed transactions only.

Inconsistent analysis   Analysis based on data where data changes between reads of the same data set.

Incremental backup   A backup of changes made to data pages since the most recent full, differential, or incremental backup.

Index   Database object use to sort and organize data.

Indexed view   View on which you have created a clustered index.

Information   Data that has been organized in such a way as to be meaningful and useful to people.

Inner join   A query in which only qualifying results are returned from the joined tables.

Input parameter   Data value provided to a function or procedure.

Instant messaging (IM)   Communication software allowing communication between users over a network or through the Internet.

Integrated security   Security based on Windows authentication and using Windows security principals.

Interactive SQL   Statements executed directly through an interactive user interface, such as a command prompt, for immediate execution on the database server.

Intersection data   Data that is part of a many-to-many relationship and associated with a specific, unique instance of related entities.

Isolation   Referring to the fact that a transaction must appear as though it executed by itself without interference from any other concurrent transaction.

Join   A query combining columns from two or more data sources.

Joining   Combining the data from two tables based on linking columns.

Key column   Column used to define index sort order.

Keyword   A part of a command identifying a clause to either supply parameters or define command actions.

Kill   Exit a process without completing any open transactions.

Large object data   Data requiring a large amount of storage space.

Latency   The time between when data changes and when the change is replicated to the destination servers.

Leaf node   A node located at the lowest level of an index and representing the actual data.

Local area network (LAN)   An arrangement of personal computers connected together by communication lines.

Local autonomy   Delegated responsibility for database server security, backup, recovery, and concurrency control.

Local variable   Object used to store a value in memory temporarily.

Localized management with central oversight   Management model with local autonomy that includes centralized management control over management decisions.

Lock level   The level at which a lock is acquired, typically database, table, or row.

Lock   A restriction placed on access to database objects.

Lock scope   See lock level.

Logical design   Design process that includes identifying entities and describing the data model.

Login   Security principal used to manage server access and server-level security.

Login credentials   Information identifying a user to the database server and used to set server access permissions.

Lost update   A condition where one transaction overwrites another transaction's changes, causing the first transaction's updates to be lost.

Main memory   Provides temporary storage of data and programs.

Maintenance plan   A defined set of maintenance tasks executing on a periodic schedule. Management model with local autonomy that includes centralized management control having the final say over management decisions.

Manual failover   The process of switching control to a secondary (backup) database server with operator intervention.

Manual task   A task that requires operator intervention.

Many-to-many relationship   A relationship in which any number of referenced entity instances can be related to any number of referencing entity instances.

Memory buffer   Dedicated area in main memory used for temporary data storage.

Merge replication   See change replication.

Merged scan join   Highly efficient join algorithm that requires either sorted or indexed join columns.

Metadata   Data about data, or the data describing a database and database objects.

Microsoft Distributed Transaction Coordinator (MS DTC)   Microsoft component that manages distributed transactions.

Middleware   General term referring to software components located in the "middle" of a multi-tier application.

Minimally logged operation   The fact that the operation ran is logged, but not its affect on the database or data.

Mirror image   An exact duplicate of a database or other data file.

Mixed authentication   SQL Server configuration option supporting Windows and SQL Server authentication.

Modality   Value setting the minimum number of entities that can be involved in a particular relationship.

Modem   Communication device that performs digital to analog and analog to digital conversions.

Multi-purposed server   A server computer running multiple server applications.

Mutual authentication   A process by which a client and server are able to identify each other before establishing a connection.

Nested loop join   Join resolved by looping through a Cartesian product.

Nested procedure   A procedure called and executed by another procedure.

Nested transaction   O\occurs when you explicitly start a new transaction while already operating within the scope of a transaction.

Network database model   Database model based on data organization supporting flexible owner/member relationships between data entities. This is primarily a legacy mainframe database model.

Node   Data stored at a hierarchical level within an index.

Nonclustered index   An index used to logically, but not physically, organize and sort data.

Noncorrelated subquery   A subquery where the inner query is not dependent on values from the outer query.

Nondeterministic function   A function that might return different results, even if called with exactly the same arguments.

Non-logged operation   That means that the change isn't written to the transaction log, but instead is made directly to the database.

Non-loss decomposition   Normalization process in which neither data nor relationships are lost.

Nonrepeatable read   A condition where data changes between reads of the same data set.

Nonvolatile storage   Storage media that continues to hold the data it contains when power is lost or the computer is turned off. The most common example is disk drives.

Normal forms   Defined rules for data normalization.

Null value   An undefined value, usually used to identify that no value is provided for that attribute

Nullability   Column definition as to whether or not a column can accept null values.

Object-oriented database model   Database model where entities are treated as objects, which are individual items that can be defined and described more completely than in a relational model.

Object-relation model   Data model based on both relational and object modeling concepts.

Object-relational database model   Hybrid database model based on the relational model, but integrating features and functionality from the object-oriented model.

OLE DB   A Microsoft data access API.

One-to-many relationship   A relationships in which one referenced entity instance can be related to any number of referencing entity instances.

One-to-one relationship   A relationships in which one referenced entity instance can be related to one referencing entity.

Online transaction processing   Database type characterized by the need to support data update, change, and delete data, the need to optimize for support of concurrency and throughput, and the requirement to scale to meet the needs of a large number of users.

Open Database Connectivity (ODBC)   An industry standard API Supporting data connectivity.

Open transaction   A pending transaction that has not been committed or rolled back.

Operating system software   Software that controls the computer hardware, provides an interface to the user, and provides an environment in which applications can run.

Operator precedence   Operator ranking used to determine the order in which operators are processed.

Optimistic processing   Transaction control method that assumes that conflicts are unlikely and does not check for conflicts before processing the transaction.

OR   Boolean operator used to test conditions in which the result is true if either condition is true.

Outer join A query returning qualifying rows from one table and all rows from the second "outer" table.

Output parameter A value returned by a procedure.

Packet size Network communication parameter setting the maximum amount of data that can be sent at one time.

Paging file An area of hard disk storage set aside for use as system memory.

Parameters Values provided that help determine how a command runs.

Partial functional dependency A dependency where data is dependent on part of the primary key.

Partial rollback A process by which part, but not all, of the statements in a transaction are reversed.

Partial update A condition when only part of the tables involved in an operation are updated instead of updating all tables.

Performance baseline Performance data you collect to use for comparison later when performance problems are suspected.

Performance counter Module designed to monitor a specific aspect of system or application performance.

Performance object A group of related performance counters.

Phantom read A condition where a row appears or disappears in subsequent reads of the same data.

Phantom A data row that has appeared or disappeared in a subsequent read of the same data.

Physical data pointer Value used to link and associate data in the hierarchical and network database models. Values to link data values to physical storage locations in many implementations of the relational database model.

Physical design Design process that includes identifying and implementing the physical database and database objects.

Physical security Protecting data against physical corruption or loss; typically involves protecting the server, ensuring the storage media and duplicating data.

Precedence constraint Decision point within a maintenance plan used to control execution.

Prepare phase Initial phase of the two-phase commit process where the databases are prepared for update.

Primary index Index for a table's primary key.

Primary key Database object used to enforce uniqueness in a table.

Procedure Compiled set of executable statements.

Processor affinity Configuration settings relating to multiple processor use.

Production database Database that provides support for day-to-day business activities.

Protocol   Rules defining data format and transmission enabling computers to communicate.

Proxy server   Support server that, among other functions, can cache copies of recently retrieved Web pages.

Public   SQL Server database role to which all database users belong.

Publicity   Informing potential users about available data and database structure.

Qualifying conditions   See search argument.

Query cache   Area of dedicated memory associated with the Web server that is used to temporarily hold query results.

Query mode   Interactive mode of SQL statement execution.

Query optimizer   See query processor.

Query processor   DBMS component responsible for parsing, optimizing, and compiling queries for execution. Also known as a query optimizer.

Query   Executable statement written in a DBMS language and typically used to retrieve or manipulate data.

RAID   Redundant Array or Inexpensive (or Independent) Disks, disk configurations commonly used with database systems that provide enhanced performance and, in most configurations, fault tolerance.

Read committed   Transaction isolation level that prevents dirty reads by not reading uncommitted data.

Read uncommitted   Least restrictive isolation level that does not acquire locks and ignores exclusive locks during reads.

Recovery   The process of updating database tables based on committed transactions in the transaction log.

Referenced entity   The entity to which another entity refers in a relationship.

Referencing entity   The entity which refers to and is associated with another entity in a relationship.

Referential integrity   Another name for relational integrity, referring to the fact that you are maintaining the relationship between referencing and referenced tables.

Relational database   Database based on the relational model.

Relational database model   Database model based on entities that are associated with each other through relationships.

Relational integrity   Ensuring that relationships between tables are correctly created and maintained.

Relational result   See result set.

Relationship   An association defined and established between two data entities.

Removable media   Media that can be physically removed from the computer.

Repeatable read   Transaction isolation level that prevents dirty reads and nonrepeatable reads by not reading uncommitted data and not allowing changes to data read by the transaction.

Replication   Means by which a database server updates one or more destination database servers.

Report writer   DBMS component responsible for designing and processing reports.

Reporting database   A decision support database designed to support report generation.

Response time   The delay from the time that the request is made (such as when the Enter key is pressed) to execute a query until the result appears on the screen.

Response time   The elapsed time required for a Web server's response to display in the client's browser.

Result set   Rows and columns returned by a SELECT command.

Role   In SQL Server, login or data user groups with defined permissions.

Roll forward   A recovery process that updates database tables based on committed transactions in the transaction log.

Rollback   The process of backing out the changes made by an unsuccessful transaction so that they are not written to the hard disk.

Sa account   SQL Server administrator account.

Scalable   Term describing a solution that can grow to meet business needs.

Scaling out   The process of partitioning data and a database application across multiple distributed database servers.

Scaling up   The process of upgrading the database hardware platform by improving the processor, memory, disk subsystem, or other hardware resources.

Schema   Metadata used to describe database objects.

Schema binding   Prevents you from making any changes to the structure of the base tables, such as adding columns or changing column data types.

Script   A set of executable statements saved together as a file.

Search argument   Logical and conditional operators used to filter the rows processed by a command.

Search attribute   A value used to retrieve particular records.

Second normal form   Every nonkey attribute must be fully functionally dependent on the entire key.

Secondary index   Additional database indexes (other than the primary index).

Secondary storage   Nonvolatile data storage such as disk and tape drives.

Securable   Server or database object over which you have control over permission assignments.

Security context   The security default for a connection based on the security principal's assigned rights and permissions.

Security principal   Refers to an entity that can be uniquely identified through authentication and sets a connection's security context.

Selectivity   Referring to the number of different values in a table column.

Serializable   Most restrictive transaction isolation level designed to prevent dirty reads, nonrepeatable reads, and phantoms.

Serialization   Non-concurrent transaction processing (serial processing).

Server instances   Multiple, separately-managed database servers running on a single computer.

Shared lock   A lock that allows other transactions to access the same data for read.

Snapshot replication   Configuration where an entire table is copied to the destination server.

Snapshot   SQL Server-specific transaction isolation level in which the transaction uses a snapshot of database data taken at the start of the transaction.

Split read   Read request serviced by multiple hard disks.

SQL Native Client   OLE DB-based data access technology that supports the full features set of SQL Server 2005.

SQL Server authentication   Authentication method based on SQL Server logins and database server authentication.

Sqlcmd   The command used to launch the preferred character-based command line interface for Microsoft SQL Server 2005.

Stakeholder   Any person with a personal interest in or who is affected by database design and implementation.

Strategic data planning   Data planning relating to long-term data use issues.

Strong password   Password that includes mixed case letters, numbers, and "special" characters.

Subquery   A way of retrieving information where one query is dependent on another query.

Surface area   A term referring to how exposed an database is to access and manipulation.

System analyst   IT specialist responsible for analyzing complex systems and how they interact, in order to determine how computers can best be used to meet business requirements.

System stored procedures   Predefined procedures that install with SQL Server.

Table   Fundamental database object in the relational database model where entities are described as rows and columns.

Table alias   A value used to replace and represent a table name when writing queries.

Table order   The order in which rows are physically stored in a table.

Temporary table   A table created in memory only and having a limited scope.

Ternary relationship   A relationship between three different entities.

Third normal form (3NF)   Referring to a database normalized to the third normal form. Transitive dependencies are not allowed.

Three-tier approach   Data configuration where data is located on the database server, the local computer, and a mainframe computer.

Threshold value   A specified minimum or maximum value that, when exceeded, indicates a potential problem.

Throughput   Relating to the volume of data moved and processed by an application.

Timeout   Occurs when a transaction is unable to complete processing within a specified time

Timestamp ordering   Schedule-based concurrency method that enforces serialization and preserves order of execution of transactions and transaction statements.

Transaction   A series of statements or commands that execute as a group. All of the statements must either run successfully or all must be rolled back, as if they were never run.

Transaction isolation   Ensuring that one transaction does not interact with other transactions.

Transaction isolation level   Connection-specific setting that defines default lock behavior.

Transaction log backup   A backup that backs up, and then clears, completed transactions in the transaction log.

Transaction replication   Configuration where completed transactions are copied from the source database's transaction log to the destination database's transaction log.

Transaction scheduling   A concurrency method that serializes transaction execution by scheduling when a transaction executes relative to other transactions.

Transactional datase   Database type characterized by the need to support data insert, change, and delete and needing to optimize for support of concurrency and throughput.

Transitive dependency   One nonkey attribute is functionally dependent.

Transmission Control Protocol/Internet Protocol (TCP/IP)   The communication protocol suite on which the Internet and most current PC networks are based.

Trigger   Specialized procedure that runs in response to an event.

Trusted connection   Server connection using the currently logged on Windows user as the basis for authentication.

Two-phase commit   Transaction processing method used to commit distributed transactions through a two-step process.

Two-tier approach   Data configuration where data is located on the database server computer and on the local computer.

Unary operator   An operator applied to only one operand at the time; typically in the format operator operand.

Unary relationship   A relationship between different entities instances within the same entity.

Uncommitted dependency   A data read based on data that has been updated, but the update has not been committed.

Unicode   A universal encoding system capable of encoding any written language.

Unified Modeling Language (UML)   Language created to design and model object-oriented systems, including object-oriented databases.

Unique constraint   Column constraint requiring unique values.

User   Security principal used to manage database access and database-level security.

User-defined function   Custom function that you can create that accepts input parameters and returns either a scalar value or a table.

Variable   Named temporary storage area in memory used for data manipulation.

Vertical partitioning   Filtering or splitting a table by column.

View   Relational database model database object that provides custom data retrieval.

Virtual desktop   A utility that lets you have the command running on one computer, but see the screens and control the command remotely from another computer.

Virtual private network (VPN)   Provides a secure, reliable communication path. VPNs can be used over the Internet, or over a private LAN or WAN.

Well-connected   Referring to a full-time, reliable, high-bandwidth connection between servers.

WiFi   Term referring to wireless communication technologies.

Windows authentication   Authentication method based on Windows users and groups.

Working database   See default database.

XML document fragment   A portion of an XML document containing data organized in a hierarchical fashion.

INDEX